Information Storage and Retrieval:

tools, elements, theories

Information Sciences

Advisory Board

JOSEPH BECKER AND ROBERT M. HAYES:
Information Storage and Retrieval

CHARLES P. BOURNE:
Methods of Information Handling

HAROLD BORKO AND ROBERT F. SIMMONS:
Automated Language Processing In preparation

ROBERT M. HAYES:
Mathematics of Information Systems In preparation

Information Storage and Retrieval:

tools, elements, theories

JOSEPH BECKER, *Data Processing and Library Consultant*

ROBERT M. HAYES, *Advanced Information Systems, Inc.*
University of California at Los Angeles

John Wiley & Sons, Inc., New York · London · Sydney

SIXTH PRINTING, FEBRUARY, 1967

Library of Congress Catalog Card Number: 63-12279

Printed in the United States of America

Information sciences series

Information is the essential ingredient in decision making. The need for improved information systems in recent years has been made critical by the steady growth in size and complexity of organizations and data.

This series is designed to include books that are concerned with various aspects of communicating, utilizing, and storing digital and graphic information. It will embrace a broad spectrum of topics, such as information system theory and design, man-machine relationships, language data processing, artificial intelligence, mechanization of library processes, non-numerical applications of digital computers, storage and retrieval, automatic publishing, command and control, information display, and so on.

Information science may someday be a profession in its own right. The aim of this series is to bring together the interdisciplinary core of knowledge that is apt to form its foundation. Through this consolidation, it is expected that the series will grow to become the focal point for professional education in this field.

Dedicated to our families:

Alice and Bob Hayes

Arlene, Jane, Wendy, Bill, and Sara Becker

Preface

This textbook grew out of some discussions between the authors about the interdisciplinary character of the field of information storage and retrieval. We both felt that the need existed to show what each professional group concerned with the solution of information storage and retrieval problems could contribute. A university-level course was developed, based on the concept that each person should be made aware of how others could help him. The course was presented about a dozen times over the ensuing years, and this book is based on it.

In one sense the book is intended for the newcomer to the field of information storage and retrieval, but this is not to say that it is intended for the beginner. Its purpose is to provide an overview of all the aspects of the field and how they relate to each other, but at this stage in the development of the field, the newcomer is probably an expert in some particular aspect. Essentially, therefore, the book is intended as a road map, guiding the newcomer through the maze of scattered development that has characterized the early growth of this field.

In conformity with the approach of the book, the work and educational background of the authors differ sharply. One of us is a librarian with an engineering education, and the other is a mathematician with systems and equipment experience. We are good friends and professional colleagues of long standing, and this book has represented the opportunity for the two of us to join forces, combine our knowledge, and make a special effort to explain things with simplicity and care. If we have done our job well, librarians, documentalists, mathematicians, system designers, equipment manufacturers, operations researchers, and computer programmers should see how interwoven are their interests and how overlapping their responsibilities.

We are grateful to many individuals who made constructive suggestions in the course of text preparation. Among them are Foster E. Mohrhardt, Librarian of the U.S. Department of Agriculture, who reviewed the material in its very early stages and guided us in the development of it so that it would be most understandable to the librarian, Richard S. Angell, of the Library of Congress, who reviewed the chapter dealing with subject classification for its completeness and accuracy, John A. Postley, of Advanced Information Systems, Inc., who reviewed the material on system design and equipment for its practicality, Ralph M. Shoffner, also of Advanced Information Systems, Inc., who aided in the development of the theoretical material in the last chapters and provided invaluable comments on the character of cost accounting.

We wish to make special mention of the University of California at Los Angeles. The idea for this book was conceived there. More particularly, the staff of the Western Data Processing Center, under the direction of George Brown, gave Joseph Becker both the opportunity and the encouragement to explore nonnumerical aspects of computer application. The Mathematics Department and its Extension Division gave Robert Hayes the opportunity to test the approach of this book in a teaching environment.

We wish also to acknowledge gratefully the support given by the United States Air Force through the Rome Air Development Center and the National Science Foundation through the Office of Science Information Service. The theoretical work discussed in the third section of the book could not have been possible otherwise.

Several wonderful secretaries aided us in preparation of the manuscript at the various stages of its production; each deserves our gratitude. Mary Osgood and Gail Motteler helped Joseph Becker, and Ruth Alvarez helped Robert Hayes. Without their ability to bring order out of the chaos of our constant revisions, we could never have completed this book. And, amazingly, throughout they remained cheerful and tolerant.

JOSEPH BECKER
ROBERT M. HAYES

Bethesda, Maryland
Sherman Oaks, California
March, 1963

Contents

SECTION I

Tools

— 1

Introduction

During the last several years the problem of designing systems for storing and retrieving information has been the subject of investigation by many diverse groups. What is this problem? Why is so much effort now being spent on its investigation? Why are so many different disciplines concerned with its solution? This textbook is intended to provide an answer to these questions. It is based on the philosophy that different backgrounds, different experiences, are an essential ingredient to the solution of the problems in information system design.

But why this explosion of new effort and why should a book be needed now? Information storage and retrieval is certainly not a new concept; it is an integral part of the communication process, a direct outgrowth of the desire among men to communicate with one another. Knowledge has been recorded throughout the ages, and techniques and methods for storing and retrieving it have long been available.

Information is the basic ingredient of decision making. As the situations in which decisions must be made become more complex, the need for information correspondingly increases. And it has been characteristic of modern life that it is complex. Business, science and technology, government—each is concerned with a world encompassing more and more interrelationships, and the need in each case has therefore become ever greater to provide the decision maker with more information.

Yet, as the amount of information which might be relevant to decisions increases, the processes of obtaining, examining, and selecting the information required for the particular decision become very large tasks. In many situations it has seemed as though the size of these tasks has become greater than that which previous techniques could handle. Equally important, not only has it appeared that new techniques were needed but also that the tools for them were available in modern data processing equipment and systems. The computers, photographic processes, and magnetic recording developed over the past twenty years provide, in a very tantalizing way, the prospect of capability for information storage and retrieval comparable to that given to the scientist in the solution of his computational problems and to the businessman in the solution of his data processing problems.

THE IMPACT OF TECHNOLOGY

The resulting impact of technology has been due to two basic characteristics of equipment: the need for precision and the need for economic utilization. Thus the nature of data processing equipment is that it is both unintelligent and expensive. It cannot operate without being told what to do, and the costs of mechanization are so great that procedures must not only be specified in detail, they must also be optimally designed. The need to define precisely the operations which data processing equipment is to handle has forced a very careful examination of the characteristics of complex decision making problems and the role which information plays in them. On the other hand, the need to utilize equipment economically has required a similarly careful analysis of the problems of system design and equipment evaluation.

Thus the combination of complex, critical, decision making problems with the appearance of machines which seem to be capable of providing the information required for their solution is the cause of the great explosion of activity in the area of information system design. Workers on the problems in the field have included users of information, librarians, documentalists and other system designers, and engineers. Each technical background has provided a body of available knowledge and techniques applicable to some aspect of the field.

This type of "interdisciplinary" effort is probably an essential characteristic of such a new field. But, as a result of the diversity of backgrounds, capabilities, and interests, evident problems in communication and understanding have continually arisen. Each worker is to some extent unfamiliar with others' language; he lacks facility with others' techniques; he is unacquainted with others' concerns. Each individual approaches the problem from his own experience and is, in a sense, unfamiliar with the other aspects of the problem. Unfortunately the inherent bias produced by specialized training makes it extremely difficult to overcome this lack of awareness; each worker continues to filter the problem through the screen of his own interests and experience.

The difficulties in communication are thus the result of a complex interaction of a number of factors. They cannot be resolved merely by improved appreciation of the language and interests of others. In fact, one of the significant causes of difficulty in communication—the tendency to step outside one's area of responsibility—seems to be compounded as knowledge grows concerning other areas. Another, far more serious factor is the use of the same language for superficially similar concepts which are, in fact, fundamentally different. Attempts to resolve the consequent confusion introduce a further complicating factor—the tendency to become more abstract rather than more concrete when communication becomes difficult.

One need merely listen at any of the numerous symposia and conferences on the information storage and retrieval problem to appreciate that a serious difficulty exists in communication and understanding. This difficulty has itself been the subject of some discussion. John Henry Merryman's paper [1] has described some of its manifestations, and Y. Bar-Hillel's paper [2] has pinpointed some of its more unfortunate results.

The purpose of this book is to demonstrate that these different backgrounds are essential in the solution of this type of problem. The intent has been to show the contribution which each can make and the means for facilitating communication among them. The authors themselves represent the different backgrounds involved; each of us tends to approach the problem in the characteristic ways of those backgrounds. In attempting to resolve our own difficulties in communication, we feel that great insight has been gained into the contribution which each type of background can best make, the tools and techniques which each provides, and how they fit together in the solution of any job.

---

[1] John Henry Merryman, Tactics and Terminology in Information Retrieval: A Summary of Recent Work, *College and Research Libraries,* January 1958, v. 19, pp. 33–37.

[2] Y. Bar-Hillel, A Logician's Reaction to Recent Theorizing on Information Search Systems, *American Documentation,* April 1957, v. 8, pp. 103–122.

UNDERLYING PROBLEMS

One of the significant insights gained is into the near universality of the underlying characteristics of information systems. Thus the techniques applicable to a scientific library are fundamentally the same as those applicable to a business record file or to a military intelligence file. The basic problems, the sources of difficulty, in each case partake of the same essential features. There is nothing revolutionary in this; on the other hand, it is important to recognize what these basic sources of difficulty are. The basic characteristics of information storage and retrieval problems, which appear to be common to all situations wherein new approaches must be considered, include on the one hand extremely rapid growth in the amount of information and, on the other, fragmentation and specialization in the immediate application of particular pieces of information with the probable eventual need for multiple application.

The feature of extremely rapid growth has been recognized for some time as a basis for the need to develop more adequate solutions. It has been pointed out that information today is printed and disseminated in such vast quantities that unless a systematic way is found to organize it there is real danger human effort will be wasted over and over again simply because it is not possible to determine what work has already been done. The current rate of publishing is indeed staggering. The United States alone produces 5 million books a year, and World Almanac circulation statistics report that Americans read about 25 billion newspapers and 60 million magazines each year. Foreign sources of publication are similarly heavy contributors to the tide.

Verner W. Clapp, President of the Council on Library Resources, described the rate of growth of library collections and publishing in the following terms.

> World publication has been doubling every forty-five years during the five centuries since Gutenberg and Coster labored—doubling roughly three times as fast as the growth of the world's population. . . .
>
> Were there no other considerations, the mere rate of publication and acquisition would create problems of the resultant size of collections. The world's population is laid to rest each generation; the world's books have a way of lingering on. How at one and the same time to extract profit and usefulness from this inheritance of the past and yet to prevent it from

clogging the channels of present information is another aspect of the problem.[3]

Burton W. Adkinson, Head of the Office of Science Information Service, National Science Foundation, in an article appearing in *Special Libraries,*[4] described the present situation in the field of science and technology.

During the past 100 years the United States and foreign professional scientific organizations, both private and public, have developed systems of publication and communication that until recently kept pace with scientific research. However, the tremendous expansion in research and development during and following World War II has produced a veritable flood of published material. This growth has induced a demand that information be produced and disseminated more speedily, be better organized, and be better summarized and indexed. As a result, the inadequacies of present services have been emphasized.

The problem which the nation faces in this area has two principal aspects—first, improvement of present information services that use known and tested techniques and, second, development of new and more effective techniques for coping with the rapidly expanding body of scientific and technical literature.

As early as 1945 Vannevar Bush made reference to the expanding publishing rate and suggested the value of machine application.[5]

There is a growing mountain of research. But there is increased emphasis today that we are being bogged down as specialization extends. . . . The investigator is staggered by the findings and conclusions of thousands of other workers—conclusions which he cannot find time to grasp, much less to remember as they appear.

The difficulty seems to be not so much that we publish unduly in view of the extent and variety of present-day interests, but rather that publication has been extended far beyond our present ability to make real use of the record. The summation of human experience is being expanded at a prodigious rate and the means we use for threading through the consequent maze to the momentarily important item is the same as was used in the days of square rigged ships.

---

[3] Third Annual Report, Council on Library Resources, Washington, D.C., 1959, pp. 13–16.

[4] Burton W. Adkinson, United States Scientific and Technical Information Services, *Special Libraries,* November 1958, v. 49, No. 9, pp. 407–414.

[5] Vannevar Bush, As We May Think, *Atlantic Monthly,* July 1945, v. 176, pp. 101–108.

A Royal Society Scientific Information Conference, one of the first international conferences of its kind, was held in London in 1948 and all facets of the documentalist's interest in both publications and research methodology were presented. J. E. Holmstrom summed up the scientific researcher's dilemma at that time when he remarked:

> The problem is a formidable one. We have heard estimates of how anything up to a million or more scientific papers a year are poured like rain over the scientific world and of how formidable are the difficulties of ensuring current awareness, by scientific men, of the *new* publications which may concern them in the particular fields of research which these publications serve to irrigate; . . . these torrents and rivers of current literature pour themselves into Libraries adding, without cease, to what is already there. . . . Our problem is founded on the fact that on the one hand every man's reading time is limited whilst on the other hand there must exist, somewhere among the millions of items of literature available, the particular ones which contain the ideas most apposite to his needs if only there was some means of singling these out from the mass. The scientist's time and power of attention are precious things which need to be husbanded; and to do this we need techniques of controlled selectiveness in supplying his needs.[6]

More than any other factor this concept of voluminous alphabetical data outpouring from our printing presses and of the consequent inability to find much of it again after it appears in print has been emphasized as the prime mover behind major information storage and retrieval efforts. Yet mere volume alone would not in itself be sufficient to warrant new approaches. It is the combination of volume with fragmentation and with multiple utilization of the information which really creates a problem. The growth of specialization is a well-recognized phenomenon which is probably an essential part of the solution of complex decision making problems. Yet the effects of specialization are to create specialized terminology and jargon so that the communication of information outside the specialized field becomes increasingly difficult. A classical example is the somewhat facetious title of a hypothetical paper in mathematics: "Analytical Algebraic Topology of Locally Euclidean Metrization of Infinitely Differentiable Riemannian Manifolds."[7] The difficulty is that although such a paper may well contain information relevant to a decision in some very different area, the specialization of both the in-

---

[6] Royal Society Scientific Information Conference, 21 June–2 July 1948. Report and Papers submitted. London, The Royal Society, Burlington House, 1948, p. 78.

[7] Tom Lehrer, Lobachevsky (song).

formation and the language lays almost insurmountable barriers to the recognition of this relevancy. Even if relevancy were easy to recognize, the very specialization of the field of coverage would make it unlikely that the paper would ever be examined.

Furthermore, each specialized area represents a new focal point for exponential growth. This was pointed out by Louis N. Ridenour ten years ago,[8]

> The problem is that the size and cost of every research library are growing, not at a constant rate, but at an ever-increasing rate. With fluctuations caused by wars, depressions, and local conditions, every library is, on the whole, following an exponential law of growth. . . . Other fields, such as atomic energy and television, are piling up enormous new masses of material with which librarians must deal, and no slackening of this trend is to be expected.

Illustrations of the influence of these problems in science and technology are readily at hand. The exponential growth of the scientific publishing rate has already been pointed out. The specialization of scientific disciplines is well recognized. The multiple application of information is evident in the growth of interdisciplinary fields, such as biochemistry or mathematical psychology.

It must also be emphasized that they are equally apparent in business and government. The flood of paperwork in modern industrial and governmental organizations is well known; the growth of population and the effects of "Parkinson's law"[9] are very powerful forces in this direction. Both specialization and multiple usage of information are also very evident in business and government. Thus, although most of the rationale for work in the field of information storage and retrieval has been based on the needs of science and technology, these other areas partake of the same characteristics and will benefit in much the same way. In fact, from an economic standpoint it seems probable that business and government are more likely to be capable of paying the price involved.

RESULTING AREAS OF WORK

Developing an adequate solution to any particular information system design problem requires answers to many questions which

---

[8] Louis N. Ridenour in *Bibliography in an Age of Science*, Urbana, University of Illinois Press, 1951.

[9] Cyril N. Parkinson, *Parkinson's Law and Other Studies in Administration*, Boston, Houghton Mifflin, 1957, p. 112.

result from the underlying three characteristics of volume, specialization, and multiple application. Answering each question requires specialized knowledge and understanding of particular aspects of the situation.

Some of these questions relate to the decision making process itself and the role which information is to play in it. Thus, how much of the information stored is really useful for the purposes of the decision maker? More basically, how do we measure value at all? Many of the illustrations of the need for information retrieval systems have emphasized the importance of the obscure fact or relation—usually with the implication that vast sums of money would have been saved if it had been recognized. Is this really significant, and how much is it really worth to be able to provide the obscure fact? It has been suggested that information retrieval is not really a significant problem, for its real solution is in developing a set of "generalists" to filter all of the information and provide the expert answer. Is this true for a particular situation, or does it merely beg the question?

A second class of questions relates to communication with the mass of data. How serious is the effect of specialized jargon and hence how accessible is the data from an intellectual standpoint? What should be the role of various methods of communication, such as dissemination, reporting, and request answering? Is an intermediary needed between the user and the file in order to provide the means for communication? If so, what are the difficulties in the tasks assigned to the intermediary?

The third class of questions relates to the problem of organization. Thus, how does the system accommodate the multiple usages to which it may be put—the specialist, the generalist, the suddenly relevant discipline? What are the limitations imposed by economics? How should the needs for efficiency be weighed with the demands of usage? What about the uncertainty of future needs—should the system be designed to accommodate them or even to anticipate them?

Another set of questions relates to the role of mechanization. Have the increasing size and complexity of information retrieval problems put them out of the reach of direct human control? Some years ago the Bell System was concerned with its inability to provide efficient service through the use of operator-manned switchboards. It was apparent that the telephone business would grow rapidly and that the number of operators required would increase proportionately just as rapidly if manual systems were continued. This kind of growth pressure had considerable influence on the development of advances in switching theory which, in turn, ultimately led to automatic dialing systems. Is information retrieval faced with the same type of situation? With the exponential growth in the literature, for example, can we reasonably expect to double the number or effectiveness of personnel every twenty years? On the other hand, does machinery really represent the answer? Can it be economically justified with its high initial and unit cost? Whether manual or mechanized systems are involved, perhaps the real answer is less service at the same cost. If mechanization is chosen, what criteria are there to weigh the relative merits of alternative systems? Mechanization introduces a highly impersonal element. How can the human being be reconciled with the operation of the machine?

All of these questions must be understood and adequately answered if an effective information system is to be designed. It seems that no single group is now in a position to provide all the answers. The needs of usage, of communication, of efficient organization, and of equipment design cannot now be evaluated without the cooperative efforts of experienced people from each of the areas involved.

PURPOSE OF THE BOOK

The purpose of this book is to show how these areas interrelate with one another and hence why it is essential that competent people, each contributing his own experience and background, must cooperate together if good information systems are to be developed. To show this cooperative interrelationship, the next six chapters describe the present state of work in the field of information storage and retrieval. They cover the contribution which people with operating experience have made; they describe the various systems for organization which have been proposed and developed; they describe the broad range of equipment which can be used. In this way the individual with experience in any one of these areas can quickly be brought up-to-date on the work being performed in the others.

Section II analyzes all of this work within the framework of the total problem of implementing an information system. This analysis shows the main areas of difficulty and the relationships among those groups concerned with their solution. It thus shows how the tools and techniques developed by each group can be brought to bear on the development of a particular information system.

The final section, Section III, attempts to provide a theoretical foundation on which the information system design can be built. It does so by describing the mathematical tools which can relate quantitatively the results from each of the contributing groups.

The authors specifically designed this book as a text for instructional use at the university level. Although many papers have been written on various aspects of information storage and retrieval, the field needs textbooks. Content selected for inclusion in the text has been carefully considered from a teaching point of view, and in fact is based upon several years of teaching experience. This book attempts to weave together relevant material into an organized, unified, logical structure that would make sense to a newcomer, from whatever field he may come. Students entering the field can thus learn of the work of others and more surely prepare themselves for interpreting future developments. It is further anticipated that those peripherally concerned with the information area—executives, research administrators, manufacturers, etc.—will also find the text a useful means by which to grasp the subject matter and draw abreast of a rapidly expanding field.

For the book to achieve its purpose as a text, it has seemed important both to avoid some of the controversies present in this field in the past and to introduce topics which ought to be controversial in the future. For example, there has been a good deal of controversy on the relative merits of various systems for organization of information. It would seem that the need for such controversy is now past, and each of these systems should be viewed for its unique and significant contribution. We have therefore tried to avoid, as far as possible, evaluating the relative merits of these systems and have instead tried to emphasize their individual characteristics, worth, and difficulties.

There are a number of areas in this field which we feel ought to be controversial but which are not now so, and here we have taken a position which is almost deliberately at odds with the established trend in the field in the hope that by so doing light would be generated from the resultant heat of controversy. For example, we have defined a meaning for the term "documentation" which is very much at odds with the generally accepted one so that the meaning of this term will be clarified by discussion. Similarly, in the definition of areas of responsibility we have defined roles in a rather unequivocal manner in order to stimulate discussion concerning the true role of each discipline.

This almost deliberate effort to introduce controversy is perhaps most evident in the last part of the book, which is concerned with the theoretical foundations of this field, for it is here that the greatest effort and open discussion are required. In particular, we have assumed that certain matters of judgment which presently are treated in a completely unquantified manner can, in fact, be measured. That such an assumption is highly controversial is almost self-evident, but it is only by introducing an assumption which can be explicitly attacked that any progress will be made.

REFERENCES

Three comprehensive bibliographies are available, as sources of additional information, for those who enter the field and are anxious for more familiarization.

C. P. Bourne, *Bibliography on the Mechanization of Information Retrieval,* Feb. 1958–1961. This bibliography and three supplements are available from Stanford Research Institute, Menlo Park, Calif.

IBM Corp., *Bibliography and Auto-Index. Literature on Information Retrieval and Machine Translation,* 2nd ed., 1959. IBM Service Bureau Corporation, New York, N.Y.

Paul C. Janaske (ed.), *Information Handling and Science Information. A Selected Bibliography, 1957–1961.* Washington, D.C., Am. Institute of Biological Sciences, 1962.

Government documents which are excellent surveys of the information processing and retrieval programs underway in the United States have also been published.

Documentation, Indexing, and Retrieval of Scientific Information. Prepared by the staff of the Committee on Government Operations, U.S. Senate, 86th Congress, 2nd Session, Doc. No. 113, GPO 1961.

Research on Mechanical Translation, U.S. House of Representatives, Committee on Science and Astronautics, 86th Congress, 2nd Session, No. 9, GPO 1960.

Finally, the National Science Foundation's Office of Science Information regularly issues several publications which list new research and development work reported to it on a continuing basis.

Current Research and Development in Scientific Documentation. National Science Foundation, Office of Science Information Service, Washington, D.C. This series appears several times per year and contains reports of progress and new research in the field. It provides the reader with a description of the research work, the names of the principal investigators, and the address location of the effort.

Non-Conventional Technical Information Systems in Current Use. National Science Foundation, Office of Science Information Service, Washington, D.C. This series includes a description of those technical information systems which have come to the attention of the National Science Foundation. It is a good source for locating actual applications in the United States which embody new principles for the organization of subject matter or the employment of automatic equipment for storage and search.

Several of the national and international conferences that have taken place over the past fifteen years have resulted in the publication of proceedings or preprints which stand out as milestones of organized effort to come to grips logically with the various facets of the field. Two such outstanding sources of reference are

Royal Society Scientific Information Conference. Report and Papers submitted. Burlington House, London, 1948.

Preprints of the Proceedings of the International Conference on Scientific Information, Washington, D.C., Nov. 16–21, 1958. Two volumes, 1635 pages.

Some of the principal journals and periodicals appearing regularly, and which review ideas, discuss new techniques, and describe achievements, include

American Documentation. Published by the American Documentation Institute, 1728 N St. NW, Washington 6, D.C. It is issued quarterly and its purpose is to be a scholarly journal in the field of documentation and to serve as a forum of discussion and experimentation.

Automation Reports. A new publication which gives timely, comprehensive indexing and abstracting coverage to the entire field of automation including automatic controls, analog computers, digital computers, and a special division devoted entirely to the information sciences. It is published by the Commerce Clearing House, 4025 W. Peterson Ave., Chicago, Ill.

Computer Review. Association for Computing Machinery. P. O. Box 1184, Chapel Hill, North Carolina. Published bimonthly, this began in 1960 and provides comprehensive coverage of new information appearing in the broad area of computers.

Journal of Documentation. Published by the Association of Special Libraries and Information Bureaux, 3 Belgrave Square, London S.W.1. This appears quarterly and is devoted to matters concerning the recording, organization, and dissemination of specialized knowledge.

— 2

The librarian and recorded knowledge

The most fundamental objective of information retrieval is to help Man make fullest use of the knowledge he discovers and records. When studying information retrieval, it is essential to understand the ways in which knowledge has been recorded and the techniques developed and used which make it available to mankind.

HISTORY OF RECORDING MEDIA

From earliest time Man has attempted to preserve his thoughts for posterity. A brief sketch of the history of early writing is useful in gaining an appreciation of the development of recorded knowledge.[1]

Archeaologists have unearthed many examples of various forms of writing chiseled into stone. Samples of Egyptian pictographic writing, known as hieroglyphics, were found cut into building stone dating back to 3 or 4000 B.C. They represent one way in which Man devised a shorthand method for conveying ideas and concepts to future generations. The translation of hieroglyphic characters on the Rosetta Stone in the early nineteenth century paved the way for increased understanding and knowledge of Egyptian civilization by modern scholars.

Clay was widely used for recording information during the Sumerian-Babylonian-Assyrian civilization. Writing on clay was less arduous than chipping away at stone because writing was done with a stylus of wood when the clay was soft; then the clay was baked

---

[1] Elmer D. Johnson, *Communication: An Introduction to the History of the Alphabet, Writing, Printing, Books & Libraries*, New York, Scarecrow Press, 1955.

for permanence. The writing is known as cuneiform (Latin for wedge shaped), which refers to the shape of the strokes made by the stylus. A vast amount of historical knowledge became available when cuneiform inscriptions were translated in the nineteenth century.

Clay tablets were awkward to transport and took considerable time to prepare for use. Consequently Egyptian papyrus, the forerunner of paper, evolved as a light-weight, convenient medium for both inscription and communication. However, the papyrus plant could only grow in certain geographical areas. Its source of supply was limited. Parchment, or dried animal skin, was plentiful and later replaced papyrus as the chief recording medium. Although the Chinese had already invented the art of paper making, its use had not yet spread westward during the Egyptian period.

The Romans sparked considerable writing activity. Cities were heavily populated, and government paperwork probably had its origin during that day. The needs of commerce and government made writing an essential ingredient to the culture of the time. Roman parchment books were rolled into scrolls and tied with a ribbon. When more than one copy was required, hundreds of scribes or slaves made the required duplication. Papyrus and parchment served as fixed media for recording. Once written, the record could not be erased and reused without considerable difficulty. The pressure of commerce and trade was probably responsible for the development of the "tabula," which consisted of a wooden board or metal sheet covered with wax. Writing was accomplished by using a metal pointed stylus, and a smooth blunt instrument served as an eraser. The "diptych" is the forerunner of our modern book. It consisted of two tabula hinged together at the center; when closed, the writing was protected. The diptych was a popular form of letter communication in its time. During this same period there evolved a book form known as the "codex," which consisted of strips of papyrus or parchment folded into accordion pleats. Eventually one side of the pleats was sewn, and this, of course, was the beginning of our modern book form.

The Dark Ages which followed the fall of the Roman Empire witnessed very little writing activity. Churches maintained the best and only continuity in the field of historical recording. Church sermons, travel reports, exploration findings, and comments on human behavior were among the kinds of information recorded. Toward the latter half of the medieval period, church manuscripts, artfully styled and beautifully decorated, began appearing. Hand illumination enhanced the value of a book, and books were treasured as much for their artistic quality as for content.

In about 1440 A.D. Johannes Gutenberg invented the movable-type printing press.

> In the cultural history of mankind there is no event even approaching in importance the invention of printing with movable types. It would require an extensive volume to set forth even in outline the far reaching effects of this invention in every field of human enterprise and experience, or to describe its results in the liberation of the human spirit from the fetters of ignorance and superstition.[2]

The combination of paper and the printing press has probably done more to preserve Man's accomplishments than any other single human achievement. Without question it is largely responsible for the mountain of recorded information extant today.

In addition to printing, other media have recently been employed to record knowledge. They include (a) *film*—and the methods of photography, (b) *wax*—as used for the recording of sound, (c) *near-print methods*—which flourish as a result of the introduction of the mimeograph stencil, the ditto master, and the offset plate, and (d) *magnetic*—wherein digital, video, and audio signals can be recorded on tapes, disks, wire, cards, drums, etc.

HISTORY OF THE LIBRARY PROFESSION

Librarians have developed, over many years of operational experience, techniques for making this recorded material available. These techniques have weathered the storm of operation—they work. Libraries, generally speaking, are successful information systems; they provide their customers with information, and they do this with reasonable speed and at minimal cost; they excel at storing information and providing easy and often open, unlimited access to printed material. In fact, they are our main centers of recorded information, and librarians represent the only single source of professional experience on which we can draw to learn about the various kinds of activities normally associated with the organization of information files.

The library profession is a well-knit group, and the network of library activity in this country is highly organized, thriving on mutual interest and interlibrary cooperation. Standardized practices are

---

[2] Douglas C. McMurtrie, *The Book: The Story of Printing and Bookmaking,* New York, Oxford University Press, 1943, p. 136.

common, so that a workable technical improvement in one library, for example, usually serves as a pattern for improvement in others. Therefore, while today's information storage and retrieval interests have machine overtones, it is well to understand established library structure, to study proven methods and techniques, and to become familiar with the tools which librarians have fashioned for the conduct of their work.

The American library system is an institution normally taken for granted. It is an active environment for self-education, recreation, and research having an immeasurable effect on our personal lives and educational development.

Present-day library tools—the card catalog, the subject classification scheme, periodical indexes, etc.—had their origin during a brief period of half a century, from about 1840 to 1900. It was during this time that subject cataloging rules were first formulated in Great Britain; the concept of a "union catalog" to cover the total listing of literature in the United States was proposed; subject heading lists were developed for periodical indexing, etc. The year 1876 was a particularly noteworthy one in American library history, for it was then that Melvil Dewey published the first edition of his now famous decimal classification scheme and the American Library Association was founded.

The most fertile period of library development took place shortly thereafter, from 1876 to 1900. This period is marked by the rise of the American university library, the wide adoption of card catalogs, the definition and introduction of the Library of Congress' subject classification scheme, and the initiation of a centralized distribution service by the Library of Congress for library catalog cards.

Since 1900 the library profession has seen a continual growth in the development of special library tools and in the area of documentation. At the turn of the century an international organization, Federation Internationale de Documentation (FID), was created. In 1909 John Cotton Dana founded the Special Libraries Association, and later in Great Britain the Association of Special Libraries and Information Bureaux (ASLIB) was organized. Another important professional organization founded in the United States several years later was the American Documentation Institute.

In 1944, with the publication of Fremont Rider's *The Scholar and the Future of the Research Library* [3] the impact of modern research

---

[3] Fremont Rider, *The Scholar and the Future of the Research Library,* New York, Hadham Press, 1944.

on the library was clearly described. Since 1950 the library profession has seen a mature and systematic attack on library problems and tremendous advances in the field of documentation and in the development of new techniques.

In September 1956, with the aid of a grant from the Ford Foundation, the Council on Library Resources was established. This is an independent, nonprofit corporation whose aim is to assist in the problems of libraries generally, and of research libraries in particular, and to aid in improving the resources and services of libraries. Its primary interests include the following:

1. Basic research in the processes of distribution, organization, storage, and communication (including transmission) of knowledge as these affect libraries.
2. Technological development looking to improvements in the physical-mechanical apparatus of library work (including the collections themselves) and to the application of mechanisms not yet utilized.
3. Methodological development looking to improvements of technique (as contrasted with improvement of apparatus, although frequently closely related thereto), including improvements effected through coordination of effort as the result of cooperation, standardization, etc.

The Council works principally through grants or contracts to qualified individuals or institutions. It has been an important force in the library profession and responsible for considerable investigation and research in the areas of information retrieval and library technology.

An activity of the federal government which is of special interest to libraries, and to the entire field of information retrieval for that matter, is the Office of Science Information Service of the National Science Foundation, which is headed by Burton W. Adkinson.

NSF has been very active in the field since 1958 at which time Congress established the Office of Science Information Service to give concentrated attention to ways and means by which the methods of storing, translating, abstracting, retrieving, and disseminating information could be improved.

The three main functions of this Office are

1. coordinating the scientific information activities of governmental agencies.
2. supporting grants to organizations performing research or working on advanced methods of indexing, abstracting, translating, and publishing scientific information.

3. publishing timely reports on the advances being made in the field of information retrieval.

LIBRARY FUNCTIONS

The aim of any library is to obtain, preserve, and make available the printed materials required for use by its patrons and in so doing to store recorded knowledge for future generations. In order to do this, libraries are generally divided into several key functions which, although performed separately, are interrelated.

Selection

The primary aim of this activity is to develop a usable collection of material, on a continuing basis, that will satisfy the information needs of the library's users. In a general library, for example public libraries, such needs are wide in scope because of the broad range of reading wants of the general public. In a special library, the collection will be built around a narrowly defined subject field and selection focused carefully to ensure adequate depth of coverage.

At the time a library is first established, the librarian will usually prepare an "acquisitions policy," setting forth the selection criteria by delineating primary and secondary fields of interest. The policy statement is interpreted by the selection personnel in making their day-to-day judgment as to which items are to be acquired and added to the main collection. The procedure consists of regular screening of book-announcements and book-reviewing media which describe available material. Items considered pertinent to the library acquisition policy are ordered. The policy is normally broad enough to include publications in adjacent fields of interest and flexible enough to allow for modifications and adjustments as subject fields of new interest evolve.

The quantity of material ordered depends on the size of the budget. The process of selection is therefore vital and critical because the library's growth and development will largely depend on the results of efforts expended here. When selection is too broad, the library may be inundated with a flood of material of limited usefulness. Yet, if selection is too restrictive, it results in an incomplete collection, and this ultimately reduces the effectiveness of service to readers. Thus it is obvious that, quantitatively, the material selected for acquisition regulates how fast the library will grow in terms of the size of its collection and the number of people required to do processing work and, qualitatively, that the human judgment exercised in the selection process determines how worthwhile library service is likely to be.

The recommendations of the selection personnel are turned into action by the acquisition process. Libraries employ two main methods of procurement. One is by purchase and the other by "gift and exchange." Most purchasing is done from book dealers and involves the routine operations of order preparation, fund allotment, payments, accounting, etc. Although purchase is the most important method, libraries also obtain printed material as gifts from benefactors or in an exchange with other libraries. In addition to its ordering function, acquisition also includes responsibility for the receipt of the printed material, assignment of an "accession," or sequence, number to each piece, and routing it on to the next processing stage.

Cataloging

Librarians distinguish between two kinds of cataloging—descriptive cataloging and subject cataloging. The former refers to the process of identifying the book and selecting the appropriate bibliographic elements for recording, whereas subject cataloging includes processes of classification and the assignment of subject headings. Essentially both processes provide the library with its main searching tools, and all subsequent use of the material will depend on the adequacy and accuracy of these tools.

Recording of bibliographic information is made on cards after the selection of pertinent elements from the title page of the book. Author's name, the title of the book, date, publisher and place of publication, number of pages, etc., represent the kinds of items selected. To ensure a consistent approach during this process, catalogers follow prescribed rules (e.g., American Library Association Cataloging Rules, Library of Congress' Rules for Descriptive Cataloging, etc.[4]) which fix the format of the recorded information. Cards are

---

[4] American Library Association, Division of Cataloging and Classification, A.L.A. Cataloging Rules for Author and Title Entries, 2nd ed., edited by Clara Beetle, Chicago, American Library Association, 1949.

U.S. Library of Congress, Descriptive Cataloging Division, Rules for Descriptive Cataloging in the Library of Congress (adapted by the American Library Association), Washington, D.C., U.S. Government Printing Office, 1949.

Cataloging Rules of the American Library Association and The Library of Congress, editions and changes, 1949–1958, Washington, D.C., Library of Congress, 1959.

later prepared for filing by author and title into an alphabetical file known as a "dictionary" catalog.

No cataloging operation is complete until the book is classified. The process of classification is defined as the systematic placement of the books of a library into related subject groupings based on a prearranged subject plan or scheme. The classifier peruses the contents of the book and, after referring to the subject classification scheme, selects and assigns a symbol, known as a "class number," which corresponds to the main subject theme of the book. This number is amplified by distinguishing symbols, usually for author, to form the "call number," which is recorded on all catalog cards and serves as the book's permanent address. Before the book is actually placed on the shelves, the call number is recorded conspicuously on its spine to ensure that it will continue to be returned to that address. A library may use any classification scheme, but the Dewey Decimal Classification [5] and the Library of Congress' Classification Schedule [6] are the two most popular ones in the United States.

In addition to assigning the call number, the classifier also selects appropriate subject headings from a prescribed list (Library of Congress' List of Subject Headings, Sears' List of Subject Headings, etc.) in order to reflect in the catalog the main subjects treated by the book. Duplicate catalog cards are used, the subjects noted as words along the top of each card, and the cards filed in the dictionary catalog along with the title and author cards.

The Library of Congress prepares and sells catalog cards for most American books and for many foreign ones. Card sets provide full bibliographic information including suggested subject headings plus Dewey and Library of Congress call numbers.

Reference

Using the library's resources for the purpose of providing service is the function of the reference activity. "Reference work" was defined by Bishop [7] as follows: [reference work as] the service rendered by a librarian in aid of some sort of study, the reference librarian as an

---

[5] Melvil Dewey, *Dewey Decimal Classification and Relative Index,* 16th ed., Lake Placid Club, N.Y., Forest Press, 1958.

[6] U.S. Library of Congress, Subject Cataloging Division, Classification Schedules, Washington, D.C. (Classification Schedules have been published for Classes A–Z in various editions at various times.)

[7] William Warner Bishop, Theory of Reference Work, *Bulletin of the American Library Association,* Chicago, June 1915, v. IX, pp. 134–139.

interpreter of library resources, and reference literature as "dictionaries, almanacs, catalogs, cyclopedias, compendia," and other books held in the library for consultation.

The reference staff consists of a unit of trained librarians who give professional assistance to users in selecting and obtaining documentary source materials which are needed for research and other purposes. In some research and special libraries the reference staff plays a particularly active role in linking the information resources of the library to the needs of the requester. Reference librarians are constantly experiencing lessons in human communication as they work with requesters and attempt to express their information requirements in clear and meaningful terms. They soon discover, too, that each requester considers his own need for service not only justified but also important, and it becomes exceedingly difficult or impossible for the staff to distinguish between marginal and worthy service requests. Consequently the reference librarian normally tends to treat all requests with equal effort.

Staff services take many different forms. "Ready-reference" service is one. It consists of giving spot answers to questions. Reference librarians will also perform extensive searches for groups of facts. They compile lists of references to literature in various subject fields, called "bibliographies." These are sometimes annotated as well. In fact, under certain circumstances (the work of the Legislative Reference Staff of the Library of Congress is a good example), the staff may even be asked to prepare articles for a requester which synthesize information on a given subject from many sources.

Not only does the experienced reference librarian have an intimate understanding of the library's own technical tools, but he also develops an over-all personal appreciation for the general content of the library's collection and sometimes along with it an almost uncanny sense of knowing just where to go to get the desired information.

Circulation

When the exact reference to a piece of printed material is known, the circulation staff routinely provides it for library users. Circulation activity consists in getting the book from the shelf, charging it out to the reader, receiving it on return, and, finally, reshelving it. The greatest number of daily-user transactions in a library occur in the circulation department. Printed materials removed from the shelves in response to individual requests are either examined on the library premises, photoduplicated, or sent or taken elsewhere for use. An extensive interlibrary loan network exists in the United States, which makes the resources of every library more widely available. Established procedures and standardized forms are used for transmitting printed materials between libraries.

An important function associated with circulation work is record keeping. Statistical records are maintained on borrowers, overdue books, and the rate at which books are issued, returned, and shelved. These records are useful to management in planning, in personnel administration, and in analyzing the nature and amount of usage made of the collection.

LIBRARY TOOLS

Early libraries concentrated on the physical arrangement of books on shelves in prescribed order, sometimes according to size and color. As the number of books increased, however, additional organization was necessary to make the content of the library collection more accessible. To provide this organization, librarians developed subject classification schemes, the card catalog, and other tools. These bibliographic tools now constitute the keystone of the structure for control of the library collection and are the basic finding aids employed by librarians to assist scholars and researchers.

The Catalog

This is by far the most important tool available to the library in the management of its collection of printed material. It serves as the library's main index to the printed contents of its collection by indicating what material the library holds and where it may be found. The form of the catalog can either be card or book. Cards are generally the preferred form because of the interfiling advantage which they have when adding new material and making changes. Book catalogs, although more compact and thus more easily disseminated, do not possess this flexibility and are essentially outdated when printed. Library catalogs are placed in conspicuous locations to facilitate consultation. A "union catalog" is a special type of catalog which records the location of printed material on an interlibrary basis irrespective of geographic location.

The practice followed by most libraries in developing their "dictionary card catalog" is to include, in addition to an entry for author and one for title, an adequate number of entries for relevant subjects, filed under one or more visual headings. Such subjects are drawn from an established list so as to best represent the information content of the book.

A typical set of Library of Congress catalog cards which are used in its unit card system is shown in Fig. 1.

The establishment of an appropriate list of subject headings and their organization and sequence in a catalog have been the subject of much discussion in the library literature. A subject heading system consists of the selection of words or phrases as main headings and the use of additional words and phrases as subdivisions. Subject headings are usually arranged in alphabetical order, and the subdivisions within each heading are also arranged alphabetically. Thus, for example, if one were to list all of the branches of chemistry, the subject heading would be CHEMISTRY, and five subdivisions might be Analytical, Inorganic, Organic, Physical, Physiological.

An oft-referred to subject heading system, and one we are accustomed to using, is the yellow page section of the telephone directory. Here words and phrases are used as subject headings, and within each heading there is an alphabetical list of the commercial firms associated with the business or service listed.

One of the drawbacks of a subject heading system is the arbitrary or artificial decisions which the indexer must make at the input stage when he makes his initial assignment of subject headings to documents. The user will not always agree with the indexer's choice—the semantics of the heading may change with time, and the concepts underlying the indexer's choice may themselves change. While the subject heading system has the virtue of expandability, it has the corresponding disadvantage of increasing rapidly in terms of size and complexity. Inevitably this leads to a disproportionate rise in subject heading maintenance costs. Norbert Wiener in 1960 remarked to the author, in this connection, that "labels are only good for preserve jars."

The subject headings used by most large American libraries are those in the Library of Congress subject authority list. This subject heading list sets the standard for most libraries and serves as the official set of headings for a large share of published materials. The Library of Congress maintains the list, keeps it up-to-date, and makes changes and additions as required by the appearance of new material or changes in terminology. The Library of Congress has devoted considerable attention and professional skill to the orderly development of the headings for organizing its own collections; the headings chosen

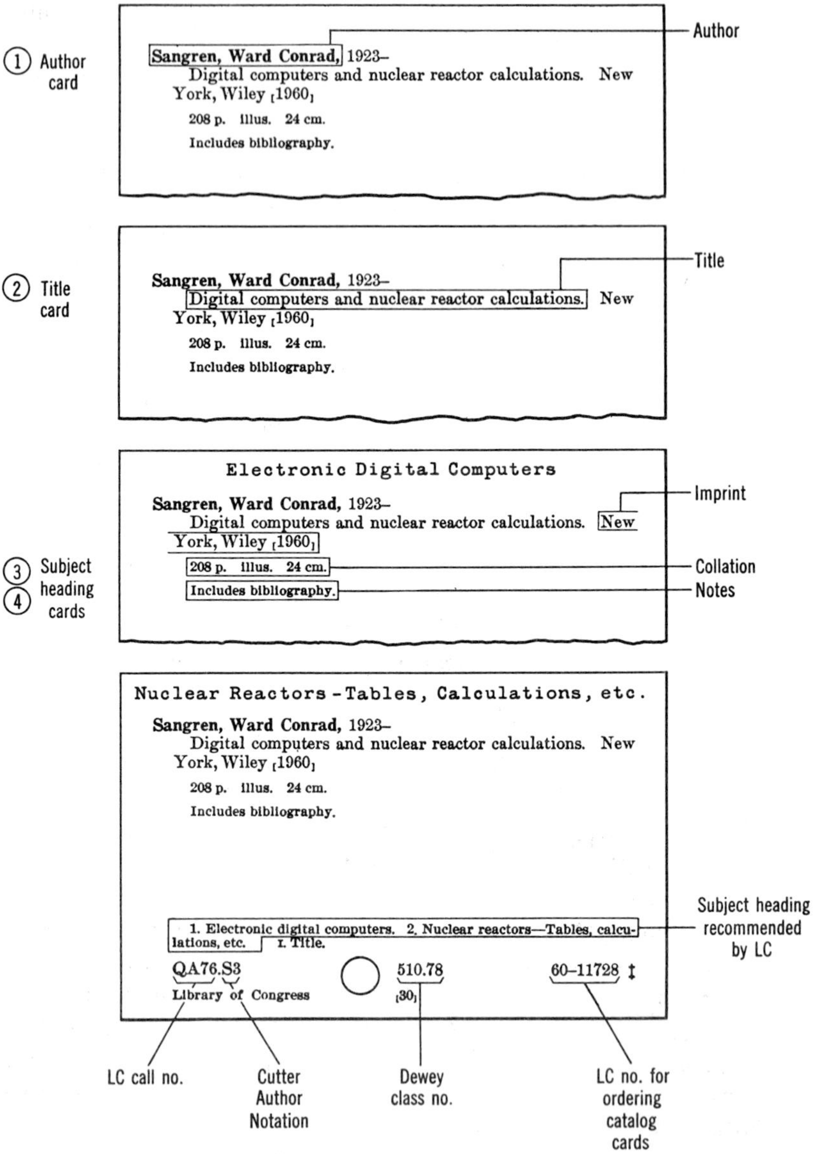

FIG. 1. Contents of a set of Library of Congress printed catalog cards.

by them for application to particular books appear at the bottom of the printed catalog cards distributed by the Library of Congress. While many libraries use the headings supplied with the cards, nothing prevents a library from developing its own list of headings to meet special needs, perhaps with the Library of Congress List as a guide. This has been the case, for example, in scientific and technical libraries, where research interest has been highly specialized. There is great danger, however, in using a subject heading list for which there are no rules of practice and no mechanism for evolving a systematic and consistent pattern of changes.

The introduction to the Library of Congress List contains the following paragraph describing the character of the work.[8]

> [The List is] a record of the headings traced on the Library of Congress' printed catalog cards and used in its card catalogs and cumulative Catalog series. [It] is the product of evolutionary forces, among them the growth of the Library's collections, semantic change, and varying theories of subject heading practice over the years. As a consequence, the list is, at any point in time, an accurate reflection of practice but not a complete embodiment of theory.

Liberally interspersed in the Library of Congress List are "scope notes," which draw distinctions between headings and provide suitable explanation of their usage. Also included are many types of references. "See" references direct the reader to preferred synonymous terms, so that the user is led from his subject to the terms employed by the system (for example, "Ex-serviceman *see* Veteran"). The "see also" reference brings related headings together and directs the user to more specific subjects or topics and to applications of the subject; the aim of a "see also" reference is to coordinate subjects which are suggested as likely to be of interest to the user (for example, "Transistors *see also* Tunnel Diodes"). Reference may also be made to the Library of Congress Classification number when there is a close correspondence between a specific heading and the classification tables; the Library of Congress subject heading list in this way serves as a partial or limited index to the Library of Congress Classification. Three key symbols are used in the list: sa for see also; x to indicate which headings were referred from a "see" term; and xx to indicate which headings were referred from a "see also" heading. Thus, as shown in the entry below, a main subject heading carries with it all

---

[8] *Subject Headings Used in the Dictionary Catalogs of the Library of Congress,* 6th ed., Library of Congress, Washington, D.C., 1957, p. iii.

TABLE 1

Library of Congress Subject Authority List (excerpt).*

Evolution (*Continued*)
  Statics and dynamics (Social sciences)
  Teleology.
  Variation (Biology)
x Darwinism.
  Development.
  Epigenesis.
  Mutation (Biology)
xx Biology.
  Botany—Variation.
  Creation.
  Genetics.
  Heredity.
  Historical sociology.
  Man—Origin.
  Natural selection.
  Ontogeny.
  Philosophy, Modern.
  Phylogeny.
  Religion and science.
  Teleology.
  Transmutation of animals.
  Variation (Biology)
  Zoology.
  Zoology—Variation.

Evolutionary ethics. *See* Ethics, Evolutionary.

Ewe (African people) (*DT500; DT511; DT582*)

Ewe language. (*PL8161–4*)
sa Fon dialect.
  Mina dialect.

Ewes.
xx Sheep.

Ex libris. *See* Book-plates.

Ex post facto laws. (*Direct*)

SPECIAL TOPICS

1. Lower schools.—General works on examinations, whether for teachers or pupils, are entered under Examinations. Compilations of questions and answers for such examinations are entered under Examinations—Questions; when confined to a single country, state, or city, the subdivision Questions is added to the local subdivision, *e.g.* Examinations — Ohio — Questions. Compilations limited to a county are entered under state subdivision.
2. Universities and colleges.—Works on examinations in universities and colleges, as well as compilations of questions and answers for these examinations, are entered under Universities and colleges, with subdivision Examinations. If limited to a single country, state, or city, the subdivision Examinations is added to the local subdivision, *e.g.* Universities and colleges—U. S.—Examinations. Works limited to a specific college or university are entered under that college or university, with subdivision Examinations. *e.g.* Harvard University—Examinations. If limited to a specific branch of study, that branch is added as a further subdivision, *e.g.* Universities and colleges — Wisconsin — Examinations—English; Harvard University—Examinations—Mathematics, and duplicate entry is made under the specific subject.

Examinations (*Continued*)
sa Civil service—Examinations.
  Law examinations.
also subdivision Examinations *under armies and navies, e.g.* France.
  Armée—Examinations.
x Achievement tests.
  Competitive examinations.
  Teachers—Examinations.
xx Education.
  Educational tests and measurements.
  Teaching.
Notes under Examinations—Questions; Universities and colleges—Entrance requirements; Universities and colleges—Examinations.
—Questions. (*LB3051–9*)
  Cf. note under Examinations.
sa Mental tests.
  Note under Examinations.

* * *

—Ohio.
  —Questions.
  Note under Examinations.

Examinations, Medical. *See* Diagnosis; Insurance, Accident [Health, Life]—Medical examinations; Pensions, Medical examinations for; Premarital examinations.
  Examinations in medicine are entered under Medicine—Examinations, questions, etc.

Examinations, Preparation for. *See* Study, Method of.

Examinations before trial. *See* Preliminary examinations (Criminal procedure)

x Nulla poena sine lege doctrine.
Nullum crimen sine lege doctrine.
xx Criminal law.
Due process of law.
Retroactive laws.

Ex post facto laws (Canon law)

Ex-service men. *See* Veterans.

Ex-votos. *See* Votive offerings.

Exakta camera.
Example under Cameras.

Examination of conscience. *See* Conscience, Examination of.

Examination of mines. *See* Mine examination.

Examination of the blood. *See* Blood—Analysis and chemistry; Blood—Examination.

Examination of witnesses. *See* Cross-examination.

Examinations. (*Direct*) (*College, LB2353, LB2367; Professional courses, LC1070–1071; School, LB3051–3060; Teachers, LB1763–5*)

Here are entered works on examinations in general, *e.g.* discussions on the value of examinations, statistics, history, and similar general topics.

3. Universities and colleges—Entrance requirements.—Works in which the requirements for admission to college or university are stated or discussed are entered under the heading Universities and colleges—Entrance requirements, subdivided in the same manner as Examinations, *e.g.* Universities and colleges—Entrance requirements; Universities and colleges—Austria—Entrance requirements; Pennsylvania. University — Entrance requirements; Smith College—Entrance requirements—Mathematics. Compilations of questions and answers for entrance examinations are entered under the subdivision Examinations.
4. Particular branches of study.—Compilations of questions and answers for examinations in a particular branch of study are entered under the specific subject, *e.g.* English language—Examinations, questions, etc.; Law—U. S.—Examinations, questions, etc.; Medicine — Examinations, questions, etc. General discussions, including the rules governing these examinations, are entered either under the appropriate phrase, *e.g.* Law examinations, or under the subject with subdivision Examinations, *e.g.* Accounting—Examinations.

Examiners (Administrative procedure) (*Direct*)
x Hearing examiners.
Trial examiners.
xx Administrative courts.
Administrative procedure.

Example.
sa Exempla.
Ideals (Psychology)
Influence (Psychology)
x Model.
Pattern.
xx Authority.
Ethics.
Exempla.
Ideals (Psychology)
Imitation.
Influence (Psychology)

Exanthemata. (*RC106*)
sa Fever.
also names of eruptive diseases, e.g. Erysipelas, Measles.
x Eruptive fever.
Fever, Eruptive.
xx Fever.

Excardination (Canon law) (*BX1939.E*)
sa Incardination (Canon law)
xx Benefices, Ecclesiastical (Canon law)
Clergy (Canon law)
Incardination (Canon law)

* *Subject Headings Used in the Dictionary Catalogs of the Library of Congress*, 6th ed., Library of Congress, Washington, D.C., 1957

other associated terms or headings which may be used or found elsewhere in the system.

INCANTATIONS (BF 1558; GR540)

sa Blessing and cursing
x Spells
xx Folklore
Magic
Occult sciences
Superstition

The shelf list is an internal library catalog generally available only to librarians. It consists of one entry for every item in the collection and is arranged in a sequence which duplicates the order of the books on the shelves. For this reason librarians often refer to the shelf list as an "inventory catalog."

To a limited extent the shelf list can also serve as a "class catalog." Since cards in a class catalog are arranged by class number, a user is able to examine material in one general subject category just as he customarily does when he browses through a shelf of books in the library stacks.

The Classification Scheme

Classification is designed to organize books on shelves in a manner most conducive to their use. Many books and ideas are related either by subject or by some accidental property of the things beings classified. Thus books can be separated by such characteristics as language, alphabet, form, and date. Fiction in most libraries, for example, is arranged by author's name, and biography is also treated alphabetically by the name of the individual written about. Book collections have also been arranged by color, size, financial value, the language in which the material is written, etc.

Subject classification concepts involve the use of a systematic plan for arranging subject matter according to some preconceived order. This generally requires the preparation of a subject plan known as a classification scheme, which organizes knowledge to a prescribed depth of detail. Plans of this kind vary from the ideal subject classification scheme, which embraces all knowledge in what has been referred to as the "tree of knowledge" structure, to more utilitarian arrangements, which attempt to organize knowledge according to patterns of user interest.

An examination of a typical classification scheme will reveal the following. The scheme will comprise those entries (words) which make up a given subject field. The entries will be arranged according to an organized structure which divides them into main classes and then into subdivisions of classes. The main class covers the more general concepts, whereas the subdivisions embrace areas of specificity. Each entry in the classification scheme carries with it a unique numerical or alphabetical notation. A "relative" index usually appears at the end of the scheme. Included in a "relative" index are the entries found in the scheme plus synonyms for the words used and related subject entries.

Classification schemes are used in libraries to place books acquired for the collection into an order which enables users to find books on the same subject in one place.[9] The librarian, faced with the prospect of classifying a book, will have already been indoctrinated in the classification scheme employed by his library. The book is examined, its key subject noted, and the pertinent entry found in the schedule. The notation symbol given for the entry is assigned to the book as the basic part of its call number. The call number is then recorded on all catalog cards made for the book; it also appears on the book's spine to facilitate shelving and finding.

Several well-known and conventional classification schedules are in use in American libraries. A general understanding of their structure is a prerequisite to full appreciation of the nonconventional schemes described later.

Melvil Dewey prepared the first edition of his Dewey Decimal Classification in 1876. The oldest of the modern bibliographical schemes, it is in widespread use. The scheme has nine main classes with an additional one for General Works.

000	General Works	500	Pure Science
100	Philosophy	600	Technology
200	Religion	700	Fine Arts
300	Social Science	800	Literature
400	Language	900	History

The individual classes are represented by decimal integers from 000. to 999. Extensions, additions, and finer subdivisions are indicated by digits to the right of the decimal point. Most such use is limited to a six-digit notation. However, the requirements of certain

---

[9] Maurice F. Tauber et al., *Technical Services in Libraries,* New York, Columbia University Press, 1954.

subject fields have extended the notation to as much as nine digits to the right of the decimal point.

An interesting feature of the Dewey Decimal Classification is the recurring use of mnemonic aids. For example, the digit 5 is used in some portions of the schedule to refer to Italy, and thus 450 means Italian language and 850 Italian literature. Similarly, under languages, a 3 stands for dictionaries, 4 for synonyms, 5 for grammar, etc. A book on synonyms of the Italian language would therefore be 454. Other classes also use special mnemonic aids. Librarians trained in the classification eventually learn to deduce considerable information about a book merely by examining its call number.

"Form Divisions" are still another technique used in the Dewey Decimal Classification to facilitate the like grouping of subject matter. The standard form divisions are

01	Philosophy and Theory
02	Handbooks and Outlines
03	Dictionaries and Encyclopedias
04	Essays and Lectures
05	Periodicals
06	Organizations and Societies
07	Study and Teaching
08	Collections and Polygraphy
09	History and Local Treatment

These numbers are used with any subject as appropriate. Thus 503 is a dictionary of science, and 850.09 means a history of Italian literature.

The Dewey Decimal Classification is divided into two main sections, the tables and the relative index. The tables are arranged in numerical sequence according to the main classes. By examining any section of the tables one can well determine the logic which caused a particular subject to be placed in a particular location. The tables are replete with helpful annotations to guide the classifier in making correct decisions and judgments. For example, certain terms are defined if for some reason there is doubt about the clarity of their meaning. Scope notes also appear to indicate to the classifier just which aspects of a given subject are intended to be embraced by a specific number. Other notes in the classification supply specific directions or instructions to the classifier. In addition to these instruction notes, the classification is generously supplied with cross reference notes which refer the classifier to other numbers where he should consider placing related material.

The second section, the relative index, is an alphabetical arrangement of subjects indicating their corresponding numerical location in the tables. The index performs two important functions: (1) It brings together various aspects of a subject to show their dispersion in the tables, and (2) it employs synonyms to assist the classifier in finding the main word used by the classification to describe a given subject.

Sixteen editions of the Dewey Decimal Classification have been published. Few libraries follow the classification precisely. Small libraries have no need for the detailed expansions, and the large or specialized libraries have need for expansions in certain subjects beyond the standard ones. For the sake of consistency in the evolution of the classification, a Dewey editorial office was established in 1958 under the administration of the Library of Congress to coordinate expansions.

In 1889 Herbert Putnam, then Librarian of Congress, reorganized the Library and introduced a new classification scheme. This was done after careful and extensive review of the Dewey scheme and others. The formulation of the new scheme, known as the Library of Congress Classification, utilized the best features of existing subject classification plans and was designed to satisfy the classification needs of the *actual* contents of the Library of Congress' book collection rather than to meet a theoretical situation.

The classification is composed of several individual classes.[10] There is no special relationship among classes, each being chosen in a fairly arbitrary way. The Library of Congress is responsible for the consistent and continuing development of the classification, and through the U.S. Government Printing Office it distributes at low cost copies of each of the classes, separately bound, each with its own index. In this way libraries with special subject needs may use only those classes which apply to their particular interests.

Main classes are grouped as follows:

A	General Works, Polygraphy
B	Philosophy and Religion
C	History, Auxiliary Sciences
D	History and Topography (excluding America)
E–F	America
G	Geography, Anthropology
H	Social Science, Economics, Sociology
J	Political Science

---

[10] U.S. Library of Congress, Subject Cataloging Division, Classification Schedules, Washington, D.C. (Classification Schedules have been published for Classes A–Z in various editions at various times.)

K	Law
L	Education
M	Music
N	Fine Arts
P	Language and Literature
Q	Science
R	Medicine
S	Agriculture, Plant and Animal Industry
T	Technology
U	Military Science
V	Naval Science
Z	Bibliography and Library Science

As can be observed, the letters I, O, W, X, and Y are not used, these being reserved for future expansions. Actually K is not in being at the present time either, but it is under development. The notation followed is alpha-numeric; thus Q means Science, QA Mathematics, QB Astronomy, QC Physics, QD Chemistry, etc., and QD181.C1 means Carbon. Although the form of notation employed has little mnemonic value, the notation is simple. The classification carries many forms of references, all designed to clarify intent, meaning, and usage for the classifier.

Because the Library of Congress classification was prepared by specialists and is patterned for the use and subject content of a very large initial collection, many large libraries in America and others throughout the world use it. Special libraries have found the separate, detailed classes to be complete in themselves, and consequently of great value, and all who use it are assured that it will be kept up-to-date and revised by professionally skilled persons.

The Universal Decimal (Brussels) Classification (UDC) is an adaptation of the Dewey Decimal Classification. UDC was originally developed by two Belgians, Paul Otlet and Henry La Fontaine. Their initial purpose was to design a universal classification scheme for bibliography and it was only later that the scheme came into use as a shelf location of books. At first the UDC flourished under the sponsorship of the International Institute of Bibliography, but in recent years it has been placed under the aegis of FID. An abridgement of the UDC describing its relationship to the Dewey Decimal Classification and providing the reader with a lucid introduction to its structure and principles was published in 1957 by the British Standards Institute.[11] UDC uses general principles of classification similar to

[11] *Universal Decimal Classification,* abridged English edition, 2nd ed., British Standards Institute, London, revised 1957.

Dewey's but employs special symbols to permit detailed classification expansions. The notation can become exceedingly long and involved. However, libraries already utilizing the Dewey Decimal Classification have found UDC to be a logical way to achieve detailed expansion within their existing main structure. The classification has appeared in several languages and is controlled by FID.

Main classes include:

0 Generalities
1 Philosophy, Metaphysics, Psychology, Logic, Ethics and morals
2 Religion, Theology
3 Social Sciences, Economics, Law, Government, Education
4 Philology, Linguistics, Languages
5 Pure Sciences
6 Applied Sciences, Medicine, Technology
7 The Arts, Entertainment, Sport
8 Literature, Belles Lettres
9 Geography, Biography, History

Although the UDC was based largely on the Dewey Decimal Classification, it has departed from the original work in terms of its comprehensiveness and the notation system employed. For example, it uses a plus sign (+) to unite two subjects contained in one book; thus 52 + 53 indicates that both Astronomy and Physics are described in the content. A slash sign (/) indicates that constituent subjects run in sequences; thus 52/58 is the same as 52 + 53 + 54 · · · + 58. The colon (:) is employed to show relationships, e.g., Lives of Astronomers would be 52:92. These are but a few of many signs used by the system. Together with the auxiliary tables, which increase the comprehensiveness of the main classification and aid in specifying subjects more precisely, they allow for many different combinations of notation and consequently more flexibility in the assignment of the final number, complex as it may appear. Table 2 shows a typical example.

Some libraries append an additional notation to the classification number of a book. This notation (e.g., Cutter author marks) represents a code for the author's name and facilitates the shelving and finding of a book in a large collection. In the biography sections of most public libraries, for example, books are arranged on the shelf according to the names of the individuals written about. Thus books from Adams to Washington are arranged in alphabetical sequence, and books about the life of a given individual can be found grouped together on the shelf. The Cutter author marks also serve as a sec-

TABLE 2

Universal Decimal Classification (excerpt).*

625		Railway, highway engineering
625.1		Railway engineering track
625.2		Rolling stock, locomotives, etc.
625.3		Railways of special construction
	(23)	Mountain railways
.31		Narrow gauge railways
.32		Adhesion railways for steep gradients
.33		Rack railways
.35		Broad gauge railways (over 5 ft 6 in.)
.36		Moving platforms
.37		Railways with driverless trains
.39		Other railways of special type

* International Federation for Documentation, Universal Decimal Classification, 2nd ed., revised 1957, London, British Standards Institution, 1957.

ondary filing mode to facilitate the physical arrangement of books on a shelf when many books by different authors are to be filed within the same subject classification number.

Cutter author marks are assigned from tables based on the statistics of distribution of names.[12] They are so constructed as to allow a two- or three-digit code number to represent a limited range of alphabetically allied surname spellings. The following portion of the tables is taken from the "W" section.

480	WEN
481	WENCKS
482	WENDELA
483	WENDLI
484	WENDS
485	WENGEN
486	WENI
487	WENL
488	WENR
489	WENY

[12] Charles A. Cutter, *C. A. Cutter's Cutter-Sanborn Three Figure Author Table,* distributed by H. R. Huntting Co., Springfield, Mass.

In applying the code from the table, the classifier uses the first letter of the author's surname and then the number which covers the range within which the surname can be located. For example, an author named WENTHORP would be assigned a Cutter author mark of W488.

THE PROBLEM AREAS

As we have indicated, mainstays of the traditional library approach have been the subject catalog and the classification scheme. They establish the principles of use and set the rules for subject application to individual material. However, their use has some serious limitations. At best, content analysis, as a human process, is subject to a wide range of interpretation because of individual differences in the education, experience, and psychological orientation of the indexers. Despite the best training efforts, inconsistent application of subject headings or numbers invariably occurs among personnel using the same list. Consequently, information scattering that eventually affects the system's reliability results.

An even more critical limitation can be described as *impermanence.* Time has an adverse effect on the meaning of terms applied from a subject list. Knowledge and language are dynamic processes, and accurate labeling of information at one point in time may later be imprecise and out of context. The strictest form of administrative control and systematic review becomes essential in order to counteract a general wearing away or weakening of the meaning of terms as originally applied. Revision must take place continuously in order to define more precisely the limits of related subjects, to adjust to subject expansions and atrophy, and to clarify language ambiguities.

Librarians have not been unaware of these inadequacies in conventional tools nor of the difficulties encountered in applying them in practice. Kelley [13] as early as 1937 described the basic elements affecting the usefulness of conventional classification. Her description sums up what many others have been repeating many different ways in recent years. She pointed out that the changing order of knowledge makes the static perfection of any classification scheme impossible. The need, the interest, the material—all will change with time; any fixed classification scheme will be outdated almost from the moment of its creation. Any single hierarchical representation

---

[13] Grace Osgood Kelley, The Classification of Books, doctoral dissertation, New York, the H. W. Wilson Co., 1937.

of subject matter is usually inadequate for expressing the great variety of relationships of interest, and the nature of systematic classification is to separate parts from whole. It thus breaks apart concepts when they do not need to be broken apart and, in fact, when it would be preferable that they were not.

Any classification or systematic order, in comparison with other more easily comprehended orders, such as the alphabetical or the chronological, has been artificially created, and, although to the creator it is the most natural classification, for the general user it may not be a natural way of viewing the world. Thus the tendency of any specialist is to organize a field of subject matter about his own special and immediate interest.

To develop a classification scheme that will meet the needs of all potential users in any given organization is exceedingly difficult if not impossible. Tough semantic questions enter into the problem, and they are inflamed by the belief of every specialist that he and he alone is competent to classify the field of his own specialty. It is noteworthy that no two such specialists, even when working together in precisely the same field, can come to 100% agreement on how their data should be categorized.

Furthermore, the content of books interferes with the satisfactory application of any system of classification, for typically they cut across a number of categories. It is impractical to reclassify old books on any wide scale, so expansions and reconstructions are difficult. The poor and faulty work of the classifier in applying a classification scheme produces almost insurmountable difficulties, particularly when complex and unfamiliar subject fields are involved. Too frequently the tendency is to determine the classification of a particular book by the use or purpose for which it was written rather than by the use which will be made of it. Finally, the long and confusing notation for very specific subjects in some of the classification schemes, involving some fifteen to twenty decimal and alphabetic characters, makes communication difficult at best.

However, it must be emphasized that the aim of classification schemes, as used in libraries, is to place books acquired for the collection into an order which enables the user to find in one place books which treat the same subject. In this way books which the user is likely to want together he will find together. This is the basic and crucial question in the organization of any library system whether it is by classification or by any other scheme. Organization has the purpose of bringing physically together material likely to be wanted together.

Aside from these problem areas, which are a result of the basic characteristics of the material a library handles, there are other problem areas which are a result more of history and tradition. For example, the library traditionally has been regarded as a service organization. It has therefore never developed a significant degree of financial support, nor has it introduced normal cost accounting procedures. The result is that even today there are few accurate pictures of precisely what the costs of individual library operations are.[14,15] This lack of a cost accounting approach is perhaps not serious when the demands are limited and can be satisfied by the dedicated service of a limited number of people. But in the functioning of large information centers, particularly when equipment is involved, the question of costs and economic operation becomes a paramount one.

SPECIALIZATION IN LIBRARY AND INFORMATION SERVICES

Although the traditional library tools make location of a particular title from among miles and miles of shelving a routine and simple task in libraries today, by and large they are not designed to provide more than a rough-cut approach to the subjects covered by the printed material in their vast collections. In terms of the clientele served by general libraries, this may indeed be all that is needed, but when the same conventional general library techniques are applied to highly specialized collections of nonbook, technically detailed data, the weaknesses in precision of retrieval are keenly observed. Library techniques are serving as a springboard from which researchers are seeking more advanced techniques to cope with rapidly emerging requirements for more subtle and detailed access to information.

During the past quarter century, the library profession has therefore seen more and more specialization of information services. This development had its start in industry and government, where the need first existed to organize more minutely the recorded information of a narrowly defined subject field in support of intensive research demands.

As the areas of inquiry grow more specialized, research becomes more complex and the consequent library problems increase. The

---

[14] Catherine Maybury, Performance Budgeting for the Library, *ALA Bulletin*, January 1961, pp. 46–53.

[15] Catherine MacQuarrie, Cost Survey: Cost of Ordering, Cataloging, and Preparations in Southern California Libraries, *Library Resources and Technical Services*, Fall 1962, v. 6, No. 4.

emergence of new ideas produces new facts together with new terminology, and the task of organizing them in proper relationship to each other poses a real challenge. There is an awareness among librarians that the selection and manipulation of fragments of information rather than entire documents will require unconventional tools. The traditional approach, exemplified by the subject classification scheme and the card catalog and based on a preconceived arrangement of knowledge, is believed too confining.

Emphasis thus has been on finding new ways and means of codifying or indexing data so that they will lend themselves more to correlation than to group selection. The trend has been toward greater depth of content analysis. In addition to exploring new analytical methods, investigations have also been made of employing electronic machines for analysis, storage, and retrieval. It is reasoned that, because of the mass of data involved, storage and handling techniques may have to be of a more advanced character than those customarily used for manually shelving books and filing documents. Vannevar Bush said [16]

> A record, if it is to be useful in science, must be continuously extended, it must be stored, and above all it must be consulted. Today we make the record conventionally by writing and by photography, followed by printing; but we also record in film, on wax discs, and on magnetic wires. Even if utterly new recording procedures do not appear, these present ones are certainly in the process of modification and extension.
>
> The repetitive processes of thought are not confined, however, to matters of arithmetic and statistics. In fact, every time one combines and records facts in accordance with established logical processes, the creative aspect of thinking is concerned only with the selection of the data and the process to be employed and the manipulation thereafter is repetitive in nature and hence a fit matter to be relegated to the machines.

Some librarians have become particularly sensitive on the subject of the mechanization of information and library processes. They believe, and rightly so, that they have been retrieving information for years—and that it is basically a human process. In library terms they call it "reference work," and most librarians trained in this field are very skillful information hunters. Their pride is therefore legitimately disturbed by suggestions made by some naive persons that a mechanical cure-all just over the horizon will place the Library of

---

[16] Vannevar Bush, As We May Think, *Atlantic Monthly,* August 1945, v. 176, pp. 101–108.

Congress in a small black box, increase efficiency a thousandfold, and do all this at less cost!

It is generally recognized, however, that during the next quarter century libraries will undergo changes comparable only to those that occurred in the years from 1875 to 1900, when a group of American pioneers changed the whole character of world librarianship. The basis of all modern library work was developed during that last quarter of the nineteenth century, but the pace then was leisurely and there was no noticeable outside pressure for rapid or drastic change. By contrast, the transformation of present-day librarianship is certain to be made under increasing pressures of output of publications as well as the urgently mounting needs of research workers.

Ridenour summed up the view of the library problem clearly when he said in his article in *Bibliography in an Age of Science:*

> . . . What is needed is a re-evaluation of the whole fabric of the library, from the bottom to the top. In making this analysis, no prejudice should enter, nothing should be taken for granted.
>
> To mention only one thing, a [research] library should no longer necessarily be regarded as a place where books are stored. Perhaps it is entirely something else. Possibly a library is a combination of study rooms, seminars, and a first-rate communication center of a specialized sort.

Machines are already playing an important role in many library and information situations.[17,18] They are handling quantities of recorded knowledge and supplying necessary information, often more speedily and efficiently than the human librarian. Some organizations are using machines experimentally for indexing, abstracting, and translating. Unfortunately, most of the information concerning the present-day activities of electronic machines in the information field is highly technical and in some cases so evidently promotional that even those familiar with the work and intellectually sympathetic to it find it difficult to distinguish fact from fiction. All too typical is the type of advertising exemplified by

> The computer department is presently engaged in the design and development of an extremely high-volume, high-speed information storage and retrieval system. The ultimate system will not be bound by the present state of the equipment art. The problems involved cannot be stated in

---

[17] The State of the Library Art, edited by Ralph R. Shaw, v. 4 [Retrieval Systems], New Brunswick, N.J., Graduate School of Library Service, Rutgers–The State University, 1961.

[18] *Nonconventional Technical Information Systems in Current Use,* National Science Foundation, September 1959, and supplements.

terms of the standard data handling system—nor is it expected that the solutions shall be.

Exciting progress is being made. Already, under pressure of research, conceptual boundaries are disappearing and the limits of the possible are expanding. Further intensive research into new concepts—and effective translation of these concepts into equipment—promise major breakthroughs in this area.

Librarians, educators, engineers, manufacturers, documentalists—all those engaged in the information field—require a basic common source of knowledge which will enable them to develop workable solutions jointly. Professionals in each field particularly need a level of intellectual and technical briefing that will enable them to visualize themselves and their work in this new environment.

It would seem that today's aim in information storage and retrieval should not be to find a mechanical substitute for public or university or special libraries but to devise a complementary electronic organization which can keep pace with the expanding publishing rate in specific fields and provide means for automating technical library processing operations. There is every reason to believe that just as handwriting continued to flourish after the invention of the printing press, so general book libraries will remain a life necessity even though various forms of mechanization may be introduced.

3

The documentalist and the development of new techniques

Several groups of people, recognizing the need for new and different techniques for organization of information and equipment, have devoted themselves to research into the problems of information system design. Since they are interested in finding new ways by which specialized information can be organized and used, they tend to view information systems in a broader sense than traditional librarianship by including the entire process from original publication of material to its ultimate dissemination from the information system. With such a broad scope of interest, this field of study has become a rather amorphous one. Since librarianship is closely related to it, there is no sharp dividing line between the traditional librarian and those, called the documentalists, concerned with this kind of research. Similarly, there is no sharp dividing line between the standard data processing system designer and the system designer concerned with information storage and retrieval.

In fact, a great deal of confusion has existed as to just what constitutes the defining characteristics of this field of effort. Some of the attempts to define documentation have instead tended to increase the degree of confusion and obscure the boundaries between it and librarianship. For example, Jesse H. Shera implies [1] that documentation is simply a different type of librarianship when he describes it as

[1] Jesse H. Shera and Margaret E. Egan, Prolegomena to Bibliographic Control, *Journal of Cataloging and Classification,* 1949, v. 5.

. . . distinguished from general library work in being more intensive—i.e., subject analysis is carried further, the range of resources accumulated is greater, etc. And documentation has the quality of special, as distinguished from general, library service in its relationship to the specialized needs of particular uses and users.

Similarly, Mortimer Taube defined documentation [2] as

. . . the designation of the total complex of activities involved in the communication of . . . specialized information . . . including the activities which constitute special librarianship plus the prior activities of preparing and reproducing materials and the subsequent activity of distribution.

Again, the implication is given that documentation is simply an extended form of traditional librarianship.

The use of the word "documentation" with this implication would be acceptable provided it truly represented the character of the work of the documentalists. However, careful examination of their work will show that the concern is rarely with the problems of operating libraries or even technical information centers. Instead it is concerned with the analysis of information systems and the development of techniques for new systems. Thus documentalists seem to share the common purpose of creating new tools which can be meaningfully applied to the mass information problems of our times. The fact that such system design tends to be concerned with the entire range of information handling, from its initial creation to its final dissemination, is characteristic of the systems approach to any problem. The significant thing is that documentation is *not* best differentiated from normal library service by this concern with the complete cycle; rather, it is best differentiated from normal library service by the fact that it is primarily concerned with system analysis and design rather than system operation.

A third definition of documentation was given by James D. Mack and Robert S. Taylor.[3]

The group of techniques necessary for the ordered presentation, organization, and communication of recorded specialized knowledge, in order to give maximum accessibility and utility to the information contained.

---

[2] Mortimer Taube et al., *Studies in Coordinate Indexing,* Documentation Incorporated, 1953–57, v. 1–4.

[3] James D. Mack and Robert S. Taylor, A System of Documentation Terminology, p. 20, in *Documentation in Action,* by Jesse H. Shera, Allen Kent, and James W. Perry, New York, Reinhold, 1956. Based on 1956 Conference on Documentation at Western Reserve University.

In this sense, Cutter, Putnam, Dewey, and the other pioneers in developing tools for library organization were all functioning as information system designers when they established their techniques for library organization. On the other hand, present "documentation centers" are in no essential respect different from any library—they partake of the same operating problems.

A review of the domestic and international conference papers written by documentalists shows their preoccupation with the development of techniques for the reproduction, duplication, and dissemination of printed material, with study of application of mechanical devices and methods of storage and retrieval, with research into the theory of subject classification. FID (Federation International de Documentation) was mentioned earlier in the text as the organization abroad which pays particular attention to the field of documentation. UNESCO has also been active in supporting international discussion and cooperative work among the several interested countries. Since 1937 the American Documentation Institute has been the organization in the United States which has pursued documentalist objectives. All seem to share a common purpose—to create new tools which can be applied to the mass information problem of our time.

Thus there is at present a great deal of activity going on in the United States and throughout the world in an attempt to resolve the difficulties in the traditional library tools. Unfortunately, this activity is very diffuse and ill-defined. Brian Vickery [4] comments that "for too long, the features which distinguish one particular system from others have been emphasized at the expense of principles common to all systems." The need certainly exists for a clearly defined integrating theory for the field. The purpose of the last two sections of this book is to fill this need by formalizing "principles common to all systems."

As the basis for discussions to come, it seems desirable to present the work of some "schools" of documentation, schools usually identified with a particular organization and creative individual. Each has been concerned with the analysis of some critical aspects of organizing information; each has proposed a technique for answering the particular critical problems of concern to him. Frequently the resulting "system" has been presented as the final solution to the entire information retrieval problem, but it seems clear that such a

---

[4] Brian C. Vickery, *Classification and Indexing in Science,* 2nd ed., enlarged. London, Butterworths Scientific Publications, 1959.

panacea cannot be expected. The real contribution made by each school is the deeper understanding given to the particular area investigated. The immediately practical by-product from this deeper understanding has been, in each case, a useful technique which should be appreciated for its value and utilized where it is most effective.

COORDINATION OF SUBJECTS

The first of the four groups to be discussed is Documentation, Inc.; the president of this organization is Mortimer Taube.[5] He has been particularly identified with the concept of coordinate indexing, under the title of "Uniterm." Basically an extremely simple scheme, it was developed in an attempt to answer one of the principal difficulties in traditional subject heading catalogs and classification schedules. In particular, with these traditional tools, while it is theoretically possible to include entries for each permutation of a combination of fundamental subjects, it is economically impractical to do so. In view of this, a library will make a choice among the possible permutations to accommodate the usage which appears most likely. For example, it may have seemed that the users of a technical library would be primarily interested in the particular discipline covered by a document and not in the country where the work had been performed. The library might under these circumstances reasonably limit the subject headings to, say, "Atomic Energy, Russia," and not include "Russia, Atomic Energy." If the character of the usage changed and it became important to recover all documents relevant to Russian activity, the subject heading catalog would be virtually worthless as an aid.

Coordinate indexing is intended to bypass this difficulty by providing a method of coordinating concepts as a combination rather than a permutation.[6] It does this in the following way. Document content is to be represented by terms chosen from a prescribed list of subjects which are, to the maximum extent possible, in the form of single words or concepts, called Uniterms. The terms are thus not subject headings in the sense used with a card catalog, since no effort is made to combine words into phrases covering complex concepts; in fact, a positive effort is made to avoid doing so. The "coordinate index" to docu-

---

[5] Documentation, Inc., 4827 Rugby Ave., Bethesda, Md.

[6] Mortimer Taube et al., *Studies in Coordinate Indexing,* Documentation Incorporated, 1953–57, v. 1–4.

ments is then based on assigning to each subject a card on which will be placed the identification number of every document to which that subject is relevant. For example, a new document, numbered 12345, might be concerned with subjects A, B, C, and D, such as the *growing* of *red wheat* in *Afghanistan.* For the subject A, which might be "grow," there is a card to which will be added the particular document number 12345, etc. The set of documents which come in during a day, 12345, 12346, etc., will therefore be scanned by the indexer for those terms from the subject list which are significant in the documents. The cards for the set of terms related to the set of documents are pulled from the file of such cards; for ten documents a day, each covering, say, ten terms, one might have to pull as many as fifty, sixty, or even a hundred cards from the files. On each of these cards will then be placed the particular document number for which that subject is relevant.

When a need arises—due to a request expressed as a combination of subjects—to recover relevant documents, the cards corresponding to the requested subjects are pulled from the file. Where a document originally involved each of them, the document number will be on each card. The search operation is therefore simply to scan through the sets of document numbers on each subject card, effectively correlating the numbers on each card with those on the other cards. Wherever a match occurs, it represents the number of a document for which these terms are simultaneously relevant. Hence it will presumably be a document significant to the request.

Certain factors must be considered in establishing a coordinate index system based on these principles. One relates to the choice of terms; another to the choice of format and representation on the term cards; a third relates to the operations required to post onto the cards and handle searches.

With respect to the choice of terms, it must be recognized that the initial aim in developing coordinate indexing was to eliminate any precoordination of concepts such as is represented by a traditional subject heading. The philosophy of Taube was therefore to reduce terms, as we have indicated, to single words and concepts. This has been a point of considerable controversy, and it is debatable whether it is an essential characteristic. In fact, recent developments—in trying to answer some of the objections to Taube's Uniterms—have introduced increasingly many *a priori* relations among the subject terms. In this respect research work by Taube and his associates has tried to show, and correctly so, that any particular choice of terms is merely one from a whole spectrum of possible choices—from the single concept Uniterms to precoordinated subject headings to the entries in the most highly organized of hierarchical classifications.[7]

From this standpoint, the only theoretical difference between a subject heading catalog and a Uniterm file is the "length of the term," and the set of catalog cards behind a subject heading card is the complete equivalent of a Uniterm card. Another difference between the two is highlighted in practice. Customarily the subject catalog card contains more information about the document—its author, title, etc.—than does the Uniterm card. Thus the catalog card can provide a user with an opportunity to sift references before going to source material; Uniterm cards, on the other hand, provide document numbers only and require the user to examine all documents uncovered in a search. Although this difference in usage exists, other factors enter into an evaluative comparison, and the principal conclusion to be drawn is that the differences between the two are not clean-cut and that one approach in certain cases may prove better than the other.

J. Albert Sanford[8] has written the results of his experience in using the techniques of a Uniterm system. Referring to the problem of generating terms, he says

> Let the documents themselves generate their own uniterms. Catalog one thousand documents. They will produce about one thousand uniterms. Weed this list carefully, combining synonyms. With this core, catalog another one thousand reports, using the "approved" basic list where possible, and then repeat the weeding operation.

In other words, do not start with a prescribed set of terms. Let the documents themselves generate the terms but control this generation by combining synonyms. Once some 8000 Uniterms have been chosen, it has generally been found that addition falls off very rapidly even with highly varied subject matter. The curve for size of the term file begins to grow nearly flat when between 40 and 50,000 documents have been cataloged.

---

[7] Frederick Jonker, The Descriptive Continuum: A "Generalized" Theory of Indexing, *Preprints of Papers for the International Conference on Scientific Information, 1958,* Washington, D.C., National Academy of Sciences, National Research Council, 1958.

[8] J. A. Sanford and Frederick R. Theriault, Problems in the Application of Uniterm Coordinate Indexing, *College and Research Libraries,* January 1956, v. XVIII, pp. 19–23.

Sanford continued:

From the start, use "see" and "see also" references on the headings of uniterm cards, in accordance with standard library practice. We have found no other satisfactory solution for problems of near synonyms, for synonyms-in-some-meanings of words, and for all the other perplexities born of the fact that uniterm coordinate indexing uses the living fabric of language for its base.

The second consideration—the choice of format and document representation on the term cards—has been far less controversial than the choice of terms. Several formats have been successfully used and adequately appreciated for their individual advantages. The original Uniterm system simply posted document numbers on the term cards. In most cases these were organized in columns by the terminal digit of the document number for ease in visual correlation. Somewhat earlier, Batten in England and Cordonnier in France had proposed dedicating a position, at which a punched hole could be placed, to each possible document and punching the hole if the document number was to be posted. Based on this approach, several recent mechanizations of such "peek-a-boo" cards have appeared.

The third consideration—the operational one—is the most critical in terms of system effectiveness. Sanford's article presents the operational picture particularly with respect to posting and problems which arise.

Our next problem was the discovery that we needed to develop satellite indexes around our coordinate index. Here the needs of libraries will no doubt differ, but we soon found that in the coordinate index we were building a heavy-duty machine unsuitable for light work. We decided to employ traditional library methods for all types of document reference questions they served best, and to turn to the coordinate index where traditional methods broke down when laden with the peculiar burdens which documents engender. The combination of old and new methods has turned out to be an unexpectedly harmonious arrangement.

Our system as it finally evolved represents the solution of a series of problems in practical operation and hence may be of interest. Because the approach lends itself so readily to rapid processing, attention paid to "time and motion" pays large dividends in total production.

(The routine in the central office is primarily concerned with the posting operation.) The "posting" operation, as the process of recording document numbers on uniterm cards is called, caused real trouble. Here lay the most formidable problem we encountered in the application of coordinate indexing. The process seems simple enough, but once it is begun difficulties multiply. Each card must be pulled, recorded upon, and refiled. The work is boring

```
LAMINATES
  68150       69472       67224       68226

LANDING
  68080 68081 67652 68333 67284 67885 68326 67227 67518
  68090 68091       68873 68334 68495 69076 68217
        68111             69524 69075
        68481

LANDING GEARS
                                                  67968

LANGLEY RESEARCH CENTER
                                      68326

LANGMUIR
  67500

LANGUAGES
        68101       67493 69384       •67796•68467•68468
        68271•                         67956
```

(a)

```
RETRIEVAL
              67942                   •67796•68467•68468
              68102                                69388

REVERBERATION
                          68115

REVERSAL
                                68296 68167

REVOLUTION
                                67436       67418

REYNOLDS NUMBER
        67851 68012
        68801 69222

RIEMANN
                    68294

RIGIDITY
  68550             69563
```

(b)

```
SUSPENSIONS
  69320 69321 69322       69564             67547 69318 69319
                                            68897       69359

SWEEP
                    68013                               67819

SWITCHES
  67280 67531 68132 67933 69484 67785 68256 67377 67588 68259
  68260 68151 68262             68075 68736 67677 68278
        68671 68522             69445 69276 68257 69278

SYMBOLS
        68271•67492 69003                   68467

SYMMETRY
              68422 69183 67244       67836       69128 68119
              68952

SYNCHRONIZERS
                    69443

SYNCHRONIZING
  67250       67782             68325
              68872             68565
```

(c)

FIG. 2. Printed uniterm cards. Courtesy Pacific Aeronautical Library, Los Angeles, Calif.

PHYS REV, Jan. 1, 1962

68443. Thermal conductivity of Ge-Si alloys at high temperatures. Abeles, B. p.44-46. bibliog. HEAT - TEMPERATURE - CONDUCTIVITY - GERMANIUM - SILICON - ALLOYS

68444. Theory of field emission from semiconductors. Stratton, Robert. p.67-82. bibliog. EMISSION - SEMICONDUCTORS - CURRENTS - DENSITIES - ELECTRONS

68445. Laser and two-photon processes. Kleinman, D.A. p.87-88. bibliog. LASERS - PHOTONS - RAYS - ABSORPTION

68446. Double injection in insulators. Lampert, M.A p.126-141. bibliog. INJECTION - INSULATORS - ELECTRONS - HOLES - CURRENTS

68447. Nuclear spin-lattice relaxation in superconducting aluminum. Masuda, Yoshika. p.159-163. bibliog. NUCLEAR - SPIN - LATTICES - RELAXATION - TIME - ALUMINUM-SUPERCONDUCTIVITY

68448. Plasma theory of the many-electron atom. Levine, P.H. p.207-213. bibliog. PLASMA - ELECTRONS - ATOMS - HARTREE FOCK EQUATION - VLASOV EQUATION

68449. Resonant scattering of gamma rays from Nuclear levels with a linear accelerator. Seward, F.D. p.335-340. bibliog. RESONANCE - SCATTERING - GAMMA - RAYS - LINEAR - ACCELERATORS - NUCLEAR - BREMSSTRAHLUNG

68450. Primary cosmic-ray and solar protons. Vogt, Rochus. p.366-377. bibliog. COSMIC - RAYS - SUN; SOLAR - PROTONS - FLUX - SPECTRUM - ENERGY

68451. Mach's principle and the locally measured gravitational constant in general relativity. Brans, C.H. p.388-396. bibliog. MACH PRINCIPLE - GRAVITATION - CONSTANTS - NEWTON - EINSTEIN, ALBERT - RELATIVITY

SPACE WORLD, Mar. 1962

68452. Moon vehicles. p.30-31. MOON VEHICLES

68453. Life on Venus. Rublowsky, John. p.34- VENUS (PLANET) - LIFE

68454. Launching pad in space. Binder,O.O. p.38- LAUNCHING; LAUNCHERS - PADS - SPACE VEHICLES - ORBITS - RENDEZVOUS - BASES (AIRCRAFT, MISSILES, ETC.)

68455. Can space prolong your life? Page, Walter. p.42- HUMANS - SURVIVAL - ZERO - GRAVITY - WEIGHTLESSNESS - OUTER SPACE

68456. America's underground missilemen. Baar, James. p.45- INTERCONTINENTAL - BALLISTICS - MISSILES - SITES

ROYAL AERON SOC JL, Jan. 1962

68457. Structural weight estimations for novel configurations. Burt, M.E. p.15-30. bibliog. WEIGHT - ESTIMATION

68458. The response of a typical aircraft structure to jet noise. Clarkson, B.L. p.31-40. bibliog. JETS - NOISE - VIBRATIONS

AEROPLANE, Dec. 14, 1961

68459. Sperry's first helicopter autopilot. p.759. SPERRY - HELICOPTERS - AUTOPILOTS

68460. Future plans for the X-15. p.766-767. X-15 - ALTITUDE - TESTING

68461. Progress with the OSO satellite. p.767-768. ORBITS - SUN; SOLAR - SPINNING - OBSERVATORIES - STABILITY

68462. Contract for Apollo. p.768. NORTH AMERICAN - APOLLO - CONTRACTS

OPERATIONS RESEARCH, Jan-Feb 1962

68463. A generalized network approach to the planning and scheduling of a research project. Eisner, Howard. p.115-125. bibliog. PROGRAM EVALUATION REVIEW TECHNIQUE - PLANNING - RESEARCH

MISSILES & ROCKETS, Feb. 12, 1962

68464. Centaur slippage drag on Apollo. Taylor, Hal. p.13-14. APOLLO - CENTAUR

68465. Pogo-Hi boosts sea-launch stock. Wilks, Bill. p.24-25. LAUNCHING - POGO-HI - WATER

68466. Device will keep watch on astronaut's telltale eyes. David, H.M. p.27. EYES - OPTHALMOSCOPES

ASSOC COMPUTING MACH COMM, Jan. 1962

68467. COMIT as an IR language. Yngve, V.H. p.19-28. bibliog. LANGUAGES - SYMBOLS - INFORMATION - RETRIEVAL

68468. Language problems posed by heavily structured data. Barnes, R.F. p.28-34. bibliog. INFORMATION - RETRIEVAL - LANGUAGES

MATERIALS IN DES ENG, Feb. 1962

68469. Stainless steel rolled ultra-thin for B-70 bomber skin. p.87. STAINLESS - STEEL - B-70 - SKINS - THICKNESS - STRENGTH

(d)

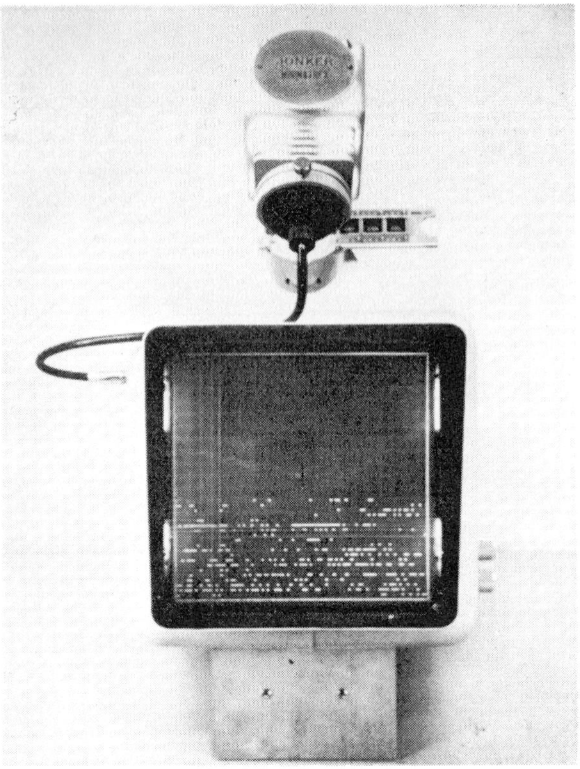

FIG. 3. Peek-a-boo cards (matrex system). Courtesy Jonker Business Machines, Inc., Gaithersburg, Md.

and fatiguing. Errors are easy to make and difficult to detect. Workers get in each other's way. While posting is going on, any reference use of the index usually means that one or the other operation must stop. (This was the real operational source of trouble.)

The solution proved to be a simple one. We installed an IBM punch in the catalog department and equipped it with standard "programs." A document number punched (and verified) on the first card is automatically reproduced on all ensuing cards until the operator wishes to change it. In changing from one document number to the next higher one, the operator touches only the final digit keys. (The posting operation called for the sorting of the cards into subject number sequence and then a manual posting.)

One particular criticism, which has been quite frequently quoted, is based on an experiment run by the Los Alamos Scientific Laboratory. According to the report of their experiment, Uniterm rules were followed as closely as possible. It was found that indexing was rapid but posting was slow and liable to errors which were not easily discovered.[9]

The operational handling of requests has been particularly subject to considerable criticism from a number of places, including the Los Alamos experimenters. They found that a large number of irrelevant retrievals were obtained. The test indicated that in spite of the use of an above-average number of Uniterms, only 11% of the reports could be retrieved completely and without false drops. The reasons for failure in the remainder were analyzed and all suggested means for improvement applied. These included the use of "poly-terms," which combined terms to form a single concept, and the splitting of a report into two or three sections with separate accession numbers. This removed most of the simplicity of the scheme, but even then Los Alamos statistics indicated that it could satisfactorily handle only 61% of the reports. It permitted false drops from 22½% and entirely lost 16½%. The system therefore was considered unsatisfactory for solving the problem of a large library, although the staff working on this experiment expressed the opinion that Uniterm could have application to collections of reasonably small size, limited to one subject field with a simple standardized vocabulary, having a uniform level of specificity.

There is a good deal of doubt concerning the validity of such test results, but there is no question that some major difficulties in the Uniterm system are certainly evident. For example, suppose that a request came in for the *growth* of *Red Afghanistan*. Document 12345, on *growing* of *red wheat* in *Afghanistan*, referred to previously, would be recovered due to the match on "grow," "red," and "Afghanistan." The probability of such a "false drop" because of an inappropriate relationship among the terms is one of the difficulties with the concept of coordinated indexing. Many of the schemes proposed by other workers on coordinate indexing, in recognition of this, have been concerned principally with the problems of reducing such false coordinations. They are all based on an attempt to introduce into the basic Uniterm system some means for representing the syntactical role played by the term. One way of doing this is to provide a separate term card for each possible syntactical role of a term, but it would seem that, in general, such an approach would result in a

[9] I. A. Warheit, A Study of Coordinate Indexing as Applied to U.S. Atomic Energy Commission Reports, *College and Research Libraries,* July 1955, v. XVI, No. 3, pp. 278–284.

chaotic file. Another possible approach, which is only now being explored in any depth, is to introduce a "link" or "role indicator" as part of the document number recorded on the subject card, indicating the role played by the subject within a standard syntactical pattern. Such an approach requires the definition of the standard syntactical patterns of significance to the library and its usage. It must be recognized that this approach will enormously complicate the operation of the system; yet it does provide a mechanism for handling the syntax where the false drop problem makes it significant to do so.

Another way in which false coordination can arise might be the following. A document is concerned with iron mining in Poland and with uranium mining in Czechoslovakia. A request for all documents relevant to uranium mining in Poland will again give rise to a false drop due to the false coordination of ideas from logically separate parts of a document. Thus prevention of such false coordination is also an important problem.

The most satisfactory approach for handling this type of false coordination is to define for each document a set of logical subunits or phrases, each of which represents a unified thought. Thus, in the foregoing example, iron, mining, and Poland would represent one such unified thought, and uranium, mining, Czechoslovakia, a second one, both with respect to the same document. Each such unified thought is then separately identified by the addition to the document number, when it is recorded on the subject card, of a "phrase" number identifying the particular logical unit of thought within which the term occurs. Superficially this kind of "link" appears to have the same form as the one designed to answer the syntactical problem, and some workers have tended to confuse the two, at least in their choice of terminology. It should be recognized, however, that the identification of phrases in no way answers the syntactical problem, for it does not prevent false relationships among correlated terms; it does prevent uncorrelated terms from being related.

Another area of major difficulty in the Uniterm system is the handling of generic requests or, in general, any requests formulated in terms of a preconceived organization of the prescribed list of terms. The very character of the terms in the Uniterm system is that they are treated as logically independent of each other. Thus there is no degree of organization among terms explicitly stated. In order to handle generic requests, the specification of the particular terms covered must be provided externally, as part of the request, since the terms themselves will in no way exhibit the desired relationships to the generic concept. A possible approach would be to indicate a structural relationship among the terms. This would permit the handling of any type of question related to the prescribed structure. As yet no substantial amount of effort has been spent in this area, although the use of "see also" references represents a step in this direction.

The problems involved in coordinate indexing are present and they must be taken care of. The handling of generic searches, the reduction in the number of false drops—each significant problem must be answered and techniques for handling it must be developed. The significant point is this: Uniterming, or coordinate indexing, like any other tool, is a very legitimate technique. It should be understood as such; it should be used as such.

EFFICIENT MECHANIZED CODING

A second documentalist is Calvin Mooers, president of the Zator Company.[10] Like Taube he is greatly concerned with the concept of coordinating terms. However, he has considered the reverse approach of listing the subject terms for a single document on a single card and in doing so has been concerned with the question of efficient storage of the subject information. The placement of these terms on the card then becomes a basic problem. One cannot assign a "fixed field" or prededicated space to each possible subject, for this would in most cases use far too much space. On the other hand, it is extremely expensive to allow "open fields" with arbitrary location for a given subject. As Mooers points out,

> . . . Scanning is a very powerful technique [but it requires] an elaborate and expensive sensing mechanism because of the need to search many alternative locations.[11]

These costs are substantially reduced if reading is restricted to invariant or fixed locations, and hence Mooers proposed the concept of storing the codes for all of the subjects related to a document in the same invariant place—one superimposed on top of the others—the concept of "superimposed coding." The identification of each subject is thus recorded in the same field in exactly the same physical location.

To illustrate, let us say that most documents will cover five sub-

---

[10] Zator Company, 140½ Auburn St., Cambridge, Mass.

[11] Calvin N. Mooers, Zatocoding Applied to Mechanical Organization of Knowledge, *American Documentation,* January 1951, v. II, No. 1, pp. 20–32.

jects. Normally, without the use of superimposed coding, each subject will be represented, depending on the size of vocabulary, by perhaps four characters. If a separate field were provided for each subject, at least twenty character positions—five fields of four characters each—would be needed. To handle a request for subject A and subject B, it would be necessary to compare each of them with each of the subject fields, since there is no way of knowing in which of the positions either may actually have been placed. Mooers suggested storing all of the subject codes in the same field, essentially by providing a twenty-character code for each subject. Then one need not worry about the fields in which particular subjects are coded but can merely match all desired subjects over the entire field.

It is immediately evident that this approach, although reducing the problems of comparison, substantially increases the probability of false drop due to the possible generation of the code of a nonrelevant subject from the superimposed codes of the actually relevant subjects. Thus if the system is to be effective, the choice of codes must be made in such a way as to minimize the probability of producing such false subjects. That this is possible can be demonstrated by the following simple analysis of possible combinations. If there are, say, 1000 possible subjects and any document will be represented by about, say, 5 subjects, the system will be concerned with at most the number of possible combinations of 1000 subjects taken 5 at a time. This number is less than 10^{13}, while with 20 decimal characters it would be possible to represent 10^{20} different such combinations with no possibility of introducing false subjects.

The problem lies in generating the codes for combinations of subjects from those for the individual subjects.[12] It can be shown—and Mooers has spent a great deal of investigation in demonstrating—that the most appropriate choice of subject codes for this purpose is a random one. This results, in principle, from the fact that random codes are the most efficient, for any organized coding is almost certain to dedicate some ranges of codes which will be overutilized and other ranges which will be underutilized. The classic example is the necessity, in the Dewey Decimal Classification, of representing subjects in engineering by extremely long (nine decimal digits in some cases) —and thus inefficient—codes, because three decimal digit numbers have been previously spent on subjects such as "Angels, Devils, and

---

[12] R. S. Casey, J. W. Perry, M. M. Berry, and A. Kent, *Punched Cards: Their Application to Science and Industry,* 2nd ed., New York, Reinhold, 1958.

Satan."[13] By introducing efficient random codes the available coding space will be better utilized, and the probability of generating identical codes from two combinations of subjects will be minimized.

Another, and independently useful, method for reducing the effects of this problem is to limit the number of terms very drastically. It has therefore been a part of Mooers' system to define very carefully the "descriptors" in terms of the subject field involved and in this way to limit their number substantially. In fact, whereas the Uniterm system may well generate 5000 to 10,000 terms, a superimposed coding system will limit their number to perhaps 300.

The scheme of superimposed coding proposed by Mooers is subject to the same criticisms as that of coordinate indexing, that is, generic searches are difficult and false drops will occur because of improper coordination and the lack of syntax. The previously discussed approaches to answering these criticisms are probably not easy to use with superimposed coding. In fact, Mooers himself points out that random coding and classified coding probably cannot be reconciled. In addition, the possible generation of irrelevant subjects represents an additional source of false drops. Despite these difficulties, however, the technique of Mooers is a useful one, particularly applicable where coding space is at a premium, as is the situation with the use of edge-notched cards, such as the McBee-Key-Sort or those developed by the Zator Company itself.

Mooers, in parallel with Taube, has been conducting theoretical investigations into the mathematical structure of coding systems. Generally speaking, each has tended to direct his theoretical efforts toward investigation which will support his studies in the particular approach which he has developed. For example, most of Mooers' study has been theoretical investigation into the advantage of this type of document-organized system with this type of coding. Most of Taube's theoretical investigations have been directed toward supporting the concept of the aspect card development.

FORMALIZED ABSTRACTS

The third documentation group is the Center for Documentation and Communications Research of the Western Reserve University. The main participants in their program have been James W. Perry and Allen Kent. They became particularly concerned with the prob-

---

[13] John Metcalfe, *Information Indexing and Subject Cataloging. Alphabetical: Classified. Coordinate: Mechanical,* New York, Scarecrow Press, 1957.

lem of false drops and the difficulties with subject interrelationships which occur in the coordinate index or superimposed coding types of schemes. They have therefore studied means of representing highly complex abstracts of documents in an effort to reduce these problems. In many respects the results are not abstracts but analytical studies in their own right in that information can actually be added to that of the document by the abstract description. The significant contribution is that they have developed tools for description which can be utilized by virtually any system.

The Western Reserve system has perhaps best been described by Brian Vickery in a paper published in *American Documentation,* v. X, 1959, entitled "The Structure of 'Semantic Coding,' A Review." The tables and examples presented in the following material are excerpted from his paper.

The structure of their so-called "telegraphic abstract"[14] is based on a number of elements for describing the information content of a document. The first is the "phrase"—a logical unit of thought within the document. Within a phrase, "subphrases" are individual words, or concepts, together with "role indicators" describing the particular role which the term plays in the phrase.

The primary significance of the role indicators is that they provide a mechanism for handling syntax of the type required in particular subject matter. For the particular subject matter with which Western Reserve has been most concerned in their study for the American Society of Metals some twenty separate role indicators have been identified.

The individual terms are produced from "semantic factors" which are then particularized by "analytic infixes," modifiers, and numerical suffices to pinpoint the particular term of interest within a group of terms. These semantic factors and analytic infixes thus represent a means of defining terms by their relationship to very general concepts. Western Reserve has defined some 214 semantic factors.

These semantic factors can be grouped as shown in Table 4 (the number of semantic factors and an example is added in each case).

Each semantic factor is represented by a code consisting of four alphabetic characters, the second of which is blank and will be filled by a letter representing the analytic relationship of a specific term to the semantic factor. Examples are given in Table 5.

---

[14] J. W. Perry, A. Kent, and M. M. Berry, *Machine Literature Searching,* New York, Interscience, 1956.

TABLE 3

Role Indicators for the Field of Metallurgy *

Applied to terms denoting material:
1. KOV (*property given for*)
2. KEJ (*material processed*)
3. KAJ (*starting material*)
4. KUJ (*component*)
5. KWJ (*product*)
6. KQJ (*by means of*)
7. KAD (*machine* or *device*)
8. KAG (*subassembly*)
9. KAL (*influenced by*)

Applied to terms denoting property:
1. KWV (*given*)
2. KUP (*determined*)
3. KAP (*influenced*)
4. KAL (*influencing*)

Applied to processes:
1. KAM (*process*)
2. KXM (*negation*)
3. KAL (*influencing*)

Representing an attendant condition:
1. KAH (*attending condition*)

Miscellaneous indicators:
1. KIS (*location*)
2. KWB (*direction from*)
3. KWC (*direction to*)
4. KAB (*field*)
5. KIT (*time occurring*)
6. KIG (*geographic location*)
7. KIB (*organization involved*)
8. KEP (*person involved*)

* Note that each role indicator is represented by a code consisting of three alphabetic characters, the first of which is a K. *American Documentation,* July 1959, v. X, No. 3.

TABLE 4

Classification of Semantic Factors *

General concepts:	*Ideas* (4, e.g. *Theory*)
	Relationships (10, e.g. *Agent*)
	Properties (4, e.g. *Chemical*)
	Fields (9, e.g. *Law*)
	Classifications (27, e.g. *Mineral*)
Relationships:	*Economics* (36, e.g. *Buying, Mining*)
	Physical (27, e.g. *Bones, Growth*)
	Social (32, e.g. *Security, Religion*)
States:	*Psychological* (4, e.g. *Emotion*)
	Action (16, e.g. *Disease*)
	Physical
	Sensible (12, e.g. *Color*)
	Conditional (12, e.g. *Weather*)
	Properties (11, e.g. *Fluid*)
Processes:	*Physical* (19, e.g. *Diffusion*)
	General (20, e.g. *Detection*)
	Material
	Change (33, e.g. *Concentration*)
	Constructive (41, e.g. *Building*)
	Destructive (29, e.g. *Cutting*)
	Industrial (15, e.g. *Printing*)
Substances:	*Generalized* (21, e.g. *Fuel*)
	Specific
	Organic (14, e.g. *Oil*)
	Inorganic (13, e.g. *Glass*)
	Preparations (9, e.g. *Paint*)
Objects:	*General*
	Natural (14, e.g. *Muscle*)
	Products (7, e.g. *Explosive*)
	Specific
	Natural (28, e.g. *Fiber*)
	Products (17, e.g. *Cosmetic*)

* *American Documentation*, July 1959, v. X, No. 3.

TABLE 5

Sample Semantic Factors *

Factor
Body fluid, B-FL
Ground, G-RD
Electrolysis, L-TL
Device, M-CH
Motion, M-TN
Release, R-LS
Arrangement, R-NG
Iron, R-RN
Plastic, R-SN
Fish, F-SH

* *American Documentation*, July 1959, v. X, No. 3.

The analytic relations and the corresponding alphabetic code for each are presented in Table 6.

Each term is represented by a semantic factor and the analytic relation which the term bears to it (or a set of these). Examples are given in Table 7.

TABLE 6

Analytic Relations *

A	*Categorical:* the coded term is a species of the genus denoted by the factor.
E	*Intrinsic:* the coded term is something of which the factor is a component.
I	*Inclusive:* the coded term is a component of the factor.
O	*Comprehensive:* the coded term is made up of several members of the class represented by the factor.
U	*Productive:* the coded term helps to produce the factor.
Q	*Affective:* the coded term makes use of, is determined, or is influenced by the factor.
W	*Instrumental:* the coded term is produced by, acts on or is acted on by the factor.
X	*Negative:* the coded term has a characteristic whose absence is denoted by the factor.
Y	*Attributive:* the coded term is characterized by the factor.
Z	*Simulative:* the coded term resembles, but is not, the factor.

* *American Documentation*, July 1959, v. X, No. 3.

TABLE 7

Sample Term Codes *

(based on semantic factors of Table 5)

Term	Relation to Factor	Code	
Blood	Categorical	BAFL.	005
Soil	Intrinsic	GERD.	030
Electrolyte	Inclusive	LITL.	005
Machinery	Comprehensive	MOCH.	047
Propulsion	Productive	MUTN.	015
Extrusion	Affective	RQLS.	010
Spaced	Instrumental	RWNG.	023
Nonferrous	Negative	RXRN.	001
Copolymer	Attributive	RYSN.	011
Whale	Simulative	FZSH.	014

* *American Documentation,* July 1959, v. X, No. 3.

This method of producing terms, since it is based on a highly organized concept of the relationship among terms, allows for recovery in response to questions phrased within this structure of terms. Thus generic questions within this framework will be handled without difficulty. However, it must also be recognized that relationships outside the structure defined by the chosen semantic relations will be as hard to handle in the Western Reserve system as they are in any other system and perhaps more so.[15]

Western Reserve has used the term "machine language" to describe their particular coding of the terms as represented by semantic factors and infixes. It is somewhat difficult to understand the basis for such usage, but apparently it is due to the fact the codes are designed to be "self-separating," so that it is obvious where one term ends and another begins without the need for "space" characters.

This approach has certain problems. Ambiguity is possible in the generation of term codes. In particular, how does one decide what semantic factor to use for a term and what particular analytic relation

[15] J. W. Perry and A. Kent, *Tools for Machine Literature Searching. Semantic Code Dictionary, Equipment, Procedures.* New York, Interscience, 1958. Library Science and Documentation, v. I.

is involved? Two different analysts examining the concept as it appears in a document could well come up with two different representations. This is characteristic of virtually all abstracting schemes, but perhaps this scheme is more subject to it than others, for determining the semantic factor and the analytic relation which are to represent the term is a process involving a substantial expenditure of intellectual effort. Another problem is the question of compromises in coding depth. One can represent a term by combining several factors which represent different aspects of this same concept. How many of these should be provided? The principal difficulty is the effort involved in creating the abstract. It is a substantial analytical process to create such an abstract from a document. In certain circumstances it may be well worth this effort. However, with any appreciable volume of documents, each with a fairly small probability of retrieval, it is probably not worth the effort.

In certain respects all these problems can be reduced by the use of a dictionary, and thus by standardizing the terms used, indexing or abstracting then becomes a matter of determining which among the possible standard terms is related to the given document, and the method of their generation is no longer significant in the indexing process. For the field of metallurgy, the Western Reserve group has developed such a dictionary of terms based on the specific semantic factors and analytic relations. However, if this approach is chosen, the process is as circumscribed as any other scheme and must be evaluated on these terms.

Even though these difficulties must be recognized and understood, it seems evident that the analysis made by the Western Reserve group has helped to increase our understanding of the syntactic problems in data representation. While the particular problem with which they have been concerned is that of metallurgy, their results should make easy the development of similar analyses in other process-type industries. Their analysis of semantic relations seems to parallel the work of others, such as Ranganathan, and thus is not quite so unique a contribution. The main emphasis of their writings seems to have been in this area of their work.

A step-by-step outline of the procedure for the "automatic encoding of telegraphic abstracts" can be found in "Information Resources; a challenge to American science and industry," by Jesse H. Shera, Allen Kent, and James W. Perry, Western Reserve University Press, 1958. This monograph is based on the proceedings of a special meeting of the Council on Documentation Research in the same year.

ANALYSIS OF SUBJECT RELATIONSHIPS

The final school of study in organization of knowledge and representation of information is that of Ranganathan and others concerned with "facet analysis." Vickery probably presents the faceted classification approach in the clearest terms when he says: [16]

> Traditional classification does not begin with individual terms as in Mooers, Taube, and Perry, but it starts from above, by division of an original universe of knowledge. The advocates of faceted classification, however, have begun to modify this pattern. Thus, terms can be sorted into groups, each of which has been differentiated on the basis of a different characteristic. This sorting of terms into groups is called by Ranganathan, "facet analysis." Instead of trying to construct from the original universe one vast tree of knowledge, facet analysis first deals with the terms and groups them into categories [kinds, state, property—much related to the "semantic factors" with which the Western Reserve group is concerned] and then arranges the terms within each category into the form of a classificatory map.

An explicit use of "fundamental" categories in classification was made by Ranganathan.[17] His colon classification exhibited, from the start, a division of classes into facets. Whenever Man attempts to sort out knowledge he invariably develops some categorical framework into which he can fit what he knows. Ranganathan, in his quest for a categorization that would be explicit, exhaustive, and uniform, chose to establish five fundamental facets: time, space, energy, matter, and personality.

The basis for this concept is the intellectual idea that one can describe the relationship among things in a universe in terms of their positions with respect to each of a set of fundamental facets. Within each facet, a set of specified values or terms is prescribed for representing the position of a given concept. To illustrate, consider literature on types of data processing storage media. It can be grouped in terms of one facet, the form of the medium, with possible characterizations as "card," "strip," "reel," "drum," etc. Similarly, it can be grouped on the basis of a second facet, the information rate, as low speed, medium speed, high speed. In effect, the combination of them

---

[16] Brian C. Vickery, *Classification and Indexing in Science,* 2nd ed., enlarged. London, Butterworths Scientific Publications, 1959.

[17] S. R. Ranganathan, Colon Classification and Its Approach to Documentation, in *Bibliographic Organization,* edited by Jesse H. Shera and Margaret E. Egan, University of Chicago Press, Chicago, Ill., 1951. (Papers presented before 15th Annual Conference of the Graduate Library School, July 24–29, 1950.)

is a classification of the storage media; one can describe a particular medium as being, for example, a low-speed card or a high-speed drum.

The main effort of the principal schools of facet analysis is to make evident the facets which will best characterize a field of interest. To illustrate the aims of such effort, consider the example given above. It may well become clear after a careful examination of the field of data processing storage media and of its literature that, say, some of the documents concerned with cards are about magnetic cards, some about punched cards, some about photographic cards. Initially these might well be treated as possible values within the facet "form." But if it also became evident that similar terms were arising in the facet of "information rate," an effort would be made to extract another facet—in this case obviously "recording" or something similar, with possible values of "magnetic," "punched," "photographic," etc. The example is of course quite trivial, but the principle is essentially that of facet analysis—the extraction of basic criteria for differentiation.

Once a facet schedule exists, a complex concept is represented by the particular combination of facet values which most adequately describes it. Document content is represented by the combination of such concepts—the coordination indicated, in the case of Ranganathan, as in Universal Decimal Classification (UDC), by a colon and other arbitrary signs between each two terms.

In order to store items in well-defined locations for later recovery by their faceted classification, it is necessary that the facet terms be put into a preferred indexing order. In other words, one must pre-establish the order in which the facets for a given item are to be listed. Effectively this results in a hierarchical classification of the literature covered.

Recovery from such a classification leads to the concept in facet analysis of "chain indexing" or the production of subject index entries from the individual terms describing the item. It involves the production of a subject heading index or subject heading catalog by, in effect, a mechanical rearrangement of the facet classification codes assigned to the documents. A discussion of this is given in "Classification Research Group Bulletin No. 5 on 54th meeting of CRG, ASLIB Research Project, College of Aeronautics, Cranfield," as follows: [18]

> Since the object of faceted classification is to be able to express complex subjects by a single notation showing the terms involved in a preferred order

---

[18] Bulletin No. 5, Classification Research Group, *The Journal of Documentation,* v. 5, No. 1, pp. 39–57.

(that which appears most logical and helpful to the user), it follows that provision must be made for finding the position of terms distributed in the subordinated positions. This is achieved by *chain indexing*. In the complementary alphabetical index the concepts in a given coded subject are cited (as words) in the reverse order of the code, together with the full code. Further entries are then made for each facet in turn, omitting one facet word on the left each time, whilst quoting the code number with one less facet code term on the right each time. The final card will thus be the first facet term (of the complete coded notation) alone, with its facet notation, and this is equivalent to the card appearing in a straightforward alphabetical index to all the terms in the classification. A complex example follows:

Classified index entry:	Ca (Cd-n-ea)	Nbj-bk-vh	Ogb
Facets:	part	physical properties	parameters

Chain structure

(1) C, structural part of aircraft; (2) a, combination; (3) Cd, wing; (4) -n, tail; (5) -ea, body; (6) N, aerodynamics; (7) Nb, aerodynamic entities; (8) Nbf, flow; (9) Nbj, transonic; (10) -bk supersonic; (11) Np, aerodynamic forces; (12) Nv, pressure on body; (13) h, center of pressure; (14) Og, aerodynamic reference parameters; (15) b, angle of attack

It may also be decided that certain links in the chain (i.e., certain terms in the Schedules) should be omitted as "unsought." Steps 1, 6, 7, 11, 14 might perhaps be so designated. We are left with steps 2 to 5, 9, 10, 12, 13, and 15 to use in the chain index.

Alphabetical index entries

(1) Angle of attack: center of pressure: supersonic, transonic flow: body, tail, wing: combination = Ca (Cd-n-ea) Nbj-bk-vh Ogb.
(2) Center of pressure: supersonic . . . combination = Ca (Cd-n-ea) Nbj-bk-vh.
(3) Pressure on body: supersonic . . . combination = Ca (Cd-n-ea) Nbj-bk-vh.
(4) Supersonic, transonic . . . combination = Ca (Cd-n-ea) Nbj-bk.
(5) Transonic flow . . . combination = CA (Cd-n-ea) Nbj.
(6) Body, tail wing: combination = Ca (Cd-n-ea).
(7) Tail, wing: combination = Ca (Cd-n).
(8) Wing: combination = Ca (Cd).
(9) Combination = Ca.

The technique of faceted classification for representation of concepts has a great deal of intellectual appeal. It has its philosophical origin deep in the history of the organization of knowledge. It also appears to be of immediately practical value in sufficiently circumscribed fields wherein facets can be well defined in terms of usage needs. In particular, it seems to be well suited to mechanical reorganization of the basic files to accommodate changing usage. Thus, although initially one sequence of facets may have seemed appropriate, new needs might imply the desirability of a different sequence. Although mechanical reorganization may not have been an initial objective of faceted representation, the nature of the scheme makes it easy to change the file structure, based on the change of facet sequence, by simple sorting without complex decision processes.

The essential simplicity and usefulness of faceted classification for representation of terms have been almost completely obscured. The psychological appeal of the extraction of facets is to continually extend the universe over which they are to apply—and eventually to encompass all of knowledge in one completely uniform system. The result of Ranganathan's attempt to do this is a metaphysical rationale which starts with the total universe. Many students therefore find Ranganathan's vocabulary and writings very difficult to grasp, and his faceted classification is not widely understood. Easy reading on this subject, however, can be found in a book on *Faceted Classification* [19] by Vickery, a chapter in Palmer and Wells,[20] and Ranganathan's own article in Shera and Egan's book, *Bibliographic Organization*.[21]

Although Ranganathan says "the only sensible course is to confine ourselves to the fundamental constituent terms and leave the derived composite terms to individual classifiers" and "the same class number should be arrived at by anybody following the prescribed rules," the facts of life are that ambiguity is as likely in facet classification as it is with Western Reserve's semantic factors. It is almost certain that, in any operational system, a prescribed dictionary or schedule of terms must be used to ensure some uniformity of coding. This schedule may well have been created by a facet analysis, just as it might have been created from semantic factors or any other analytical technique, and to that extent will exhibit the interrelationships inherent in the particular analytical technique used. However, as soon as such a dictionary is introduced, it immediately limits the flexibility of representation.

---

[19] Brian C. Vickery, *Faceted Classification—A Guide to Construction and Special Schemes,* ASLIB, London, 1960.

[20] Bernard I. Palmer and A. J. Wells, *The Fundamentals of Library Classification,* Allen and Unwin Ltd., London, 1951.

[21] Jesse H. Shera and Margaret S. Egan (eds.), *Bibliographic Organization,* Chicago, University of Chicago Press, 1951.

In other words, none of the techniques for term specification can simultaneously eliminate ambiguity and retain flexibility. The choice must be made as to which is important for the particular information system. Given that choice, each of the means for defining terms can be evaluated for the degree to which it represents the character of the field of knowledge covered by the information system.

In this respect the efforts of Western Reserve, Ranganathan, UDC, and others to develop new means of representing terms and their interrelationships must be evaluated, particularly in comparison with the traditional library tools. One of the most interesting efforts in making such a comparison is by John Metcalfe in his *Information Indexing.*[22] It would be impossible to give here the flavor of this book, or even to summarize its contents, but it should be read carefully for its insights into this comparison.

---

[22] John Metcalfe, *Information Indexing and Subject Cataloging. Alphabetical: Classified. Coordinate: Mechanical,* New York, Scarecrow Press, 1957.

4

The information framework and the user

The implications of the information storage and retrieval problem for the usage and possible sale of equipment have been well recognized by the data processing industry. Over the past five to ten years a veritable explosion of effort on the part of the computer manufacturers to understand the problems in utilizing equipment for information retrieval and to develop new equipment to fill the needs has been underway in the United States. In many cases this work has taken the direction of developing total systems to satisfy the needs of specific problems. In other cases the efforts have been to develop markets for existing equipment. In nearly all cases the manufacturer has been faced with a threefold problem: the engineering development of equipment, the systems research into how to use it, and the implementation of operating systems.

It is not surprising that the data processing specialists have been so active in the information storage and retrieval field. Having achieved spectacular successes in handling numerical information and business data by electronic means, and recognizing the potential market which similar treatment of alphabetical information would serve, they are understandably willing to devote vast resources to the analysis and solution of the fundamental problems in developing this market.

Despite this effort, however, thus far the equipment built and the research performed have been largely segmented. No one general purpose machine or complex of machines yet exists which meets all the requirements inherent in most information systems. Where total systems have been developed, the efforts by equipment manufacturers have been largely specialized, based usually on the specific needs of a specific customer at a specific time.

It is therefore somewhat difficult for the general customer or the system designer to determine the suitability of this great array of specialized equipment for his total job. It is essential, in view of this, to provide a framework within which to interrelate each of these specialized areas of equipment development, the individual inventions, the special component development, and the type of research which has characterized the work of equipment manufacturers.

THE INFORMATION FRAMEWORK

The technical contributions can be divided into three key areas of activity: printed data, analysis and logical processing, index and document files. Figure 4 illustrates, in simplified block diagram form, this Information Framework, which is a convenient general structure within which to view all information storage and retrieval systems. Typical of many storage and retrieval applications, *printed data* are received and *analyzed* to determine which index terms are to be associated with the document. An *index* code pattern is determined and the document is placed in a *file*. A user interacts with the index and the file; to use the index he must employ certain *logical processes*. He obtains ideas and facts from the system and eventually starts the cycle over again by generating a new document.

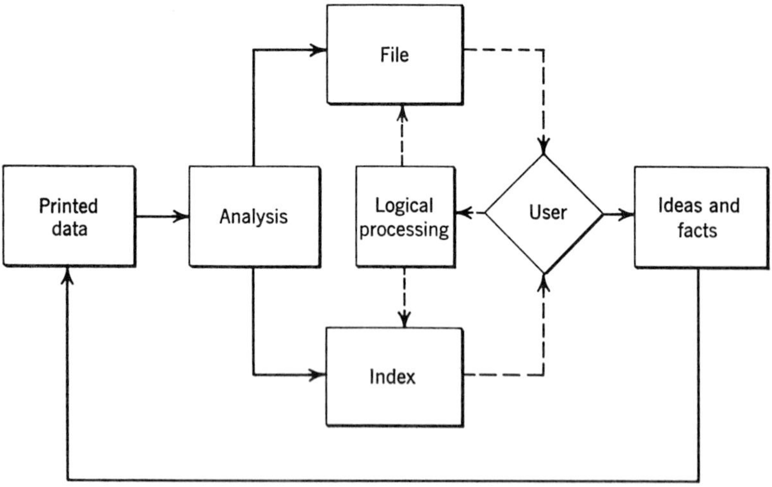

FIG. 4. The information framework.

The Information Framework can serve as a simple, useful outline for bringing into focus the main parts of any information storage and retrieval system. Also, it will be used to help categorize new equipment research and development and their application. The examples of information systems given below should be viewed in terms of this block diagram. By essentially "walking through" the Information Framework in each case, these examples illustrate the essential processing similarities which exist in creating both library-type subject files, with their characteristic intellectual complexity, and commercial-type named object files, with their characteristic volume of activity. Thus a basic frame of reference is provided for later interpreting the applications of machine research and development activities in the entire information system field.

The first example is that of a *local public library.* Here the printed data are the information recorded in books, periodicals, and other publications acquired or produced by the library. The analysis required to make this material usable involves the intellectual processes of examining each new piece of printed material, assigning classification numbers, and preparing title, author, and subject cards for inclusion in a card catalog. The index is then the accumulation of cards in the card catalog. This is usually the first place a user of a public library goes to find a book and determine its shelf location. The document file is then the collection of publications themselves, filed on the shelves according to a prescribed order as indicated on each card in the catalog. The users are the library patrons who will consult the index and from it, by logical processes, determine the material they want; frequently they will query the reference librarian to obtain her assistance, and she must then logically process their questions to recover the desired material.

Another example is that of the *scientific research library.* Here the printed data may appear to be quite similar to that in the public library—books, periodicals, and similar publications. However, they will generally be more detailed, with much greater depth of coverage in the particular technical field. Data may include confidential reports, working papers, foreign literature, etc. The process of analysis again involves the intellectual effort of reading the document, assigning classification numbers or subject headings for each important fact, and preparing cards to be used in the index. The library operation may well require abstracts of the more significant articles, and these would be prepared and processed at this stage. The index then contains the data which result from the process of analysis.

This index may be on manual cards, punched cards, magnetic tapes, depending on the complexity of operation and the volume of activity. The information in the index can include merely a reference to the location of the information in the document file or an entire abstract of the document. The document file itself contains the basic source material, perhaps in hard-copy form, perhaps on microfilm or even on magnetic tape. It is arranged in an order most convenient for access, usually by preassigned number. The document file will most often contain the full length document to which the index refers, but it may contain individual pieces of information grouped together in convenient form. The users of such a library are the researchers, workers, and employees of the organization which it serves. They will logically process their requests by referring them to the index, obtaining references from it, and then consulting the document file.

A third example is a *personnel record file* such as would be maintained by commercial, governmental, or military organizations. The printed data consist of all recorded information or paperwork associated with the chronology of service for each man. This may include forms, correspondence, orders, efficiency reports, etc. The process of analysis involves the extraction from the source material of pertinent facts about each man, such as name, birth date, employee number, grade, and address. The accuracy of this process is crucial because spelling errors and numerical coding errors made at this time are almost certain to result in failures at the time of retrieval. The index is then a personnel record on each man which includes, in fixed subfields, key characteristics about the man. These may be either information vital for searching purposes or data subject to change through personnel activity. The manual cards, punched cards, or magnetic tape which may be used to store these data will be organized in a manner that will satisfy most retrieval demands. For such a situation, the document file will consist of the collection of source dossiers kept on each man. This will contain all the original documents affecting his service. The file is usually organized by an address system tied into the index record. The user activity results in additions, corrections, deletions to the file, and searches for information concerning the man and his past or present activities.

The fourth example is represented by the *title insurance* business. Here the printed data consist of recorded transactions and other legal actions affecting the rights of individuals to convey real property. They may include transfers of property or property rights, financial transactions and liens, court cases of several kinds, etc. [In one particular example (Title Insurance and Trust Co. of Los Angeles), these transactions amount to over 50 million covering a period of 100 years.] The process of analysis involves the identification of the property and the individuals affected. The relevant facts are then extracted from the source material in the form of an abstract. (In the case cited there are over 5000 such transactions each day.) The index is a record maintained for each parcel of land (over 2 million in the case cited), with a posting for each transaction affecting its status. The document file is then the set of abstracts of each transaction arranged in strict chronological order and grouped by daily activity. The index record defines the exact chronological position of the abstract. The users of this file include the title officers of the company, other company officials concerned with property data, and municipal employees. Requests are normally processed by reference to the index, producing a list of references to abstracts which are then collected for documentation as necessary to handle the request.

A fifth example is represented by the *cataloging* operation in the Department of Defense. The term "cataloging" is used by supply people in the military to describe the method by which materiel, such as equipment parts, is described and referenced in published indexes. Here the printed data consist of the description, both in words and pictures, of inventory items, including major assemblies, subassemblies, component parts. Each of these approximately 2½ million individual items is assigned a unique identification number. The purpose of the cataloging operation is to assign these numbers and provide them in response to requests. The process of analysis covers the description of items in standardized form for processing against the stored descriptions to determine whether the item has previously been assigned an identification number. These standardized item descriptions are based on a set of patterns, each suitable for a particular class of items. There are presently some 12,000 such descriptive patterns. Each item description involves the specification of parameter values within the pattern appropriate to the item. This sequence of assigned parameter values is called the "signal" for the item and can be anywhere from 50 to 250 characters long, with the average of about 100 characters. A number of indexes are provided. One is in sequence by the assigned identification number so that the description can be quickly located if the identification number is known. A second is arranged in sequence by the part numbers of the various manufacturers so that the identification number for a specific part can be quickly located if the manufacturer's part number is known. The document file consists of a set of item descriptions arranged in sequence by their signals. This rather odd arrangement

Federal Item Identification Guides for Supply Cataloging—PART II

DP 1193A

23 April 1953

FSC Group 74

Supersedes DP No. 1193a

1. Item name (obtain from Alphabetic Index of Names, Section A, Cataloging Handbook H 6–1)
2. Specify whether portable or nonportable (e. g., portable)
3. If noiseless, so state (e. g., noiseless)
4. If nonportable, give carriage size (e. g., 11 in. carriage size; 33 in. carriage size)

   NOTE.—*Carriage size is equivalent to maximum width of paper accommodated, disregarding fractions. For example, 11-¾ inch maximum width paper accommodated gives an 11 inch carriage size; 11.2 inch maximum width paper accommodated gives an 11 inch carriage size.*
5. Type data
   - a. Style (select from list below)
     - academic no. 21
     - bold face no. 16
     - bulletin
     - documentary no. 40
     - elite
     - executype no. 516
     - facsimile gothic
     - gothic
     - gothic no. 4
     - large vogue
     - large bulletin
     - modern no. 32
     - modern gothic
     - pica
     - pica gothic
     - pica double gothic
     - pica single gothic
     - small bulletin
   - b. Type of characters (select from list below)
     - upper-case and lower-case
     - upper-case only

     NOTE.—*Lower-case refers to small (noncapital) characters.*

1 November 1954 (Continued)

DP 1193A

6. Keyboard data
   - a. Type (select from list below)
     - air navigation
     - American Standard
     - French
     - Greek
     - Russian
     - Spanish
     - telegrapher
     - United States Navy telegraph
     - United States Weather Bureau
   - b. Number of keys (e. g., 42 keys)

     NOTE.—*Include character keys only.*
7. If electric, so state (e. g., electric)
   - a. State whether alternating and/or direct current (e. g., ac; dc; ac, dc)
   - b. Frequency (e. g., 60 cycles)
   - c. Voltage (e. g., 115v)
   - d. If shielded to prevent radio (electronic) interference, so state (e. g., shielded to prevent radio interference)
8. Special features (list in tabular form)
9. SR–1 Specifications data
10. SR–5 The manufacturer's data

A. *Deleted*

FIG. 5. Typical descriptive pattern (pattern for typewriters and similar devices). U.S. Department of Defense, Assistant Secretary of Defense for Cataloging.

in effect treats the entire signal as though it were a number and arranges these numbers in increasing order. The users of this file are governmental groups and individuals concerned with the standardized identification of inventory items. To utilize the file they must process the item description and check its validity by comparison with standard permissible ranges of parameter values and their interrela-

Federal Stock Number		FEDERAL SUPPLY CATALOG ITEM IDENTIFICATION CARD		
FED SUPPLY CLASS	FED ITEM IDENTIF NO.	STD COMMODITY CLASS	FED DP NO.	ACTIVITY STOCK NUMBER
7430	282–1984		1193A	

1. TYPEWRITER — QM: 54-T-4712 19-00-01240
2. non-portable
3. N/A
4. 12 to 14 in. carriage size
5. type data
   a. elite style
   b. upper-case & lower-case characters
6. keyboard data
   a. American Standard keyboard
   b. 42 keys
7. electric
   a. ac
   b. 60 cycles
   c. 115v
   d. N/A

8, 9, 10. N/A

DD FORM 1 FEB 54 146 PREVIOUS EDITIONS OF THIS FORM MAY BE USED	TYPE OF ITEM IDENTIF	DATE		PREPARED BY
	TYPE 1	ORIGINAL 1 Dec. 54	REVISED	19-00-01240

7430	164-1420			1193A	
STD COMMODITY CLASS	FED ITEM IDENTIF NO.	STD COMMODITY CLASS	PC NO.	DP NO.	ACTIVITY STOCK NUMBER

1. TYPEWRITER — QM: 54-T-17450
2. portable
3. noiseless
4. N/A
5. type data
   a. gothic style
   b. upper-case only
6. keyboard data
   a. telegrapher keyboard
   b. 42 keys

7, 8, 9, 10. N/A

DD FORM 1 APR 50 146	TYPE 1 ITEM IDENTIFICATION CARD	DATE ORIG16Jun50 REV5Jun53	PREPARED BY QM-14160

FIG. 6. Typical item descriptions. U.S. Department of Defense, Assistant Secretary of Defense for Cataloging.

tionships. Each potentially new signal must then be compared with the signals stored in the document file to determine if it matches any one of them. If it does, the presently assigned identification number is used; if it does not, the new description is added to the file, a new number is assigned to it, and appropriate references are inserted in the index. The logical problem in determining whether a given signal matches any of the stored signals is an extremely complex one.

REVIEW OF RESEARCH AND EQUIPMENT DEVELOPMENT

In the following chapters, the work in each of the key activity groups—printed data, analysis and logical processing, index and document file—will be treated individually. In each case the developments can fall within any of three main areas: the development of equipment, the development of programs and procedures for satisfying defined tasks, and the development of total systems of operation. These activities will be explained in detail, the nature of the process will be described, and the aim of research will be discussed, including a survey of the more significant developments. Frequently the techniques used in the solution of information storage and retrieval problems are among the most spectacular developments of modern science and engineering. The explanation of each activity group will therefore include descriptions of the fundamental technical notions when they seem essential to clear understanding. The machine developments chosen for explanation in the survey have been selected to illustrate areas of work; they do not necessarily represent a complete inventory of all the great variety of experimental efforts conducted in the field.

— 5

Printed data and the creation of a machine language

Printed data, considered in terms of input for mechanized information storage and retrieval, have four prominent characteristics.

1. *They are voluminous*—there are lots of data and their rate of growth is astronomical.
2. *They are alphabetical*—letters and certain special symbols are involved, numbers playing a relatively small part.
3. *They have differing type fonts*—original copy may appear in any type font, italics, upper and lower case, or in the alphabet of any language.
4. *Their preparation is varied*—standardization of printing type or format is not always possible or even desirable.

To help in illustrating the various forms which printed data take in modern systems, it is necessary to explain the primary methods used for document preparation and reproduction and the means available for capturing a suitable machine language by-product. A fundamental appreciation of each technical process is essential to the student of information storage and retrieval because of the vital, originating role which documentary reproduction plays in all information systems. The description of the processes is not intended, however, as a substitute for technical reading on the subject. For more detail, a comprehensive current source on processes and equipment in the field of documentary reproduction can be found in the looseleaf service of the FID [1] and in Fussler's [2] textbook on reproduction.

PRIMARY PUBLISHING

The mass publishing of books, magazines, journals, newspapers, and other printed documents has come far since the development of movable type by Johannes Gutenberg so many years ago. A great variety of techniques for reproduction and composition is now available to the publisher.

Letterpress

Letterpress is printing from a raised surface. This raised surface can be either type, plates made from type, or illustrations. These surfaces are raised in relief, and in printing, the raised surface is coated with ink and the paper pressed against this inked surface.

The type for letterpress printing can be set by hand or by a number of machines. Best known of the typesetting machines is the Linotype. This machine is widely used for setting type for newspapers, books, etc. Type set on this machine is formed in a solid slug and the line is automatically "justified." This justification produces the even right-hand margin to which readers have become so accustomed.

Another machine widely used in setting type is the Monotype machine. This machine produces individual pieces of type for each character and space. This makes the Monotype method of composition readily adapted to the production of tabular material and other fine printing requiring various length lines, letter spacing, etc. Setting type for the Monotype method requires two machines, a keyboard-operated tape perforating machine and a casting machine activated by the perforated tape.

Offset

Offset printing has become a significant factor in the printing field in recent years because of its numerous advantages over other methods. In offset printing, typesetting is not necessary.

---

[1] FID, Manual on Document Reproduction & Selection, FID Publication No. 264, 1953.

[2] Herman H. Fussler, *Photographic Reproduction for Libraries, A Study of Administrative Problem,* Chicago, University of Chicago Press, 1942.

The concept of offset as a technique for mass printing was first raised in 1818. Alois Senefelder, the inventor of lithographic printing, published a handbook on lithography [3] in which he mentioned the possibility of using zinc plates for the process instead of stone. It was not, however, until a hundred years later that the principle of *offset duplication* was developed. United States manufacturers who are known for their equipment in the field are the Addressograph-Multigraph Corporation, the Davidson Manufacturing Company, the A. B. Dick Corporation, and others.

The theory of offset is based on the mutual antipathy of water and grease and the disposition of greasy substances to adhere to each other. Preliminary steps in the preparation of the plate are taken to ensure that the image will receive greasy ink. Generally a grease-base ribbon is used on typewriters preparing paper plates. More recently, Xerography has been used successfully as a dry-process method for transferring an image directly to a paper plate (see Xerography, p. 89). When camera negatives are involved, metal and paper plates can have a grease receptive image burned into them. In the latter case, the negative is placed over plates which have been treated with a photo-sensitive, grease-attracting chemical. Arc light exposes the negative; light passing through the transparent areas of the film fixes the grease receptive chemical on the plate. After washing, the plate is left with an image that will repel water and attract oily ink.

Equipment which implements the printing process is constructed basically with four features: an ink fountain, a water source, a plate cylinder covered with a rubber blanket, and an impression cylinder. These are so synchronized that, as the plate cylinder turns, the plate is first washed with water which adheres to the nonprinting areas only. Then it passes the grease-base ink fountain, where the ink is repelled by the water except in the image area, where it is attracted. As the cylinder revolves further, the inked image is transferred to the rubber blanket which in turn deposits the impression on paper. The plate never comes in contact with the paper but is offset by the rubber blanket; hence the origin of the name "offset duplication." For each new plate, the rubber blanket must be wiped clean.

The fact that the master is a direct (not mirrored) image of the final copy in offset printing allows the use of a wide range of techniques, from the simplest to rather sophisticated, in composition and

---

[3] Alois Senefelder, *A Complete Course of Lithography,* London, R. Ackerman, 1819.

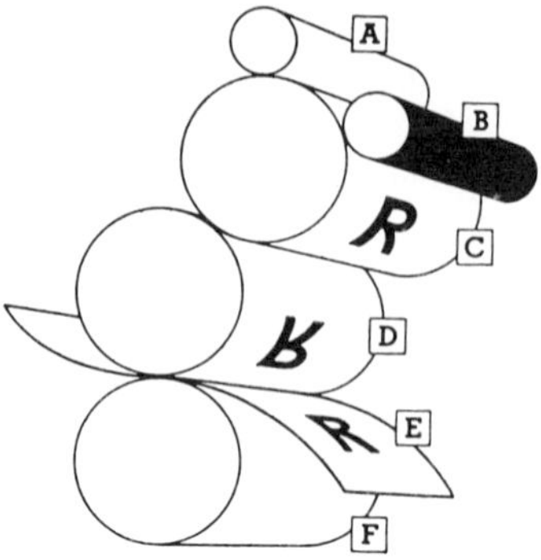

FIG. 7. Offset printing. The multilith process is based on the principle that grease and water do not mix. The positive image area of the paper or metal duplicating master has a grease base and, therefore, attracts inks but repels water. Moisture (A) and ink (B) are automatically applied to the entire surface of the master every revolution of the master cylinder. Moisture is repelled by the grease base image area but adheres to the nonimage area. Ink is repelled by the moistened open area but adheres to the grease-base image area. The master (C) contacts another cylinder covered with a rubber blanket (D). The inked image is transferred to the blanket cylinder in negative or reverse form. The inked image is then "offset" or transferred to a sheet of paper (E) in positive form as it passes between the rubber blanket cylinder (D) and an impression cylinder (F).

offset master preparation. Printing on small presses or duplicating machines is most often done by use of a paper master. A master is usually prepared on a typewriter. It may even be handwritten or drawn. When quality or volume is an important consideration, the offset master is more likely to be made on a metal plate and the printed copies on large presses. The metal plates are made from a negative obtained by photographing the original. This type of printing is frequently referred to as photo-offset.

Punched Card Composition

Paradoxically, in the context of this chapter where we are discussing *printed data as a source of machine language,* it is worth noting that data processing machines can be used very effectively in the composition and preparation of masters for offset printing. Punched card and electronic data processing techniques provide a great advantage for organizing a large volume of data, printing offset masters at high rates of speed, and for effecting revisions and preparing updated masters periodically. The printed output (in this case offset masters) from the data processing machines is generally limited in format variations, type fonts, variety of characters, etc.

A number of devices have also appeared for producing photo-offset directly from lines printed on individual cards. In normal practice, the cards are punched cards. One such device is the List-o-matic camera manufactured by Eastman Kodak; another is the Foto-list of Varityper Corporation; a third is Composo-list of Lithoid. Each of these uses a card as the vehicle for the introduction of data in the system. The text imprinted on the card is photographed by the device to produce a photograph of a single line of print, in other cases of several lines. In this way a photo-offset master can be created, producing a single page from the individual lines occurring on several cards. By thus utilizing the data handling facility afforded by cards —and particularly punched cards—they make mass reproduction of information from a data processing file rapid and convenient.

The Linofilm photocomposition system, developed by Mergenthaler Linotype Company, is now being used to convert automatically the output of an experimental Russian translating computer into a reproducible English text. Until recently an electric typewriter was used for output; since the typographic quality was not satisfactory for wide circulation, it was necessary to redo the material completely prior to distribution. Substituting a Linofilm photo unit results in a book quality print-out on film or paper suitable for reproduction by offset or letterpress printing.

Another device which has been specifically designed for photo com-

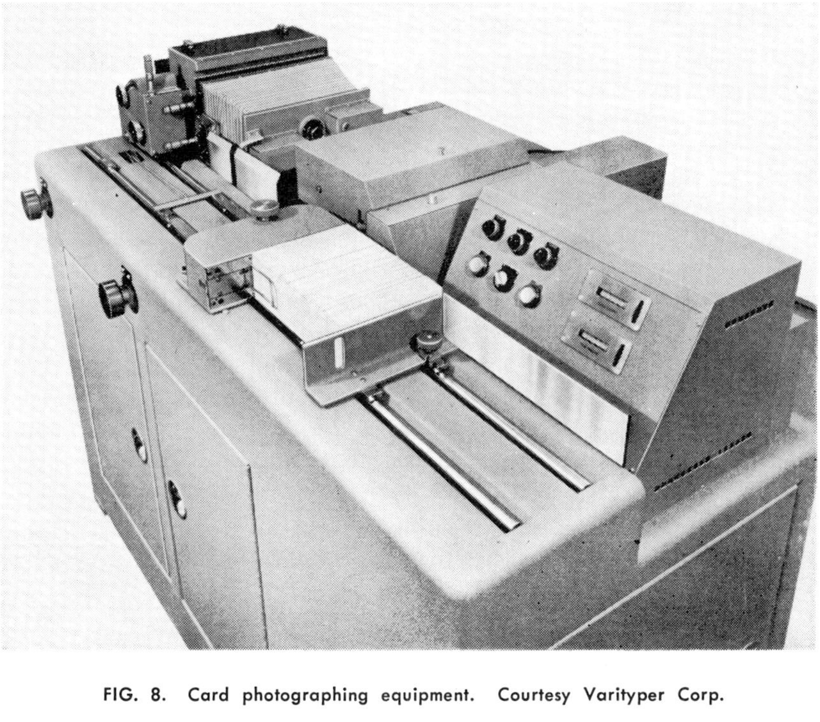

FIG. 8. Card photographing equipment. Courtesy Varityper Corp.

position purposes is the Photon. This equipment includes the capabilities for handling multiple fonts, for justifying the line, and for all the other features of high quality printing. As currently used, the Photon accepts instructions from punched paper tape or from a keyboard and prepares a photographic negative, a line at a time, for subsequent printing use. The term "photo composition" describes the general process of placing type images on photographic film or

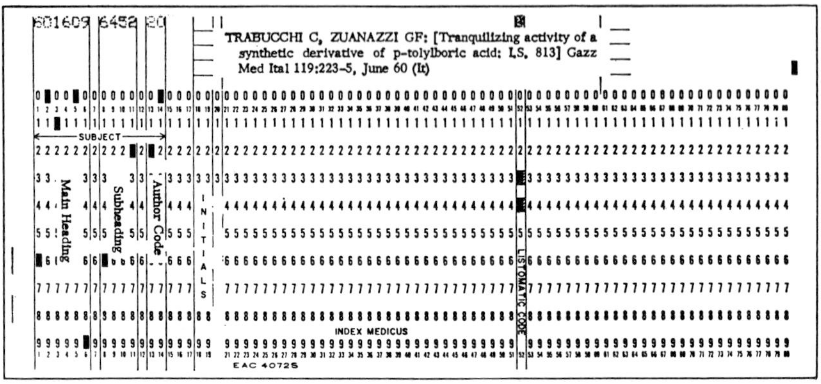

FIG. 9. Index Medicus citation-subject card. The National Library of Medicine, Index Mechanization Project, *Bulletin of the Medical Library Association,* January 1961, v. 49, No. 1, Part 2 (of 2 parts).

paper. In the Photon machine, characters to be photographed are selected at the keyboard in the style and size desired. The machine permits the operator to select the type style and type measure required to do a specific job, and then it automatically spaces and justifies the line. Mixing of style and sizes in the same line is possible, thus providing the operator a great composing flexibility.[4]

The use of such equipment is now well proven by the experience of many organizations. For example, the Atomic Energy Commission,[5] for publication of the indexes for *Nuclear Science Abstracts,*

---

[4] Photon, Inc., 355 Middlesex, Wilmington, Mass.

[5] Documentation, Indexing, and Retrieval of Scientific Information; A Study of Federal and Non-Federal Science Information Processing and Retrieval Programs. Committee on Government Operations. U.S. Senate, 86th Congress, 2nd Session, Document No. 113, Government Printing Office, Washington, D.C., 1961, p. 43.

Time-Life, Inc., for production of certain of its book material, and the National Library of Medicine,[6] for publication of its *Index Medicus* are each using this type of approach. In each case the index entry is typed on a prescribed area at the top of an electric-accounting machine punched card using proportional spacing typewriters. Data for sorting and other card manipulation operations are then punched into the cards in standard form. The cards can

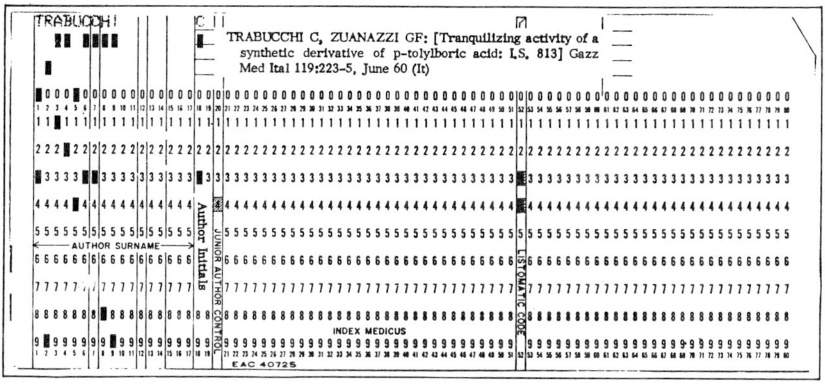

FIG. 10. Index Medicus citation-author card. The National Library of Medicine, Index Mechanization Project, *Bulletin of the Medical Library Association*, January 1961, v. 49, No. 1, Part 2 (of 2 parts).

then be mechanically rearranged into publication sequence and merged with standardized subject heading cards of the same character. A mechanized camera, of the type described earlier, then photographs the composed lines typed at the top of each punched card.

Intaglio

Another technique for printing, which is of interest primarily because of the high quality print image which results, is Intaglio. This technique is based on transferring ink not from the surface of the master plate but from the nonraised surfaces, that is, in the master plate, the raised surfaces are coated with a protective surface to

[6] The National Library of Medicine, Index Mechanization Project, *Bulletin of the Medical Library Association,* January 1961, v. 49, No. 1, Part 2 (of 2 parts).

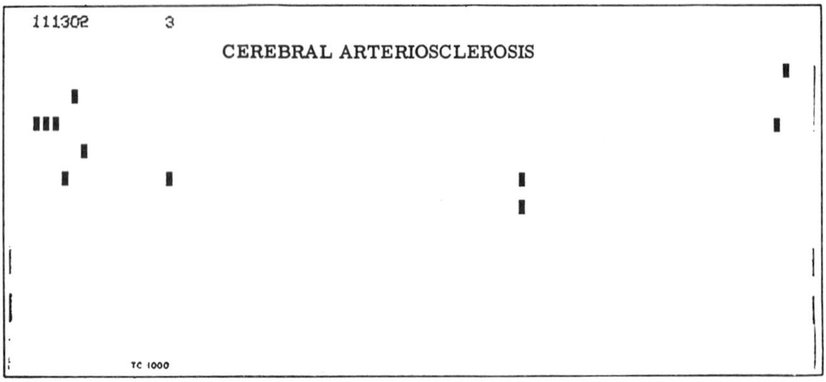

FIG. 11. Index Medicus subject card. The National Library of Medicine, Index Mechanization Project, *Bulletin of the Medical Library Association,* January 1961, v. 49, No. 1, Part 2.

which the ink will not adhere, whereas the depressions or holes in the printing surface are not so protected. The ink will therefore collect in these depressions and will not be on the raised surfaces. When the paper is brought in contact with the printing surface, the ink in the depressions will be transferred by capillary action, thus producing the printed image.

The great advantage of Intaglio is that the amount of ink transferred is dependent on the depth of the impression and can therefore

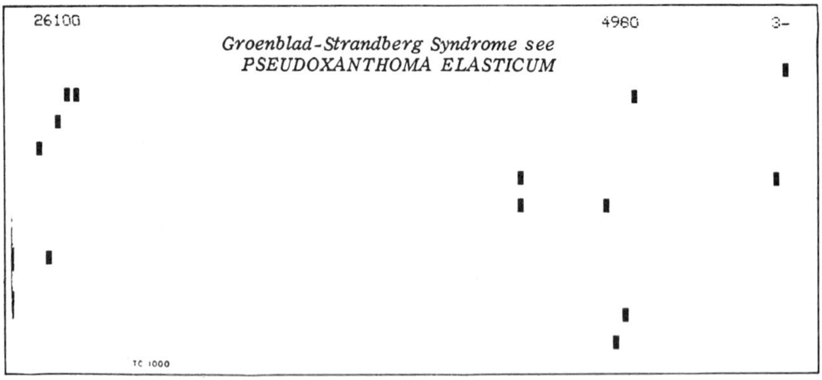

FIG. 12. Index Medicus reference card. The National Library of Medicine, Index Mechanization Project, *Bulletin of the Medical Library Association,* January 1961, v. 49, No. 1, Part 2.

be varied in this way. The technique of Intaglio is used principally for the reproduction of paintings, where such high quality is so desirable.

OFFICE DUPLICATION

With the growth of modern communication through paper, the need for techniques of duplication suitable for the office and the library became evident. Today a great variety of equipment exists for reproduction in relatively small quantities. One such technique is offset, already described, utilizing small-sized office printing equipment and short-run master plates. Others are listed below.

Spirit Duplication

Ditto, a trade name used by the Ditto Corporation, is the term most popularly used to refer to the *spirit duplication* process. Ditto Corporation, however, is only one of several firms which manufacture spirit duplicators. The A. B. Dick Company, for example, markets a product known as Azograph which also utilizes the spirit process.

The master used in the spirit duplication process is produced from two sheets of paper. The upper sheet, which will become the master, is coated on its verso with wax; the second sheet is coated with aniline dye, which faces the upper sheet. Copy is prepared by typing or hand drawing on the impression side of the master. Any instrument, such as a pencil, ballpoint pen, and stylus, can be used provided it is sharp enough to exert point pressure between the wax and dye coatings. After preparation, the second sheet is torn away from the master and destroyed. The master is then fastened to the drum, dye image outward, ready for running.

The spirit duplication process basically involves transferring part of the dye, which was deposited on the wax coating, onto another sheet of paper. This is accomplished by lightly saturating the blank paper with an alcohol mixture (hence the basis for the name, spirit process) and, through use of contact rollers, pressing the paper against the dye deposits on the master. The image forms as dye on the paper. By chemical transfer there is a gradual wearing away of the dye image through interaction with the alcohol in the paper, since each piece of paper which comes in contact with the master dissolves some of the dye. The prints therefore are more legible at the outset and become lighter and fainter as additional copies are run. Purple dye is used almost exclusively because it will produce a greater number of legible copies than other colors.

Stencil Duplication

Stencil duplicating is among the most widely used of all office duplicating methods. Mimeograph, the trade name adopted or the product manufactured by the A. B. Dick Company, has come into common usage to refer to the duplicating process as well as the company. Printomatic, Speed-O-Print, Rex Rotary, and Roneo are also well known in the stencil duplication field. Gestetner is an English firm which is a strong competitor on the American market.

Stencil sheets are made of a porous base tissue covered with a waxy substance which is impervious to ink. The tissue is attached by perforation to a harder stock sheet in order to facilitate handling and storage of the stencils and to serve as a backup for proofreading and a cushion for typing. An insert is sometimes used between the tissue and the backup sheet serving as an additional cushion to prevent deep cutting of the tissue. The backup sheet and the tissue are both used in the preparation of copy. By typing or drawing on the stencil with a hard instrument, the coating is pushed aside and the porous tissue exposed. After preparation and proofreading, the hard backup sheet and the stencil are around the drum; the backup sheet is removed before running. The readable image is always faced toward the drum.

The drum is covered with an inked pad; inking is accomplished by pouring the ink into a cylinder located inside the drum (A. B. Dick) or by inserting a tube of ink into the machine and using a plumbing system to coat a silk screen immediately beneath the stencil (Gestetner). In each case the ink is centrifugally forced through the drum roller and thence through the porous openings of the tissue stencil. Paper is pressed against the stencil, and the result is a duplication of the original text or drawing.

Office Photocopy

There are many indirect photocopying methods which use sensitized paper as the intermediate master, the "negative." The negative is exposed to the original. It then is inserted into a developing solution with a piece of chemically treated positive paper. The sheets are rolled into contact after immersion and then peeled apart to produce a positive copy. A detailed, up-to-date description of such equipment is given by W. R. Hawken in his recent book.[7] In it he includes considerable data on equipment specifications and operating costs.

The Photoclerk, known widely in library circles,[8] is perhaps the best example of a *direct photocopying* method. It employs an optical system for copying the original directly onto sensitized paper. On exposure, the camera lens with a mirror serves to place the original image in readable form on the face of the sensitized paper. Chemical development and drying of the sensitized paper give a direct, negative copy of the original.

Direct contact copying involves only the original and the copy. Contact printing in photography is a good example of the method. A negative is placed on a piece of sensitized paper; the two are held together under pressure; a light source passes visible light through the image area of the negative onto the paper; the paper is developed chemically in a darkroom and dried, and the result is a positive photograph. The aim of direct contact copying in documentary reproduction is to make a positive copy from another printed sheet without using a negative, without immersing prints in chemical solutions and without too much delay. In the last five years technical strides have been made toward perfecting the technique.

Direct contact copying must involve two things—light and a sensitized coating on the paper used to make the copy. Methods have been developed using each end of the light spectrum and corresponding receptive coatings. One uses infrared light waves plus a heat-sensitive coating. The paper used to make copy has a coating which blackens upon application of sufficient heat. The copy paper is placed on top of the original, both being right side up and in firm contact with one another. Infrared rays are passed through the copy paper to the original. The rays are absorbed by the text image, and the resultant heat blackens the corresponding areas of the copy paper to produce a positive copy. This form of direct contact copying takes about 4 seconds; opaque or translucent originals can be used. Originals with good black text produce the best results. Pigment of ink must be carbon or material that will retain infrared. Most colored inks are pigmented with vegetable dyes which pass infrared. The

---

[7] W. R. Hawken, Full Size Photocopying, New Brunswick, N.J., Graduate School of Library Service, Rutgers University, 1960.

[8] R. R. Shaw, *The Use of Photography for Clerical Routines,* Washington, D.C., American Council of Learned Societies, 1953.

clarity and sharpness of the resultant image leave something to be desired, although the quality has improved steadily with the growth of the method. (The Minnesota Mining and Manufacturing Company produces a machine called "Thermo-Fax" for use with this method.)

The second uses ultraviolet light waves plus sensitive paper coated with diazo compounds. The original must have printing on one side only and must have opaque images on translucent paper capable of passing ultraviolet light. The original is placed, under pressure, on the paper with the image side up. Ultraviolet light is played across the original. The light passing through the translucent portions of the original disintegrate the diazo compounds, making them incapable of acting as a coloring agent. By passing the dry paper through gaseous ammonia, the dye remaining in the image area is brought out and a readable, dry positive results. The Ozalid process uses the diazo technique.

Output Printers

The growth of the modern data processing field has introduced another duplication device, the high-speed output printer, operating as a part of data processing systems. A great variety of such printers is available on the market, most of them as part of the complement of equipment provided by data processing manufacturers.

Some of these printers operate by a direct mechanical impression. Generally speaking, such machines print a line at a time, varying in length up to 100 to 150 characters. They normally operate in a range from 100 to 1000 lines per minute. Most have the capability of producing multiple copies, up to perhaps five, through the use of carbon paper. Where more copies are required, a master can be produced which is then used in one of the other printing processes.

Other types of output printers use styli to create individual characters from combinations of dots, lines, and other forms. These printers are primarily used in the high-speed duplication of printing labels and other information where quality is not of primary significance.

More recently, output printers based on the use of cathode ray tubes for the generation of individual characters have appeared on the market. These are capable of extremely high speed; one now commercially available provides a printing rate up to 5000 lines per minute.

Xerography

Xerography is a combination of the Greek words for dry printing. It uses an electrostatic process to generate an intermediate master and thus represents a departure from the standard forms of documentary reproduction. It is a fast, dry, daylight process which produces permanent paper prints or offset masters from an original. "Xerox" machines are manufactured by the Xerox Corporation of Rochester, New York.

In Xerography, a lens is used to project the image of the original onto a continuously rotating selenium-coated drum. Prior to exposure, the drum surface is made light-sensitive by the application of an electrical charge. After exposure, the light from the original causes the charge to "bleed off," retaining the charge only in the image or text areas where no light was reflected. The drum then

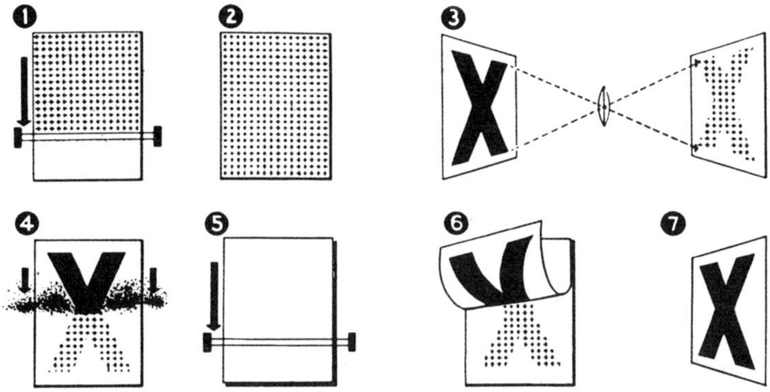

HOW XEROGRAPHY WORKS

1 Surface of selenium-coated plate is electrically charged as it passes under wires.

2 Plus marks represent positively charged plate.

3 Original document is projected through camera lens. Plus marks here represent latent image retaining positive charge. Charge is drained away in areas that are exposed to light.

4 Negatively charged powder is cascaded over plate and adheres to positive image. Latent image now becomes visible.

5 Sheet of paper (or paper offset master) is placed over plate, and paper is given positive charge.

6 Positively charged paper attracts powder from plate, forming direct positive image.

7 Print or offset master is fused by heat for permanency.

FIG. 13. Xerography. Courtesy Xerox Co., Rochester, N.Y.

rotates through a developing station where a toning powder is cascaded on the surface. The powder adheres only to the charged areas. As the drum continues to rotate, the powder image on the surface is rolled into contact with a piece of plain paper which has also received an electrical charge. The charge causes the toner powder to be transferred to the paper which is then subjected to heat in order to fuse the powder to the paper. The drum continues to rotate and the cycle is repeated for the next print or offset master. This is a versatile and convenient method of office copying.

MACHINE LANGUAGE

In an electronic machine system, in order to make efficient use of the data from the great volume of printed material created by all of these methods of duplication, ways must be found to convert the documentary production into a language suitable for machine processing.

Machine language can be thought of as electrical signals or other physical states which represent either letters of the alphabet or numbers. For example, when the letter "A" is depressed on the typewriter keyboard of an IBM key punch machine, the machine internally emits a unique set of electrical signals which cause a combination of punches to be made in a given column of an IBM card. This punch pattern or code will thereafter be recognized as the letter "A" by all other machines in the IBM electronic line. No matter how complex a given application may be, the relationship between the letter "A" and its particular punch combination will remain inviolate.

The representation of information by code of one type or another is basic to understanding how machines operate. It must be recognized, though, that it is fundamental to all communication. Our entire system of written words involves codes for the information conveyed. In the usage of codes there are two relevant considerations: one is the symbols used in the code and the other is their position. That symbols are an essential part of codes is almost self-evident. The decimal digits, the alphabetic characters, are all very familiar. The role of position is perhaps not so evident, but the difference between "god" and "dog" is entirely dependent on the differences in symbol position. Another familiar example of the role of position is the common "radix" notation used in the representation of numeric data, wherein the relative position of the digits with respect to "period" (.) determines their significance. Another example would be the punches in a punched card. The "x" punch at one column of the card will have a very different meaning from the "x" punch at another column of the card. Both are interpreted as "x" punches, but their position determines the particular significance: in one case it may identify a master card as opposed to a detailed card; in another it may be the zone choice in an alphabetic coding; and in a third case it may represent a positive sign for a particular field of numerical data.

Such is coding in general, but the type of coding particularly important for equipment considerations is the so-called "binary coding," which involves only two basic symbols, represented as "0" and "1," called "bits." The reasons for this primarily relate to the difficulties in measurement when attempting to represent more than two things. There are many familiar examples of the use of such coding in punched cards, punched tape, edge-notched cards, magnetic cards, tapes and drums, optical spots.

The language of a digital computer is usually in a binary code because circuits, switches, tubes, transistors, and other electronic components are most efficiently designed to have only two alternate states—on/off, transmitting/nontransmitting, magnetized/unmagnetized, etc.

A knowledge of binary coding, whether designed for punched cards or magnetic tape, is a vital prerequisite to understanding how information can be stored in different forms. Researchers have been ingenious in structuring patterns of this basic binary yes-no coding scheme to represent and store alpha-numeric information. For librarians, the art is thoroughly covered in a recent article by Doralyn Hickey [9] in which she describes various coding systems in use, ranging from the familiar punched card to the complex superimposed coding schemes of Mooers and Wise. Included for good measure are the binary based system used in telegraphy and the code system employed in Braille.

Binary codes, as combinations of sets of positions for these two symbols, are designed for particular purposes. A specific example is the standard "binary coded decimal" representation, where 0000,

---

[9] *The State of the Library Art,* edited by Ralph R. Shaw, v. 4, Part 5, Coding in Yes-No Form, by Doralyn J. Hickey, pp. 319–361, New Brunswick, N.J., Graduate School of Library Service, Rutgers–The State University, 1961.

0001, 0010, 0011, 0100, 0101, 0110, 0111, 1000, and 1001, respectively, represent the decimal digits zero, one, two, three, four, five, six, seven, eight, and nine. Other types of codes can be used for the representation of numeric data, depending on particular usages. One is called "excess-three," using this code: 0011, 0100, 0101, 0110, 0111, 1000, 1001, 1010, 1011, and 1100 for 0, 1, 2, 3, 4, 5, 6, 7, 8, and 9. Notice that in the one case a code 0101 is used to represent a five and, in the other case, to represent a two. How can this be done? The answer, of course, is that they are used in different contexts—one of BCD and the other of excess-three.

Now consider the question of arithmetic convenience. There are several different, but equally reasonable, ways of representing the number 22, for example. From the machine standpoint, the simplest representation for the number 22 would be a binary representation. The binary representation of 22 would be obtained in terms of the radix notation based on "zero times one, plus one times two, plus one times four, plus zero times eight, plus one times sixteen": 10110—the symbol at each position being multiplied by the power of two corresponding to its position. To add two such numbers by using binary arithmetic is extremely simple, and the implementation of arithmetic in binary representation is ideal from an equipment standpoint. In fact, most inexpensive computers are binary computers.

The problem with this approach, however, is that human beings do not normally deal with binary representation; they deal with decimals. Hence, to accommodate the human being, rather than treating 22 as a whole number and representing that binarily, each decimal symbol can be treated separately. For example, 2 can be represented binarily, in binary coded decimal, in each position. In order to do it, eight positions will be needed and each 2 will be represented as 0010, i.e., 00100010. Notice that in one case, binary representation, five "bit positions" are needed and, in the other case, eight, so that binary coded decimal representation is a far more redundant one than binary. But it has the convenience that one can easily identify the decimal characters in the number.

For the representation of alphabetical data, or alphabetical and numerical ("alpha-numeric" data), an appropriate set of codes must be chosen convenient for the purposes to which these codes will be put. The pattern choice is in part a function of the chosen data processing equipment, in part a function of convenience in communication. Some standard sets of codes are illustrated in Figures 14, 15, 16, and 17.

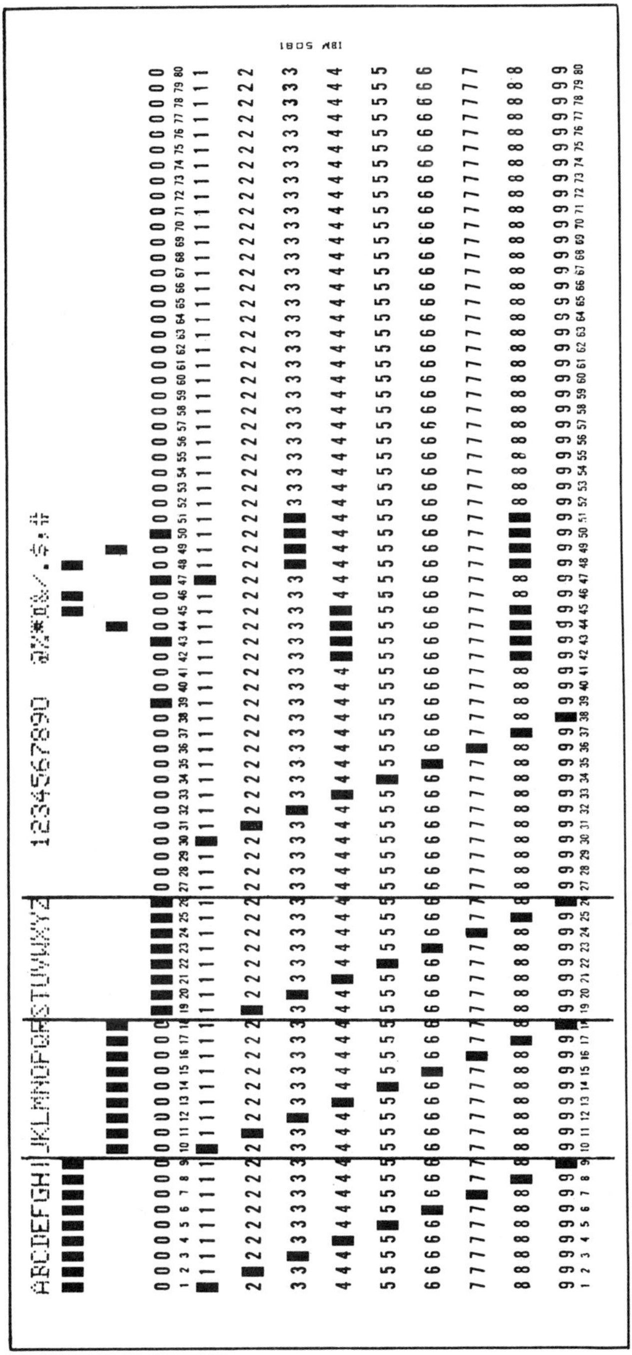

FIG. 14. IBM card code system. Courtesy IBM Corporation, New York, N.Y.

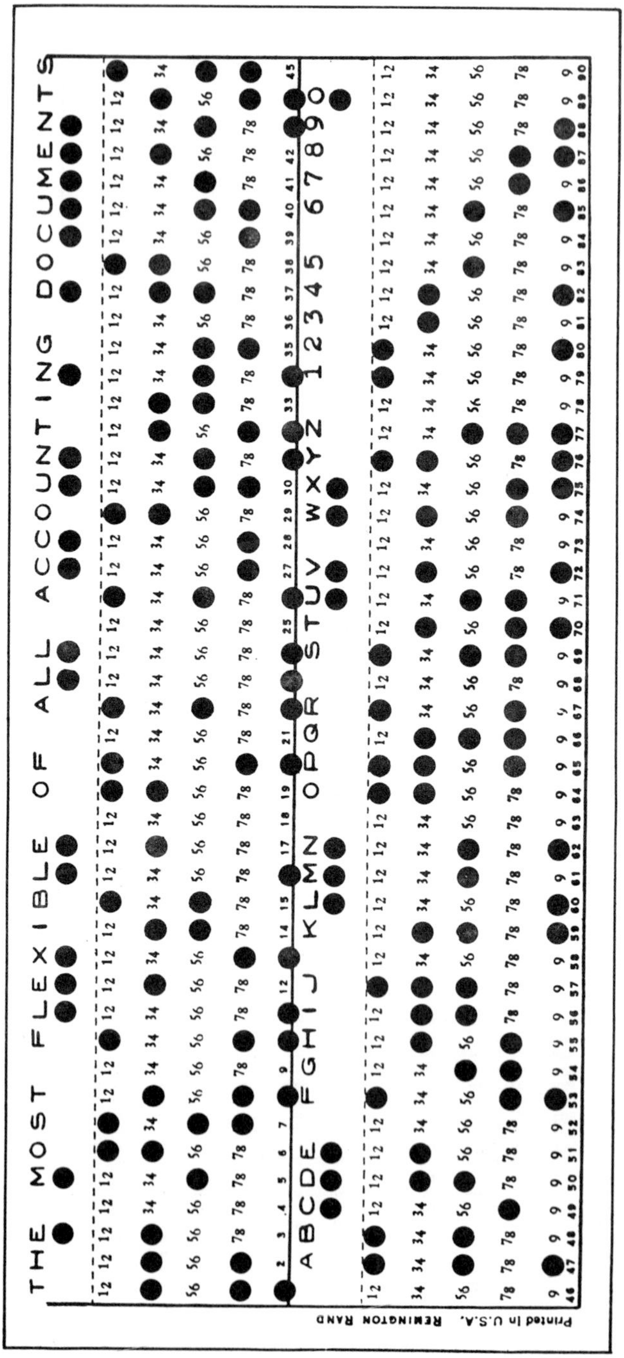

FIG. 15. Remington Rand card code system. Courtesy UNIVAC Division of Sperry Rand, Los Angeles, Calif.

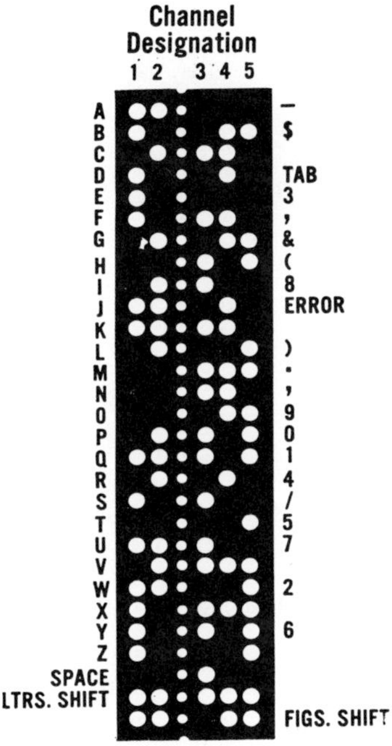

FIG. 16. Standard 5-channel punched tape code system. Courtesy Friden, Inc., San Leandro, Calif.

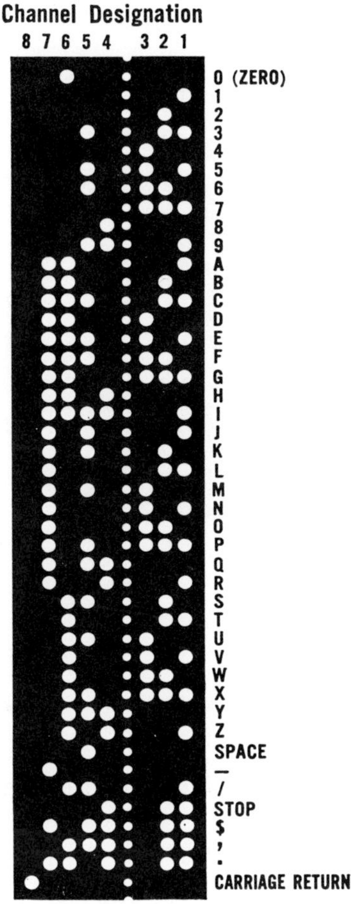

FIG. 17. Standard 8-channel punched tape code system. Courtesy Friden, Inc., San Leandro, Calif.

CONVERSION TO MACHINE LANGUAGE

Two means exist for converting documentary data to machine language: one attempts to capture the data as a by-product of the key depressions made on a keyboard at the time of composition, when the information is prepared for typesetting, office duplication, etc.; the other, based on the evolution of an entirely new set of machines, attempts automatically to scan or "read" printed information and convert it into machine language. At the present time, key depres-

FIG. 18. Flexowriter. Courtesy Friden, Inc., San Leandro, Calif.

sion is the dominant form of machine language conversion available. Machines like the Flexowriter and key punch produce perforated paper tape and punch cards, two basic machine language media. Both require the services of a human operator who performs a typing operation.

As a general rule, use of perforated paper tape proves most effective when it is prepared as a by-product of the creation of the original printed data. This means, however, that publishing must be controlled at source, and in practice this is seldom possible since, for the most part, publishing is uncontrolled. In the absence of reliable character recognition equipment, it is necessary to *rekey* or *retype* the original material in order to obtain either perforated paper tape or punched cards.

Machines such as our modern-day computers operate at speeds measured in microseconds, or millionths of a second (and more recently in terms of nanoseconds, which are billionths of a second). To take full advantage of this manipulative speed for information-processing purposes, some input means other than typing or key-punching at an average speed of 80 words per minute becomes absolutely essential. The absence of a fast, reliable input medium tends to thwart most machine applications because of the prohibitive costs to convert existing documentary data manually. A good example of this burdensome, repetitive necessity can be found in the mechanical translation field, where in many of the experimental programs each foreign language word must be punched into a separate card in order to feed the computer. The need to retype manually or keypunch every word in a foreign language article before machine processing will still exist, even when mechanized translations are acceptable, unless the original printed data can be "read" or scanned automatically.

Inasmuch as typing is tedious, slow, and error prone, ways and means have been investigated for the automatic "reading" of printed data. This research field is called "character recognition." The goal is to invent a device with sufficient discriminatory power to scan letters, words, or sentences and to produce unique electrical signals for each one that will automatically convert the text to digital code that can serve as input to a machine. There is no doubt that a break of this kind in the input bottleneck will open flood gates of data and encourage new applications in the field of information storage and retrieval. While the problem is a formidable one, efforts in the area of character, and auditory, recognition have been underway for some time.

Simply stated, the aim of machine research and development in the Printed Data area is *automatically to convert printed text to machine language.*

The primary objective of all character recognition methods is to obtain clean-cut, discrete signals for each letter, number, or special symbol scanned. Most research has been oriented toward the big problem of automatically reading large quantities of printed information on a production basis.

The possibility of small, portable, "type-reading" machines, however, has also been examined. The history of such interest dates back at least to 1914 when Fournier D'Albe invented the first known reading machine for the blind. He wanted to evolve a simple, hand-operated device which a blind person could move across the printed page and from which he could obtain meaningful aural output. With it a blind person would be able to read a wider range of printed material of his own choosing and do so unassisted.

D'Albe's machine produced five distinct tones, based on the scanning of five photosensitive elements. The machine was not quite portable, and scanning was accomplished mechanically by moving along one line of print at a time. The presence or absence of pieces of print in a letter resulted in a different set of tones being produced. In 1946 the Radio Corporation of America developed an electric pencil which could be moved across one line of print at a time and which emitted aural signals whose frequency was a function of the position of a beam of light in the pencil as it passed over segments of printed letters. Varying signals generated different sounds, and to the highly trained and sensitive ears of the blind one letter could be distinguished from another.

In 1948 Mortimer Taube suggested [10] that the signals emitted by the electric pencil be coupled to a facsimile device so that a copy of the printed page being scanned could be transmitted to a remote station. He said,

> There is, however, one development which may aid us to overcome the initial bottleneck of making the essential record. During the war the Radio Corporation of America (RCA) Laboratories worked on the development of a scanning device which could be held in the hand and which could activate a sound producing apparatus when passed over a printed text. This machine was intended as a device to enable blind people to read ordinary printed books. Unfortunately it has so far proved impossible to use the scanner on texts selected at random since the shapes of letters vary too much in different texts. For example, a letter "a" in one font may sound more like an "e" in the same font than like an "a" in a different type font. However, during a visit to the RCA Laboratories, members of the Library of Congress staff suggested to the RCA engineers the possibility of using a hand scanner as the reading end of a facsimile recorder. Such a scanner could be passed rapidly over the title pages or the table of contents of any book or journal, and material required for identification or indexing could be selected for facsimile reproduction on a tape, card or film in any order desired by the person moving the scanner. Such an instrument is entirely practical and a model of the hand scanner has already been built.

The Prosthetic and Sensory Aids Division of the U.S. Veterans Administration had Batelle Memorial Institute [11] design, under contract, a print reader for the blind in 1958. The output was to be aural, the machine portable, and the output sounds as distinct and different as possible. Five prototype "optophone" readers were designed and

---

[10] Mortimer Taube, New Tools for the Control and Use of Research Materials, Documentation, Inc., Bethesda, Md., November 5, 1948.

[11] Batelle Memorial Institute, Development and Evaluation of Aural Reading Devices for the Blind, mimeographed, June 30, 1958, U.S. Veterans Administration, Prosthetic and Sensory Aids Service, 252 Seventh Ave., New York 1, N.Y.

built, each containing 11 photoelectric cells to increase the reliability of the signal discrimination. An auditory code was produced which recorded the different sounds or tones for the different letters of the alphabet. These, in turn, were used as instructional aids to teach blind persons to recognize the letter meanings of the sounds. Some students achieved relatively good proficiency in reading, although average reading was far from perfect. Milton F. Metfessel of the University of California at Los Angeles recently described a "robot voice" capable of generating synthetic speech from human sounds. The machine was invented by Hans Mauch of Mauch Laboratories, Dayton, Ohio, and while it is not yet perfected, its purpose is to examine the letters of printed matter, translating what it scans into electrical impulses that can identify each letter. The machine, being developed for the blind, is then supposed to convert the letter signals into spelled speech.[12]

While this type of research is not directly applicable to the problems in the area of printed data, it does represent an illuminative sidelight. The printed word can be recognized by machine to produce digital code for direct machine use or aural code for human interpretation. Another type of recognition being explored is the area of auditory or speech recognition. The question posed here is whether or not a machine can discriminate phonetic sounds and in so doing produce a satisfactory, usable digital code for input to machines.

Let us, then, examine typical research work and techniques investigated in character recognition.[13] Most present techniques have been used mainly for reading numerical characters, with several practical applications of this nature in actual operation today.

Applications of existing equipment have been largely of a special purpose kind where the input is generally in a controlled type font and format and aimed mainly at solving problems associated with decentralized document recording and centralized document processing; a high transaction rate has usually been involved in such applications as banking, gasoline credit cards, and insurance. None of the methods in their present form would be used as a general purpose character recognition system for examining a typical page of printed

---

[12] Earl Ubell, A Robot Voice May Let the Blind "Read," *The New York Herald Tribune,* Thursday, June 21, 1962.

[13] Optical Character Recognition, edited by George L. Fischer, Jr., Donald K. Pollock, Bernard Raddack, Mary Elizabeth Stevens. Proceedings of the Symposium on Optical Character Recognition held in Washington, D.C., January 15–17, 1962, under joint sponsorship of Office of Naval Research and the National Bureau of Standards. Spartan Press, Washington, D.C., 1962.

text. While considerable progress is being made for the automatic reading of specially prepared numerical characters, the ability to discriminate alphabetical intermixed type fonts and sizes in a precise and reliable way is still not in sight.

Most character-reading apparatus possess three features which seem to resemble the human reading process.

1. *A Scanner:* To focus on the character the way the human eye does. In machine reading of alpha-numeric characters, each character must be scanned in two directions to provide a maximum number of distinctly different waveform combinations. Scanning may occur more than once to ensure reliable and verified input.

2. *A Signal Library:* Some reference storage which contains the rules to decide what electrical combination represents which letter or word in the signal library and auxiliary circuitry to output the results in the form required. It thus provides the ability to compare the electrical signals obtained in scanning with basic well-defined recognition criteria held fixed in storage. Three methods are presently used for making this comparison: (a) *Exact match*—requiring an absolute match with all or part of the character in the store, (b) *Best fit*—a unique identification of the character but not necessarily absolute, and (c) *Threshold*—which allows for an acceptable degree of match between the character and the store. As might be expected, Exact match is very accurate but has a high reject ratio. The Threshold method is least accurate and may produce a high rate of ambiguous identification.

3. *A Mechanical Feed:* Some *document handling* facility for moving the documents to be read past the scanner. Currently two methods used are (a) *Continuous feed*—when the original documents can be placed in reel form, and (b) *Unit feed*—when the documents being read are to be handled on a piece-by-piece basis. The way documents are handled largely determines the rate of speed at which characters can be examined by the scanner. Continuous feed is faster because data can be packed together without interruption.

The *optical scanning* technique involves projecting an image of the character by reflected light to a lens system. The optical system sharpens the image and transmits it on through two intersecting slits to a photomultiplier. Since the white parts of the image transmit light and the black portions of the image do not, the photomultiplier essentially receives a continuous stream of "spots of light." The photomultiplier is a tube capable of converting light patterns into electrical signals. Theoretically, if the combination of spots of light for each image is different, then the converted electrical signals will be different. These "differences," in effect, give the technique its power to discriminate between numerical characters. As the photomultiplier produces electrical signals, they are sent to a special purpose computer for comparison with all of the possible combinations of electrical signals, each of which identifies a given numerical character. After a number has been identified on the basis of the comparison, computer circuits are activated which trip the appropriate character on a printer, write it on magnetic tape, punch it into a card, or display it on an electrical print-out device.

The Intelligent Machines Research Corporation[14] has investigated the use of the optical scanning technique for reading alphabetical characters as well as numerals. This research is part of their program to develop character recognition equipment for the U.S. Post Office Department which will assist in the reading and sorting of mail. An interesting aspect of the work is the addition of a Comparator circuit in the optical scanning itself. The function of the Comparator is to adjust the magnitude of the electrical signals produced by the photomultiplier in proportion to the size of the first character examined in the address portion of an envelope. This yields the ability to read alphabetical characters in many styles and sizes of type without changing the logical circuitry. For Post Office applications, it was decided to have the computer "save-up" combinations of electrical signals until it could identify the signal for a city and a state as a group rather than identify a character at a time.

The purpose of the research was to provide sufficient flexibility to enable a machine to read intermixed type faces with a single logical program. This is particularly important in the automatic reading of mail because of the many different typewriters and imprinters which are used to prepare addresses. If the approach proves feasible for reading mail addresses, it may eventually have the necessary versatility to read intermixed type in other printed data.

A comparable system known as "Selfchek" was also developed by the Intelligent Machines Research Corporation. It is used by some companies as part of a credit card invoicing-accounting application and operates as follows.

Plastic gasoline credit cards are furnished to each customer. Embossed on the card is the customer's account number. (Type faces for the ten numerals were so chosen as to ensure maximum reliability by building in large differences between each of the characters.)

---

[14] Intelligent Machines Research Corporation, 7019 Edsall Rd., Alexandria, Va.

When gasoline is purchased, the customer presents his card. It is used to imprint his name and account number on a tabulating card invoice. The gasoline attendant writes in the dollar amount by hand. At a central location, Selfchek automatic character-reading machines scan the account number imprinted on the invoice and automatically punch it into a tabulating card. An operator proofreads each invoice and, as a by-product, keys in the dollar amount in an adding machine which is coupled with a card punch. Thus the dollar amount also gets punched automatically into the tabulating card. Conventional electronic accounting machines then sort, collate, and merge the punched invoices and prepare monthly billing statements for the customer.

The basic operating speed of the reading equipment is 180 invoices per minute. It has built into it sufficient error-check devices to keep the reject rate low. Dirty thumb prints and handling smears have had only insignificant effects on the system. Experience in field installations, such as that of Standard Oil Company of California, has proven it to be very reliable.

Recently the U.S. Air Force announced some new equipment developed for the Rome Air Development Center (RADC) [15] by the Farrington Company. Over a number of years the RADC Intelligence Laboratory recognized that automatic reading of information is essential to advances in information processing. Air Force Intelligence need for a Print Reader centers on a never-ending necessity for handling millions of pages of information which must be processed before being used.

The Intelligence Laboratory of RADC and Intelligent Machines Research Corporation, Alexandria, Virginia, after a two-year development program, successfully demonstrated a print reading machine in May 1959 at Rome Air Development Center. The machine, called Print Reader, reads ordinary typewritten pages, one page at a time, from the input receptacle. The Print Reader reads both the capital letters and the small letters of the alphabet. At the present it reads only one type style, which is called financial Gothic. If needed, the electronics can be programmed to read other type styles, such as Roman and italic. However, the programming of many different styles in a single machine results in a considerable decrease in speed and accuracy.

---

[15] Rome Air Development Center, U.S. Air Force Air Research and Development Command, Griffiss Air Force Base, Rome, N.Y.

The Scanner Unit has an electro-optico-mechanical scanner. As it scans the information a character at a time, it produces TV-like video pulses from the typewritten character. These electrical signals are fed into the Pattern Recognition Unit, which analyzes the video pattern for various identification clues on a "go" and "no go" basis. Recognition is accomplished by fulfilling the programmed logic for each character. This eliminates a storage unit for storing a unique video pattern for each character.

The input rate of the Print Reader is approximately two $8\frac{1}{2} \times 11$ full single-spaced pages per minute. The output rate is 240 characters per second, which is the speed of the tape perforator. Other output forms, such as punched cards or magnetic tape, are also possible.

Another approach uses a cathode ray tube which emits a moving spot of light tracing a series of parallel lines (known as raster-rows) over the character being scanned. As the spot traces out the raster, it moves over the white part of the paper and the black parts of the character. White paper reflects more light than the black character. Thus line-by-line variations in light signals are transmitted to a nearby photomultiplier where they are converted to electrical signals.

Due to the hazards of mutilation and dirt around the character, special filtering circuits are introduced to clip or "clean up" the electrical signals. The filtered signals are then passed to a special purpose computer where bit-by-bit and line-by-line they are stored for subsequent analysis. Essentially, storage occurs in grid coordinate fashion. When all of the information for a given character is in the machine's memory, logical circuits determine what letter has been identified. Table 8 shows how the recognition decision is made for the characters in one specialized font. Once a character is logically identified, its distinctive electrical signals can be used to operate a card punch, magnetic tape unit, or a printer.

The same principles are embodied in equipment manufactured by Solartron Electronic Group Ltd.[16] The Solartron Roll Reader, as it is called, is in practical use in England for reading rolls of cash-register tapes. On the tapes are printed the code for the salesperson making the transaction, a code for the item sold, and the amount of purchase. Each day the Roll Reader scans the cash-register tapes, and through coupled automatic key punch machines, produces punched

---

[16] Solartron Electronic Group Ltd., Queens Road, Thomes Ditton, Surrey, England.

TABLE 8

Character Recognition Criteria *

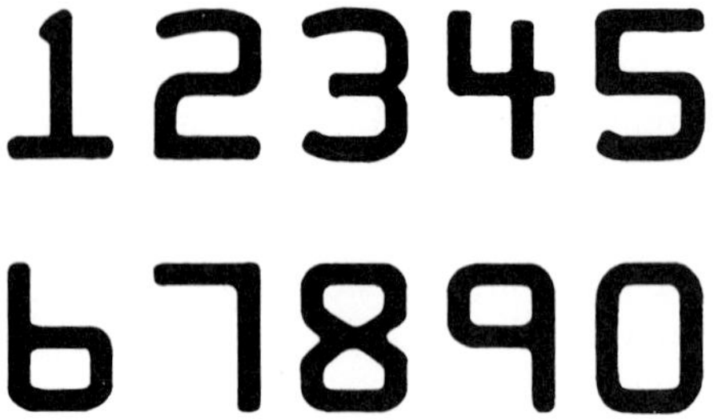

	0	1	2	3	4	5	6	7	8	9
LONG VERTICAL LEFT	+		−	−	−	−	+	−		−
LONG VERTICAL RIGHT	+	+	−	+	+	−	−	+		+
HORIZONTAL TOP	+	−	+	+	−	+	−	+	+	+
HORIZONTAL MIDDLE	−	−	+	+	+	+	+	−	+	+
HORIZONTAL BOTTOM	+	+	+	+	−	+	+	−	+	−
SHORT VERTICAL UPPER LEFT & LOWER RIGHT	+	−	−	−		+	+	−	+	+
SHORT VERTICAL UPPER RIGHT & LOWER LEFT	+	−	+	−	−	−	−	−	+	−
SHORT VERTICAL LEFT & RIGHT SIMULTANEOUSLY	+	−	−	−		−	+	−	+	+
SHORT VERTICAL UPPER LEFT				−	+					
LONG VERTICAL LEFT & RIGHT SIMULTANEOUSLY	+								−	
MIDDLE PROJECTING RIGHT					+					−

+ CONDITION MUST BE DETECTED

− CONDITION MUST NOT BE DETECTED

* Courtesy Farrington Manufacturing Co., Needham Heights, Mass.

transaction cards which are sorted and tabulated by conventional accounting machines. The system is adaptable to any other application which involves many printed transactions and which uses rolls of paper tape as the recording medium. Type style and size as well as roll tape format must be fixed within certain prescribed limitations.

The Solartron Roll Reader is capable currently of reading numerals and special symbols, but the manufacturer is investigating ways by which other alpha-numeric characters can be treated reliably. Some attention has also been given by the company to automatic reading of original data stored on rolls of microfilm.

Pattern-matching techniques have also been employed by the Rabinow Engineering Company [17] for the conversion of typewritten or printed information into digital form suitable for input to electronic data processing machines. The Rabinow Universal Reader, as it is called, employs the principle of match correlation. In other words, the machine compares the unknown character which it examines with a set of known ones and finds the best match. Thus the machine does not recognize a letter, say A, because this character meets certain specific requirements but rather because it meets the characteristics of the letter A more completely than all other letters in the alphabet. This principle of operation therefore is capable of handling relatively imperfect print and can tolerate minor defects in the characters being read. Reference storage in the Rabinow Universal Reader takes the form of master matrices. Each matrix represents the font of characters or unique symbols required for recognition. Recently the company announced the use of its Reader for converting impressions made from addressograph plates to machine language for computer use. In doing this, the company creates a set of controlled impressions from the addressograph plates on the customer's premises and uses this controlled font for reference storage in a master matrix. Reading results in converting the impression to any computer input selected by the customer—magnetic tape, punched paper tape, or punched cards.

Some of the companies known to be engaged in research and development in various forms of character recognition equipment include the Baird-Atomic Co., RCA, and Sylvania.

Bell Telephone Laboratories [18] developed a technique for the automatic reading of handwritten numerals; it is formally called Guided Arabic Double Dot (GADD). This represents the major work undertaken thus far for reading longhand writing. The research resulted in design of a prototype machine on which any operator could write any number and instantaneously view the standard digit on a lighted number panel. This proved the machine's ability to discriminate between numbers regardless of which operator did the writing. It operated as follows.

---

[17] Rabinow Engineering Company, 1025 W. Montgomery Ave., Rockville, Md.

[18] T. L. Diamond, Devices for Reading Handwritten Characters, *Communications of the Association for Computing Machinery,* February 1958, v. 1, No. 2, pp. 32–33.

1. Writing is done on a specially prepared metal surface with a metal stylus.
2. On the metal surface there are two dots, one placed above the other.
3. A prescribed set of rules determined what constraints would be used by the operator when writing the number around the dots (see Figure 19).
4. Seven sensitized lines extended radially from the dots.
5. Writing the numbers according to the rules resulted in unique vectors or different combinations of crossed lines for each number.
6. Crossed sensitized lines generated electrical signals to special logical circuitry which opened the proper switch to light the written number on a visual panel. The signals could also have been used with other output devices such as automatic key punches, paper tape punches, printing mechanisms, or magnetic tape.

This system is not limited to numerical characters. Through the use of a four-dot constraint pattern, it could accommodate a complete alphabetical scheme as well. The principle has not yet been put to use in a field situation on a large scale. An extension of this research at Bell resulted in the production of another prototype machine which "reads" ten handwritten words, "zero" through "nine" spelled out. The machine was invented to demonstrate methods which may be used to read a wider variety of handwritten material. As on the double dot machine, the handwriting machine requires the user to write his words within certain surface constraints on a metal plate. The plate is made up of 15 horizontal metal strips alternately sandwiched between electrical insulating material on the surface. Up and down movement of a stylus causes electrical signals to be emitted depending on which combination of metal strips was crossed. The sequence in which these signals are emitted enables the machine to

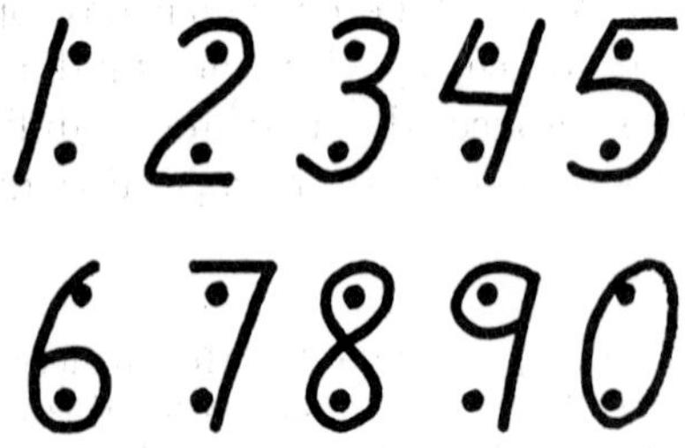

FIG. 19. Guided Arabic double dot. Courtesy Bell Telephone Laboratories, New York, N.Y.

interpret logically which word was written. Although the machine can recognize most writing styles, it has its limitations. The writer, for example, must not print his words nor lift the stylus from the plate while writing. In tests of 1000 words written by 20 different people, the machine scored 97% accuracy.

The Bank of America has been a leader in the development and application of electronic systems to banking. During the course of its research efforts, it encouraged the Stanford Research Institute (SRI) [19] to pursue automatic character recognition. The great bulk of banking business is done by check, and The Bank of America appreciated the enormous benefits which would be derived if some automatic means were devised to sort and handle checks. SRI developed a system for the magnetic reading of numerals which operates as follows.

1. Original numerals, in a prescribed type font, are imprinted on the check by using ink containing magnetic oxide.
2. The check is fed past a prereading station which essentially is a magnetic field, and the magnetically inked numerals are energized or charged.
3. Next, the numerals on the check are placed in almost direct contact with a conventional magnetic read-head of the kind normally used in magnetic tape systems.
4. The magnetic read-head senses the signals which are generated by the thin layer of magnetic ink. Since the type font of the numerals was originally designed to produce ten (0–9) distinguishable signals, each numeral produces a distinctly different signal or waveform when passed under the read-head.
5. These signals are amplified, filtered, and transmitted to correlation networks. These electrical networks have the signal characteristics of each number stored for reference in circuitry.
6. When a given signal passes through the correlation network, it exists as an output signal for a particular numerical character. This output signal is used to punch cards, write on magnetic tape, print, etc.

The American Express Company issues travelers' checks which are numbered serially. The company is anxious to reconcile these checks as quickly as possible after issuance in order to know how many checks are outstanding, to know how many checks have been used within a given period, and to detect malpractices, etc. By imprinting

---

[19] K. R. Eldredge, F. J. Kampheofner, and P. H. Wendt, Automatic Input for Business Data Processing Systems, *Proceedings of the Eastern Joint Computer Conference,* 1955, p. 94.

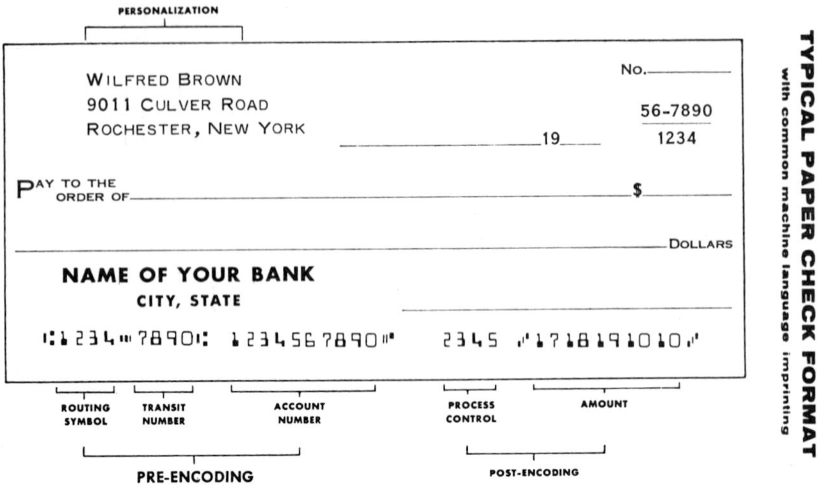

FIG. 20. "Magnetic ink character recognition" (MICR) system.

these checks with a special type font for the serial number and magnetic ink, a machine sorts the checks at the rate of 3000 a minute by using the magnetic ink-reading technique. The output signals generated by the reading system in this case are used to open or close gates in a mechanical sorting device.

Recently IBM, Burroughs, General Electric, and National Cash Register Co. have introduced electronic banking equipment that uses the principles of magnetic ink reading for sorting and other accounting purposes. The magnetic-ink character-reading system is secure against most of the common types of defacement. Overprinting, dirt, or writing across the numbers causes no trouble. Embossing, for example, by a ballpoint pen, causes no difficulty, nor does wrinkled or sharply creased paper. Even though during the reading process close contact with the read-head is desirable, a layer of transparent adhesive tape over the numbers does not prevent reliable results. This means that torn checks can be repaired without detriment to the reading system. Imprinting with magnetic ink is highly durable and can withstand thousands of transits across the read-head with no impairment of the signal.

REFERENCES

Chow, C. K., "An Optimum Character Recognition System Using Decision Function," *Convention Record WESCON*, 1957, v. 1, Part 4.

Clark, W. A., and B. G. Farley, Generalization of Pattern Recognition in a Self Organizing System, *Proceedings of the Western Joint Computer Conference,* 1955, p. 86.

Davidson, J. T., and R. L. Fortune, Automatic Translation of Printed Code to Impulses Acceptable to Computing Equipment, *Proceedings of the Western Joint Computer Conference,* 1955, p. 29.

Henaley, C. C., Jr., Selfchek—A New Common Language, Paper delivered at Western Joint Computer Conference, May 9, 1958.

Shepard, D. H., and Heasley, C. C., Jr., Photoelectric Reader Feeds Business Machines, *Electronics,* May 1955, p. 134.

Zworkin, V. K., L. E. Flory, and W. S. Pike, Letter Reading Machines, *Electronics,* June 1949, p. 80.

6

Analysis, logical processing, and the computer

Analysis of document content and logical processing of requests are the stages in the total cycle of the Information Framework in which "intellectual" effort is spent in order to ensure satisfactory retrieval results. This intellectual process is crucial and represents the heart of any information system. Adequate handling of it presents the most challenging obstacle in the path of mechanized solution to the total information retrieval problem.

To describe the document analysis process, librarians use terms such as "indexing" and "subject classification." There is a formal distinction between the two but, characteristically, they have the same aim—to represent the contents of documents and to organize the various files into information compartments suitable for retrieval. In a conventional library situation, analysis consists of reading the contents of an article to comprehend the ideas expressed in the text and then matching the ideas with headings chosen from the special lists prescribed for this purpose.

This process results in the index which is then utilized as the fundamental data for logical processing in answer to requests. Generally speaking, the contents of the index are abstractions of each of the basic source documents, that is, they can be considered a substitute for the original documents, containing only as much information as will help users to decide intelligently which documents in the document file most closely satisfy their needs. The preparation of an index would be unnecessary if the original documents could themselves be arranged in a way which would satisfy all consultative and searching requirements. However, it is clear that this is only possible when the quantity of printed material is small or when highly specialized use is all that is involved; even then it would be difficult at best to determine the most suitable document arrangement. As soon as a collection of printed material begins to grow and user needs become diverse, no single arrangement of material could possibly serve all purposes, and indexes are necessary to meet the multiple needs.

Most responses to a request can only be effective when all pertinent printed materials bearing on the subject can be rapidly listed and rapidly provided to the researcher. The researcher most often wants a complete list of all available documents which might provide background for his study and, perhaps, abstracts of the more important ones. In this way the abstracts present the user with text information and presumably help him to judge more fully which documents will most likely suit his purpose. The logical processes in handling requests attempt to provide such a list and to evaluate the probable usefulness of the documents. The index provides the searcher with the most basic tool for doing this. If the searcher does not have an index service, he must devote much time and effort, which might otherwise be applied to productive research, to bring together the source materials he needs.

Manual systems which utilize standardized indexing schemes are almost wholly dependent on them for later retrieval and processing of requests. This has somewhat obscured the importance of the intellectual processes in the handling of requests for information. It has frequently seemed as though the major intellectual effort has been accomplished at the stage of analysis and that the examination of the index to obtain desired material was a fairly mechanical process. In fact, of course, the handling of requests can be fully as complicated an intellectual task as the original analysis of documents, and the importance of the role of the reference librarian only serves to emphasize this. The translation of requests into a form suitable for processing against an index and the determination of relevancy of stored information are extremely difficult intellectual problems.

In essence, the main result of research work in development of mechanized solutions in this area has been the experimental testing of the capabilities of electronic data processing machines to determine which aspects of document analysis and logical processing of requests can be accomplished or served efficiently by using these new tools. To understand this research, and any part of the field of information storage and retrieval for that matter, it is essential to obtain a basic understanding of electronic data processing and the general purpose computer.

Computers and auxiliary machines for the electronic processing of data are emerging as revolutionary tools to extend and multiply human skills. One class of computers, the analog, processes measurements of a continuum—notably time, direction, distance, or velocity—and displays the results in some measurable form. An automobile speedometer is a mechanical form of very simple analog device; it measures the rotation of a car's wheels and continuously translates this into a miles-per-hour reading on the dashboard. For electronic computation the measurements may be represented by the voltages of electrical signals and processed by integration and differentiation of these voltages. One typical application of the analog computer is in a missile guidance system. It converts measurements of wind and missile velocity, launching angle, position, time, etc., into a chain of output signals for adjusting the valves and control surfaces of the missile. Through a feedback loop to the missile these make instantaneous correction of abnormal trajectory variations. They may also be used to drive a data-plotter on the ground for charting the trajectory or displaying it on a TV screen.

Because they work with measurements, analog computers are limited in the precision of their operation. Digital computers process discrete numbers, and since numbers may be used (as we have described) to represent the letters of the alphabet or verbal symbols, the digital computer is the machine that has the major promise for handling verbal data.

THE GENERAL PURPOSE DIGITAL COMPUTER

More than any other factor, the advent of the general purpose digital computer has represented the potential for revolutionary solutions to mechanized information retrieval systems. It has opened up a wealth of possibilities, for it provides capabilities enormously more powerful than those of any previous mechanical device for the handling of information.

These possibilities result from a combination of three basic characteristics of the general purpose computer: its built-in capabilities for performing specified elementary operations at extremely high speed, its stored program, which allows it to perform automatically a prespecified sequence of such elementary operations, and its capability for automatically modifying the stored program. Thus general purpose computers perform complex operations through a large number of simple operations, each of which represents a built-in capability of the computer. The sequence of operations for performing a given job must have been prepared and appropriately stored in the machine, but it may include the mechanism for changing these operations and the sequence in which they are performed on the basis of the data which are handled.

To understand computers it is therefore necessary to appreciate what the built-in operations are and how the computer can automatically perform a sequence of them. More than this, however, it is also essential to understand how the personnel utilizing a computer analyze a problem and determine the sequence of elementary operations which the computer is to perform. This process, called programming, turns the computer from an inert collection of hardware into a powerful tool for the handling of information.

Structure of the Computer

The block diagram in Figure 21 shows the traditional description of the parts of a computer system and their relationship to each other.

As shown, it consists of four basic elements: the operation and control unit, the memory unit, the files, and the peripheral input-output units. The operation and control unit provides the capability of executing any one of several built-in elementary operations. It does this on the basis of interpreting a "command" which essentially describes the operation to be performed and the location of the data on which it is to be performed. In carrying out these functions, the operation and control unit occupies the key role. It must interpret each command, control the memory unit for the purpose of obtaining the information involved, execute the operation on that data, control other affected elements, such as the files and the input-output equipment, and determine where to find the next command in the memory unit. In support of these functions, the memory element serves as

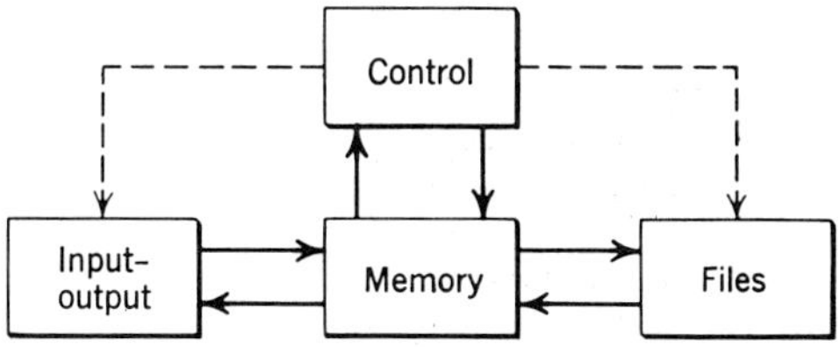

FIG. 21. Computer block diagram.

the location from which data are drawn to be operated on and from which commands are obtained in succession by the operation and control unit. The files provide for mass storage of data, available at high speed to the computer. The input-output elements, under the control of the operation and control unit, provide the capability for communication to and from the world external to the computer.

Typically a command will consist of three sections. The first specifies the operation to be performed; the second specifies the data which are to be operated on by defining their location in the memory; and the third, which may or may not be an explicit part of the command, defines the location of the next command in the memory. From this it is clear that there is a very close association between the memory and the operation and control unit.

Computer memories are usually organized into fixed locations, each of which can hold a specified quantity of data, such as six alphanumeric characters or 10 decimal digits. The specified quantity is usually called a "word" and the location of a word is called its "address." Thus, if a given word consists of a set of alphabetic characters representing a name and it is desired that an operation should compare it with another set representing another name, the command would need to specify the operation of *compare* and the addresses of the particular words to be compared.

Of even more importance—in the close relationship between the memory and the operation and control unit—is the fact that the commands are themselves stored as words in addresses of the memory. In the first place this allows the commands which are interpreted by the operation and control unit to be automatically available to the computer and successively picked up from the memory. In addition, however, since commands are stored in the same form as data, they can be operated on and changed as the result of other operations. It is this last feature, the ability to change the stored commands,

FIG. 22. Instruction format. Courtesy UNIVAC Division of Sperry Rand, Los Angeles, Calif.

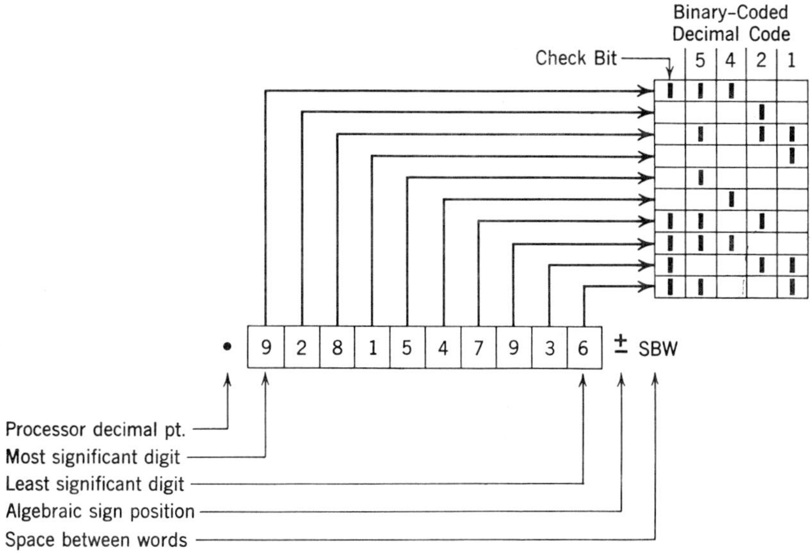

FIG. 23. Format and composition of a computer word. Courtesy UNIVAC Division of Sperry Rand, Los Angeles, Calif.

which gives the general purpose computer its greatest power and has led those involved with them to consider computers as self-regulating devices.

The built-in operations which the computer is capable of carrying out can be of a great variety. A set of typical commands is shown in Table 9. Some of these operations are arithmetic or pseudo-arithmetic in nature. Commands calling for such operations will allow numbers from specified locations in the memory to be added, multiplied, subtracted, etc. The power of these commands has led some to view the computer simply in terms of the arithmetic operations and, hence, as a glorified calculating device.

Such a view ignores the fantastically greater power for complex manipulation of data afforded by the other types of built-in operations. Probably the most significant of these operations, called the logical operations, are those which allow for comparisons to be made between blocks of data essentially independent of any arithmetical considerations. In this way data coded in any form can be compared or matched against basic criteria and alternative paths of processing chosen. Other related operations provide the capability for extracting portions of data groups, such as a single alphabet character, which

TABLE 9

Set of Typical Computer Commands *

INSTRUCTION CODES

ARITHMETIC

				WORD TIMES
70*	m	c	(rA) + (m) → rA	5
75*	m	c	(rA)— (m) → rA	5
85	m	c	(rL) × (m) → rA MSD, rX LSD	5+NDM+SDM
55*	m	c	(m) ÷ (rL) → rA Quot, rX Remain	5+2NDQ+SODQ+SNCEDQ
			* If arithmetic overflow → c + 1	

TRANSFER

25	m	c	(m) → rA	4
60†	m	c	(rA) → m	4
05	m	c	(m) → rX	4
65†	m	c	(rX) → m	4
30	m	c	(m) → rL	4
50†	m	c	(rL) → m	4
77	—	c	(rA) → rL	3
26	m	—	0's → rA, sign +	3
06	m	—	0's → rX, sign +	3
31	m	—	0's → rL, sign +	3
36	m	—	0's → rA, orig. sign remains	3
86	m	—	0's → rA & rX, sign of rL → rA & rX	14
23	m	—	(rC) → rA	3
			† m cannot be a register address	

INDEX REGISTERS

02‡	m	c	m portion of inst. word → IR:	3
07‡	m	c	m + (IR) → IR: and m of rA; 0's → OP & c of rA	4
			‡ IR selected by sign & STR-3 bits.	

Sign bit =	0	0	1	1
STR-3 bit =	0	1	0	1
	None	IR1	IR2	IR3

TRANSLATE

12	—	c	90CC (rA, rX) → MC (rA, rX)	3
17	—	c	MC (rA, rX) → 90CC (rA, rX)	3
C1	—	c	MC (rA) → XS-3 (rA)	3
C3	—	c	XS-3 (rA) → MC (rA)	3

COMPARE

82	=	≠	(rA) : (rL)	3
87	>	≦	(rA) : (rL)	3

LOGICAL

20	m	c	Superimpose (m) on (rA) → rA	4
35	m	c	Erase (m) from (rA) → rA	4
32	0n00	c	Shift right n places (rA) → (rX) → (rA)	3 + n
37	0n00	c	Shift left n places (rA) ← 0's	3 + n
62	—	c	Zero-suppress commas & zeros, MC in rA, rX	4
00	m	—	Skip to m	2
67	—	c	Stop	—

HIGH-SPEED PRINTER

11§	bbnn	c	Advance nn lines & print bb band; (rA) (rX) destroyed. For M/L, level 0197; NI, level 0189	592
16§	00nn	c	Advance nn lines	4
			§nn Maximum = 79. 50-59 lines 0101 = 5 = A; 60-69 lines 0110 = 6 = B; 70-79 lines 0111 = 7 = C	
			§If AOP, 11 or 16 not executed, (rC) → rA, NI → c + 1	
27	Yes	No	Test: Printer free? Yes, (rC) → rA	3 if no; 4 if yes

HIGH-SPEED CARD READER

72	m	c	Move cards, sense. If interlocked, (rC) → rA, NI → m. If AOR 72 not executed, (rC) → rA NI → c + 1	3 if c, 4 if m
96	bb00	c	(B) → J interlace on bb band. For M/L, level 0198; NI, level 0001	203
96	bb01	c	(B) → MC → J interlace on bb band. For M/L, level 0198; NI, level 0005	207
42	Yes	No	Test: HSR buffer loaded? Yes, (rC) → rA	3 if no; 4 if yes
47	0n00	c	Select n stacker (n = 0, 1, or 2)	3

* Courtesy UNIVAC Division of Sperry Rand, Los Angeles, Calif.

READ-PUNCH UNIT				
81¶	bb00	c	0 Interlace on bb band → B. Move, sense, punch cards. For M/L; level 0098; NI, level 0001	103
81¶	bb01	c	MC in 0 interlace on bb band → 90CC → B. Move, sense, punch cards. For M/L, level 0098; NI, level 0106 ¶If AOR-P, 81 not executed, (rC) → rA, NI → c + 1	208
46	bb00	c	(B) → I interlace on bb band. For M/L, level 0198; NI, level 0001	203
46	bb01	c	(B) → MC → I interlace on bb band. For M/L, level 0198; NI, level 0006	208
22	Yes	No	Test: RPU buffer loaded? Yes (rC) → rA	3 if no; 4 if yes
57	—	c	Select stacker 1 (sort)	3
MAGNETIC TAPE				
C2	Yes	No	Test: Synchronizer free? Yes, (rC) → rA	3 if no; 4 if yes
C6	bb00	c	Tape interlace on bb band → B. M/L, level 0048; NI, level 0053	205
C7	Yes	No	Test: Buffer free? Yes, (rC) → rA, (EFF) → rL.	3 if no; 5 if yes
F2	0xy0	c	Rewind Servo x. (x = 0 — 9) y = 0, no interlock y = 2, with interlock	600 ms
F6	bb00	c	(B) → Tape interlace on bb band. M/L, level 0198; NI, level 0003 if AOT, (rC) → rA; NI → c + 1	205
G2	0xyz	c	Read: One tape block from Servo x → TB y = mode (0 = USS or 5 = UNIVAC) + density (0 = 250 ppi or 1 = 125 ppi) z = direction (0 = forward or 5 = backward) + gain (0 = normal or 1 = low or 2 = high)	17
H2	0xy0	c	Write: (TB) → write forward 1 tape block on Servo x y = mode (0 = USS or 5 = UNIVAC) + density (0 = 250 ppi or 1 = 125 ppi) 0x61 = UFC mode, 125 ppi	17
RANDEX				
40	m	c	(m) → SIR	4
43	0n00	c	Test unit n. If head in position set Head Position Flip Flop.	3
92	Yes	No	Test HPFF. If set (rC) → rA.	3 if no, 4 if yes
F6	bb00	c	(B) → Tape interlace on bb band M/L, level 0198; NI level 0003 AOT, (rC) → rA; NI, c + 1.	205
C6	bb00	c	Tape interlace on bb band → B M/L, level 0048; NI level 0053	205
C7	Yes	No	Test Buffer Free? Yes, (rC) → rA, (EFF) → rL.	3 if no, 5 if yes
C2	Yes	No	Test Synchronizer Free? Yes, (rC) → rA.	3 if no, 4 if yes
18	OUDSSTTB		Position Read-Write Head 125-550 ms.	*
28	OUDSSTTB		Write RANDEX Blk. (B) → Blk specified. 35-105 ms.	*
38	OUDSSTTB		Read RANDEX Blk. Blk specified → B. 35-105 ms.	*
48	OUDSSTTB		Write/Check. (B) → Blk specified and check. 105-175 ms.	*
58	OUDSSTTB		Search Write. (B) → Blk identified. 35-105 ms.	*
68	OUDSSTTB		Search Read. Blk identified → B. 35-105 ms. *Instructions executed from SIR.	*

NOTE: Add 1 word time to instructions employing index-register modification

can then be handled independently and examined by other operations. By combining this operation with the logical ones, complex codes, including alphabetic ones, can be readily handled.

Other operations, which can be provided as built-in capabilities of the computer, will allow for the handling of groups of words, such as for the mass transfer of data, for the automatic rearrangement of blocks of data into prescribed order, for the automatic matching, in a "table look-up," of a given block of data against a standardized set.

A fourth class of commands, the input-output commands, provide for the control of peripheral devices and thus allow the computer to communicate externally under its own control. In this way data can be input to the computer, processed, and organized for output without any manual intervention.

In summary, the tremendous variety of built-in capabilities of the computer makes it an extremely versatile tool for the manipulation of data coded in almost any manner and for decisions to be made on the basis of the results obtained.

Programming

A computer performs a complex operation as a sequence of the elementary built-in operations available to it. The task of analyzing a complex problem into the appropriate sequence of the elementary steps which the computer is capable of performing is the work of a professional group known as programmers. The result of their efforts, the sequence of commands which the computer will obey, is called a program. Within a program there are certain critical portions to which particular attention must be paid by the programmer. The first establishes the starting conditions. This will define certain constants, such as the number of words in a message or the maximum size of a word of text. It will establish certain controls, such as, perhaps, a critical level of relevancy. It will make certain preliminary checks for consistency and accuracy of the data and of the program itself. A second critical portion of a program is known as the "bookkeeping" portion, which allows the program to maintain control of its own operation. This will include counting the number of times certain operations have been performed; it may include timing the functions of external devices; it will include facility for handling error situations or other unusual situations. The third critical portion of the program is concerned with the decision points at which alternative paths will be chosen. The fourth critical portion of the program is the actual operation to be performed—the "heart" of the program.

Programming requires a very clear definition of the nature and purpose of the job for which the computer is to be used. This generally takes the form of a "flow chart," exemplified by Figure 24, consisting of a number of boxes connected by arrows and other symbols. This technique of analyzing a total problem by means of flow charts is standard not only for developing the program but also for explaining its function. Each box describes some major portion of the total job which, depending on the detail provided, may be at the level of the elementary operations of the computer or at the level of much more gross steps. The sequence of the boxes, as indicated by the arrows, then defines the sequence of steps in solution of the problem. A most significant set of boxes describes the basis for decisions, on the data obtained in previous steps, among several alternative successive paths.

The ability to choose among alternative paths has led to the usage in computer programs of iterations or "loops" which involve the repeated execution of a sequence of commands. At the end of each execution of the loop, the program will decide whether to repeat it again or not. The number of times which the sequence will be repeated is controlled by the program itself on the basis of several possible criteria. For example, the number of times that a loop will be repeated may be determined by preset constants or it may be determined as a result of the particular nature of the data being operated on. In any event, this technique of iteration allows a relatively few commands to perform the work not only of a very large number but even of an indeterminate number of commands, for the number of iterations actually performed may vary widely from one time to the next.

Subroutines

If each problem for which a computer were to be used needed to be programmed from scratch, it is unlikely that the computer would have achieved its present success. Fortunately there exists a technique not only for utilizing past experience in order to reduce the programming task but also, as we shall show, for doing this in such a way as to extend effectively the range of built-in operations which the computer can recognize. The basis of this technique is the concept of a "subroutine"—a sequence of commands developed as a program for handling a general class of problems. A subroutine is designed in such a way that it can be drawn on and specialized whenever a particular problem involves any situation from this general class. It is utilized by being appropriately integrated into a larger program and even combined with other subroutines.

Over the past ten years the major effort of the programming profession has been to develop increasingly more complex subroutines. The earliest such subroutines were those suitable for handling various types of situations in numerical computation. For example, subroutines were prepared to provide for the evaluation of broad classes of mathematical functions, for the solution of major classes of problems, such as integration of differential equations or inversion of

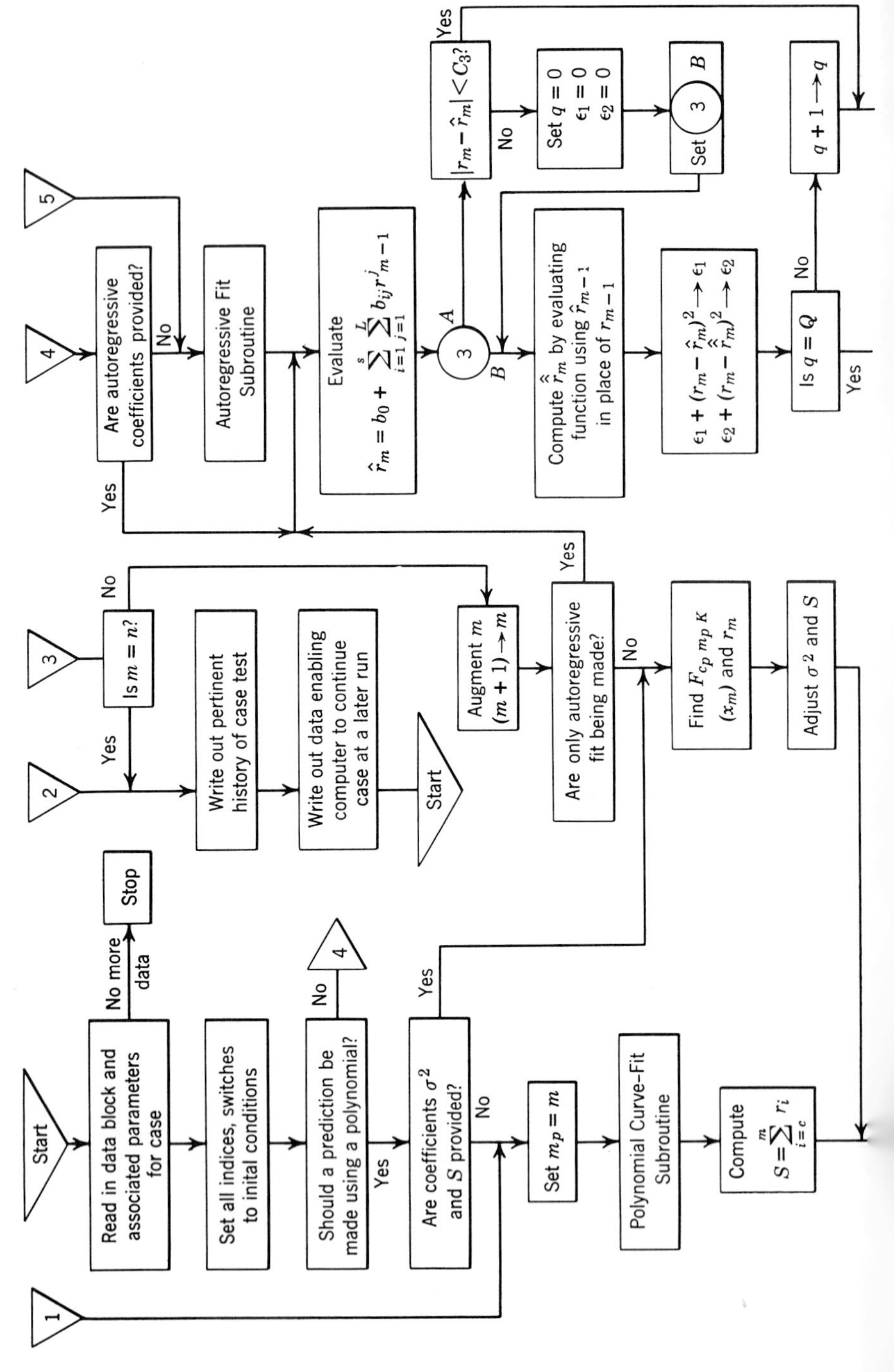
Start
Read in data block and associated parameters for case
No more data
Stop
Set all indices, switches to inital conditions
Should a prediction be made using a polynomial?
No
4
Yes
Are coefficients σ^2 and S provided?
Yes
No
1
Set $m_p = m$
Polynomial Curve-Fit Subroutine
Compute $S = \sum_{i=c}^{m} r_i$
2
3
Is $m = n$?
Yes
No
Write out pertinent history of case test
Write out data enabling computer to continue case at a later run
Start
Augment m $(m+1) \to m$
Are only autoregressive fit being made?
Yes
No
Find $F_{c_p}\, m_p\, K$ (x_m) and r_m
Adjust σ^2 and S
4
5
Are autoregressive coefficients provided?
No
Yes
Autoregressive Fit Subroutine
Evaluate $\hat{r}_m = b_0 + \sum_{i=1}^{s} \sum_{j=1}^{L} b_{ij} r^j_{m-1}$
3
A
B
$|r_m - \hat{r}_m| < C_3$?
Yes
No
Set $q = 0$ $\epsilon_1 = 0$ $\epsilon_2 = 0$
Set 3 B
Compute $\hat{\hat{r}}_m$ by evaluating function using $\hat{r}_{m-1}$ in place of r_{m-1}
$\epsilon_1 + (r_m - \hat{r}_m)^2 \to \epsilon_1$
$\epsilon_2 + (r_m - \hat{\hat{r}}_m)^2 \to \epsilon_2$
Is $q = Q$
No
Yes
$q + 1 \to q$

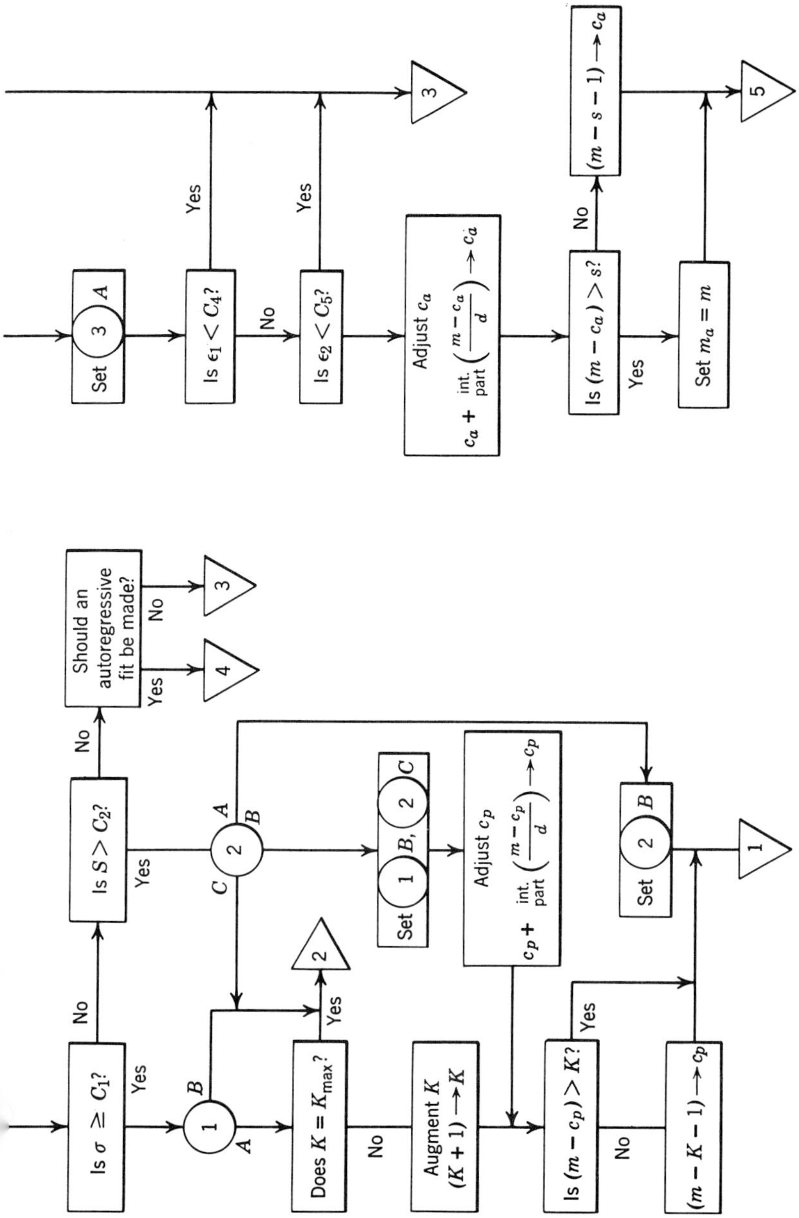

FIG. 24. Flow chart.

matrices, for recognition of various representations of numerical data and conversion from one to the other, for handling large arrays of data, such as tables and matrices. During this stage of program development, more and more was learned about the arithmetic capabilities of the computer, and subroutines now exist which can be combined for the solution of virtually any engineering or mathematical computational problem.

As computers began to be used for business data handling, a whole new class of subroutines concerned with the large-scale handling of combined numeric data and alphabetic data was developed. These subroutines provided the capabilities for sorting, collating, and searching great masses of data, for controlling input and output devices, and for developing reports in a great variety of formats. As the result of the work during this period, there exists a great wealth of knowledge and subroutines for handling masses of alpha-numeric data with the computer and its peripheral equipment.

More recently, the growing importance of information retrieval and other problems related to the handling of data concerned with "meaning" has led to the development of subroutines for language data processing. At the far end of the spectrum of such work are the efforts to develop subroutines for portions of the language translation problem but of more immediate interest are the subroutines concerned with information storage and retrieval. Although this area of language data processing is one to which the programmer has only recently turned his attention, several such subroutines for handling natural language and other semantic codes are already available.

Of a far more speculative nature are the efforts to develop subroutines which, in one way or another, simulate the thinking processes of the human being. Routines have been prepared which cause a computer to play games, such as chess or checkers; to "prove" theorems in geometry and logic; to develop concepts and recognize the occurrences of them. The enthusiasm of the computer man has led him to use such terms as "thinking" to describe these programs, and this choice of terminology frequently has caused violent reactions from others who are less enthusiastic. There is no question that there has been a tendency to overstate present capabilities and that very few programs of this nature have been written. But there is also no question that such subroutines do exist, that others are being developed, and that they are more and more capable of handling situations which, from any reasonable standpoint, involve really complex judgments.

Compilers and the Extension of Built-in Capabilities

The concept of the subroutine alone, however, would not result in a real extension of the built-in capabilities of the computer, since the determination of the subroutines to be used and the recording of them as part of the sequence of instructions for a given problem would still be the job of the programmer. Thus, although the subroutine can perform a job which is more complex than those of any elementary built-in operations, in order for it to represent directly an extension of the computer capabilities there would need to exist a mechanism by which the programmer could call for the subroutine in the same way in which he would call for an elementary operation. This mechanism has been developed and has indeed resulted in a fundamental extension of the capabilities of the computer. It is called a "compiler" and is itself a program but one which will interpret data representing commands of a far more general nature than those which the computer interprets. This program, although a subroutine in the sense of other subroutines, is very different in the way in which it is used.

The development and use of a compiler require three things: the first is a set of subroutines to perform operations; the second is a formal language by which the programmer can define those subroutines in which he is interested and their relationship to each other; and the third is the compiler itself, which interprets this language and then determines and brings together the subroutines required to perform the operations called for by the programmer. When the compiler is in the computer, the computer has effectively become a new device capable of recognizing a totally new language. It can execute sequences of instructions expressed in that language or construct "compiled" programs for doing so. In this way the burden of bringing together the appropriate subroutines for solution of a complex problem, in a form so that they fit with each other, has been removed from the programmer and placed on the compiler. In a very real sense the new machine consisting of the old computer with the compiler communicates with the programmer at a much higher level of complexity and abstraction and much closer to natural language. The present aim in the programming field is to bring this level of abstraction ever closer to the normal communication processes of the programmer himself.

The status of the development of compilers roughly parallels the sequence of development of subroutines themselves. Thus compilers and a corresponding specialized language have existed in the field of numerical computation for some time. Such a language is one called FORTRAN; another is called ALGOL (ALGebraic Oriented Language). Compilers to interpret FORTRAN or ALGOL have been developed for major computers. On the other hand, the development of subroutines for business data handling came considerably after that for numerical computation, and the development of a language has correspondingly been delayed. There now exists, however, a preliminary language called COBOL (COmmon Business Oriented Language) as a first step in this direction. Routines have been prepared to interpret COBOL for several different computers. Similarly, it is to be expected that, as the field of information retrieval, machine translation, and language data processing in general develops, subroutines will appear, a language will be developed, and compilers will be prepared for each of the major computers. When this occurs, the user of a computer will very probably phrase his request in a form close to natural language and have it completely interpreted by the compiler. The appropriate subroutines will then be automatically brought together for execution of the request. This is no dream; it is very much a part of the growth in understanding and the increasing capabilities of computer usage.

PROGRAMS FOR ANALYSIS AND LOGICAL PROCESSING

The possibility of using computers for quasi-intellectual processes has led to a number of experiments and corresponding computer programs and subroutines to handle areas in information retrieval of increasing logical complexity. The earliest of these mechanized the relatively well-defined aspects of file searching and logical matching of request patterns of a simple form with document patterns. As the complexities in measuring relevancy, in representing documents, and in organizing files have become better understood, these experimental programs have moved increasingly into the more speculative areas.

Computer Searching Experiments

Most of the immediately useful and practical work, as we have indicated, has been directed toward mechanizing file searching of stored data based on traditional library techniques or the new methods of the documentalists for representing document content. The resulting programs have all assumed that indexing terms and abstracts have been prepared by the professional librarian staff.

In its most fundamental form, the searching process involves an examination of the indexed information in whatever form it may be stored. For example, if it is on a continuous medium like magnetic tape, then it will be necessary to scan the entire set of records in their sequence on tape. On the other hand, if the file is stored on, say, magnetic cards, strips, or disks, which can themselves be physically selected under program control, then only those portions of the index file which apply to the request need be selected and scanned, provided they can be identified and the criteria for their selection known.

While the information in the index file is being scanned, it is "compared" with the request. This includes consideration of the terms making up the request and their logical interrelationship.[1] Each record in the index file must be examined for the appearance in it of the terms in the request to see if the required logical relationships are also exhibited. Matches, based on agreement between the structures of terms in the request and those in index records, result in the output of sufficient identifying data to permit referral to the original source material in the document file. This form of output can range from a serial number address to an abstract, depending on the content and order of the source data stored in the document file.

H. E. Tillitt,[2] at the U.S. Naval Ordnance Test Station at China Lake, California, adapted the Uniterm indexing system in this way to an IBM 701 electronic data processing machine. Accordingly, Tillitt's master tape contained index records arranged in sequence by index term and, within index term, in ascending order by document number. The system allowed for an average of 8 index terms per document and had a limit of 6750 document numbers per index term.

The machine program accepted up to 75 questions as input to the machine at the beginning of each search period. Each question was punched into tabulating cards which contained all information necessary to conduct a given search, that is, the index terms defining the subject, document number, limits, etc. On input the program first sorted all questions by index term, and then the master tape was scanned completely once. During the scanning, all records on the master tape which corresponded with the sorted index terms were

---

[1] The mathematical basis for this type of request structure is discussed in Chapter 13, in the section on Boolean algebra, page 335.

[2] R. H. Bracken and H. E. Tillitt, Information Searching with the 701 Calculator, *Journal of the Association for Computing Machinery,* April 1957, v. 4, No. 2, pp. 131-136.

written magnetically on a separate tape. Thus a working tape, consisting of only those portions of the master tape pertinent to all searches, was produced. By this technique the effective average time for any one search was considerably reduced.

The process of comparison was designed to handle only the simplest of logical interrelationships among the terms in a request. It therefore was concerned only with the occurrence of the same document number in the index record for those terms described in the request. For example, if a request called for "term A and term C but not term D," then a document number appearing in index records A and C but not on index record D would represent a match, etc.

Document numbers which were found to match over the index terms defining a given search were immediately written on a result tape. The result tape therefore contained document numbers presumed relevant. It is these numbers that were printed-out and furnished to the user. While the original search experiments were conducted on an IBM 701, Tillitt at the time looked forward to faster tape drive speeds, and denser packing, available on more advanced machines. Since then the search process has been successively reprogrammed for the IBM 704 and IBM 709.

S. R. Moyer and Gwendolyn M. Bedford, as members of the Institute of Cooperative Research of the University of Pennsylvania, designed a search system utilizing the IBM 705.[3] The file organization differed from that used by Tillitt. In Moyer's system each document was indexed much as was Tillitt's, but the results for a given document remained grouped together as part of one record on the master tape. An index record consisted of the document serial number, a bibliographical facts section (identifying number, author, publisher, date, etc.), and a descriptor section, containing an average of 30 index terms to define the document content.

Moyer's index record was carefully divided into fixed fields of information. Scanning consisted of comparing prescribed fields of the record with the combination of information specified in the request. During a search, each applicable field of the record was compared with the request patterns. Thus, although every record in the system had to be examined at least once, the limited number of possible combinations of fields scanned in each record kept the time per record within reasonable bounds.

Moyer's procedure provided for considerably more information per

---

[3] S. R. Moyer, Automatic Search of Library Documents, *Computers and Automation,* May 1957, v. 6, No. 5, pp. 24–29.

index record than did Tillitt's, and, consequently, the rate of scan was slower. However, since in Moyer's method many facts about the document are carried in the body of the index record, matches between document and request result in an immediate print-out which includes all bibliographic data rather than mere document number references. Moyer contends that research library experience corroborates the necessity for such flexibility and greater capacity for satisfying user demands, and Tillitt's experience tended to confirm this contention. Thus, on request, Moyer's system can print-out the entire index record for each match, and the user can study this bibliography thoroughly before deciding which full-length documents he wants to see.

Moyer did some research on the time and cost of performing a computer search and an equivalent manual search in a card catalog in a conventional library situation. His conclusions indicate that an IBM 705 system can do a literature search of his type of index file in about 2% of the manhours required to do the same search manually, that the cost of the search by machine would be less than that of the manual search, that the search would be more accurate, and that "the electronic computer as an information storage mechanism offers unlimited possibilities for a higher potential number of descriptors and bibliographical facts per document than any other existing automatic equipment."

Barton and Caplan, of General Electric's Aircraft Gas Turbine Division at Evendale, Ohio, during 1958 evolved a two-part tape system used by their library for servicing document search requests.[4] The machine in this case was the IBM 704. The first tape contained the index file arranged by serial number with the index terms which described the document's content. The second tape was also arranged in serial number sequence. Each record carried identification information about the document—publisher, date, security classification, etc.—followed by an abstract of the document.

Since the library was one among many users of 704 time, they combined the file maintenance and searching request operations into one synthesized machine program. During its allotted time on the machine, the master tape would be updated with new information and could be searched for comparison with up to 99 different request criteria simultaneously. During the scan phase, those numbers found on the first tape which matched the request pattern were placed in

[4] A. Barton, V. L. Schatz, and L. N. Caplan, Information Retrieval on a High Speed Computer, *Proceedings of 1959 Western Joint Computer Conference,* IRE, New York, N.Y.

memory to serve as instructions for locating and printing the title and abstract information located on the second tape. The resulting output consisted of bibliographies grouped and printed on separate sheets for transmittal to requesters.

Before the machine system was installed, search time by trained personnel using a conventional manual system took an average of 14 hours. Barton and Caplan claim this was cut to less than 15 minutes by their program. The times and costs are therefore consistent with those of Moyer.

In all of these experiments the problem of matching a request with the stored document descriptions has been reduced to the simplest matching of terms. However, the problem is really extremely complicated, and the lack of any more adequate measure of relevancy has been a critical difficulty. Thus the degree of correspondence between the information content of a document and the set of terms assigned to it by the analyst is difficult to specify; the relationship between a request and its set of terms is correspondingly difficult to specify; and the resulting "noise" introduced by attempting to match the two sets of terms can prevent relevant documents from being found. M. E. Maron and J. L. Kuhns [5] proposed that the document analyst, in assigning terms to documents, apply a quantitative measure or weight of the probable relevancy which each term has for the document. To rephrase their point of view, such a weight would represent an estimate of the probability that, if a user requests a given term, he will be interested in the document. Traditional subject indexing or Uniterm indexing are special cases of this approach which assign a probability of one or zero, depending on whether the term is applied or not. By allowing a range of values to be used, a much greater capability for selection is available.

The problem of matching a document index record with a request is synonymous with estimating the probability that a library user will be satisfied with the document as an answer to his request. For each term in the request, Maron and Kuhns estimate this probability from the product of three factors. The first is the relevancy weight assigned to the document by the original indexer; the second represents the weight which the index term has to the request; and the third measures the *a priori* probability of the document based either on its intrinsic value or on its relative frequency of usage. For each

[5] M. E. Maron and J. L. Kuhns, On Relevance, Probabilistic Indexing and Information Retrieval, *Journal of the Association for Computing Machinery,* July 1960, v. 7, No. 3, pp. 216–244.

index term, the product of these three weights produces a measure of probable relevancy of the document with respect to the index term. Determining the probable relevancy of the document to a request, consisting of a set of such terms together with their logical interrelationships, requires the appropriate combination of the individual probabilities. Maron and Kuhns developed several measures of closeness or "coefficients of association." One appropriate choice might be the product of the probabilities if the associated index terms are related by logical conjunction, etc. Maron and Kuhns experimented with this technique on a small collection of articles chosen from *Science News Letter,* using five possible weightings from "very relevant" to "irrelevant." They indicated that their results showed the technique of weighted indexing, with suitable automatic elaboration of the search strategy, retrieved relevant documents that would not otherwise have been obtained.

The National Bureau of Standards and the U.S. Patent Office have also been concerned with the complexities in matching requests with stored document descriptions.[6,7,8] They considered the problem of matching request structures of a far more complex character than that provided by the simple logical connectives of "and," "or," and "not." In the Patent Office examiners must frequently perform generic searches on structural diagrams describing chemical compounds, for example. Lewis Ray and Russell Kirsch [9] of the National Bureau of Standards developed a SEAC (Standards Electronic Automatic Computer) search program which makes an atom-to-atom match between the atoms of the question structure and the atoms of the structures and substructures recorded in the index file. When a correspondence exists, the routine accepts the structure found in the file and continues the process. Making such an atom-to-atom match, however, even on high-speed electronic computers, would be altogether too time con-

---

[6] H. Pfeffer, H. R. Koller, and E. C. Morden, A First Approach to Patent Searching on Standards' Electronic Computer (SEAC), U.S. Patent Office, Research and Development, Report No. 10, 1958.

[7] B. E. Lanham, J. Leibowitz, H. R. Koller, and H. Pfeffer, Organization of Chemical Disclosures for Mechanized Retrieval, U.S. Patent Office, Research and Development, Report No. 5, 1957.

[8] H. R. Koller, E. C. Morden, and H. Pfeffer, The Haystaq System: Past, Present, and Future, International Conference on Scientific Information, Preprints, Area V, Washington, D.C., 1958.

[9] L. C. Ray and Russell A. Kirsch, The Use of Automatic Data Processing Systems in the Retrieval of Technical Information, National Bureau of Science, December 28, 1956.

suming without the use of a screening device which would reject structures on a more gross examination. They therefore included as part of the program an examination of the empirical formula of each structure together with the number of occurrences of each type of atom in the structure. In this way the program can inspect this list to determine whether there are enough atoms of the right type present to satisfy the search requirement before it searches the structure itself to determine the atom-by-atom agreement. Their experience indicated that on most searches the computer quickly rejected the vast majority of irrelevant structures.

Computer Indexing Experiments

Each of the foregoing experiments has dealt with searching and maintaining a file of index records based on document content analysis performed by human indexers. However, preparation of conventional index terms to describe the information contained in a document is a laborious, inconsistent human process. Invariably manual indexing operations require large staffs; yet they still fail to close the gap between the date of publication and the date of indexing. The attendant delay is a function not only of the increasing publishing rate but also of the personnel factors associated with the situation. Indexers are scarce, their work tedious, the pay scale low; skilled personnel find other professional pursuits more attractive and turnover is inevitably high. Also, variations in background and education mean that no two people are likely to interpret information content the same way nor to generate an equal set of index terms each time. Even with considerable on-the-job training there is uncertainty as to ultimate reliability and consistency of their decisions. Another element of difficulty is the index terms themselves. The terminology of a given discipline may change in time and new concepts may evolve which can change the sense and character of past indexing. Hence indexers need to be able to trace past indexing usage and suggest future changes. Unfortunately manual index operations are not suited to accommodating this process of continuing revision.

The aim of machine indexing is to overcome these disadvantages by introducing some mechanical controls. Mechanizing the analytical processes of indexing, abstracting, or translating would at least conserve human resources. In addition, automatic indexing is more apt to keep pace with an increasing publishing rate, for indexing can be virtually concurrent with publication. Machine-executed instructions ensure that index term selection is made on a consistent and accurate basis, by a strict interpretation of prescribed rules, so that the usual human distortions are eliminated. Machines can update and make other changes in basic indexing terminology and procedures with relative ease, and they can retrace the revisions.

A summary of the progress made in the field of automatic abstracting and indexing appeared in the Communications of the Association for Computing Machinery.[10] R. A. Fairthorne in his review of this summary defined the two terms as follows:

> "Automatic Indexing" deals with purely lexical and orthographic rules for selecting words from the complete text of a document in order to indicate its topic.
>
> "Automatic Abstracting" deals with similar rules for selecting phrases for quotation in order to describe its content.[11]

The phrase "auto-abstract" was coined by H. P. Luhn of IBM[12] to describe the end product of his research in the application of statistical methods in a machine program to develop meaningful condensations of lengthy text. Luhn proceeded on the basis that certain sentences in an article contain more information than others. His object was to identify these sentences automatically by comparing the relative rank of the "noncommon" or meaning-bearing words in each sentence with all words of the total text. By using Luhn's technique a machine program is able to isolate the several statistically important sentences in an article and to write them verbatim as they appeared in the original text. The output thus produced is representative of the general content of the original text itself. Some therefore prefer to call this process "extracting" rather than abstracting.

As the computer for his exploratory research, Luhn chose the IBM 704. He was able to obtain direct machine input for his experiments through an arrangement with a commercial publishing house. As a by-product of an original typing operation, the publisher also pro-

---

[10] H. P. Edmundson and R. E. Wyllys, Automatic Abstracting and Indexing—Survey and Recommendations, *Communications of the Association for Computing Machinery,* May 1961, v. 4, No. 5, pp. 226–234.

[11] R. A. Fairthorne, *Computing Reviews,* November–December 1961, v. 2, No. 6, No. 1246, p. 196.

[12] H. P. Luhn, Automatic Creation of Literature Abstracts, *IBM Journal of Research and Development,* April 1958, v. 2, No. 2, pp. 159–165.

duced perforated paper tape which was used in operating an automatic monotype machine for setting the text of certain journal articles. Instead of discarding the tape after the copy was set, the publisher made the tapes available to IBM. This cooperative effort is worth mentioning because it demonstrates the dual use which can be made of a single typing operation and the very close relationship which can exist between publishing and information processing. Once the typesetter tape is perforated, the information processing system has ready-made machine readable input on which it can perform analytical work with minimum human intervention.

The Luhn process is founded on two main principles—word occurrence and word proximity. Word occurrence assumes that items of importance in text are stressed by the author through his repetitive use of certain words. Word proximity assumes that the physical nearness of words to each other in sentences is indicative of the close intellectual association of the ideas they represent.

Generally speaking, the steps followed in producing an "auto-abstract" under Luhn's program are:

1. The machine program separates the text in a way which ensures that words and sentences are identifiable and available for subsequent processing on call.
2. A table look-up compares each word with those common words which rarely characterize meaning in English sentences, such as the conjunctives, articles, and prepositions, and causes them to be deleted.
3. The remaining notion words (i.e., verbs, nouns, adjectives, etc.) are then sorted alphabetically so that the total occurrences of each can be tabulated.
4. A number of statistical calculations follow:
   a. Grouping of words having the same stem—to ensure that variations of the word will still be treated as one occurrence.
   b. Tabulating the number of words at each frequency.
   c. Determining the number of words in a sentence and the average word frequency.
5. High-frequency words are then traced back to their original sentences and their position noted.
6. Proximity rules determine which high-frequency words are "bracketed" within a given sentence.
7. Finally, the sentence is assigned a value corresponding to the square of the number of high-frequency noncommon words within bracketed sections. After all sentences are assigned a value, they are ranked and the highest ones selected for the auto-abstract.

A good summary of the logic of the IBM-704 program for preparing auto-abstracts is given by T. R. Savage,[13] who concludes:

> The exploratory research carried out thus far has, in principle, confirmed the premise that the information contents of sentences is related to the occurrence within them of high frequency noncommon words and to the way in which these words are clustered. The use of statistical methods to measure these relationships appears to be effective despite the apparent simplicity of the approach. Considerable work remains to be done before a sufficient amount of data are available for the formulation of any general conclusions. Because of the wide variability of written text with respect to style, size, complexity of subject matter, etc., the major prerequisite in evaluating the effectiveness of the results is simply the collection of large samples of data.

A typical auto-abstract produced by Luhn's program appears as Exhibit 1 on pages 134 and 135.[14]

The first results of another research effort into methods for mechanizing the process of extracting and displaying the information content of a document were announced in March 1959. This work was accomplished under the supervision of V. A. Oswald of the Planning Research Corporation, West Los Angeles, Calif., in response to an Air Force contract.[15]

The objectives of Oswald's research were much the same as Luhn's —to isolate the sentences in an article which, in the language of the author, most completely expressed the subject content. Whereas Luhn stressed the word frequency count, and word correlation—the concurrence within a sentence of single noncommon high-frequency words—Oswald expanded this to include "all juxtapositions of meaning bearing forms of highest frequency" which he called "multi-terms." His hypothesis was that the most significant sentences in a document would be those in which the maximal concurrence of high-frequency multi-terms would be found.

The research procedure was performed manually but was obviously suitable for computer programs. It operated as follows:

1. The text of the document was examined and all articles, prepositions, conjunctions, were culled. In addition, high-frequency quali-

---

[13] T. R. Savage, The Preparation of Auto-Abstracts on the IBM 704 Data Processing System, Yorktown Heights, N.Y., International Business Machines Corp., 1958.

[14] *IBM Journal of Research and Development,* April 1958, p. 163.

[15] Interim Report, The Automatic Extraction and Display of the Content of Documents, PRC-R-91, March 15, 1959, Contract AF 30(602)–1748.

Exhibit 1

Source: The Scientific American, Vol. 196, No. 2, 86–94, February, 1957
Title: Messengers of the Nervous System
Author: Amodeo S. Marrazzi
Editor's Subheading: The internal communication of the body is mediated by chemicals as well as by nerve impulses. Study of their interaction has developed important leads to the understanding and therapy of mental illness.

Auto-Abstract *

It seems reasonable to credit the single-celled organisms also with a system of chemical communication by diffusion of stimulating substances through the cell, and these correspond to the chemical messengers (e.g., hormones) that carry stimuli from cell to cell in the more complex organisms. (7.0) †

Finally, in the vertebrate animals there are special glands (e.g., the adrenals) for producing chemical messengers, and the nervous and chemical communication systems are intertwined: for instance, release of adrenalin by the adrenal gland is subject to control both by nerve impulses and by chemicals brought to the gland by the blood. (6.4)

The experiments clearly demonstrated that acetylcholine (and related substances) and adrenalin (and its relatives) exert opposing actions which maintain a balanced regulation of the transmission of nerve impulses. (6.3)

It is reasonable to suppose that the tranquilizing drugs counteract the inhibitory effect of excessive adrenalin or serotonin or some related inhibitor in the human nervous system. (7.3)

* Sentences selected by means of statistical analysis as having a degree of significance of 6 and over.
† Significance factor is given at the end of each sentence.

fiers of minimal semantic importance like "good," "very," etc., were also discarded.

2. Occurrences of high-frequency words were posted and ranked, and multi-terms were noted whenever two or more high-frequency words were in juxtaposition.

3. Significant sentences for display were selected each time a given sentence contained at least three multi-terms.

Both Luhn's noncommon high-frequency words and Oswald's multi-terms can be used not only for the selection of significant sentences in a document but also as an automatic method for preparing a practical substitute for traditional subject headings. Further research is necessary to test the efficacy of such uses by comparing them with the product of conventional manual methods of preparation.

In the techniques discussed thus far, automatic examination of full-length document text resulted in a ranking of noncommon high-frequency words or high-frequency multi-terms. A novel approach was taken in 1958 when Phyllis Baxendale of IBM tested the value

Significant words in descending order of frequency (common words omitted).

46	nerve	12	body	6	disturbance	4	accumulate
40	chemical	12	effects	6	related	4	balance
28	system	12	electrical	5	control	4	block
22	communication	12	mental	5	diagram	4	disorders
19	adrenalin	12	messengers	5	fibers	4	end
18	cell	10	signals	5	gland	4	excitation
18	synapse	10	stimulation	5	mechanisms	4	health
16	impulses	8	action	5	mediators	4	human
16	inhibition	8	ganglion	5	organism	4	outgoing
15	brain	7	animal	5	produce	4	reaching
15	transmission	7	blood	5	regulate	4	recording
13	acetylcholine	7	drugs	5	serotonin	4	release
13	experiment	7	normal			4	supply
13	substances					4	tranquilizing

Total word occurrences in the document:	2326
Different words in document:	
Total of different words	741
Less different common words	170
Different noncommon words	571
Ratio of all word occurrences to different noncommon words	~4:1
Noncommon words having a frequency of occurrence of 5 and over:	
Total occurrences	478
Different words	39

of the prepositional phrase as a construction which could reflect subject content more so than words alone.[16]

Baxendale suggests that phrase selection has appealing advantages. First, the phrase is an active form of construction in both reading and writing. Phrases which the eye can easily scan, and the mind quickly comprehend, are fundamental to good writing. Newspaper column widths, for example, are so constructed as to permit scanning of phrase groups in 6 to 8 word lengths. Secondly, English grammar has always emphasized the important role of the coordinated use of modifier and noun in sentence structure; the prepositional phrase is known as a "unit of expression" in syntactical structure. Thirdly, the prepositional phrase lends itself to flexible sentence usage more than any other grammatical unit. Finally, the index terms derived from each phrase unit remain in context because of the availability of

[16] P. B. Baxendale, Machine-made Index for Technical Literature—An Experiment, *IBM Journal of Research and Development*, October 1958, v. 2, No. 4, pp. 354–361.

the adjacent modifier. The absence or presence of an adjective can sometimes make a vast difference in the meaning of the noun.

The machine available for Baxendale's research was the IBM 650. Her procedure consisted of the following steps:

1. The machine program examined the running text and performed simple deletion of all parts of speech of the connective or reiterative type. This step reduced the volume of the text to an average of 52% of the original.

2. Using the 50 common prepositions of the English language as indicators, the machine selected each indicator and stored the next four words which followed it. These represented the prepositional phrases contained in the text.

3. Words contained in a phrase unit were then ranked on a frequency of occurrence basis.

In addition to the prepositional phrase, Baxendale also investigated the topic sentences as a meaning-bearing element in text. She corroborated the long-standing composition rule that prime thoughts are expressed by an author in either the first or last sentence of a paragraph. After examining 2000 paragraphs, she determined that in 85% of the cases the initial sentence was the topic sentence and in 7% of the cases the last sentence was the topic sentence. Her results indicated that a machine could be programmed to identify and operate on these and similar phrases as meaning-bearing forms in running text.

Another mechanical rule by which documents can be indexed utilizes as index headings the "citations" that the author makes to other papers. This approach has been extensively exploited in the legal profession, where Shepherd's Citation Index is a traditional tool. The value of such an index in law is that it leads the legal researcher from a given known case to later cases which reference it and may therefore modify its results. Presumably, similar indexes for scientific and technical literature would lead the searcher from a given technical paper to later work which modified or extended its results. Some research has been done, by the Institute for Scientific Information, Philadelphia, Penna., and others, on the value of a citation index for scientific literature searching.[17]

As Garfield has described citation indexing, it seems particularly

---

[17] E. Garfield and I. H. Sher, New Factors in the Evaluation of Scientific Literature through Citation Indexing, presented at the 1962 annual meeting of the American Documentation Institute, December 1962.

applicable to scientific literature because it capitalizes on the research practices of the scientist. At the time a scientist prepares a paper he methodically reviews all pertinent previous work relating to his theme and conscientiously records meaningful citations either in his footnotes or in his bibliography. In essence, this methodology then utilizes the fact that the scientist knows his field, knows the authors in his field, and can sift those references highly important to his own work. Since the end product of a citation index is a listing which collects in one place the *bibliographical descendants* of a given cited author, bringing these titles together helps to illuminate for the searcher the extent and nature of information association patterns employed by other authors who had a similar or related interest to his own. Its development therefore serves as an approach to the user's frame of reference not the indexer's.

Garfield compares the citation index to the subject index as follows: [18]

> . . . the Citation Index helps to overcome the problem of changing terminology, time, and the other inherent limitations of *a priori* indexing. The beauty of a citation index is that it achieves *a posteriori* indexing because a citation is *experiential*. The "logic" of all conventional scientific classifications has inevitably broken down with experience. Aristotelian logic has been a chain around the neck of the scientist and classifier alike. . . . Citations are permanent and unique, as are the works they identify. The significance of men's writings may change, but their identities are fixed.

The preparation of a citation index is an arbitary construct rather than a logical one. It involves the coding of the elements of the citation only and does not include any reading or interpretation of subject matter. Coding of a cited author, journal, volume, page, etc. is essentially a clerical operation and is thus susceptible to machine treatment. As citations accumulate, it becomes possible to output a variety of citation arrays or presentations in different formats.

Language Data Processing [19]

Another area of research has been concerned with computer programs for working on raw information in machine-coded natural

[18] E. Garfield, Citation Indexes—New Path to Scientific Knowledge, *The Chemical Bulletin,* April 1956, v. 43, No. 4, p. 11.

[19] Research on Mechanical Translation, U.S. House of Representatives, Committee on Science and Astronautics, 86th Congress, 2nd Session, No. 9, Government Printing Office, 1960.

language by linguistic analysis rather than by the simpler statistical techniques. The desired end product may take one of the forms of index terms, abstracts, or partial or full translations. In all instances the machine approach also addresses attention to accurate spelling, abbreviation, punctuation, arrangement, and completeness of information.

The most significant efforts in this area are those concerned with mechanized language translation. Their results have obvious application to the information retrieval problem, for indexing can be regarded as a translation process from document language into retrieval language. Virtually all this research is still in a highly speculative stage although claims of varying degrees of success have been made. At present more than ten separate research efforts on the problem of language translation are underway in the United States alone. The groups have been remarkably diverse, not only in the languages examined—which have included Russian, French, German, Chinese—but also in the variety of approaches utilized. There have been substantial differences with respect to the type of program prepared, the utilization of a dictionary, and the experimental approach itself.

Programming efforts in the handling of natural language have generally adopted one of two approaches: word-by-word analysis or complete sentence analysis. The aim of the first approach is to determine the meaning of each word in succession as it appears in the text. Variations in meaning are handled by a predictive technique which determines the meaning for a given ambiguous word at the time of examining a later word whose occurrence was predicted in terms of one of the possible meanings of the given word. The second approach applies traditional linguistic analysis to entire sentences, determining the role of each word with respect to every other word much as traditional "parsing" would do.

Whichever of the two approaches is adopted, the word-by-word analysis or the complete sentence analysis, the size of the program required to perform the analysis is largely determined by the size of the dictionary of word forms provided to it. Thus the larger the dictionary, the more the burden of translation can be placed on table look-up operations; the smaller the dictionary, the greater the burden which must be placed on the analysis of the word forms appearing in the natural language text. There has been a noticeable tendency on the part of those concerned with linguistic analysis to utilize small dictionaries and place the major burden on the analytical program. On the other hand, one of the major efforts in the field, that by IBM under the sponsorship of the Rome Air Development Center, has adopted the opposite approach of making the dictionary as large as possible, thus including virtually all possible variants of the source language vocabulary. In this case the approach is a result of the IBM program for development of an extremely high-capacity, high-speed device for the storage of the dictionary.

The experimental work for any of these efforts, whatever the programming approach or the dictionary size, must be based on the examination of texts. Here again, however, two fundamentally different approaches have been adopted by researchers. The first is essentially experimental and attempts to arrive at a final operating program by a process of successive approximation. The researchers do this by establishing a relatively simple program utilizing limited analysis of a small body of text and then testing the program on a major body of text to determine where differences in meaning result. The differences are analyzed and the program corrected, in as simple a way as possible, to accommodate the apparent errors in the original program and the process reiterated. The opposite approach, which might be called the "scholastic" one, attempts to establish as nearly perfect an operating program as possible based on a complete linguistic analysis of the languages involved in the translation.

The problem of evaluating the success of these efforts to develop useful mechanized language translation programs is a difficult one, for no criteria exist by which to measure adequacy of translation. There are even those who would claim that Putnam's translation of *Don Quixote* did not really represent the flavor of the original and they would, of course, be correct. Some have gone so far as to claim that mechanized language translation is actually an impossibility and that the present efforts to develop programs are fruitless.[20] This seems to be a little extreme, although it may be a reaction to the over-inflated claims of some of the groups working on the problem. A rational evaluation would probably be that translations adequate for conveying the general sense of a foreign-language technical article in a sufficiently circumscribed field can now be prepared by any one of several operating programs and that the quality of the translation will significantly improve with time.

In making this evaluation several problems concerned with the very philosophical foundations of language structure are essentially ignored.

---

[20] Y. Bar Hillel, Report on the State of Machine Translation in the United States and Great Britain, Report on NOR Contract No. NONR-2578(00), 15 February 1959.

If these problems are considered, then the evaluation that present mechanized translation efforts are fruitless is probably valid but would apply in the same sense to human translation. The real breakthroughs, if they are to occur, will result from the efforts of several groups concerned with the logical analysis of language rather than the linguistic one. Although these studies are significant, they begin to fall outside the scope of what can be covered in this book; however, they are of such significant importance that the reader is referred to the following additional references.

Y. Bar Hillel and E. Shamir, Finite-State Languages: Formal Representations and Adequacy Problems, *Bulletin of the Research Council of Israel,* February 1960, v. 8F, No. 3, pp. 155–166.

R. A. Brooker and D. Morris, A General Translation Program for Phrase Structure Languages, *Journal of the Association for Computing Machinery,* January 1962, v. 9, No. 1.

R. Carnap, *The Logical Syntax of Language,* Littlefield, Adams, and Co., 1959.

N. Chomsky and G. A. Miller, Finite-State Languages, *Information and Control,* 1958, v. 1, pp. 91–112.

N. Chomsky, *Syntactic Structures,* Mouton & Co., 'sGravenhage, 1957.

H. B. Curry and R. Feys, *Combinatory Logic,* North Holland Publishing Co., Amsterdam, 1958.

W. N. Locke and A. D. Booth, *Machine Translation of Languages,* John Wiley, New York, 1957.

Information Retrieval and Machine Translation, edited by Allen Kent. Based on the International Conference for Standards on a Common Language for Machine Searching and Translation held at Western Reserve University, Cleveland, Ohio, September 6–12, 1959, vols. 1–3.

R. M. Smullyan, *Theory of Formal Systems,* Princeton University Press, Princeton, 1961.

Automatic File Organization

A subject heading authority, a classification scheme, or the fixed dictionaries of documentalists provide reasonably static frameworks against which incoming information may be identified. The fact that they may undergo revision by no means implies any dynamic change in their conceptual foundation; rather, revision reflects a patch-quilt method for accommodation to new subject crystallizations, old subject incrustations, and atrophied terms. Another area of computer research has been in development of programs to analyze information independent of its preclassification so as to adjust, in a more dynamic manner, to demands as they arise. This would indeed make for a radical departure from existing techniques. With this type of logic available, it would be possible to discover new relationships and express patterns now recognized only through the intuition of the individual researchers instead of depending on a fixed classification of information based on what has already transpired.

To make the distinction clear, traditional subject classification schemes, alphabetic subject heading listings, and even the prescribed vocabularies of the documentalists tend to pigeonhole information and restrict its use. It is hoped that the results of research work in the field of artificial intelligence and self-organizing systems will provide a mechanism by which this strait jacket can be removed. Such systems would be capable of evolving with the future. The real trick in accomplishing this is to develop the machine programs that would be capable of logically reorganizing stored information.

Although much of the work in this area is highly speculative and in the conjectural stage, some of the efforts are of immediate practical application. For example, in 1958 a computer was used to produce indexes to the *Dead Sea Scrolls* and prepare concordances and other specialized word lists as an aid to textual criticism. The effort required the establishment of analytical ground rules defining the kind of information which scholars wanted to know about each word. The scholars then marked the text according to their evaluation of the relationship of each word to these ground rules. This, in effect, provided the machine with the linguistic analysis required for successful cataloging and indexing. Among the ground rules were identification of biblical words or biblical quotations, words "cancelled" but still legible, reconstructed words, words in a different alphabet, word forms peculiar to the particular scribe, missing letters of indefinite number, etc. Since the compilation of concordances is essentially a straightforward sorting task once linguistic difficulties have been resolved, the machine processing was highly successful.[21,22]

Of the same general character are the computer programs (such as those which of necessity must be part of the experiments by Tillitt, Barton, and Caplan) for the generation of coordinate index records by successive posting of document numbers when relevant. These programs involve a similar straightforward sorting of document numbers into sequence according to the assigned index terms and then a posting of them to each index term record.

---

[21] P. Tasman, Indexing the Dead Sea Scrolls by Electronic Literary Data Processing Methods, International Business Machines, World Trade Corp., New York, 1958.

[22] W. R. McCulley, UNIVAC Compiles a Complete Bible Concordance, *Systems,* 1956, v. 20, pp. 22–23.

```
HENRIT-60-EPR  HENRIKSEN T        PIHL A
                 ELECTRON PARAMAGNETIC RESONANCE OBSERVATIONS ON IRRADIATED
                   THIOLS AND DISULPHIDES.
                 NATURE, 185, 307-8 (1960).
HENRMC-60-IAS  HENRY MC           NOLTES JG
                 INFRARED ABSORPTION SPECTRA OF SOME FOURTH GROUP
                   ORGANOMETALLIC COMPOUNDS.
                 J. AM. CHEM. SOC., 82, 555-8 (1960).
HENRMC-60-NSO  HENRY MC           NOLTES JG
                 NEW SIX-MEMBERED ORGANOMETALLIC RING SYSTEMS.
                 J. AM. CHEM. SOC., 82, 561-3 (1960).

HEYNAH-60-SMS  HEYN AHA           FINSTON HL
                 SEPARATION OF MAGNESIUM FROM SODIUM AND POTASSIUM.
                   TRACER STUDY.
                 ANAL. CHEM., 32, 328-32 (1960).
HEYNSK-60-ADF  HEYNS K            SCHULZ W
                 1-N- AMINO-ACID-1- DESOXY- FRUCTURONIC ACID
                   ( FRUCTURON-AMINOACID) FROM GLYCINE, ALANINE, AND D-
                   GLUCURONIC ACID.
                 CHEM. BER., 93, 128-32 (1960).
HIETLA-60-RBW  HIETT LA           BEERS WL           ZACHARIASEN KA
                 RELATIONSHIPS BETWEEN WOOD DENSITY AND OTHER WOOD AND PULP
```

A. Citation

```
KALINE-EARTH METALS AND MAGNESIUM.                                FESCHH-60-SSC
UM PHASE DIAGRAM OF THE MAGNESIUM- TITANIUM- OXYGEN SYSTEM.       YOSHIT-60-EPD
 OF DILUTE SOLUTIONS OF MAGNESIUM AND CADMIUM CHLORIDES IN E      GOLBEM-60-CSD
     THERMAL EFFECTS IN MAGNESIUM AND CALCIUM OXIDES.             RAOC  -60-TEM
IMINES WITH MIXTURES OF MAGNESIUM AND MAGNESIUM IODIDE AND A      THIESH-60-RKM
 EFFECTS OF CHOLINE AND MAGNESIUM CHLORIDE ON COMPENSATING H      BINETL-60-ECM
              ACTION OF MAGNESIUM COMPOUNDS ON ETHOXY- TRICH      NORMAH-60-AMC
SPHORUS AND SYMPTOMS OF MAGNESIUM DEFICIENCY.                     ODELBL-60-MRG
OMIUM(III) FLUORIDE AND MAGNESIUM FLUORIDE, DISSOLVED IN CER      MERGAP-60-ICF
          SEPARATION OF MAGNESIUM FROM SODIUM AND POTASSIUM.      HEYNAH-60-SMS
MINATION OF CALCIUM AND MAGNESIUM IN GENERAL BIOLOGICAL MATE      HUNTEG-60-MMD
MINATION OF CALCIUM AND MAGNESIUM IN WATERS BY AUTOMATIC TIT      HASLAJ-60-DCM
XTURES OF MAGNESIUM AND MAGNESIUM IODIDE AND ALUMINUM AMALGA      THIESH-60-RKM
HERMAL DECOMPOSITION OF MAGNESIUM OXALATE.  (GER.)                PONECV-60-FAM
RANSITIONS OF NICKEL IN MAGNESIUM OXIDE.                          ORTOJW-60-DES
 MANGANESE-(+2) IONS IN MAGNESIUM OXIDE.                          COLEBA-60-AEI
DES.  CALCIUM OXIDE AND MAGNESIUM OXIDE.                          BORCHJ-60-RSA
                        MAGNESIUM REQUIREMENT OF GUINEA PIGS      ODELBL-60-MRG

TICE OF POLAROGRAPHY IN MELTS.  (ENG.)                            HILLGJ-60-TPP
RPTION OF ULTRASOUND IN MELTS AT HIGH TEMPERATURES.               BESSMV-60-AMS
                NUCLEAR MEMBRANE AS A BARRIER TO THE FREE DI      FELDCM-60-NMB
MPARTMENT PERMSELECTIVE MEMBRANE CELLS FOR THE PREPARATION O      RAFFLM-60-MPM
LATION IN MITOCHONDRIAL MEMBRANE FRAGMENTS.                       PACKEL-60-LSC
 ACIDS IN THE VITELLINE MEMBRANE OF A CHICK OVUM.                 SHALVN-60-SFF
   SELECTIVE BIOLOGICAL MEMBRANE TRANSPORT OF INDIVIDUAL AMI      HARDSM-60-SBM
 THE PLACENTA AND FETAL MEMBRANES.  OF THE RABBIT.                TERRCW-60-TZA
RMEABILITY OF CAPILLARY MEMBRANES.                                GABORM-60-ATP
OTILITY, OF CYTOPLASMIC MEMBRANES.                                HUTTWE-60-IES
S THROUGH ION-SELECTIVE MEMBRANES BY ELECTRO-OSMOSIS.             JARVJW-60-TNT
 LINOLEATE, LINOLENATE, MENHADEN AND TUNA OILS.                   PEIFJJ-60-DLH
 AND U-15,442 IN NORMAL MEN.                                      KUNICM-60-AUE
 ROLE OF THE SOLVENT IN MENSHUTKIN/S REACTIONS.                   GONIMG-60-RSM
LE PLANT MATERIALS.  P- MENTHADIENOL OF THE ESSENTIAL OILS O      NAVEYR-60-VPM
VATIVES AND ANLOGUES OF MEPHENESIN.                               PETROV-60-DAM
 IN VITRO METABOLISM OF MEPHENESIN, 3-O- TOLYLOXY-1,2- PROPA      MAASAR-60-VMM
                     W- MERCAPTOALKYLAMMONIUM SALTS AND THEI      BOHMEH-60-WMS

THE FERROUS CHELATES OF POLYAMINO CARBOXYLIC ACIDS AS INITIA      BONDJ -60-FCP
OF ULTRAVIOLET LIGHT ON POLYBENZENOID HYDROCARBONS ADSORBED       VOYATE-60-AUL
ETERMINATION OF BENZENE POLYCARBOXYLIC ACIDS.                     GERMJE-60-SOC
E POPULATION OF SEVERAL POLYCHETES.                               AMOURL-60-POC
XCHANGE RESINS BY PEARL POLYCONDENSATION RELATION BETWEEN FU      LESEKF-60-PIE
P-PRIME)- CALCIUM-40 IN POLYCRYSTALS.                             JAOUMB-60-PDR
         OZONOLYSIS OF POLYCYCLIC HYDROCARBONS.                   COPEPG-60-OPH
CS OF EXTRACTION FROM A POLYDISPERSE MIXTURE OF POROUS PARTI      AKSEGA-60-TDE
NTERION DISTRIBUTION IN POLYELECTROLYTE SOLUTIONS BY THE RAT      MORAWH-60-CCD
M ALBUMIN AND SYNTHETIC POLYELECTROLYTES IN VARIOUS BUFFER S      NOGUCH-60-ISA
RON MODEL.  CASE OF THE POLYENES AND POLYACETYLENES.              BARF  -60-NFE
 TRANSFER TO CONJUGATED POLYENES BY TERMINAL PHENYL GROUPS.       WASSEA-60-IPT
N OF STYRENE MONOMER IN POLYESTER RESINS.                         AYREWM-60-PDS
E OF THE COMPOSITION OF POLYESTER RESINS ON OPTICAL PROPERTI      HUDECZ-60-ICP

POLYDISPERSE MIXTURE OF POROUS PARTICLES.                         AKSEGA-60-TDE
          ADSORPTION ON POROUS SOLIDS.                            CLAMBH-60-APS
                        PORPHYRIN BIOSYNTHESIS IN THE LEUCOC      CULLIB-60-PBL
CE OF HYPOPHYSECTOMY ON PORPHYRIN SYNTHESIZING ENZYME ACTIVI      FIGGFH-60-IHP
T EFFUSIONS OF PICRITIC PORPHYRITES ON THE TERRITORY OF THE       STARNP-60-AEP
      OSONHYDRAZONES.  POSITIONAL ISOMERIC MIXED OSAZONES A       HENSEG-60-OPI
 ALANINE OR TYROSINE IN POSITIONS-2-OR-3.  (FR.)                  BOISRA-60-SAO
                        POSSIBILITY OF ELIMINATING THE NEGAT      ROZAYM-60-PEN
                        POSSIBILITY OF SIMPLIFYING THE GROUP      DAVTOK-60-PSG
E OF ACETYLCHOLINE FROM POSTGANGLIONIC PARASYMPATHETIC NERVE      EMMELN-60-ITL
GNESIUM FROM SODIUM AND POTASSIUM.   TRACER STUDY.                HEYNAH-60-SMS
DIUM ACID PHOSPHATE AND POTASSIUM ACID PHOSPHATE SOLUTIONS.       TATABP-60-EHD
                        POTASSIUM AND THE TRANSMUCOSAL RESIS      HARRJB-60-PTR
NE ATOMS IN CRYSTALLINE POTASSIUM BROMATE.                        HARBOG-60-HCB

 REACTIONS OF DIAZONIUM SALTS WITH NUCLEOPHILES.   SUBSTITUT      LEWIES-60-RDS
ION OF TETRAVALENT LEAD SALTS WITH TRIETHYL ALUMINUM AND OTH      FREYFW-60-STL
 MATERIALS CONTAINED IN SALVIA-OFF.-L.                            BRIECH-60-AEO
L AUGER SPECTRUM OF 62- SAMARIUM-152.                             FWANGT-60-KAS
ELLS. ELECTRODES OF THE SAME NATURE. DETECTORS OF GASES. LIQ      BERTUA-60-GCE
EFFECT OF FLOW-RATE AND SAMPLE-SIZE ON COLUMN EFFICIENCY IN       BERNRA-60-EFS
          CORRECTION OF SAMPLE ABSORPTION OF RADIOACTIVITY.       BERSSA-60-CSA
S, THINNED FROM MASSIVE SAMPLES.  SUBSTRUCTURE OF THE DISLOC      SAULNA-60-EMB
AMINATED ACIDS OF THREE SAMPLES OF CHICKEN-EGG LYSOZYME.          JOLLEJ-60-CAA
AND USE OF A CONTINUOUS SAMPLING DEVICE.                          THOMCJ-60-DUC
ANCE PROPERTIES OF SOME SANDWICH COMPOUNDS.                       ROBERE-60-MRP
    COURSE OF ALKALINE SAPONIFICATION OF POLY(VINYL-ACETATE       GRIGOF-60-CAS
 FRACTION ISOLATED FROM SASSUREA-LAPPA-(CLARKE).                  DUTTNK-60-PAA
       SALTS OF HIGHER SATURATED ALIPHATIC DIACIDS AND MULT       PAQUOC-60-SHS
             EFFECT OF SATURATED AND UNSATURATED FATTY ACID       HERTDC-60-ESU
SM OF SUBSTITUTION AT A SATURATED CARBON ATOM.   NUCLEOPHILI      HUGHED-60-MSS
Y TO WATER OF PARTIALLY SATURATED GLASS FIBER BEDS.               PARKJD-60-PWP
RSE OF THE OXIDATION OF SATURATED HYDROCARBONS BY CHROMIUM(V      FOSTEG-60-BHC
SYNTHESIS OF THE HIGHER SATURATED STRAIGHT-CHAIN ACIDS CONTA      GERSOT-60-RNV
 FROM A FREE RADICAL BY SATURATION OF ELECTRONIC RESONANCE.       TCHAYH-60-DPP

ON AMBERLITE- IR-120.  SEPARATION FROM MIXTURES.  (ENGLISH)       KHOPSM-60-CER
UTILIZATION OF ISOTOPE SEPARATION METHODS.                        MURIAN-60-CUI
                       SEPARATION OF 2 GLUTAMIC- OXALACETIC       FLEIGA-60-SGO
                       SEPARATION OF 7-TO-14-CARBON ALKYLPH       MACAKJ-60-SAM
                       SEPARATION OF ALKALINE PHOSPHATASE F       BAMANE-60-SAP
                       SEPARATION OF ANALOGS AND ISOMERS IN       TIROUJ-60-SAI
                       SEPARATION OF A PEPTIDE WITH INSULIN       HUGGAK-60-SPI
                       SEPARATION OF CADMIUM FROM URANIUM.        STREFW-60-SCU
      CHROMATOGRAPHIC SEPARATION OF FRANCIUM FROM CESIUM A        LAVRAK-60-CSF
                       SEPARATION OF HALOGENATED PHENOLS BY       CHOGHS-60-SHP
                       SEPARATION OF MAGNESIUM FROM SODIUM        HEYNAH-60-SMS
LEXES IN POLAROGRAPHY. SEPARATION OF MANGANESE FROM ITS COM       BIERNJ-60-KEP
          VAPOR PHASE SEPARATION OF METHYL- OR ETHYL- MERC        KIMURY-60-VPS
      CHROMATOGRAPHIC SEPARATION OF MICROQUANTITIES OF BUT        LIPITG-60-CSM
                       SEPARATION OF NIOBIUM FROM TANTALUM        ZIEGLM-60-SNT
 ISOTOPE EFFECT FOR THE SEPARATION OF OXYGEN ISOTOPES OXYGEN      BAERTP-60-IES
EE RADICALS AND ATOMS.  SEPARATION OF POLAR AND RESONANCE EF      RUSSGA-60-SER
      CHROMATOGRAPHIC SEPARATION OF SOME ALKALI METALS. (E        MARTEC-60-CSS
     INFLUENCE OF THE SEPARATION OF THE ELECTRODES IN ALKA        QUINTM-60-ISE
                       SEPARATION OF THE HYPNOTIC POTENTIAT       BAXTRM-60-SHP

  GASIFICATION OF EAST SIBERIAN BROWN COAL UNDER PRESSURE.        DERBMI-60-GES
ENT OF HUMAN FOETAL AND SICKLE-CELL HAEMOGLOBINS.                 ALLIAC-60-SGC
ANALOGS WITH UNBRANCHED SIDE CHAINS. (GER.)                       SMOLIS-60-VVS
UTERIUM EXCHANGE IN THE SIDNONE SERIES.                           IASHVG-60-ADE
 DESCRIBED AS MOLECULAR SIEVES.                                   MIRSJV-60-VAC
 AND LAMBDA HYPERONS BY SIGMA-MINUS CAPTURE IN DEUTERIUM.         DAHLO -60-PSL
         PRODUCTION OF SIGMA-O AND LAMBDA HYPERONS BY SIGMA       DAHLO -60-PSL
M COMPOUND CONTAINING A SIGMA-TYPE METAL PHENYL BOND.             LIEFMH-60-SOV
ETIC ROTATION OF BOND.* SIGMA BONDS IN THE ALIPHATIC SERIES.      GALLAF-60-ESM
OMERS FROM METHYLCHLORO SILANE.                                   PONOVA-60-OSM

    INTERACTION BETWEEN SODIUM ALUMINO SILICATE AND CALCIUM       MALYMF-60-IBS
                        SODIUM AMALGAM IN THE FORM OF PELLET      ISBEHS-60-SAF
                        SODIUM AND LITHIUM HEXAFLUORO RUTHEN      BOSTJL-60-SLH
ATION OF MAGNESIUM FROM SODIUM AND POTASSIUM.   TRACER STUDY      HEYNAH-60-SMS
 THE TOTAL EXCRETION OF SODIUM AND POTASSIUM IN RATS EXPOSED      BOCCIM-60-ETA
THE 3(2)P(3/2) STATE OF SODIUM AND THE QUADRUPOLE MOMENT OF       DODDJN-60-HSP
ION OF DIFFUSE BANDS OF SODIUM BEHIND SHOCK FRONTS.               TAKEYH-60-EDB
                        SODIUM B- SODIO METHACRYLATE, A NEW       DEPRDO-60-SBS
CATALYZED HYDROLYSIS OF SODIUM BOROHYDRIDE.                       LEVYA -60-CHS
 OF INORGANIC ANIONS IN SODIUM CARBONATE SOLUTION.  (ENGLISH      BELLCB-60-PEI
```

B. Permuted title entries

FIG. 25. Typical permuted title index entries. ***Chemical Titles,*** **No. 1, April 5, 1960, The American Chemical Society.**

A somewhat related technique is that of the permutation index which, by sorting operations, produces an index of the individual words appearing in document titles or abstracts. One such index, called by Luhn the "key word in context" (KWIC) index,[23] is illustrated in Figure 25. It has been successfully applied to titles for *Chemical Abstracts.* The resulting index, called *Chemical Titles,* provides a listing of titles in alphabetical order, with an entry for each word in the title. A permuted title index can be prepared on punched card equipment or on more elaborate electronic data process-

[23] H. P. Luhn, Keyword-In-Context Index for Technical Literature, IBM, August 1959.

ing machines. When using a computer, it becomes possible to compare words in a title one by one with words in a table in the computer's program. Insignificant words can thus be ignored and remaining key words accepted for rotating into a sorting position. The process results in a line entry for each key word in the title so that at time of print-out each key word is sorted into an alphabetical list and is presented to the user in the context of its surrounding words in the title. The preprints of the International Conference on Scientific Information were subjected to this kind of program and the resulting print-out served as a specimen of the permuted title method.[24]

Automatic file organization is not limited to manipulation of subject and title information only. Surname indexing can often be another important element of a mechanized system. This is true, for example, in large name files which are maintained for motor vehicle registration, social security, insurance and banking records, veterans administration files, etc. The chief problem associated with these large name files rests with the misspelling or misunderstanding of names at time of input and with the possible variations in spelling at the time of search. In order to overcome such difficulties, various coding systems have been devised to permit filing and searching of large groups of names phonetically as well as alphabetically. Thus names which sound or appear alike can be grouped together within the same file structure. Names like Burke, Berck, Birk, Bourke, Birque, Burck, Bherk, Borck, Bircke, Bourk, Borke, and many others, can be filed together as one group. Soundex, developed by Remington Rand, is perhaps the most popular of the codes used in conjunction with large name files. A Remington Rand Univac computer program capable of performing the phonetic coding of input names has been prepared. An extension of the program operates on the name information in its homogeneous groupings for searching, comparing, and print-out.

The Soundex code represents a name by an alphabetic character followed by three decimal digits. The alphabetic character is chosen as the initial letter of the name. The successive decimal digits are chosen according to the following rules. (1) Double letters are treated as single letters. (2) A-E-I-O-U-W-H-Y are always ignored. (3) Letters with similar sounds are then identified by the appropriate code number.

---

[24] J. Citron, L. Hart, and H. Ohlman, A Permutation Index to the Preprints of the International Conference on Scientific Information, System Development Corp., No. SP-44, November 1958.

B F P V	1
C G J K Q S X Z	2
D T	3
L	4
M N	5
R	6

(4) If there are less than three such consonants after the initial letter, zeros are added to produce the three digit code. To illustrate:

Name	*Soundex Code*
Kuckuck	K220
Swinhart	S563
Whiffen	W150
Wullenwaber	W451

Although the use of the computer for sorting and rearranging natural language words and titles, as used in the development of concordances and permuted word indexes, is a useful technique, it hardly seems to provide a powerful tool for handling the really difficult problems in file organization. There are, however, some extensive experimental efforts in the more speculative areas. For example, Maron and Kuhns,[25] in their work on probabilistic indexing, proposed techniques for automatic grouping of documents and index terms based on the statistical relationship among the usage of index terms as applied to documents.

Lauren Doyle is another researcher who has advanced the hypothesis that the laws of probability, rather than pure chance, are responsible for the frequency of subject word coincidence in a document.[26] He has also been among the most stimulating of the researchers into the use of associations among indexing terms.[27]

The work by Maron and Kuhns can best be described in the following way.

The set of documents, together with the weights assigned to the

---

[25] M. E. Maron and J. L. Kuhns, On Relevance, Probabilistic Indexing and Information Retrieval, *Journal of the Association for Computing Machinery,* July 1960, v. 7, No. 3, pp. 216–244.

[26] L. Doyle, Programmed Interpretation of Text as a Basis for Information Retrieval Systems, *Proceedings of the Western Joint Computer Conference,* San Francisco, March 1959, pp. 60–63.

[27] Lauren B. Doyle, Indexing and Abstracting by Association, *American Documentation,* October 1962, v. 13, No. 4, pp. 378–390.

relevant index terms, can be represented in the form of a matrix whose rows correspond to the individual documents and whose columns correspond to the entire set of assignable terms. The element appearing at any row and column of this matrix then represents the weight assigned by the indexer to represent the relevancy of the particular term to the particular document. In the traditional case, this matrix would consist of a very large number of zeros and a relatively small number of ones for the index terms assigned to the document; utilizing probabilistic indexing or any other type of weighted indexing, a range of values might appear at any given point. On the basis of this matrix, several measures of distances between documents related to the degree of similarity between rows can be derived, each of which provides a criterion for grouping documents on the basis of their similarity.

H. E. Stiles [28] proposed a technique for a similar grouping of index terms based on the same set of data represented by the matrix of document—term relationships. He developed a list of terms arranged according to the number of times they had been associated with a given term in assignment to documents, normalized by the product of the total number of assignments of each term to any document. These "term profiles," as Stiles called them, are thus derived from the document collection by a statistical analysis of term assignment. This technique can be extended to further degrees of association, such as the extent to which two terms have high degree of association with a set of third terms. Based on these association factors, groupings of terms on the basis of their mutual association can then be derived.

Maron and Kuhns, on the one hand, and Stiles on the other, have all used a measure of relevancy derived from the degree to which documents had index terms in common. Given such measures of closeness, documents can be grouped and classifications assigned to such groupings or terms can be grouped and generalized subject headings assigned. The experimental work in this area provides the rudiments of a method for automatic file organization.

SEARCHING USING SPECIAL PURPOSE DEVICES

It has been felt by many that the general purpose computer was, despite its great power and flexibility, unsuitable for information

[28] H. Edmund Stiles, The Association Factors in Information Retrieval, *Journal of the Association for Computing Machinery,* April 1961, v. 8, No. 2, pp. 271–279.

retrieval. It seemed to many that it was too expensive a device, with too much of its capability devoted to the computational area. Furthermore, even considering its great speed, it was too slow a device because of its serial processing in executing one command at a time. For example, in 1951 Phillip R. Bagley of MIT prepared a master's thesis entitled "Electronic Digital Machines for High Speed Information Searching," in which he came to this conclusion.[29, 30]

The object of Bagley's thesis was to examine methods and machines designed to make possible the high-speed location of related items in a large body of suitably indexed material. He considered the application of a general purpose computer for the searching of a large-scale index on magnetic tape. His objective was to determine what kind of computer would be necessary to search a total collection of index records derived from 50 million documents. He concluded, using Whirlwind I as the sample general purpose machine, that a search of 50 million records of 30 index terms each would take 41,700 hours. Based on this fact, Bagley disqualified the general purpose computer as an effective searching device, since considerable time was spent internally in the machine due to its sequential nature and the need to move and shift information around in memory during the compare part of the search.

To overcome this disadvantage, Bagley proposed that a special purpose "information searching machine" be built which would be engineered to compare large blocks of information simultaneously, thus reducing over-all search time. His calculations for doing substantially the same job as that contemplated on Whirlwind I resulted in an over-all estimate of search time of approximately 11 hours.

The immediate basis of Bagley's conclusion, which involved the characteristics of the Whirlwind I computer, is no longer valid. Computers now have internal operating speeds and magnetic tape data rates greater by several orders of magnitude. However, many other people have come to similar conclusions based on economic considerations or specialized requirements. Machine research and development in this area have been quite varied. The following are some representative examples of this type of work undertaken by manufacturers and individual research workers.

---

[29] P. R. Bagley, Electronic Digital Machines for High Speed Information Searching, Report R-200, Digital Computer Laboratory, MIT, Cambridge, 1951.

[30] P. R. Bagley and J. W. Perry, Application of Newer Electronic Techniques to Information Searching, American Chemical Society, Division of Chemical Literature, New York, 1951.

IBM 9900 Special Index Analyzer

In 1957 Taube [31] proposed a new special purpose machine, which he called COMAC—COntinuous Multiple Access Collator. It was designed to handle a collection up to one million items and to employ collation, as in coordinate indexing, rather than linear searching. The 9900 Special Index Analyzer was a unique machine configuration developed by IBM to meet COMAC objectives.

It was designed by IBM to make more efficient the machine operations required in searching large index files of punched cards arranged in sets according to Uniterm indexing.[32] This seemed necessary because conventional electrical accounting machines methods have limitations when it becomes necessary to collate three trays to find the documents which they have in common, that is, the basic file order in the trays is disturbed when a match occurs because the common cards are removed when they match; later the cards must be resorted into their original sequence. Furthermore, the number of logical operations which a standard collator can perform are few. The IBM 9900 Special Index Analyzer is made up of several conventional units including a key punch, a card reader, an intermediate storage unit containing control equipment and a perforated paper punch and reader, and a typewriter for printing-out final results.

By using the 9900 with a coordinate index system, punched cards can be arranged by index terms. Within each index record are the document number references arranged in ascending sequence. For example, one tray of punched cards may deal with the index term "Jet" and each card in the tray may contain numerical references to documents (up to 12) where information on "Jet" exists. Another tray may contain cards on the subject of "Air Traffic Control," another on "Domestic Airports," etc.

A typical matching operation on the Special Index Analyzer to find the document numbers common to the three terms would proceed as follows:

1. The cards for "Jet" are read into the storage unit by the card reader.

2. The control unit produces an equivalent perforated paper tape.

---

[31] M. Taube, The COMAC: An Efficient Punched Card Collating System for the Storage and Retrieval of Information, AF OSR TN 58-365, ASTIA No. AD 154, 271, 1957.

[32] R. W. Murphy, The IBM 9900 Special Index Analyzer, IBM Corp., Poughkeepsie, N.Y., 1958.

3. The cards for "Air Traffic Control" are read in as is the perforated paper tape for "Jet"; the result is a new paper tape containing those document numbers common to the two terms.

4. The cards for "Domestic Airports" are read in as is the paper tape containing the results of the previous match. A new paper tape results which contains only those document numbers common to the three index terms.

5. The typewriter prints-out the numbers contained in the final paper tape which would presumably deal with the control of jet air traffic at domestic airports.

The operations performed by the Special Index Analyzer are of the type found in the theory of sets: the range of operations which can be performed on two sets (A and B) of cards are equivalent to those on the items in sets; the items found in one set but not the other (A and not B); the item in either set but not in both (A or B, but not A and B); and the item in either one set or the other (A or B), etc. In planning a search, the user usually states his problem in words which can be reduced to logical combinations of one or more index terms. Since his logic can be expressed as different modes of operation on the machine, they can be ordered, or programmed, to produce a sequence of machine operations equivalent to the logic of the original search request. Programming the various modes of operation can either be performed manually by an operator or automatically, using command or control cards.

In addition, the Special Index Analyzer also assists in index file maintenance by providing a systematic means for uniting new information with its related master cards already in file.

WRU Searching Selector

Based on the experience of Bagley and some preconceptions of Perry concerning the suitability of general purpose computers, the Western Reserve group decided to develop a specialized searching device especially designed for their particular technique of coding document abstracts.[33,34] The device was intended as an experimental

---

[33] A. Kent, J. Melton, and C. Flagg, Abstracting, Coding, and Searching the Metallurgical Literature for A.S.M., *Information Systems in Documentation, Advances in Documentation and Library Science II,* New York, Interscience, 1957.

[34] J. H. Shera, A. Kent, and J. W. Perry, The WRU Searching Selector, *Information Systems in Documentation, Advances in Documentation and Library Science II,* New York, Interscience, 1957.

unit and was built from relatively inexpensive relay-type equipment. It used punched tape as the medium for storage of document abstracts and compared each term, subphrase, and phrase with the stored counterparts representing the request.

The logic of a search request was programmed into the WRU Searching Selector via conventional wiring or plugboard panels. Due to its relays, the device's speed was very slow. It was able to search one abstract per minute and handle 10 questions simultaneously. The end result of a request or search varied. It either provided the address number of an abstract, its bibliographic citation, or the complete abstract itself.

GE 250 Selector

The General Electric Company initiated the design of a similar device based on electronic components with magnetic tape as the storage medium and embodying the same technique for representation of document content. However, presumably because the device in this form would be too specialized for the costs involved in its design, the project was abandoned in favor of a more general purpose computer based on the same philosophy.

Minicard Selector

Based on the specific concepts of file searching logic in the Minicard development (which will be discussed in more detail below), Eastman Kodak designed a specialized searching device. The device utilizes a plugboard on which the relationships between various terms in a request were specified. Up to 20 terms can be handled and two levels of logical interrelationship. The device is limited, primarily by the handling rate of the Minicard handling equipment, to a maximum scan rate of 20 cards per second.

Question term codes are input to the selector by means of punched paper tape. The logical relations and conditions of assertion, negation, and other boundary requirements connecting the terms together are all specified by means of the plugboard. The plugboard also provided the capability of controlling the stacking of Minicards, selected for their matching with a request, into particular magazines and for controlling various counters and indicator lights. A copy of the Minicard selector plugboard is shown in Figure 27 and a summary of its selecting capabilities can be gained by a study of Figure 28. The plugboard is organized into four major sections, each pro-

FIG. 26. Minicard selector. Courtesy Eastman Kodak Co., Rochester, N.Y.

viding a means of specifying the logical conditions and connections for the codes of the questions. As shown in the diagram, up to 20 terms may be set up in a question code register from the input codes in the punched paper tapes. The selecting operation involves a comparison of data read from the Minicards with terms stored in the question code register for match according to the logical relations specified.

To understand the functioning of the selector, it is important to appreciate that the Minicard system is based on "phrases" as groups of terms, just as in the Western Reserve system. Thus the logical relations between phrases in a question are specified by wiring the level one section of the plugboard. The logical relations between the terms within a phrase are specified by similarly wiring in the level two section of the plugboard.

CCC Index Searcher

In 1958 the Computer Controls Company of Framingham, Mass., produced a machine, called the Index Searcher, that was similarly

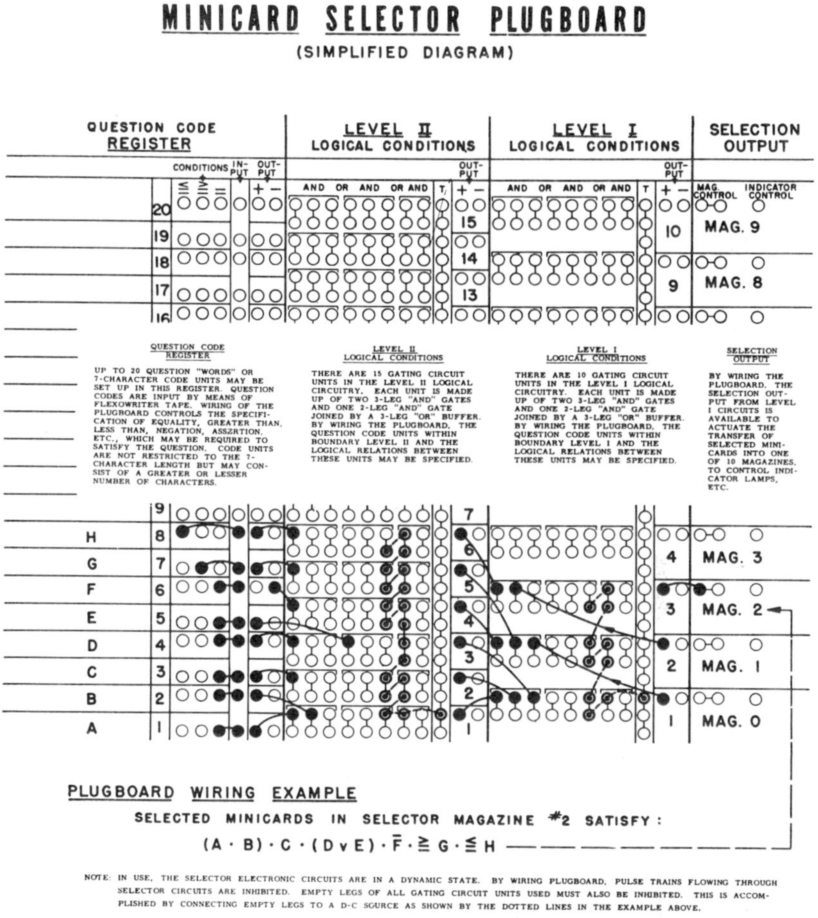

FIG. 27. Minicard selector plugboard. J. W. Kuipers, A. W. Tyler, and W. L. Myers, A Minicard System for Documentary Information, *American Documentation*, October 1957, v. 8, No. 4, pp. 246–268.

designed to perform exclusively search and file operations, but on continuous tape media.[35] It evolved as a result of the company's experience in building the Minicard selector under subcontract for Eastman Kodak Company.

The Index Searcher uses continuous magnetic tape rather than

---

[35] B. Kessel and A. de Lucia, A Specialized Library Index Search Computer, *Proceedings of 1959 Western Joint Computer Conference*, IRE, New York.

Let A, B, C, ... etc., be index code units.

Typical Question: Select documents from the file which satisfy the following:

A and B present within a "phrase", and C present, and D or E or both present within a "phrase", and not F present, and a code unit present which is equal to or greater than G, and a code unit present which is equal to or less than H.

Question in Logical Notation:

$$(A \cdot B) \cdot C \cdot (D \vee E) \cdot \bar{F} \cdot \geqq G \cdot \leqq H$$

Analysis of Question for Preparation of Plugboard:

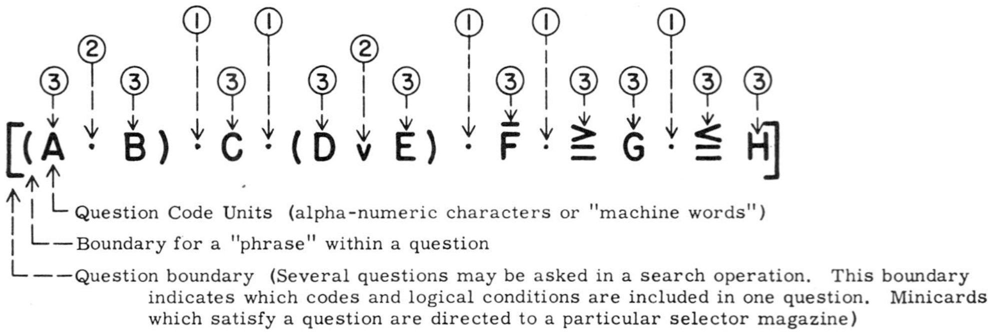

(1) = Logical relations which may be specified by wiring Level I plugboard circuits.
(2) = Logical relations which may be specified by wiring Level II plugboard circuits.
(3) = Codes and code conditions specified in the Question Code Register.

FIG. 28. Analysis of a question for preparation of minicard selector plugboard. J. W. Kuipers, A. W. Tyler, and W. L. Myers, A Minicard System for Documentary Information, *American Documentation*, October 1957, v. 8, No. 4, pp. 246–268.

Minicards as the storage medium. On the tape, indexed information can appear in most any form—from brief coded notations of data to the complete text of an article—depending on the nature of the application. Each 2400-foot reel of magnetic tape 1 inch wide can store 57,600,000 bits. As in most magnetic tape systems, an alpha-numeric character is represented by a six-bit code plus one bit for a parity check, for a resulting maximum capacity of about 8 million characters.

The Index Searcher has six different modes of operation. A very brief description of each mode will give the salient features of the machine.

1. *Document insert.* Perforated paper tape is used as input, and this mode converts the paper tape code to machine language and stores the new information on the main storage tape via a tape buffer.

2. *Regenerate tape.* This mode allows for a simple conversion from magnetic tape to magnetic tape which can be used to duplicate the entire main storage tape as insurance against loss or damage.

3. *Question insert.* Question words containing the search criteria for one or more requests are prepared on perforated paper tape and via this mode are sent to the Index Searcher's memory. At the same time, plugboard connections are made which reflect the logical operations to be performed for each search request, such as the nature of the comparisons to be made. The plugboard is wired manually, of course, and inserted in position in one rack of the machine's main mechanism.

4. *Search.* This is the primary mode of the machine. The tape can move forward or backward during a search. While the tape is being scanned, comparisons are made with the question words stored in memory according to the logic wired in the plugboard. Matches are stored in a buffer, and at the end of a completed scan through the tape, answers are printed-out on a Flexowriter. Answers can take the form of document numbers plus other identifying data. When a tape end-of-file is reached, the machine automatically positions itself for the next search in the opposite direction, thus avoiding time normally lost in rewinding.

5. *Print.* This mode allows for the complete print-out of all information in the magnetic tape index record associated with a given index term. Thus, if an abstract followed the indexed information, the print mode would print-out both the indexed information and the abstract on command.

6. *Edit.* This allows for the removal or deletion of unwanted indexed information records from the main storage tape.

The six operating modes and the flexibility of manual plugboard wiring for specifying the combination of logic required for each request serve the same purpose as the appropriate subroutines used on general purpose machines. The power of the Index Searcher and similar special purpose devices lies in its economy of design, stressing only those operating functions needed for scanning, searching, comparing, editing, and printing. It can thus be much smaller than a general purpose machine and can be produced more cheaply.

7

Indexes, documents, and the storage of data

The basic index record data resulting from the processes of analysis must be stored in a form compatible with the data processing equipment which will operate on it to answer requests. Similarly, the documents and other source data which will be supplied in answer to requests must be stored in some way so as to be easily made available to the user. For example, in manual systems the index record data is stored as typed or printed information on cards in a subject card catalog, on the pages of a book catalog, on the term cards in a Uniterm coordinate index; the document file is the set of physical books or journals stored on shelves or in cabinets.

These printed forms of data storage for index records and documents may be very suitable for manual systems, but they are space consuming and generally unsuitable for mechanized handling. A very crucial part of the entire effort to mechanize information retrieval has therefore been the development of new storage media and new recording methods for data and image recording. Some of these developments have been among the most spectacular technological advances in modern engineering. Some have been prosaic improvements in existing methods. The results, in any event, have provided a great variety of methods for storing all forms of data at high density and for reading them automatically at high speed. In this way the great mass of data which the computer and its more specialized cousins must analyze and provide in response to requests can be readily available for processing.

In the following material, illustrations of the most significant developments in data storage are described so as to provide a picture of the great variety of available methods. In each case the method involves a storage medium and a means of representing coded or image information.

Before considering these developments in detail, it is important to recognize that although the relationship between the logical equipment and the storage medium in an information system is a close one almost any of the storage media we will discuss could be used with almost any of the various logical devices previously described. The possibility of various combinations of equipment is important because the unique features of each possible method of storing information should be considered for the advantages independent of the particular equipment chosen for logical processing. Unfortunately the possibility of various combinations of equipment has been ignored in many cases; the advantages of a particular system have been attributed to its approach to the problems of logical processing when they were really due to the significant features of the storage medium. Awareness of the relative independence of logical processing and the storage medium is a particularly important consideration when the problem is one of evaluating proposed new approaches.

ORGANIZATION

Generally speaking, the contents of the index record are an abstraction of an item from the file of basic source documents, that is, they can be considered a sort of shorthand substitute for the original document, containing only as much information as will help users to decide intelligently which documents in a document file most closely satisfy their needs. Normally the index and the document files are kept separate; however, they can be consolidated in machine systems like Minicard and File-Search, which are discussed later. The preparation of an index is unnecessary, of course, when the original documents can be arranged in a way which itself satisfies all consultative and finding requirements. However, it is clear that this is only possible when the quantity of printed material is small and when specialized use is all that is involved. As soon as a collection of printed material begins to grow and user needs become diverse, no single arrangement of material is able to serve all multidimensional purposes.

Equipment manufacturers have been particularly fascinated by the notion of an index for several reasons.

1. Operations here are typical of the normal data processing routines performed on existing equipment for numerical applications. Inasmuch as alphabetical information also can be expressed in machine language, they can see no technical obstacle in the path of achieving similar electronic advantages (speed and accuracy) with general or special purpose machines.

2. A conventional index has physical limitations in the sense that users must come to it in order to consult it. Technical advances in communications and particularly in television suggest to equipment people that technical ingenuity can make the contents of information indexes more widely available to people irrespective of physical location. Such widespread and effective use of an information system would, in turn, most certainly strengthen our national resources.

3. Equipment manufacturers are aware of the exponential publishing rate and the concomitant increase in the number of people required to do information work if the index is manual. They draw an analogy to other fields, like the banking business, where machines have been introduced to cope with fast-growing, complex, large-scale record keeping problems.

A combination of the above elements, the rapid and intense pull of our expanding technology, and the normal competitive motivations of equipment manufacturers are all responsible for the considerable machine research and development in the index area. The aim has been to devise equipment for the rapid maintenance, sort, search, and automatic display of alphabetic data.

To provide background for considering the specific developments for the storage of index and document files, it is useful to review some examples of the kinds of content arrangements available for use. A researcher or a library may start a private file of source material by just placing the original documents in random order in a file drawer. As the quantity of material increases, however, one is forced to develop either some kind of preferred filing arrangement or an index to avoid the necessity of searching through everything in the cabinet each time a demand materializes. It is true that some individuals perform such a search very well, and, in fact, it has been claimed that such an arrangement is the most suitable for mechanized systems. However, it does seem that sooner or later a point of diminishing returns is reached and either items are invariably missed or the cost of the search becomes too great.

If the source material can be arranged in some preferred physical order which suits principal user demands well, then an intermediate index may appear to be unnecessary. This type of arrangement is usually accomplished in a manual system by using an established list of subject headings and writing the appropriate heading on the outside corner of the document. The document, of course, can usually only be filed in one place and therefore receives only one subject heading unless multiple copies are available. This may sound quite restrictive, but there are times when the practice serves its purpose well. A newspaper morgue file is typical of this filing technique. Clippings are filed away by names of people, of things, or of organizations appearing in newspaper articles. Most scientific and technical research workers use this method in constructing their private document files according to personalized classification schemes.

Even in the preferred order organization, however, some elementary degree of analysis is required in order to prejudge the categories into which the material should be filed. Locating this position in the file requires at least a rudimentary index. A record in the index thus may be very simple, serving merely as a reference to the document file. Alternatively, it may include characteristics of, and information about, the source document designed to help the user of the index file filter irrelevant references to the document file during his logical processing at the time of a search. For example, a simple catalog card might contain only the author's name and the call number of the book; however, usage would probably dictate the need to record title information also. This information aids immeasurably in identifying the material and evaluating its potential usefulness. Some applications also include an abstract of the document as part of the record in the index file in order to provide the user with as much information about the content of the document as possible, short of

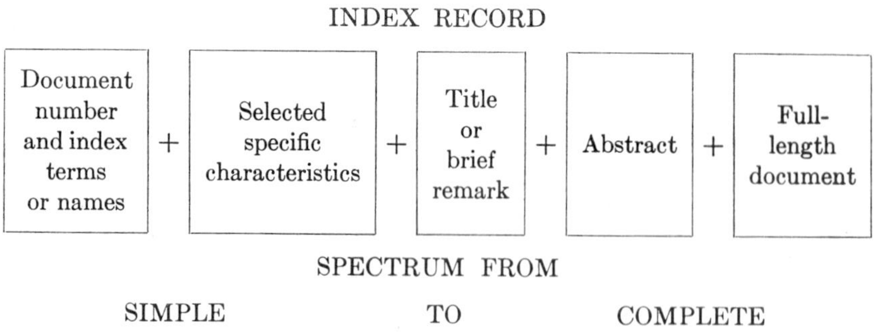

FIG. 29. Spectrum of abstraction.

SOME POSSIBLE PHYSICAL FORMS

INDEX	DOCUMENT FILE
Manual cards Punched cards Printed books Magnetic tape, strips, or disks Digital code on film, video tape	Hardcopy originals Continuous microfilm Unitized microfilm Magnetic tape, strips, or disks Video tape

FIG. 30. Some possible physical forms.

actually seeing the full report. The content of an index file can thus run the gamut from a highly abbreviated and single purpose record to a very complete and multipurpose one.

The fuller and more complex the index record, the more intellectual effort is required during the analysis and processing work but the more accurate the processing of the requests. How much a more complete index record provides to the user is a question on which too little research has been done to draw good conclusions. There are some who believe than an ideal system should retain all of the text of the original document, whereas, at the other extreme, others feel that the most abbreviated content provided during indexing and abstracting is adequate. Don R. Swanson has described the nature of the dilemma as follows:

> Intuitively one knows the larger and more detailed the index and catalog, the less the information loss, but the greater the difficulty in searching.

SOME POSSIBLE COMBINATIONS OF ARRANGEMENT

INDEX		DOCUMENT FILE
By word with references to one or more numbers By number with references to words	+	By number in sequence By hierarchical classification By word categories, subjects, or names of persons or things

FIG. 31. Some possible combinations of arrangement.

Indeed, in the extreme, if each sentence of an article of a collection were cataloged, the "representation" of the library so created might approach high fidelity but would be almost as impractical as the library itself for conducting searches.[1]

The combination of an ordered document file and an ordered index is by far the most popular in libraries and commercial file installations. The physical form and arrangement of both the index file and document file vary depending on the specific application and need.

PERFORATED RECORDING

The use of perforations in card and tape for storage of information, for communication, and for process control has a long history that dates back to the time of the Jacquard loom, if not earlier. Basically the concept in perforated recording is the representation of information by binary codes, using the punching or lack of punching at specified positions in the storage medium. Since this form of storage is readily acceptable to both the human being and the machine, it has found widespread use in the information retrieval field and seems to be particularly applicable to the mechanization of small library problems.

Punched Tape

In certain respects the simplest form which this method of recording takes is that represented by punched tape. With punched tape, individual alphabetic or numeric characters are represented by the combination of punched holes occurring in parallel "channels" across a narrow strip of tape. These punched holes can occur at any one of the several fixed positions, with respect to the sides of the tape, defined by the channels. Index information thus can be stored as a sequence of coded characters along the length of the tape. In fact, the entire content of a document can be so represented. For example, in the discussion of H. P. Luhn's experiments with automatic indexing, his use of the monotype tape was mentioned; this particular form of tape is 31 channels wide and can be used to control the setting of pages of type in multiple fonts. In the case of Luhn's experiments, it contained the entire text of the journal articles to be abstracted.

---

[1] Don R. Swanson, Searching Natural Language Text by Computer, *Science*, October 21, 1960, v. 132, No. 3434, pp. 1099–1104.

In this same connection, the use of punched teletype tape in telecommunication is standard in many phases of the publishing field. It is particularly used by national magazines for transmission of magazine content from editorial offices to the nationally distributed publishing points. Again, the existence of complete text data in machine language teletype tape makes it possible to consider mechanized literature retrieval with it as a storage medium.

In the experimental work of Western Reserve University to test their method for document representation and the functioning of their experimental searching selector, punched paper tape was used for the storage of the document abstracts. The sequence of alphabetic characters along the tape in this way represented the sequence of term codes and associated indicators for each document. An entire reel of tape would contain the set of documents received during a period of time, such as a week or a month.

Despite these examples, however, punched paper tape is unlikely to be widely used as the basic medium for either index or document storage in large information retrieval systems. Fundamentally, as a medium, its storage density is far too low and, although the possible reading rate has been increased several orders of magnitude over the past few years—from 10 characters per second to over 2000 characters per second—it is still a relatively slow information transmitting method. In addition, punched paper tape is difficult to correct if it is in error; unlike magnetic tape, it cannot be changed; and unlike cards, it cannot be sorted, interfiled, and otherwise rearranged.

Notched Cards

An entirely separate line of development is the edge-notched card. In edge-notching, information is represented by binary codes in the form of the notch or lack of notch at each of specified positions along the edge of a card. Because this technique of recording is almost inherently a low density one, the amount of information which can be recorded on an individual card in this way is relatively small. Problems of efficient coding of the data to be represented have therefore been of predominant importance. Several manufacturers have developed coding systems and card punching and searching equipment. Among these are the McBee Key-Sort system, the E-Z Sort system, the Zator system of Calvin Mooers, etc.

It has been said by many authors that a realistic upper limit for

Matrix Case Arrangement 7C1a (Job)

Function keys Nos. 31, 41, 52, 144, 149, 216, and 293 are not shown in Matrix Case.

Row	NI	NL	A	B	C	D	E	F	G	H	I	J	K	L	M	N	O	
1	‘ 296	’ 297	l 280	i 268	*l* 203	*t* 188	‘ 63	’ 64	. 142-214	, 141-213	, 290	l 131	i 119	] 48	[47	· 45 150-291	▮ 49-56	5 Unit
2	j 278	f 275	t 265	*i* 191	*f* 198	! 61	: 98	; 99	- 97-180	j 129	f 126	I 9	*j* 201	: 181	; 182	! 215	23 ▮ 50-57	6 Unit
3	! 292	- 246	; 248	I 224	r 264	*c* 208	) 59	(58	*e* 186	*r* 187	r 115	s 124	t 116	J 19	*s* 196	*v* 209	*z* 51-206	7 Unit
4	? 281	: 247	z 283	c 285	s 273	*b* 210	*o* 192	*g* 199	? 62	I 75	z 134	c 136	e 114	*?* 24-204	s 14	. 132	*q* 53-184	8 Unit
5	9 258	7 256	5 254	3 252	1 250	0 259	q 261	*d* 197	*a* 195	*y* 189	. 147	9 109	7 107	5 105	3 103	1 101	0 54-110	9 Unit
6	$ 249	8 257	c 26	6 255	4 253	2 251	v 286	x 284	*x* 207	*k* 202	_ 65	$ 100	8 108	6 106	4 104	2 102	55 ■ 145-294	9 Unit
7	J 234	o 269	y 266	g 276	a 272	p 270	e 263	*h* 200	x 135	J 85	g 127	o 120	a 123	P 11	F 16	L 21	T 6-38	9 Unit
8	b 287	u 267	A 13	n 288	*p* 193	*u* 190	*n* 143-211	S 80	v 137	y 117	p 121	u 118	n 139	*fl* 2-161	B 28	O 10	E 4-39	10 Unit
9	k 279	h 277	D 15	d 274	*fi* 183	*I* 158	fl 78	fi 111	q 112	k 130	b 138	h 128	d 125	V 27	fi 7-260	G 17	R 5-40	10 Unit
10	Z 239	F 231	H 18	L 22-236	S 229	ff 238	*J* 168	*S* 163	*Q* 151	*C* 175	Z 90	*ff* 172	ff 89	*Z* 25-173	U 8	fl 20-227	N 29-42	11 Unit
11	X 240	C 241	E 219	P 226	T 221	V 242	B 243	A 228	Y 222	L 87	P 77	F 82	*w* 185	M 30	*F* 165	*L* 170	*O* 43-159	12 Unit
12	R 220	U 223	w 262	*G* 166	Q 68	V 93	C 92	B 94	T 72	O 76	E 70	A 79	w 113	*P* 160	*B* 177	*E* 153	*T* 44-155	13 Unit
13	K 235	Q 217	D 230	O 225	N 244	G 232	*Y* 156	*R* 154	*V* 176	Y 73	U 74	G 83	R 71	*m* 12-212	*ffi* 1-205	w 3	*ffl* 32-194	14 Unit
14	ffl 174-271	ffi 169-282	H 233	m 289	*A* 162	ffl 122	ffi 133	X 91	D 81	N 95	K 86	H 84	m 140	*H* 167	*U* 67-157	*N* 178	*D* 33-164	15 Unit
15	& 237	W 218	M 245	√ 34	¾ 37	¼ 35	½ 36	*W* 152	*M* 179	— 66	.. 148	M 96	W 69	% 60	@ 46-171	& 88	148 ■ 295-298	18 Unit

Characters in Matrix Case

ABCDEFGHIJKLMNOPQRSTUVWXYZ&
ABCDEFGHIJLMNOPRSTUVW
abcdefghijklmnopqrstuvwxyzfiflfffffiffl
ABCDEFGHIJLMNOPQRSTUVWYZ
abcdefghijklmnopqrstuvwxyzfiflfffffiffl
ABCDEFGHIJKLMNOPQRSTUVWXYZ&
abcdefghijklmnopqrstuvwxyzfiflfffffiffl
.,-:;‘’!?()[]*:;!?*-—....%@√**.,-:;‘’!?**
$1234567890¼½¾**$1234567890**

NOTE: The two Justifying-space Bars and Keys Nos. 23 and 57 produce Matrix Case position 2-O. The Space Bars and Key No. 23 also bring up the Justifying-space Punch and consequently produce Justifying Spaces. Key No. 57 produces 6-unit spaces because it does not bring up the Justifying-space Punch.

The red numbers in the squares with the characters indicate the Keys that produce these characters.

See Keyboard Arrangement at left.

Omitted characters—small caps K Q X Y Z & Æ Œ and italic caps *K X &*

fi 7-260

Two or more numbers in the same square with a character indicate the different Keys that will produce this character; for example fi will be produced by either Key 7 or Key 260.

On special work these extra Keys are used for additional characters: Thus, Key 7 might be capped with any desired character of same width body as ligature fi, for which this extra character would be substituted, without affecting the justification, when the matter is corrected.

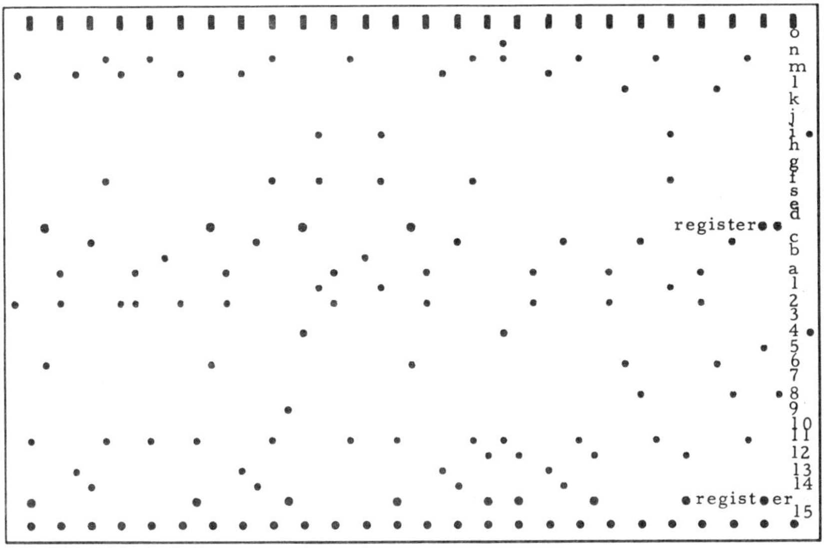

FIG. 32. On monotype tape a character is represented by two punches out of the possible 31. One of these occurs on the top side of the tape and identifies the column of a matrix; the other occurs on the bottom side of the tape and identifies a row of the same matrix. The row and column together identify the character. Courtesy the Lanston Monotype Company, Philadelphia, Pa.

files of edge-notched cards is approximately 10,000.[2] Up to that limit, however, there are some significant advantages in the ease with which these files can be handled. The value of edge-notching lies in the fact that an entire file of cards can be simultaneously interrogated and the notched codes on each card compared with search criteria. In addition, and of even more fundamental importance, the technique of interrogation not only locates the desired card but also allows for its physical extraction. In a very real sense, therefore, the technique of edge-notching represents one of the most powerful available for indexing of files. Yet, its potential use in equipment has been almost unexploited. Only recently have devices appeared which, to any significant extent, have mechanized the concepts of edge-notching. One of these, discussed later, is the CRAM development of National Cash Register.

[2] Claire K. Schultz, Limits of Mechanization for Small Applications, presented before the American Documentation Institute, Lehigh University, October 22–24, 1959.

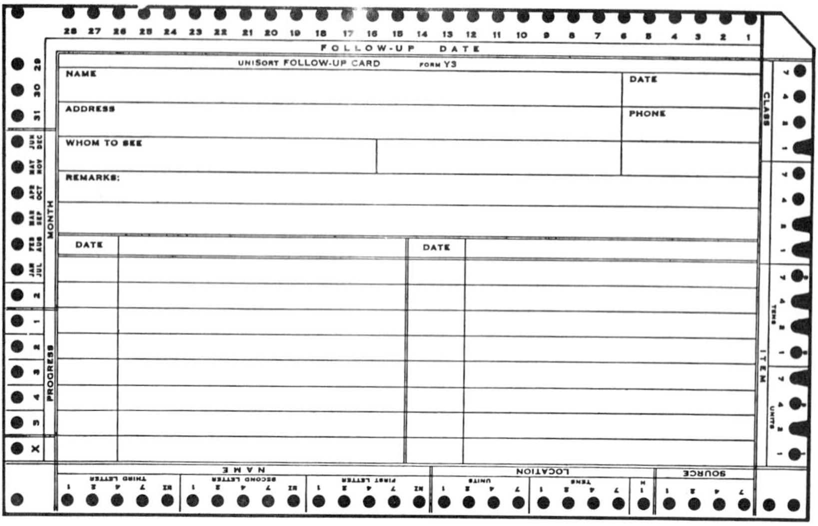

FIG. 33. Edge-notched card.

Edge-notched cards are the subject of an intensive review prepared by Felix Reichman. In it he enumerates the many different kinds of cards in use, traces their historical development, exposes several applications, and describes advantages and disadvantages of each. Appended to his text is a list of worldwide suppliers of marginal punched cards, which constitutes an excellent summary of what is available in the field.[3]

Feature Cards

A third technique of using perforated holes for representation of information is so closely allied to the Uniterm system that it can best be described in terms of it. In this approach, a fixed position on each card is assigned to a particular document number. A perforated hole made at that position will therefore indicate that the document associated with that position is in some way concerned with the term to which the card is related. If two such cards are placed together, the conjunction of holes at any point will indicate that the corresponding document is concerned with the two terms. This feature

---

[3] *The State of the Library Art,* edited by Ralph R. Shaw, v. 4, Part 1, Notched Cards by Felix Reichman, pp. 9–54, New Brunswick, N.J., Graduate School of Library Service, Rutgers—The State University, 1961.

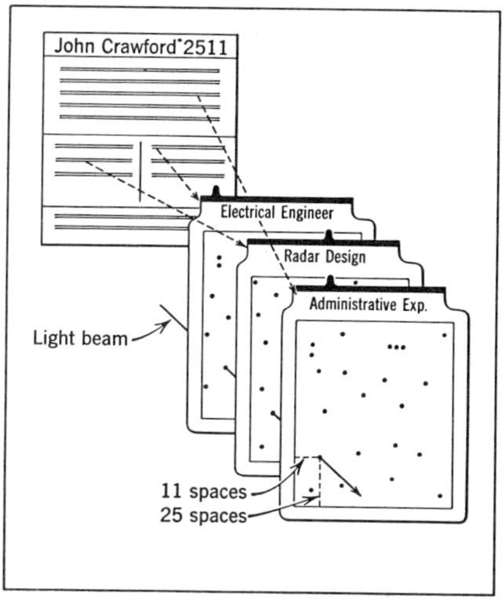

FIG. 34. Termatrex cards. Courtesy Jonker Business Machines, Inc., Gaithersburg, Maryland.

has led to the usage of the name "Peek-a-boo" to describe this technique of storing coordinate index information. The origin of this somewhat undignified term is described as follows by Lawrence S. Thompson.

Some American documentalists have used the rather ludicrous terms of "peek-a-boo," "peekable," or "peephole" for the type of punched card to be discussed in this essay. Other English-speaking documentalists have played with such other terms as "super-imposable," "optical" or "coincidentally" punched cards. Foreign terminology is less uncertain: "fitches superposables" (Fr.), "sichtlochkarten" (Ger.), "titthalkoft" (Sw.), or "onderwerpponskaarten" (Du.). They are also called Cordonnier or Batten cards after two of their leading exponents. The term "feature card" is advocated by J. L. Jolley and J. Edwin Holmstrom. Contrary to other punched card systems that use one card for one document or one item, the feature card system uses one card for one subject, characteristic, aspect, or feature.[4]

Recently there have appeared several semimechanized versions of this approach called Termatrex based on developments by Documentation, Inc., and Jonker Business Machines, Inc. In the Termatrex

[4] *The State of the Library Art,* edited by Ralph R. Shaw, v. 4, Part 2, Feature Cards by Lawrence S. Thompson, pp. 55–100, New Brunswick, N.J., Graduate School of Library Service, Rutgers—The State University, 1961.

systems, there is a Termatrex Card (term card) for every term used in the system, and the serial numbers of the "items" are "punched out" on these cards. For this purpose each card has a numbered position for every item of information. Each item has the same numbered position on every Termatrex Card.

In general, Termatrex systems may have anywhere from 500 to 5000 Termatrex Cards. These cards are kept in open files. To enter an item of information, all the Termatrex Cards describing this item of information are pulled from the file, leaving numbered Removal Markers where cards have been removed. These cards are then placed in superimposition in the Termatrex machine, and a hole is drilled in all cards simultaneously at the numerical position of the item of information that is being entered. The cards are then dropped back in the files at the position of the Removal Markers.

For the search, cards representing the search terms are placed in superposition in the machine. A light source in the base of the machine will show the coinciding holes as light dots. A grid or coordinate system allows the serial number of each light dot to be read off in a few seconds.

Electronic Accounting Machine Punched Cards

All these described usages of punches in cards for the representation of information are essentially manual. But mechanized electronic accounting machine (EAM) systems also use punched cards. Therefore, when approaches were made to the problem of mechanizing information retrieval, immediate consideration was given to the punched cards which had been so successfully exploited in business data handling.

Basically there are two versions of the EAM punched card, versions associated with the two principal American manufacturers of equipment for handling them—the IBM card and the Remington Rand card. The IBM punched card represents information by punches in the face of the card. These punches occur at fixed positions identified by one of 12 rows and one of 80 columns. Thus there are 960 positions at which a punch can be made. For most applications, alphabetic or numeric characters are represented by the combination of punches appearing in a column, and hence the rows of the card are analogous to the channels on punched tape. The Remington-Rand card similarly represents information by punches, but since it uses round holes rather than rectangular ones, there are only 45 columns, for a total of 540 positions. Two characters are usually represented

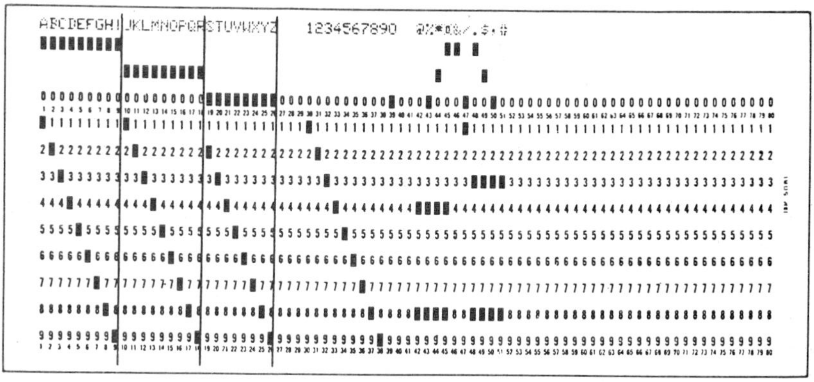

FIG. 35. IBM punched card. Courtesy IBM Corporation, New York, N.Y.

in each column, for a total of 90 characters compared to the 80 stored on an IBM card.

A great variety of equipment has been developed for handling these cards, for sorting them, for collating and merging sets of them, for reproducing them, for tabulating and printing the information from them. For the purposes of information retrieval, some specialized devices based on the same general principles as the other card-handling equipment have been built. In Chapter 6 we described the 9900 Special Index Analyzer, a machine of this type. It illustrates the basic principles of virtually all EAM punched card systems.

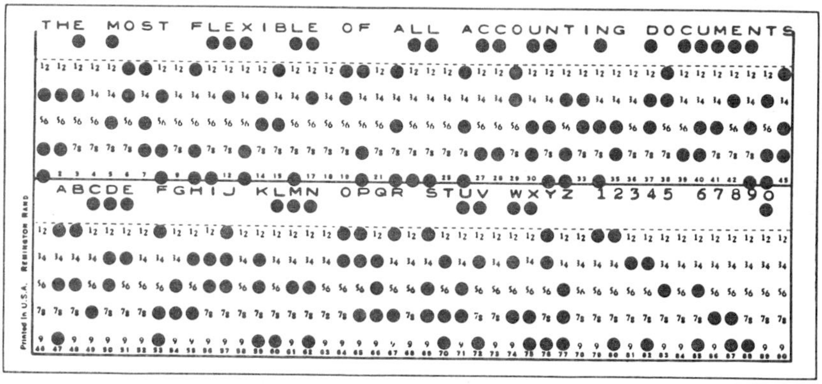

FIG. 36. Remington Rand card. Courtesy UNIVAC Division of Sperry Rand, Los Angeles, Calif.

Probably the earliest large-scale EAM punched card indexing system was that developed by the Central Intelligence Agency as an index and aid to the operation of their Intellofax system. In this use of punched cards, each card contained a set of subject and area codes in punched form identifying the coverage of a document, together with a preprinted abstract to be copied for presentation to the requestor. The file of these punched cards was arranged in sequence by associated area.

The CIA system is described as follows:

> The classified documents are received from scores of different major sources, the daily volume fluctuates and lacks uniformity in format, in reproduction media, in length and quality of presentation, and in security classification. As they come in they must be read with an eye to identifying material of interest to the many different customer receipt points; those which have future retrieval value (approximately 50%) must be indexed and stored in such manner as to provide retrieval pertinent to customer needs. This material is subject to control through IBM cards.
>
> These IBM card files now contain over 40 million cards. Since 1954 we have been miniaturizing the documents by microphotography and mounting them in apertures on IBM punched cards. Access to the document itself is indirect, through codes punched into the cards to indicate subject, area, source, security classification, date and number of each document. The data on cards retrieved in response to a particular request is reproduced by photographic means in tape form and constitutes the bibliography given the customer. This system, which we instituted in 1947 (using microfilm strips rather than aperture cards prior to 1954 and facsimile rather than photo tape prior to 1959), we call the Intellofax system; it represents pioneer work in the field of information storage and retrieval.[5]

Selection of documents relevant to a request for a desired set of subject and area codes was made by use of the Collator for relatively simple searches or of the 101 Statistical Sorter for the requests with more complicated logical combinations of codes.

A somewhat different approach to the use of punched cards as an aid to indexing has been adopted by Los Angeles County Library, Los Angeles, California, and King County, Washington. For several years they have each been preparing book catalogs of their holdings

---

[5] Documentation, Indexing, and Retrieval of Scientific Information. A Study of Federal and Non-Federal Science Information Processing and Retrieval Programs. Committee on Government Operations, U.S. Senate, 86th Congress, 2nd Session, Document No. 113, Government Printing Office, Washington, D.C., 1961, pp. 63–64.

through the use of punched card sorting and tabulating equipment. A number of cards are prepared for each title. Each contains author, title, and other bibliographic data (along with a brief one-line description of content) in punched form. New cards are sorted by major subject coverage, by title, and by author and then are merged into their respective existing files. At periodic intervals the files are tabulated to produce a multilith offset master for each page; from this, several hundred copies of a complete book catalog are printed and distributed to the various branch libraries. A similar although somewhat different approach has been adopted by the Library of the State of New York.

These examples are representative of the type of application to which punched card equipment has been put. In the case of the CIA operation and the library book catalogs, extremely large files have been indexed by using EAM punched cards. Examples of similar files of varying sizes could also be cited. Ralph Blasingame, in his history of machine-sorted punched cards, provides a framework for judging applications in terms of the library functions for which they were employed. He describes applications of machine-sorted punched cards to such library processes as circulation, acquisitions and accounting, analysis of book stock, serial acquisition and control, catalogs, shelf listing, and, finally, literature searching. In his conclusion he points out that reliable standards of measurement have not yet been established and pertinent data not yet collected with sufficient care to permit one to reconstruct accurately either cost or performance information in any given instance.[6]

In general, however, useful though the punched card has been in business data processing, and as a preliminary stage in the development of information retrieval systems, it appears to be unsuitable for any real mechanization in this field. Fundamentally, its density of storage is too low; it is not erasable and thus the information cannot be changed; and its information transfer rate is too slow. Even in business data processing, the punched card is being increasingly replaced by magnetic tape as the storage medium for files, although it will continue to find its principal application in the field of transaction recording, where its unit physical record character is of predominant importance.

[6] *The State of the Library Art,* edited by Ralph R. Shaw, v. 4, Part 3, Punched Cards by Ralph Blasingame, Jr., pp. 101–136, New Brunswick, N.J., Graduate School of Library Service, Rutgers—The State University, 1961.

MAGNETIC RECORDING

The need for a high-density data storage medium which would provide a high information transfer rate has been a driving force in the data processing business. The potentialities of magnetic recording at a very early date were recognized as the most likely to provide an effective answer. Recording of information in magnetic form has therefore been a key part of the entire development of electronic data processing equipment.

Magnetic recording is based on the fundamental relation between magnetism and electricity. Thus, if an electrical current is passed through a wire wrapped around a small "u" shaped bar, called a "writing head," a magnetic field will be created at the "gap" in the "u" which can be used to fix the magnetic state in a magnetizable surface. On the other hand, if a magnetized medium is passed by a similar (or the same) "u" shaped bar, now called a "reading head," an electrical current will be generated in the wire. On this basic relationship the entire field of magnetic recording has developed, including that of audio signals, analog data, digital information, and video pictures.

To record digital information in this way, the appropriate binary codes are represented by a corresponding sequence of two different voltages in the electrical current through the wire. The result is an identical sequence of magnetic fields and a resulting sequence of magnetically polarized spots on the storage medium as it moves under the recording head. In the reading operation, the process is reversed, and as the recording medium passes under the reading head, the succession of magnetic spots generates a corresponding succession of voltages in the wire. These are then interpreted by the logical circuitry to develop the binary coded representation of the information.

The density at which the binary coded data can be stored is described by the number of "bits to the inch" in the direction of recording and the number of "channels to the inch" across the recording medium. The densities possible in each case are determined by a number of considerations. The most fundamental of these is the basic geometry defined by the size of gap in the reading head and the distance from the gap to the recording surface. The smaller these two distances, the finer the resolution and therefore the higher the density possible; in fact, "contact" recording, with essentially zero spacing between head and surface, is standard for magnetic tape, and densities of perhaps 500 bits to the inch are not uncommon.

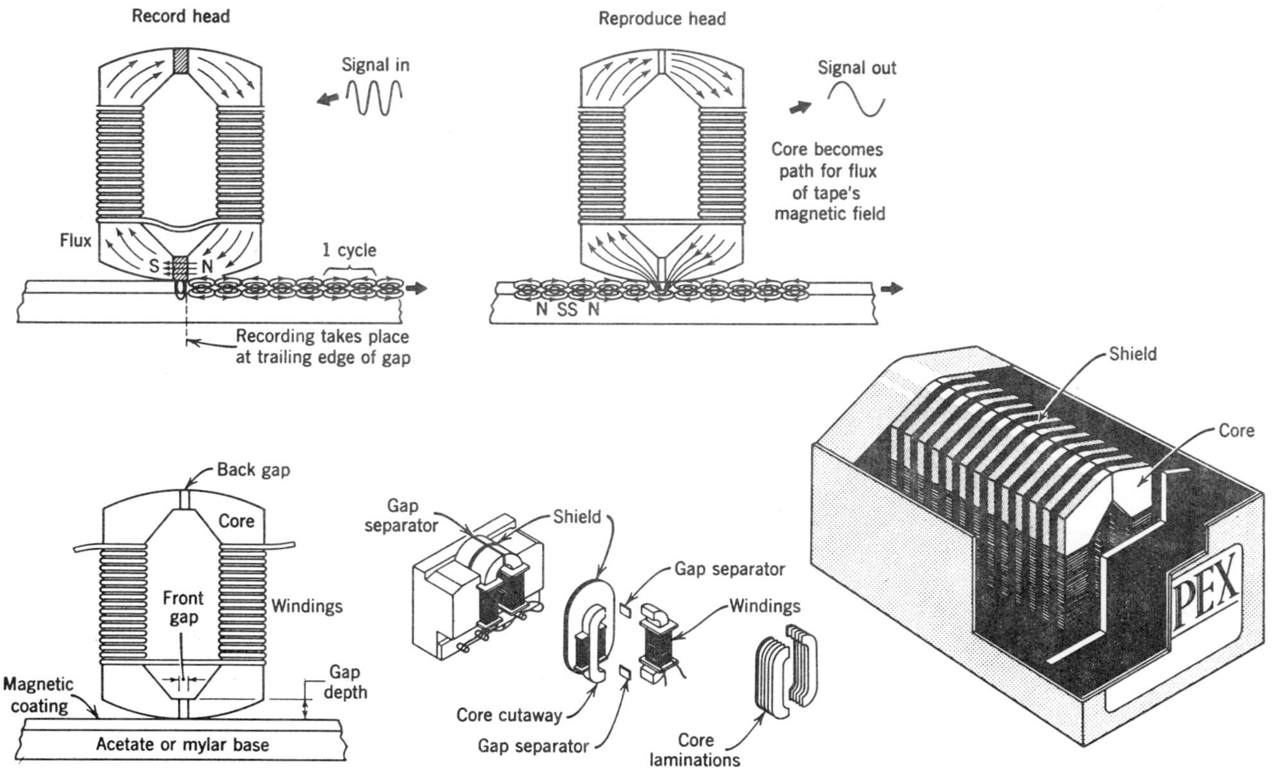

FIG. 37. Principles of magnetic recording. Courtesy Ampex Corp., Redwood City, Calif.

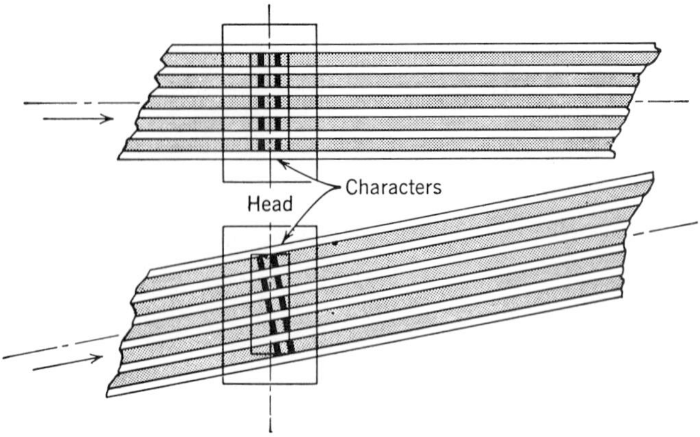

FIG. 38. Error caused by tape skew.

Another fundamental consideration is the speed at which the storage medium is moved past the reading head; the higher the speed, the stronger the signal generated and therefore the better the resolution possible. This results from the fact that the strength of the signal generated in a reading head is directly proportional to the rate at which the magnetic field on the storage medium passes by the head. In general, the signal level is on the order of perhaps $^{30}/_{1000}$ of a volt, and therefore the signal is at best difficult to distinguish

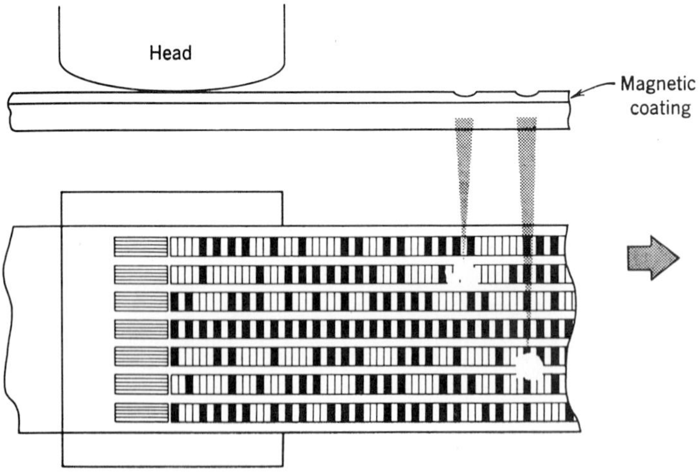

FIG. 39. Effect of drop-outs in digital recording.

from the background "noise" in the electrical circuit itself. At lower speeds and correspondingly lower voltages, dust particles, imperfections in the tape, and other sources of error could easily obscure the signal completely.

To record other than digital data, such as audio, video, and other analog information, the same techniques are involved, but different measures of storage density must be used (and fundamentally even digital storage densities must be considered in the same light). These considerations are expressed in terms of the available "bandwidth" measured in "cycles per second," which combine in a single measure the storage density and the transport rate. Typical audio magnetic tape recording provides a bandwidth on the order of 20,000 cycles per second; present video magnetic tape recording provides 5 to 10 million cycles per second. Measured in somewhat the same framework, digital magnetic tape recording presently provides up to 150,000 bits per second from each channel, which can be considered as the equivalent of perhaps 500,000 cycles per second.

Magnetic Drums

In certain respects the simplest physical medium for the recording of magnetic information is a cylindrical drum coated with material which will retain magnetic polarity. Such drums are rotated at extremely high speeds, limited only by the physical properties of the drum, so that the size of the signal will be correspondingly large. The reading and recording heads are placed in fixed positions close to the surface of the drum as it rotates under them. Each recording head will generate a "channel" of information. Most drum systems are limited by physical boundary conditions to a drum diameter of between 3 and 24 inches and to perhaps 100 channels. As we have indicated, the density at which information can be recorded is a function of the distance between the reading head and the drum surface; the smaller this distance, the higher the density. Most drum systems utilize a half mil (thousandth of an inch) spacing to provide typical densities on the order of 100 to 200 bits per inch.

One situation illustrates the type of application for which drum systems may prove suitable. In 1959 the Magnavox Company developed a specialized drum storage system for the U.S. Air Force. Its purpose was to provide a dissemination control device as an adjunct to the Minicard system. Standing requests for documents were stored on the drum as combinations of subject and area codes desired by the requesting agencies. The associated processing logic, in the

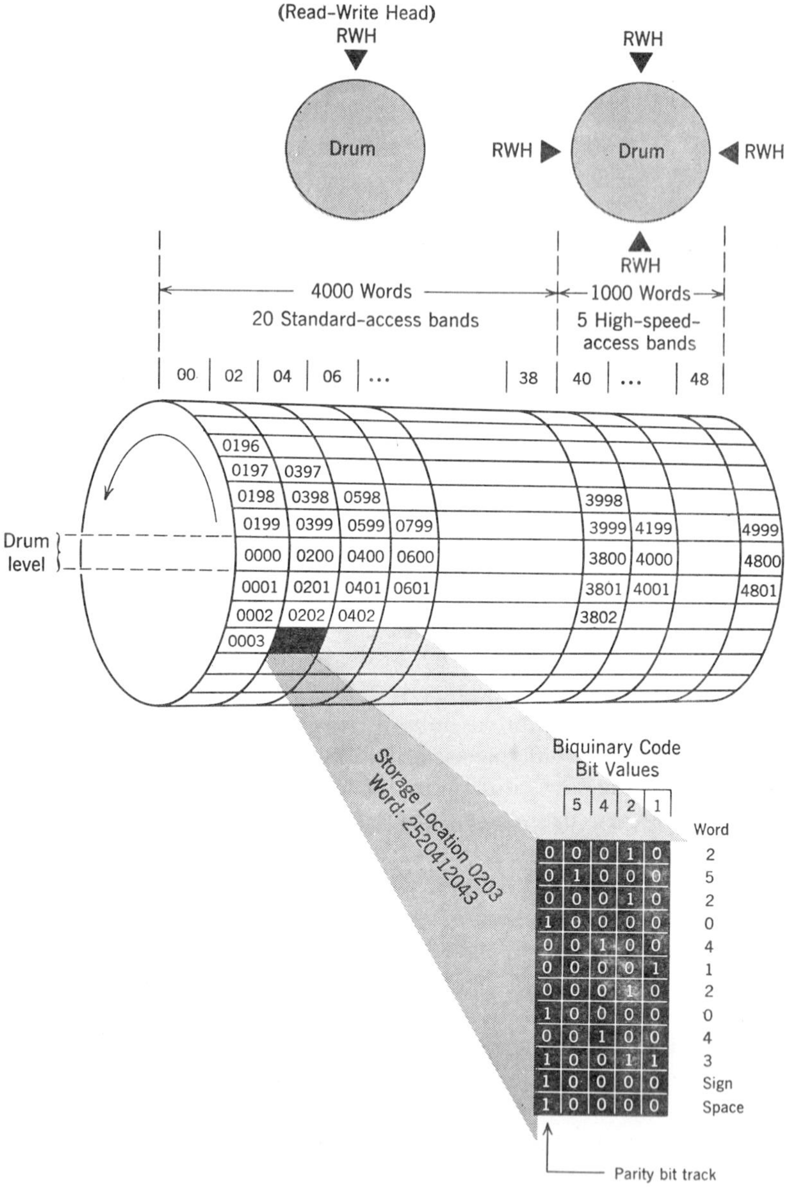

FIG. 40. Magnetic drum addressing. Courtesy UNIVAC Division of Sperry Rand, Los Angeles, Calif.

form of a general purpose computer with a specially designed program, compared descriptions of document content against the stored requests. The resulting matches between requests and documents resulted in control of the dissemination of the documents to the agencies.

For such applications, drums may be superior to other possible mechanizations. However, drums are relatively unsuitable for any large capacity storage, since they are limited to, generally speaking, less than one million bits (the equivalent of perhaps 150,000 alphabetic characters). Hence drums are probably not useful for the storage of large files and are unlikely to be significant in the solution of information retrieval problems.

Magnetic Tape

Magnetic tape, on the other hand, represents an almost ideal file storage medium. Information is stored on magnetic tape in channels, much as with punched tape, but in magnetic form so it can be erased and can be stored at much higher densities. Present magnetic tapes generally have up to 8 channels across a ½ inch tape and store at a density of up to 500 bits to the inch, utilizing contact recording. A typical reel of 2400 feet of magnetic tape may thus contain over 100 million bits of information, the equivalent of 12 million alphabetic characters. The tape handling devices transport the tape at high speed (200 to 300 inches per second) past the reading and recording head. The information transfer rate is fantastically high, in some cases over 100,000 characters per second. The entire reel of 12 million alphabetic characters can be completely scanned in less than three minutes.

In the great majority of the experiments in highly mechanized systems described in Chapter 6, magnetic tape played a predominant role. It is the basic file medium for virtually every major computer; it provides the efficient storage and high-speed transfer rate desired; it is erasable, so the stored data can be changed; its use has been well developed in both numerical computation and business data processing. Magnetic tape will probably continue for some time to be the mainstay in both general purpose and special purpose computer systems in the field of information retrieval.

In most of the work done to date in utilizing magnetic tape, the techniques of digital recording have been utilized. However, the potential of video recording for storage of document images has been recognized. RCA recently proposed a "Video File" based on their video magnetic tape recording methods. Video File is a system which

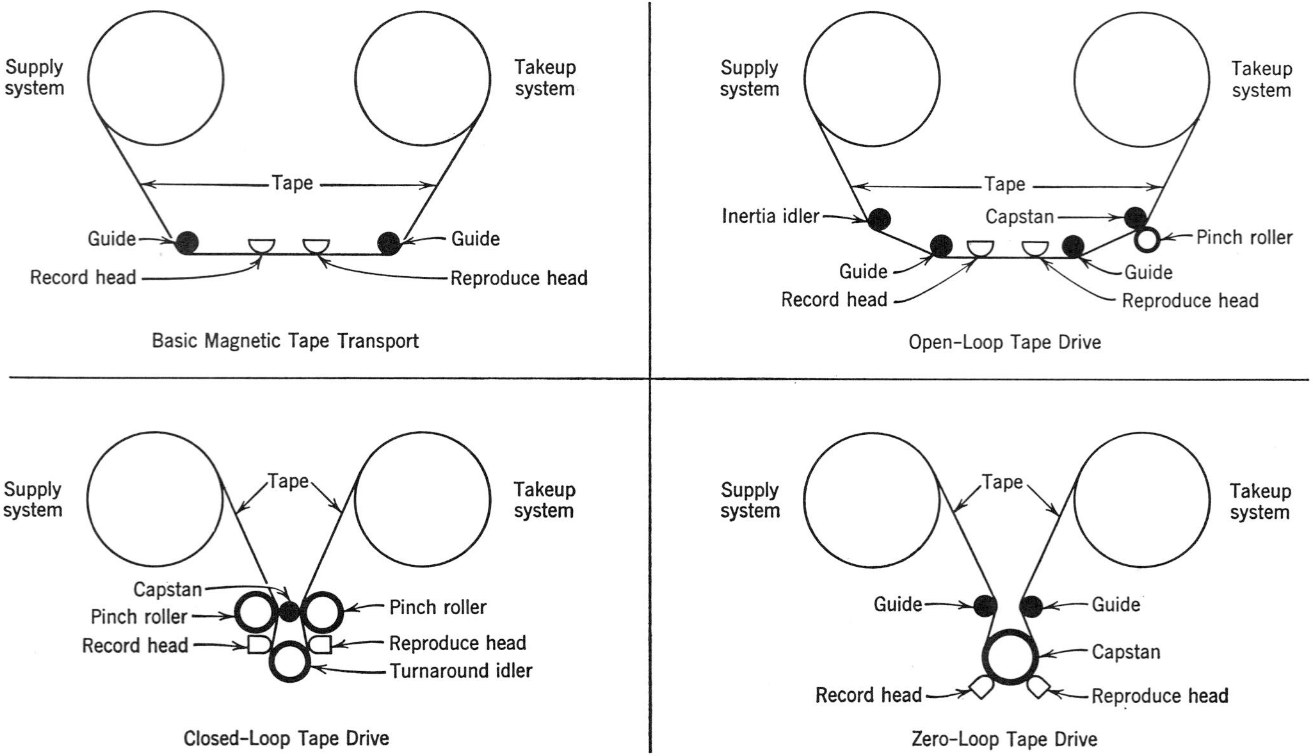

FIG. 41. Magnetic tape. Courtesy Ampex Corp., Redwood City, Calif.

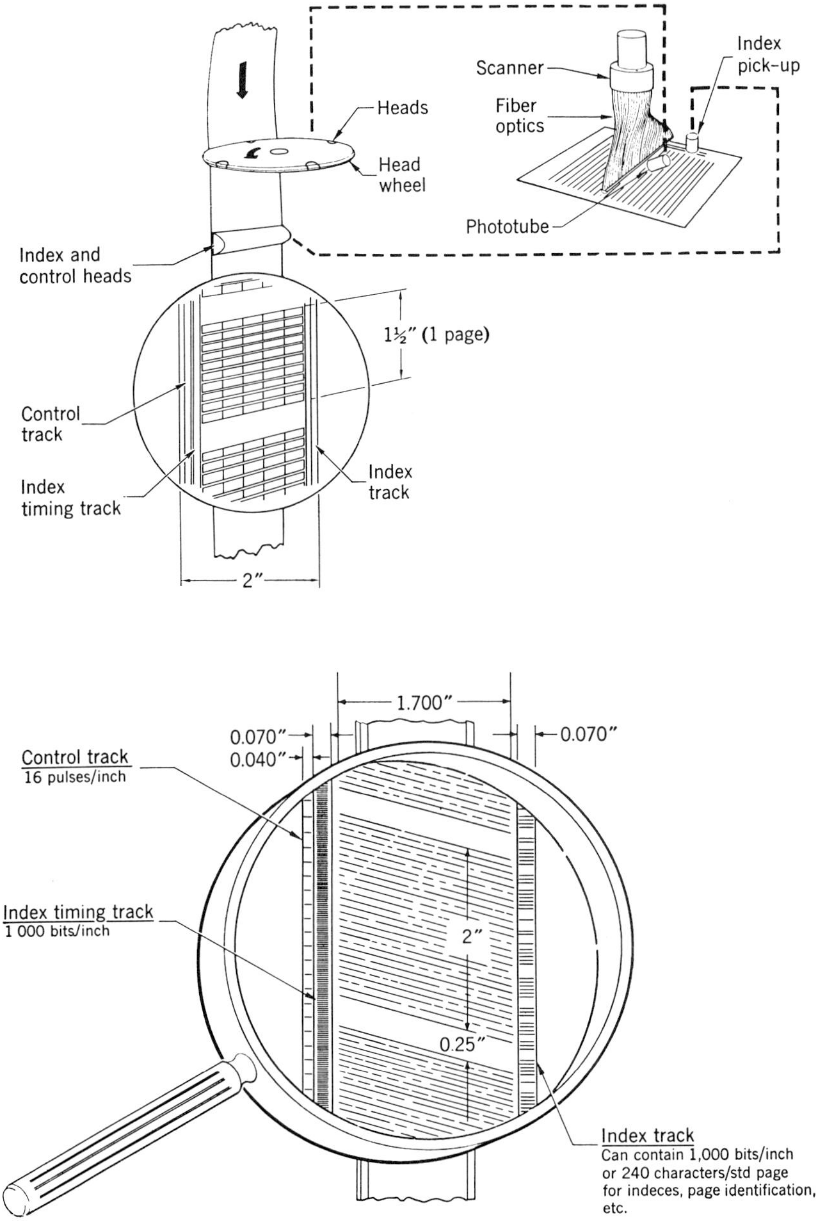

FIG. 42. Video file. Courtesy RCA, Van Nuys, Calif.

employs television recording techniques in the storage of pictorial data. The unique capability of RCA Video File is that it can store and retrieve information regardless of the nature of the data whether it be maps, charts, typewritten or handwritten, colored or black and white. The present system does not provide facility for reproduction of colored material; rather it processes colored material and reproduces it in black and white without half tones. The RCA Video File system is most efficiently utilized in those applications where there is a requirement to maintain a document facsimile file with the facility to update any or all of the documents in the file.

The system is comprised of six modular components—Camera, Recorder, Merge Control Unit, Status & Switching Panel, Electrofax Printer, and Document Reader. The automatic camera contains paper handling equipment and a flying spot scanner which develops a video signal for the recorder. The tape recorder-reproducer is capable of handling 7200 feet of standard 2 inch video tape on 14 inch reels with a capacity of 36,000 8½″ x 11″ pages. This unit provides for recording both video and digital data and has a capability for a high-speed search in either direction at 300 inches per second and a record and reproduce speed of two frames per second. The electrofax printer is driven from a video signal derived from the recorder and supplies 8½″ x 11″ printed pages at the rate of two pages per second in either cut sheet or roll form. The merge control unit is a device used to simultaneously address and control two recorder units during the process of merging information on one tape to another. The capability of selectively erasing and replacing one single frame of video data is provided. Another major component of the RCA Video File system is the status and switching panel whereby the status of each equipment is indicated and provisions are made for interconnecting all system components. There is also provided as standard equipment a document reader which is used to display any document obtained in roll form from the electrofax printer. The reader is capable of being incremented by one document in the forward or backward direction as well as a high speed search through the paper roll.

However, even at the storage densities and information transfer rates available with magnetic tape, if conventional library card catalog practice or virtually any other technique of file organization were to be duplicated, it would consume a great deal of space on the tape and increase the scanning time for any given correlative search. In fact, the character of most tape systems is that no file organization would significantly improve access times to individual items, since on continuous tape the scan time for a single search varies only with the size or length of the tape. This has led to the development of completely different physical storage media to permit direct location of a single index record or groups of similar records without having to scan the entire file. This capability would find its greatest advantage where file organization can be made to fit usage needs.

Magnetic Disks

An indexed or "random access" memory of the magnetic disk type now is a feature of several electronic data processing systems. In such memories, every unit record is stored in its own addressable location. Thus the information need not be scanned and compared in order to find a particular record. All that is required is the address which uniquely locates the desired index record.

These memories store information on the surface of disks coated with magnetic material and rotating at extremely high speeds. Typically, such a disk will be from 2 to 4 feet in diameter and store the binary coded information in perhaps 100 concentric channels across the surface of the disk. In most cases several disks are stacked, one parallel to the other (as in "juke box" record players), but physically separated so that the magnetic reading and recording head can be physically moved from one disk to another and from one recording channel to another. The movement of the head is controlled by an addressing mechanism which determines, from the disk and channel identification supplied to it, the physical position to which the head must be moved.

Best known of these disk-type memories is the IBM Ramac disk unit which consists of 50 disks, each containing 100 channels with a capacity of 6000 bits, for a total capacity of 30 million bits or 5 million alphabetic characters. The time for the reading and recording head to move from a channel on one of the disks to a randomly located channel on another disk is approximately ½ second. Other, similar units are sold by RCA, Bryant, Telex, Laboratory for Electronics, Autonetics, and Aeronutronics. Although each approaches the problem of indexing in a slightly different manner, thereby providing different capacity and access rate characteristics, they are all fundamentally similar approaches to the mass data storage problem.

To illustrate the application of such a memory to the problems

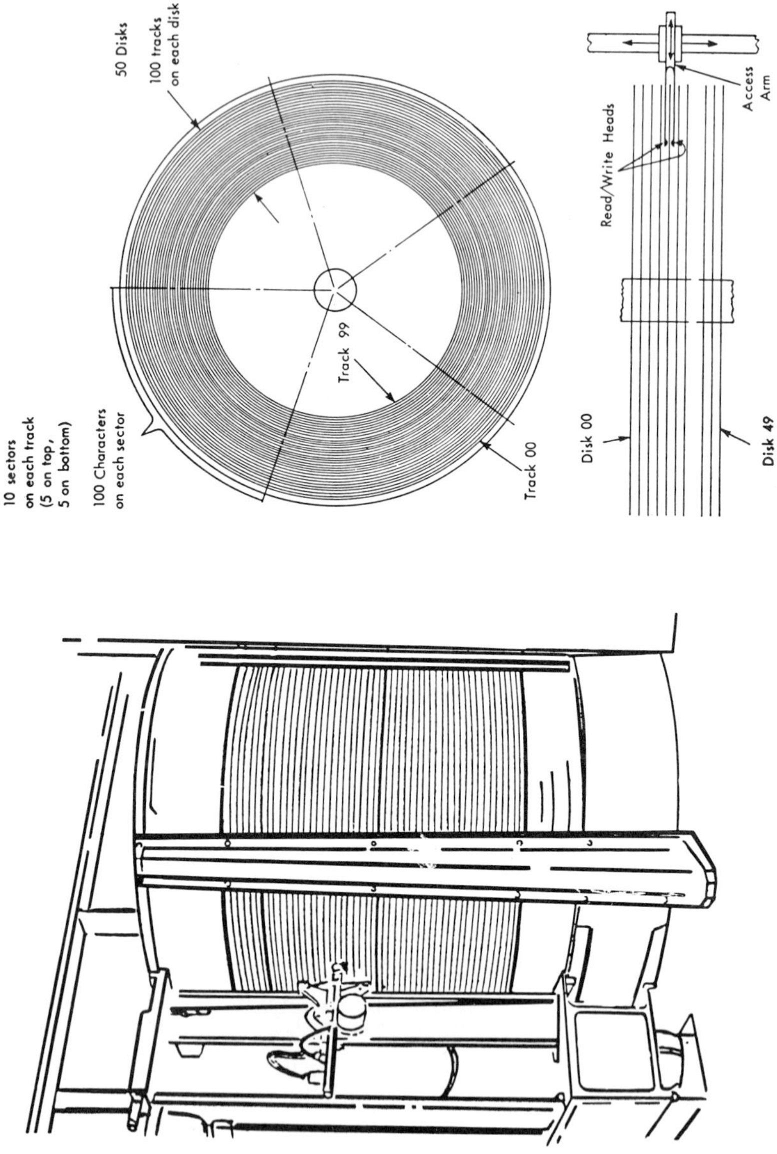

FIG. 43. Disk memory. Courtesy IBM Corporation, New York, N.Y.

of information retrieval, experiments were conducted by J. J. Nolan[7] and F. E. Firth[8] of IBM. They thought of the Ramac disk file as separated into three sections. The first was a dictionary of the index terms used in the system, each with its respective address. The second section contained the coordinate index term records of their pertinent document serial numbers. The third section contained the bibliographical reference data in the form of document titles, each of which was addressable by the number found as the result of a coordinate index search in the second disk section.

During input, new entries were checked against the dictionary section for editing of new index terms. Then the document serial numbers were automatically entered under the appropriate index terms in section two and, as part of the same operation, the new titles were entered into the bibliography section. During search, the machine first determined the addresses of the index terms involved from section one; then it went directly to these addresses. Based on the logic of the request, it performed the necessary comparison operations. This resulted in matches which yielded addresses found in section three. Finally, the pertinent records in section three were printed out as a bibliography of titles which satisfied the request pattern.

Nolan compared continuous tape to the single-entry system of bookkeeping and the random access memory system to double-entry ledger accounts. In the IBM experiment conducted at the San Jose Research Laboratory in collaboration with the Technical Library there, the 305 Ramac was found to be mechanically sound for the purpose, but the reliability and completeness of any search, as with most other systems, were found to be wholly dependent on the quality of the human indexing and the effectiveness of the decision process for compatibility of index and search terms.

The disk type addressed access approach has a great deal of appeal, and certainly where usage is well defined it provides an extremely powerful approach to replacement of scanning by indexing. However, the problems in providing the item address so essential to the functioning of the unit must be recognized. Essentially, they all are a result of the fact that, since scanning in a disk memory is an almost impossibly expensive operation, any utilization must depend on an index of some form and therefore must have been anticipated by the

---

[7] J. J. Nolan, Principles of Information Storage and Retrieval Using a Large Scale Random Access Memory, IBM, San Jose, Calif., November 17, 1958.

[8] F. E. Firth, An Experiment in Literature Searching with the IBM 305 RAMAC, IBM, San Jose, Calif., November 17, 1958.

organizer of the file. The methods for resolving this basic difficulty are many and are of varied utility, but none of them will succeed unless the activity is suitably restricted.

Magnetic Cards and Strips

As we have indicated, magnetic tape must be searched essentially in its entirety in order to locate a particular address or to compare combinations of data. Furthermore, computer processing of continuous tape is comparatively slow when called on to perform routine data processing operations, such as sorting, merging, matching, and filing. It was natural, then, for companies to consider using magnetic cards or strips as physically discrete media for storing information.

Magnacard, a development of the Magnavox Company, is one such development which, although it has never been used for an actual index file operation, does represent a technical concept with excellent potential application.[9] Essentially, this unitized tape development is based on the premise that card handling equipment can do a file processing job cheaper and can make searches faster than can a general purpose, electronic data processing machine utilizing magnetic tape.

The system uses magnetic recording of information on discrete pieces of magnetic tape. The unit storage medium is a magnetic card, 1″ x 3″, with a storage capacity in excess of 5000 bits (about 1000 decimal digits or 800 alpha-numeric characters). Information is recorded on 18 parallel channels at densities of 100 bits per linear inch, using standard magnetic reading and recording techniques.

Routine handling functions and file searches are accomplished by moving the card containing the information rather than by moving the information itself. The card transport equipment is basically pneumatic and consists of a relatively few mechanical elements—a vacuum transport drum, an automatically reversible card feeding and stacking station, a drum-to-drum transfer device, a card holding station. By combinations of these elements, handling devices can be assembled which provide for various routine card rearrangements, such as sorting, merging, and searching. The transport rate in all operations is 100 cards per second.

Large files of cards are handled by storing the cards in magazines and the magazines in file mechanisms that provide addressed access

---

9 R. M. Hayes and A. Nelson, Magnacard—A New Concept in Data Handling, *IRE Wescon Convention Record,* Part 4, 1957.

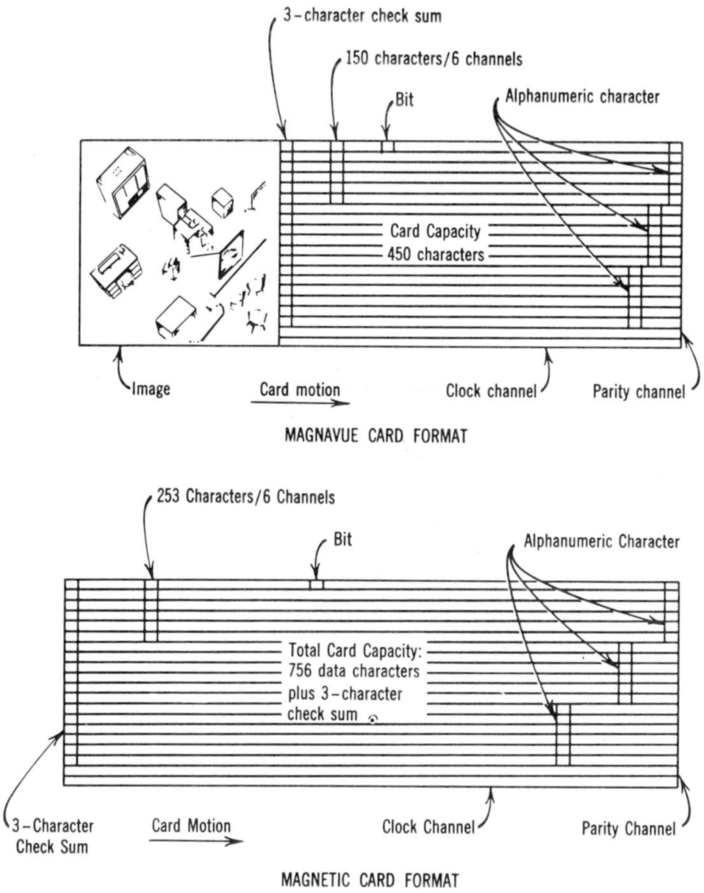

FIG. 44. Magnetic card format. Courtesy Magnavox, Ft. Wayne, Ind.

to individual magazines which can then automatically be brought to a card handler. Present Magnacard files utilize magazines with a capacity of 3000 cards and can automatically provide any single magazine in about 5 seconds. At the handling rate of 100 cards per second, the average time to scan an indexed magazine is then 15 seconds. Other files which provide smaller magazines or other indexed blocks of cards with correspondingly reduced scan times have been considered, but as yet no such equipment has been built.

The entire face of the card need not necessarily be used for recording index information in the form of magnetic code. Instead the card could be designed in two sections, one part for code and the other

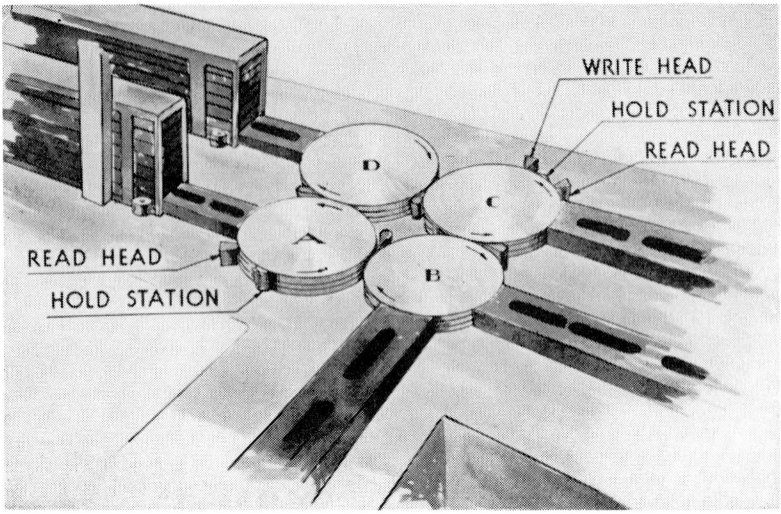

FIG. 45. Magnacard collator. Courtesy Magnavox, Ft. Wayne, Ind.

for image. Magnavox recently announced this design configuration under the tradename "Magnavue." Experimental cards of this type are reported to present no special handling problems. Similarly, the reverse side of the card could be used for additional recording of information, say in video signal form, in order to facilitate the remote display of data once searched and selected by the regular equipment configuration.

A more recent development, by the National Cash Register Company, is called CRAM (Card Random Access Mechanism) which similarly uses unitized tape for the storage medium, although in this case the card is much larger.[10] Each card is 14 inches long by 3¼ inches wide. Data are recorded on the magnetic card in 56 parallel channels divided into 7 sets of 8 channels, each set being treated as the counterpart of a magnetic tape, with the bits for each individual character recorded in parallel. Successive characters are recorded sequentially at a density of 250 bits to the inch. The total capacity of the card is over 160,000 bits; of a file of 256 cards, over 40 million bits. The information transfer from a single set of 8 channels is at the rate of

[10] Large Capacity Memory Techniques for Computing Systems, National Cash Register Company, Hawthorne, Calif., Tech. Pub. No. 4394 (see A. M. Angel, The NCR Magnetic Card Random Access Memory).

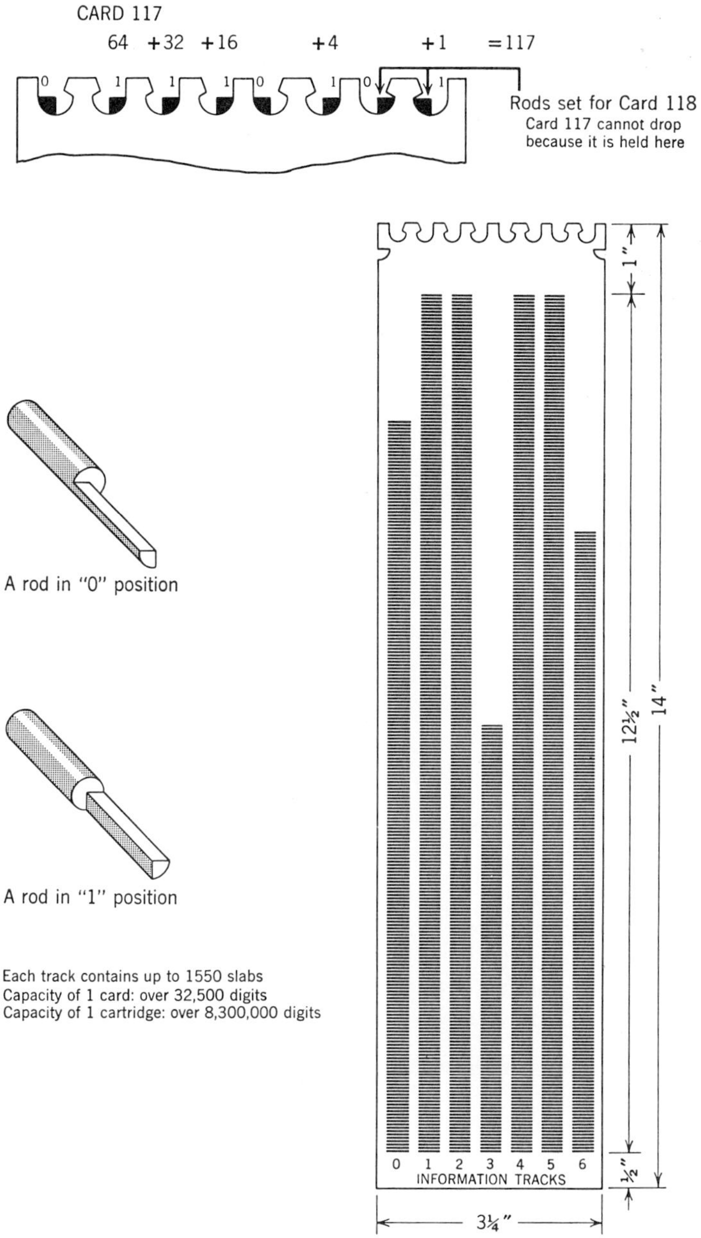

FIG. 46. CRAM card. Courtesy National Cash Register Co., Dayton, Ohio.

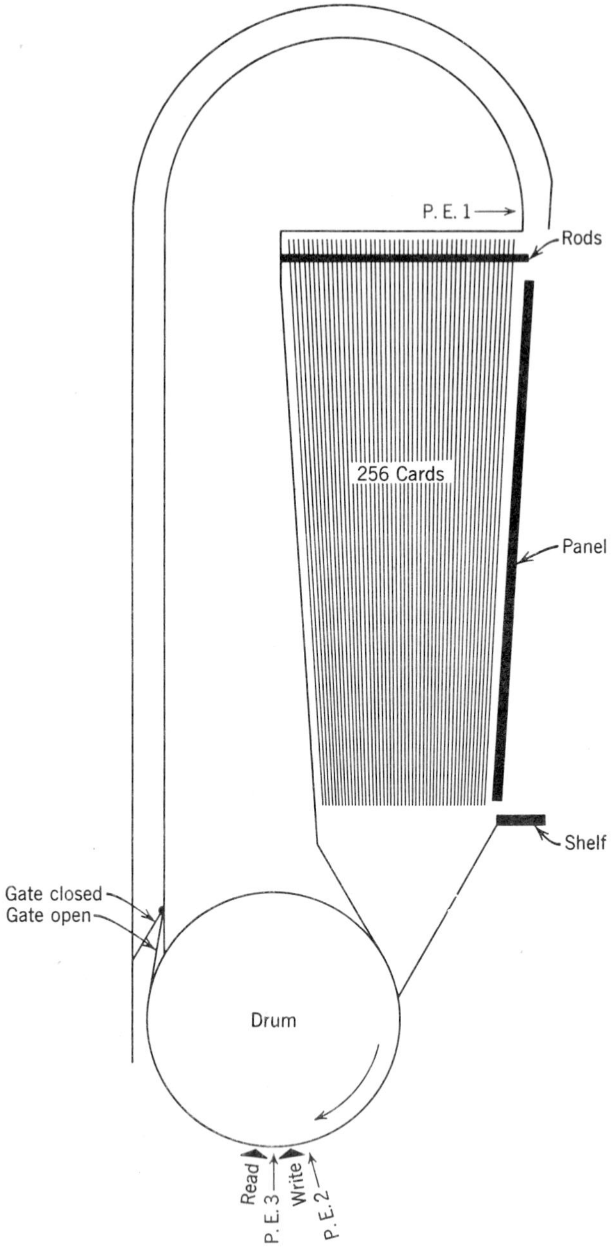

FIG. 47. CRAM handling unit. Courtesy National Cash Register Co., Dayton, Ohio.

100,000 characters per second. This is accomplished in blocks of 1470 characters, 2 such blocks being located along the length of the card.

The cards are stored in a magnetic card unit, which contains 256 cards at a time. They are suspended by 8 binary coded rods which pass through notches at the end of each card. Through edge-notched selection, by automatically setting the rods to a binary coded value from 000 through 255, any desired card from the set can be chosen for reading or recording. Cards can be successively selected, read, and returned to the file at the rate of approximately 5 cards per second.

Another approach to physical access so as to reduce the size of the block which must be scanned is the Burroughs Data File. This device stores information on magnetic tape strips, each of which is 250 feet long. The Data File unit contains 50 separate such strips and a reading head which can be positioned to any one of them. Information is stored in each strip in 12 channels at a density of 100 bits per inch.

The average time to locate an individual record from a random location in the file includes time to move the head to the appropriate strip and to scan that strip until the record of interest is located.

FIG. 48. CRAM unit in NCR 315 system. Courtesy National Cash Register Co., Dayton, Ohio.

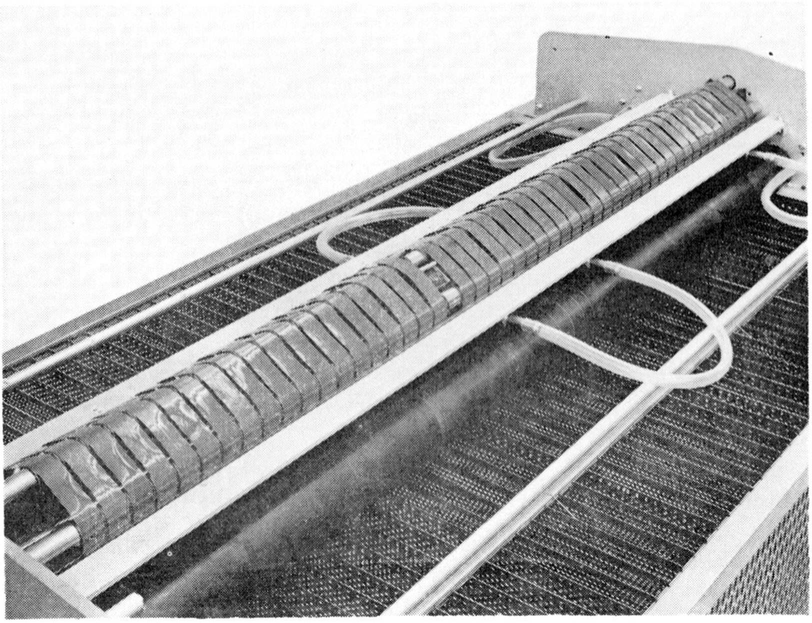

FIG. 49. Burroughs Data File. Courtesy Burroughs Corporation, Detroit, Mich.

The average random time for head movement is approximately one second and the average time to scan a single strip an additional 15 seconds; thus the average access time in a data file with a capacity of approximately 20 million characters is roughly one tenth that for a magnetic tape of approximately the same capacity.

One additional development, which attempts to provide the same type of capability, is the Facit "Carousel" memory [11] which takes an average of two seconds random access time to a record in a file of approximately 20 million bits. This device also uses tape strips, but they are 28 feet long and store data in 8 channels across the tape. These strips are stored in little spindles located around the periphery of a circular disk. To locate a desired item, the disk is turned to bring the spindle of interest to the reading head and the tape is then pulled past the reading head for the scanning operation.

Each of these systems represents a compromise between the problems and advantages of, on the one hand, scanning and, on the other,

[11] Etienne J. Guerin, International Conference on Information Processing, *Datamation,* July–August 1959, pp. 6–9.

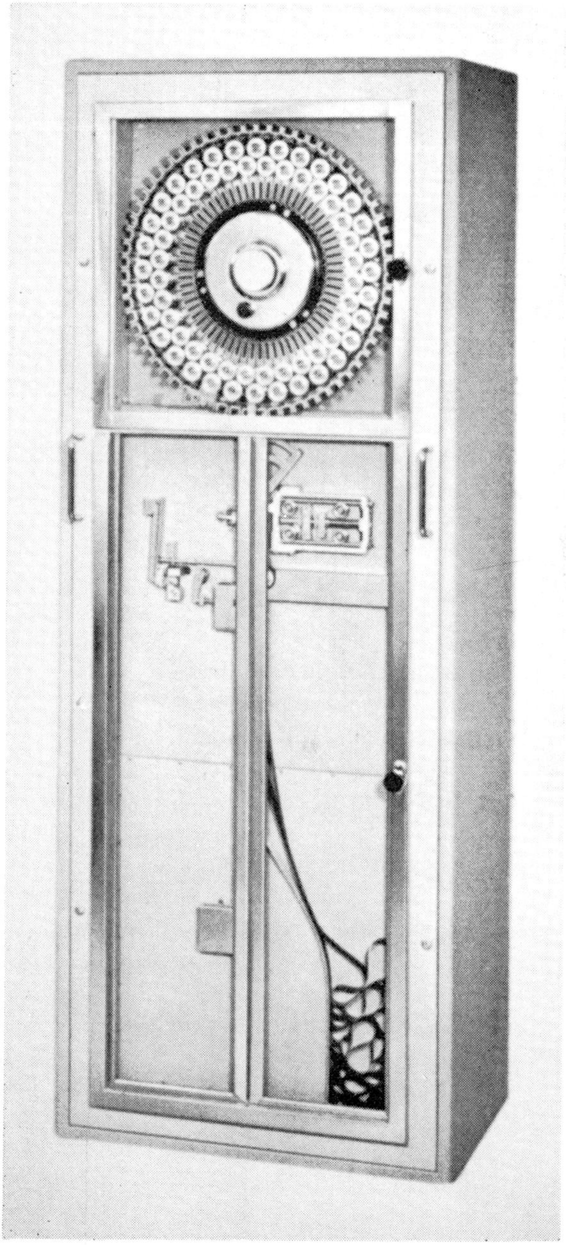

FIG. 50. Facit carousel memory.

physical indexing. In this sense they represent various points along a spectrum which, in fact, includes not only them but magnetic tapes and disks as well. Thus tapes are at one end of the spectrum, with a large unit capacity, and a long scan time (perhaps 25 million characters requiring an average scan of 100 seconds). The tape bin and the Magnacard systems substitute some degree of addressed accessing time and provide for scanning a smaller block of data (on the order of perhaps 500,000 to 2,500,000 characters requiring an average scan time of 15 seconds). The CRAM and the Carousel systems index to much smaller blocks of data (on the order of 100,000 characters requiring perhaps $\frac{1}{5}$ second of scanning time). At the far end of the spectrum are the disk-type memories which index to extremely small blocks of data (100 characters with a negligible scan time of perhaps $\frac{1}{30}$ second).

However, although all these approaches can be regarded as different points in a spectrum, to do so would hide some significant qualitative differences in the way they are used. This is particularly borne out by the way in which each of the manufacturers concerned with the card or strip approach has been led into consideration of "activity" organized files. It is almost as though the particular range of parameters involved with cards and strips has made evident the time and cost advantages in fitting the file organization to the statistical character of usage, that is, in these approaches the time for scanning a block of data is small enough (unlike magnetic tape) so that random access methods can be reasonably considered but large enough (unlike magnetic disks) so that the time in doing so cannot be ignored.

Activity organization therefore attempts to reduce the average scan time in an indexed block by taking advantage of the existing patterns of record reference. Thus, where a small percentage of records represent a large percentage of the activity, by placing the active records where they will be readily accessible, the average access, in terms of the activity, will be substantially reduced. This approach provides significant insight into the entire theoretical foundation of file organization.

MICROPHOTOGRAPHY

The document file provides the source material referred to by the index. Normally it contains copies of the documentation either in original hard-copy form or as a collection of microcopies. The character of the source material will vary from full-length documents to abstracts and digests. In all cases, however, the document file includes more printed information than is worth storing in the index.

Machine research in this area is threefold. It aims (1) to achieve more compact storage of the source material, (2) to provide rapid access to it, and (3) to display it or make it available in suitable form for use. The RCA Video File and similar developments in magnetic tape image recording represent one approach now in its preliminary experimental stage. However, the outstanding technological achievement associated with the document file has been the introduction of microphotography. This technique greatly compresses information without alteration of information content. Its impact on file storage as well as on research methodology has been revolutionary.

Microphotography is a general technique covering the use of any opaque or transparent carrier of a miniaturized permanent message, including microfilm, microfiche, film strips, film inserts, and many others. The possibility for producing miniature images is the result of developments in photographic emulsions with almost unbelievably high resolutions. The most spectacular of these are some of the silver halides, processing resolving power greater than 2000 lines per mm or potential information storage capacity over 3 billion bits per square inch.

The diazo and Kalvar dry copy processes mentioned in Chapter 5 are also applicable to film. Since the coatings in each process can be applied to a mylar base, it is possible to obtain suitable positive and negative microimages on film stock for storage. That both processes are dry gives them an important advantage over the silver halide family of films, which still require chemical development and fixing. Diazo and Kalvar films are quick, dry, and offer acceptable resolution characteristics for many applications. It is important then to point out that when the word film or microfilm is used, it actually embraces a variety of processes and not just the silver halides.

L. B. Heilprin of the Council on Library Resources, an expert in the area of microimage storage, has commented on the variety of media available for this purpose.

In their early stages microforms were confined almost exclusively to silver-halide storage. A new medium with different properties entered with the discovery of photosensitive dyes such as diazo and Dr. Chalkley's dicyanide. Since they have molecular units smaller than most silver grains, perhaps the principal gain was that more generations of photocopies could be reproduced without loss of a threshold quality of resolution. A potential gain may be their use in copying microimages. A new set of properties was introduced with discovery of photoelectrostatic reproduction, or xerography.

Here the developer is neither a liquid nor a gas, but a dry powder or toner, fixed by heat. This reduces processing time. Then it was discovered that a plastic (Kalvar) could be a recording medium through photorelease of gas bubbles which in turn form scattering centers. The film is insensitive to daylight handling, has complementary density on transmission and reflection, and is developed by heat. More recently yet it was discovered that another plastic can be made to melt locally under the action of an electron beam controlled by the signal from a scanned graphic image. This added thermoplastic recording to the list.

All of these media fit within the gross structural pattern of the microforms. The engineer now has a variety of choice for storage media, with a wide spectrum of physical properties.[12]

With fantastic storage capability of micro-recording, permanent messages can be greatly compressed. Actually, the ultimate practical limits become more a matter of the nature of optical systems, of the wave length of light, and of the techniques for developing the image than of the storage medium itself. As a result, high linear ratios for reduction in size from document to recorded image are becoming a standard part of the state of the art. For example, whereas ratios of 10 or 20:1 have been traditional in microphotography, Eastman Kodak used a reduction ratio of 60:1 in its Minicard system. More recently, AVCO Corporation has utilized ratios of 70:1 and 140:1. Others have experimented with ratios up to 1000:1, although it has been estimated that the practical limit is from 500 to 600:1, based on optical limitations in both recording and later reading.

A further consideration, which becomes particularly significant at the higher reduction ratios, is the physical size of the image carrier itself. This must remain on the order of several centimeters, no matter how many images may be stored on it, in order to be handled, whether by machines or human beings. In view of this, if the high reduction ratio is to have any real meaning in terms of storage efficiency, many, many images must be stored on a single carrier and the resulting problems in locating the desired image become very significant.

Another important problem is in the quality of the microimage. Inasmuch as there is a loss of resolution from one generation to the next, a microfilm system will, as a general rule, require exacting quality controls at all stages of the processing system—in the optics at time of filming, in the storage medium, and in the reproduction process employed to duplicate an enlargement back to its original dimensions.

---

[12] L. B. Heilprin, Communication Engineering Approach to Microforms, *American Documentation,* July 1961, v. 12, No. 3, p. 217.

A significant element to consider in evaluating microforms for documentary storage is the gradually declining cost of making hardcopy reproductions. Many companies are already engaged in commercial duplication of various microforms; in fact, some are even reproducing entire copies of out-of-print books from microfilm at reasonable cost and in bound book form. If this continues, it is very probable that in time users will be willing to forego seeing the original material "on loan" from their library in favor of getting a duplicate, expendable print for personal use. Should the user wish to avoid building up a vast paper library of his own, the alternative would be to obtain a duplicate copy of the microform for desk viewing. L. B. Heilprin makes just this distinction when he distinguishes between a D (duplicating) Library and a C (circulating) Library. He maintains that through increased microform usage, and advances in communications, we can expect to see the D-Library achieving considerable popularity and prominence in the future. "Thus many problems of storing multiple copies; of loss through wear, mutilation, and stealing; of cost and effort of charging out and charging in; of binding and rebinding, can be simplified or eliminated in a D-Library. The D-Library can combine photoreduction of scale; i.e., compact storage, high mobility through optical and electronic transmission of images, and great economy of operation. The D principle of dissemination by reproduction of expendable or vendable copies will almost certainly alleviate many present physical problems." [13]

The great variety of machine research in this area has had the purpose of exploiting the technique of microphotography, with its almost fantastic capabilities, and attempting to find the most efficient shapes, sizes, and reduction ratios for the microforms. Roll film, flat film, strips, cards, inserts—all have been utilized in an effort to meet desired objectives most effectively. Also, a variety of microreproduction equipment is commercially available to facilitate all facets of the processing operations which are involved.[14]

Microfilm

Certainly the most familiar of these various forms is the now standard microfilm which stores document images, at reduction ratios

---

[13] L. B. Heilprin, On the Information Problem Ahead, *American Documentation,* January 1961, v. 12, No. 1, pp. 6–14.

[14] Hubbard W. Ballou, Guide to Microreproduction Equipment, National Microfilm Association, Annapolis, Md., 1959, 438 pp.

typically around 15:1 to 20:1, on reels of film. At first documentation was recorded continuously on spools of film using special purpose microfilm cameras; the most common film sizes were 16 mm and 35 mm. Along with the camera, other equipment was evolved for viewing the film—first by hand with a magnifying glass and later by mechanical viewers. In early systems desired images were located by visual scanning of the set of stored images, assisted, perhaps, by an indication of their linear positions, in inches, along the film. The "Lodestar" microfilm viewer manufactured by the Recordak Corporation is a more advanced viewer, which provides a visual frame index. It uses spool film, but in cartridge form to simplify film loading and unloading. One of the most popular applications of Lodestar equipment has been as a mechanical viewing device for Sears and Roebuck catalogs and, by the company Information Handling Services, for vendors' catalogs. More recently, several developments have appeared which automate the location of particular frames by their linear position on the reel.

Among the most interesting of these linear indexing devices is a form of "teaching machine." The Western Design Company, a divi-

FIG. 51. Eastman Kodak Lodestar. Courtesy Eastman Kodak Co., Rochester, N.Y.

sion of U.S. Industries, in Santa Barbara, California, developed a machine to be used as an aid to student instruction which can select one frame or a sequence of frames based on the exact order in which the frames appear on the film. Each frame on the film is concerned with one element in the teaching pattern. At the bottom of each frame a question is posed to the student about the material presented above; his choice of answer will determine one of several other frames to which the machine indexes. (If he selects the incorrect solution, he finds himself at a frame which explains why he missed the question and which directs him to another frame containing an appropriate element of instruction to be learned. A recorder in the machine can trace the pattern of his instructional behavior by keeping track of his progress in terms of the selection of correct answers and the time taken.)

The file of instructional material is on sprocketed 35 mm film, in color or black and white, that runs at the standard movie speed of 24 inches a second. The start position on the machine is frame No. 1. Since all successive frames are of the same size, the machine is able to locate any frame on the film by using frame No. 1 as its reference. Furthermore, since the film is driven at movie speed, there is also provision in the machine for showing a movie sequence as one element of instruction when a particular frame is reached. The combination of still frame and movie display of information, plus its ability to locate and find particular frames in a well-ordered film file, make the Western Design Tutoring Machine a possible candidate for special application in the document file area even though it was originally designed as an automatic teaching machine.

However, although microfilm satisfies the basic requirements for achieving more compact storage of the printed information, its access time is slow even when the difficulty of locating a specific image on the spool is overcome (by organizing the original material in a logical manner before filming, by providing visual index marks recognizable at viewing time, or by automatic linear indexing). These technical considerations of access time and display may not be too important in routine library operations which involve microfilming sets of material like newspapers and periodicals. But when continuous film is used as the primary recording medium for storing a heterogenous collection of documents keyed to a subject or named object index, the questions of rapid access and display become very serious.

The basic principles of an electronic microfilm searching system were advanced by Vannevar Bush of MIT in the early 1940's as a means for overcoming these deficiencies. Government funds were provided for its development through the Office of Technical Services of the Department of Commerce.[15] A prototype model called the Rapid Selector was designed and built by Engineering Research Associates[16] of St. Paul, Minnesota. Ralph R. Shaw,[17] Librarian of the Department of Agriculture at the time, supervised the development and performed most of the bibliographical experimentation. The machine handled microfilm with associated patterns which described the contents of documents. Code and document images were on large, 2000-foot reels of 35 mm microfilm containing 72,000 image frames each, which went through the machine at five feet per second or 2400 identified pages per minute. Copies of the documents as selected by proper code recognition were copied "on the fly" photographically.

The code was in the form of black and clear "dots" which identified each document either by number, name, author, or contents. In this machine the code appeared on one half of a 35 mm film and a photographic image of the document on the other half, as shown in Figure 52. As the film passed through the selector, the coded area was projected on a photocell. This photocell was masked by a cutout of the complement of the projected code being sought. Recognition occurred when no light struck the photocell. This initiated a signal which fired a photographic flash lamp when the selected microfilmed document was in the copying position. The light projected an image of the desired document onto unexposed microfilm which became the output of the Rapid Selector.

In the early 1950's Yale University undertook the redesign of the selector for use with a large collection of documents which had already been abstracted and coded on IBM cards.[18] Each document required 5 cards or 4800 bits to describe its contents. The new model was required to read many more bits than the previous machine and to copy successive frames without slowing down. The designers therefore changed the arrangement of the code and documents so

---

[15] J. C. Green, The Rapid Selector—An Automatic Library, Revue de la Documentation, 1950, v. 17, pp. 66–68, reprinted from the *Military Engineer,* 1949, v. 41, pp. 350–352.

[16] Engineering Research Associates, Inc., Report for the Microfilm Rapid Selector, June 20, 1949, Contract Cac 47–24 (PB No. 97313).

[17] Ralph R. Shaw, The Rapid Selector, *Journal of Documentation,* 1949, v. 5, pp. 164–171.

[18] U.S. Department of Commerce, Report to the Secretary of Commerce by the Advisory Committee on the Application of Machines to Patent Office Operations, Government Printing Office, Washington, D.C., 1954, 76 pp.

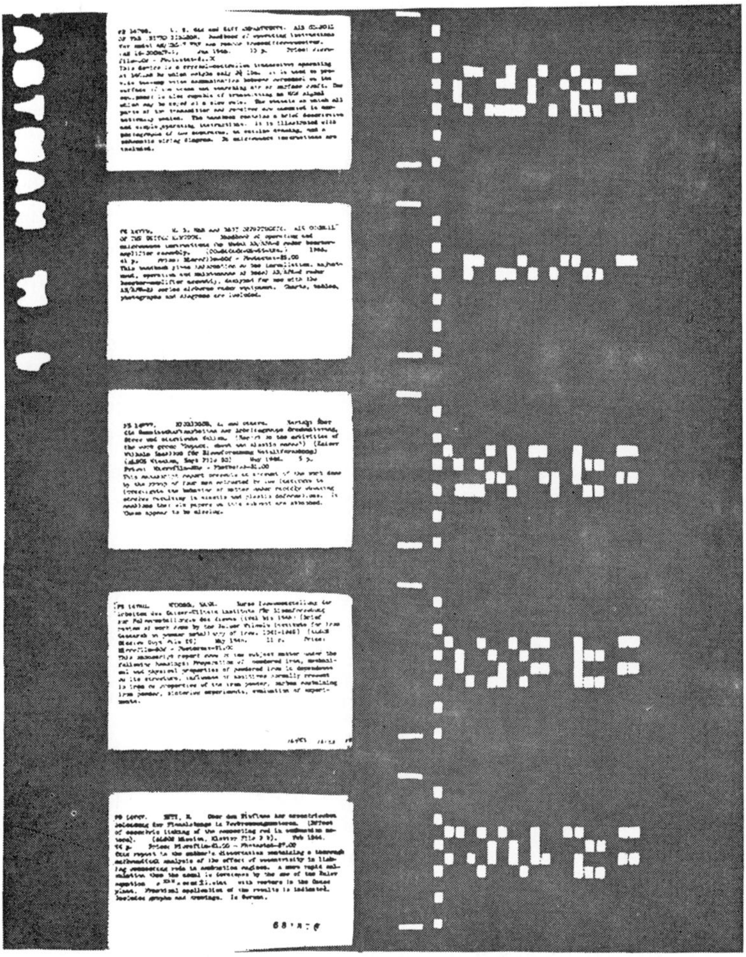

FIG. 52. Rapid selector film format #1.

that the code area covered the entire film width in 50-bit groups extended along the film as far as required. The contents of five cards made a code frame 1¼ inches long and thus occupied about the same area as a document image with an 8 to 1 reduction.

The Yale interrogator read the entire code field simultaneously, using one photocell for each bit in parallel. The copying of successive documents was achieved by using a conventional continuously lit projection lamp which illuminated the master film as it passed over a slit. The image was focused onto another slit behind which was unexposed microfilm. The selector controlled the motion of this unexposed film. When a copy was called for, the film was brought up to speed so that a 1 to 1 copy was made. After the necessary copying was finished, the film gate was cleared of exposed film and the machine waited for the next print command.

As part of the cooperative program with the Patent Office, the Data Processing Systems Division at NBS initiated a study to demonstrate the practicality of the Rapid Selector for their use.[19] For this program the laboratory obtained a portion of the Yale equipment. The master film format is shown in Figure 53. In the present design the useful film width for documents is 1 inch by whatever length can be photographed. For the usual standard or legal size letter, a 10-to-1 reduction is required. For a 2½ by 3 foot drawing the reduction is 25 to 1. Such reductions are common microfilm sizes and present no problem in the machine for copying on the fly. If the average length of each article on the film were four letter size pages and required only one code area, a 20-to-1 reduction would allow the four pages to appear in the space formerly occupied by a single page and would increase the effective speed of the machine fourfold. The present format is based on a 15-to-1 reduction for a single page per frame.

The main piece of auxiliary equipment consists of a camera for recording the index information and the image on the same frame of film. A numerical keyboard adjacent to the camera allows the operator to set up a large dot pattern on a lighted glass plate to represent the code for the index. Once the code pattern is set, the camera records this index information in one area of the frame and then records the document image in the remaining area. The Rapid Selector is today the basis for an operating information retrieval system in the Navy Department's Bureau of Ships. Recent developments in the Navy's coding formats permit the placement of all necessary machine-control signals within the limits of the document image width. This allows the use of microfilm prepared on *any* 35 millimeter camera for Rapid Selector search.

Prior to the version of the machine produced by NBS, the Rapid Selector was experimental and never put into practical operation. Technical difficulties and the basic disadvantage of having to run the

---

[19] T. C. Bagg and S. Greenwald, The Rapid Selector Development Program at the National Bureau of Standards, National Bureau of Standards, November 1958.

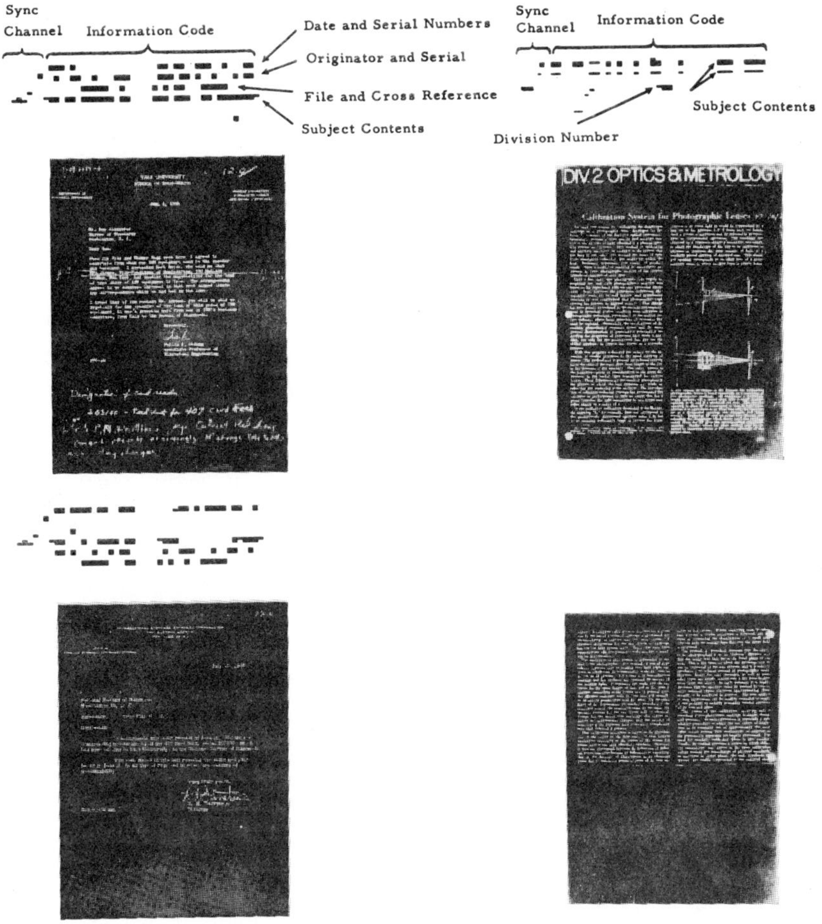

FIG. 53. Rapid selector film format #2.

entire master spool of film through the machine for each search proved to be major stumbling blocks. The machine was not able to accelerate and decelerate the film smoothly, and consequently the film broke too frequently. Although these technical problems were serious at the time the Rapid Selector was conceived, they would not be today. The machine designed by the National Bureau of Standards is now being used in a working, everyday operation. The Rapid Selector was a bold step forward in trying to combine the speed of electronic selection with film reduction.

Shaw summarized the objectives of electronic selection as follows:

It appears that there are three broad areas in which electronic selection and reproduction may be a useful aid to administration and scholarship. These are:

1. High speed finding and reproduction of any type of file material stored in a minimum of space.
2. Cumulative indexing of technical data or other materials so that complete searches may be made of all known sources as required.
3. That eventually oragnization of knowledge might be based to a much greater extent on intellectual content of material and needs of research, rather than being limited as greatly as it is now by physical factors.[20]

The general objectives given by Shaw were valid for the design of the Rapid Selector, and they are equally valid today for other electronic searching machines applicable to library-type problems.

An automatic microfilm searching machine called Flip (Film Library Instantaneous Presentation) is somewhat similar to the Rapid Selector.[21] It was developed and built by the Benson-Lehner Corporation at Los Angeles. Flip was designed to rapidly locate any desired frame, from among 72,000 frames on a 1200-foot reel of 16 mm film, and to project this frame on a built-in viewing screen. The prime design criterion was to develop a machine to search at the comparatively high speed of 300 to 600 frames per second.

Each frame contains pictorial data and 32 bits of binary coded information in the form of black bars on a clear background. Upon command to search, the machine chooses the correct direction for search and upon recognizing the frame, stops, overshoots about five frames, and returns to project the image on the screen for visual presentation. Information contained on the selected frame is projected on the viewing screen. Simultaneously, the frame identification is digitally displayed. Thus frame selection is verified and the operator signalled that a new search may be instituted.

The FMA File Search system similarly automates the storage and retrieval of written or graphic material on microfilm.[22] The system equipment is contained in two major units. The first of these is a Recording Unit, which is made up of a camera, lights, and worktable.

---

[20] Ralph R. Shaw, *Bibliography In An Age of Science,* Urbana, University of Illinois Press, 1951, p. 69.

[21] Gordon Williams, FLIP: Film Library Instantaneous Presentation, *Library Resources and Technical Services,* 1958, v. 2, No. 4.

[22] Company brochure on FILE SEARCH, FMA, Inc., 142 Nevada Street, El Segundo, Calif., 1961.

FIG. 54. FMA File-Search coded film reel. Courtesy FMA, Inc., El Segundo, Calif.

The other is the File Search Retrieval Unit, which searches the films comprising the library for the appropriate material. The Retrieval Unit also provides a viewing mechanism, a printer for producing hard copy, and a camera for making 1:1 film copies of the material. The general operating procedure by the system is as follows:

Documents or other graphic material are indexed and this descriptive information is then changed into binary coding, using a Flexowriter, and recorded beside the material which it describes. The binary code capacity of each frame is 392 bits, allowing as many as 56 alpha-numeric characters to be used for indexing. The standard system uses 35 mm film; a reduction ratio of 25:1 enables 32 legal size pages to be accommodated on every foot of film, and a library of 32,000 pages on one film reel. Requests for information in the indexing language are similarly translated into a binary description. The appropriate reel of film is selected from the library and placed into the Retrieval Unit. This unit then searches the reel and selects those documents, or other material, which have descriptive coding that matches that in the request. As the desired information is found by the machine, the film is automatically stopped and the image is projected onto the viewing screen.

The File Search film is moved past the reading station at 200 feet

FIG. 55. FMA File-Search equipment. Courtesy FMA, Inc., El Segundo, Calif.

per minute. If the documents are stored one page per frame, this corresponds to a rate of 6400 pages per minute. The code bits on the film are read at this station and the information is sent to the circuitry for comparison with the request code.

Each descriptor of a document read from film is compared with the contents of the request registers and the results are stored until the start of the next document is sensed. The comparison results are sampled and associated according to the logical structure of the request. If the document is to be selected for retrieval, the film transport is stopped and the first page is positioned for viewing and printing. A frame counter is used to count the number of pages (frames) in a document, so that all pages can be printed automatically. After the selected document is copied or examined, the circuitry is reset and the search process continues.

When the Retrieval Unit signifies that a match with a request has been made, three options are available to the requestor. In the first option, called "browsing," the selected material is displayed on the viewing screen. The requestor can then read it directly for information and also obtain hard copy, if desired. Where viewing by the requestor is not necessary, a switch selection provides automatic hard-copy production of all material satisfying the request. Finally, the copy camera attachment essential to the file expansion operation will permit automatic microfilm recording as a third option.

This capability is very useful in cases where the volume of requested information is large or where the material is to be sent to a remote location. Automatic file expansion can also be used to create subsets of files as the need arises and to reorganize all or part of the main file to meet special situations.

The Rapid Selector, the Benson-Lehner Flip, and the FMA File Search Machine all utilize microfilm with binary coded data stored for automatic searching. Thus each provides a means for mechanized

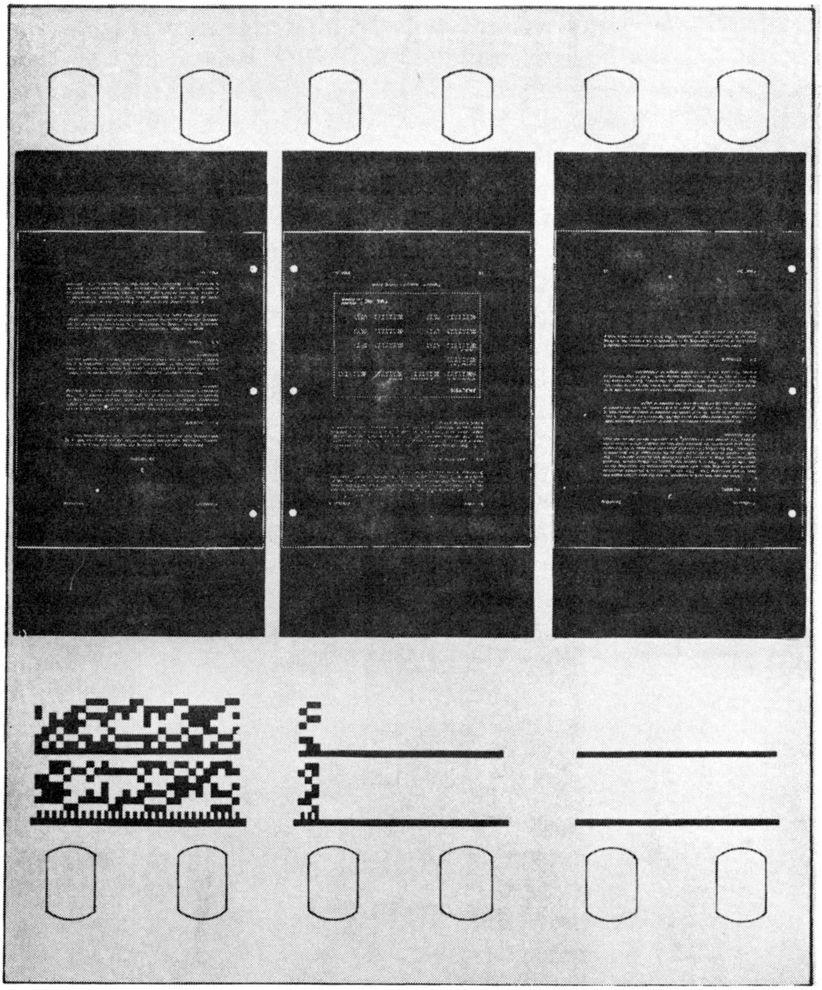

FIG. 56. FMA File-Search film format. Courtesy FMA, Inc., El Segundo, Calif.

document retrieval. However, none of them provides an answer to the basic operational disadvantages of continuous film files: it is awkward to interfile new material in an orderly sequence, and the search mechanism must examine the entire file to satisfy every search request.

Microimage Cards and Strips

Unitized film files are able to overcome many of these disadvantages. In fact, virtually every consideration which led the data processing industry to consider magnetic cards and strips as replacement for magnetic tape applies with equal force to microphotographic storage. With a discrete medium, the rigidity of sequential handling disappears and processing and finding operations become more flexible and random. Several methods now exist for placing microreductions of documents onto cards.

The Microcard is an extension of conventional microfilming to allow for combination with cards. Documents are filmed in a normal manner, then developed, cut into strips, and contact printed as opaque positive images on the face of a card. The extent of the photoreduction determines how many document pages may be contained on one card. The standard Microcard is 3″ x 5″ and at typical reductions may contain as many as 80 pages. The reverse face of the card may

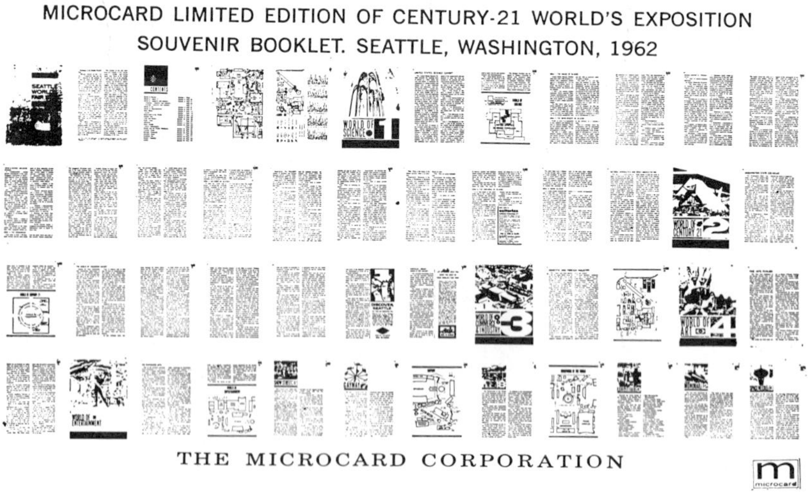

FIG. 57. Microcard. Courtesy Microcard Corp., West Salem, Wisconsin.

be used to record clear-text identification or index data. Special photographic equipment is required to process the cards and prepare them for use, and special viewers exist to assist the user in reading the card.

The color control department of the Eastman Kodak Company was among the first organizations to install a Microcard procedure for disseminating new information to its researchers as a substitute for hard-copy filing of the material in its central library. Other large users include the Atomic Energy Commission, the Bureau of Ships, university libraries, and industrial organizations.

Until 1961 the opaque nature of a Microcard made it inconvenient to duplicate and enlarge. To do so formerly required going back to the original negative film strip and employing conventional photo-enlarging techniques. Other media were invented which provided a transparent negative image in card form rather than an opaque Microcard. One such sheet film method, called "microfiche," is an approach principally adopted in Europe, and another, called CIM-card (continuous image microfilm card), a diazo impregnated mylar sheet, was originally produced by the ozalid division of General Aniline Corporation to help solve the engineering drawing problem at Douglas Aircraft Company. Microfiche and CIM-cards can be contact printed, and there are a line of equipments on the market for viewing and enlarging the microimages stored on them.

A more widely followed approach is the aperture card, which utilizes small windows in an otherwise solid card form to store pieces of film. The number of apertures can vary depending on the amount of space required for identification of the stored document images. To place the images in aperture cards, documents are filmed sequentially in microfilm form, and later chopped and mounted to fit neatly into cards with precut apertures. The Filmsort Division of Minnesota Mining and Manufacturing Company produces a mounter which cuts the frame of film, inserts it into the aperture, and presses it firmly against an adhesive frame which surrounds the aperture.

Sometimes the apertures are combined into a punched card so that a portion of the card can be used for index and selection purposes by EAM equipment. This is not altogether satisfactory, for it requires special engineering of the card handling device to ensure that cards will not be mangled or scratched during sorting operations. However, the Intellofax system of the Central Intelligence Agency is possibly the largest single installation of such aperture EAM punched

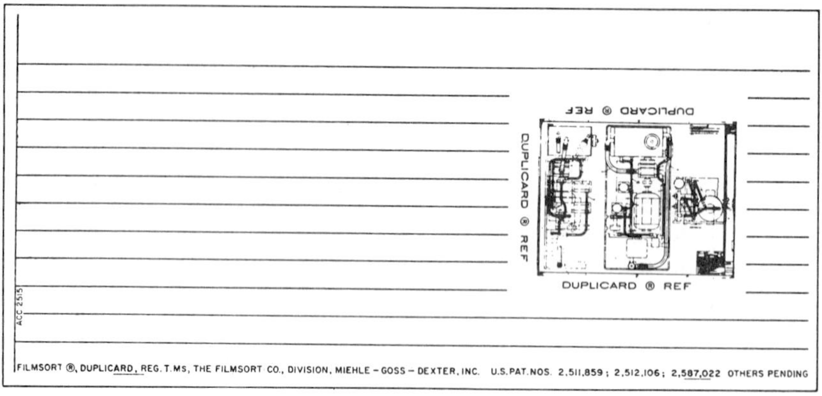

FIG. 58. Aperture card.

cards. This system was instituted in 1954 and represented an early effort in this field.

Minicard,[23] developed by Eastman Kodak Company for the Department of Defense, is an effort to go one step further than EAM aperture cards, by utilizing photographic techniques for both image and coded index data. In this sense it is like a unitized Rapid Selector, containing both index and document file information photographically on the same card. A Minicard is about half the size of a standard postage stamp: 16 mm x 32 mm. It contains images reduced at the ratio of 60:1. In the code portion of the Minicard, information is represented by small squares of black and white dots. These dots, in combinations of six, represent either a number or a letter using a binary coding system. They are arranged in 42 parallel channels and sets of 10 columns called fields. The card is divided into seven fields which can be devoted to either code or image storage. The first field is called the fixed field and must always be used for coded data storage. The remaining six fields can be either similar sets of coded data or pairs of document images. Depending on the application, therefore, a Minicard can contain a large code area and no image area or a maximum of 12 images plus about 60 alpha-numeric code characters.

Minicard, in addition to being a storage medium, is also a family

---

[23] A. W. Tyler, W. L. Myers, and J. W. Kuipers, The Application of the Kodak Minicard System to Problems of Documentation, *American Documentation,* January 1955, v. 6, pp. 18–30.

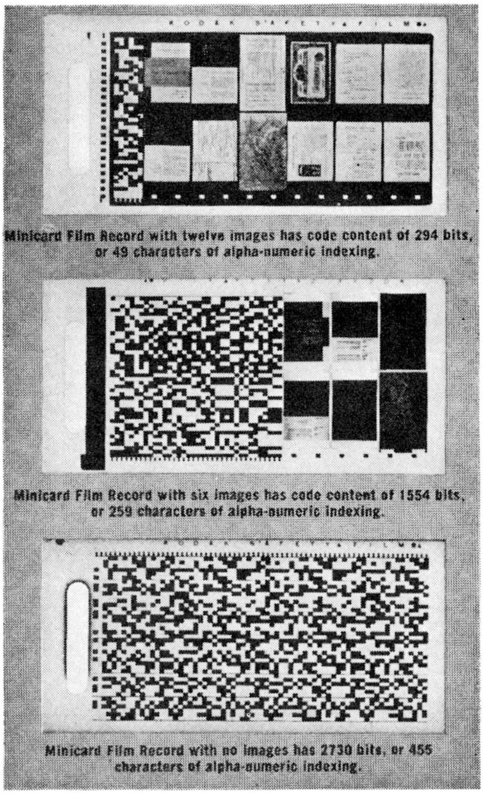

FIG. 59. Minicard card formats. Courtesy Eastman Kodak Co., Rochester, N.Y.

of equipment: the Camera, the Duplicator, the Sorter, and the Selector.[24] The camera is similar to the microfilm cameras in use today except for special optics to provide the 60:1 reduction ratio and the combination of image and code. To produce Minicards, index information is converted into punched paper tape which in turn is fed into the camera. The camera translates the punched holes in the paper tape into the black and clear patterns on the film by means of a series of small shutters which open or close in accordance with the punched information. After the index information is recorded, the images of the document are photographed by the camera in typical

[24] J. W. Kuipers, A. W. Tyler, and W. L. Myers, A Minicard System for Documentary Information, *American Documentation,* October 1957, v. 8, No. 4, pp. 246–268.

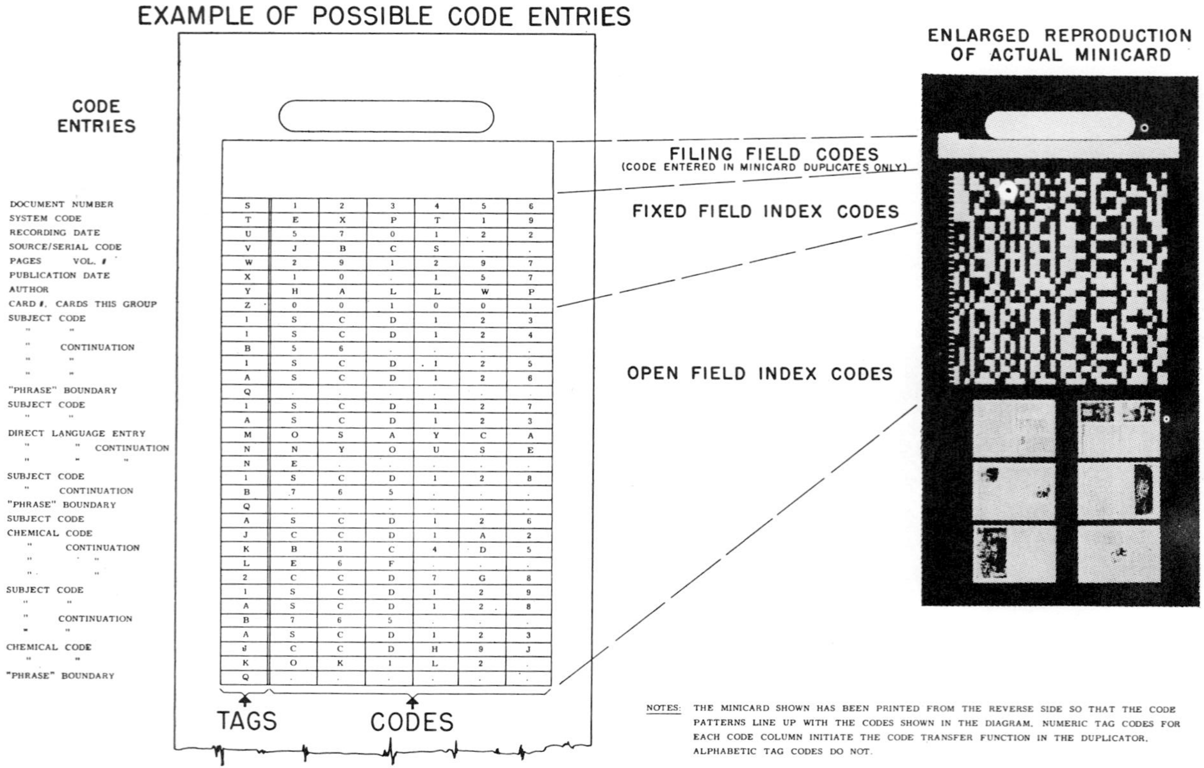

DOCUMENT NUMBER	S	1	2	3	4	5	6
SYSTEM CODE	T	E	X	P	T	1	9
RECORDING DATE	U	5	7	0	1	2	2
SOURCE/SERIAL CODE	V	J	B	C	S	.	.
PAGES VOL. #	W	2	9	1	2	9	7
PUBLICATION DATE	X	1	0	.	1	5	7
AUTHOR	Y	H	A	L	L	W	P
CARD #, CARDS THIS GROUP	Z	0	0	1	0	0	1
SUBJECT CODE	1	S	C	D	1	2	3
" "	1	S	C	D	1	2	4
" CONTINUATION	B	5	6	.	.	.	.
" "	1	S	C	D	1	2	5
" "	A	S	C	D	1	2	6
"PHRASE" BOUNDARY	Q	.	.	.	.	.	.
SUBJECT CODE	1	S	C	D	1	2	7
" "	A	S	C	D	1	2	3
DIRECT LANGUAGE ENTRY	M	O	S	A	Y	C	A
" " CONTINUATION	N	N	Y	O	U	S	E
" " "	N	E	.	.	.	.	.
SUBJECT CODE	1	S	C	D	1	2	8
" CONTINUATION	B	7	6	5	.	.	.
"PHRASE" BOUNDARY	Q	.	.	.	.	.	.
SUBJECT CODE	A	S	C	D	1	2	6
CHEMICAL CODE	J	C	C	D	1	A	2
" CONTINUATION	K	B	3	C	4	D	5
" "	L	E	6	F	.	.	.
" "	2	C	C	D	7	G	8
SUBJECT CODE	1	S	C	D	1	2	9
" "	A	S	C	D	1	2	8
" CONTINUATION	B	7	6	5	.	.	.
" "	A	S	C	D	1	2	3
CHEMICAL CODE	J	C	C	D	H	9	J
" "	K	O	K	1	L	2	.
"PHRASE" BOUNDARY	Q	.	.	.	.	.	.

NOTES: THE MINICARD SHOWN HAS BEEN PRINTED FROM THE REVERSE SIDE SO THAT THE CODE PATTERNS LINE UP WITH THE CODES SHOWN IN THE DIAGRAM. NUMERIC TAG CODES FOR EACH CODE COLUMN INITIATE THE CODE TRANSFER FUNCTION IN THE DUPLICATOR. ALPHABETIC TAG CODES DO NOT.

FIG. 60. Minicard code entries. J. W. Kuipers, A. W. Tyler, and W. L. Myers, A Minicard System for Documentary Information, *American Documentation,* October 1957, v. 8, No. 4, pp. 246–268.

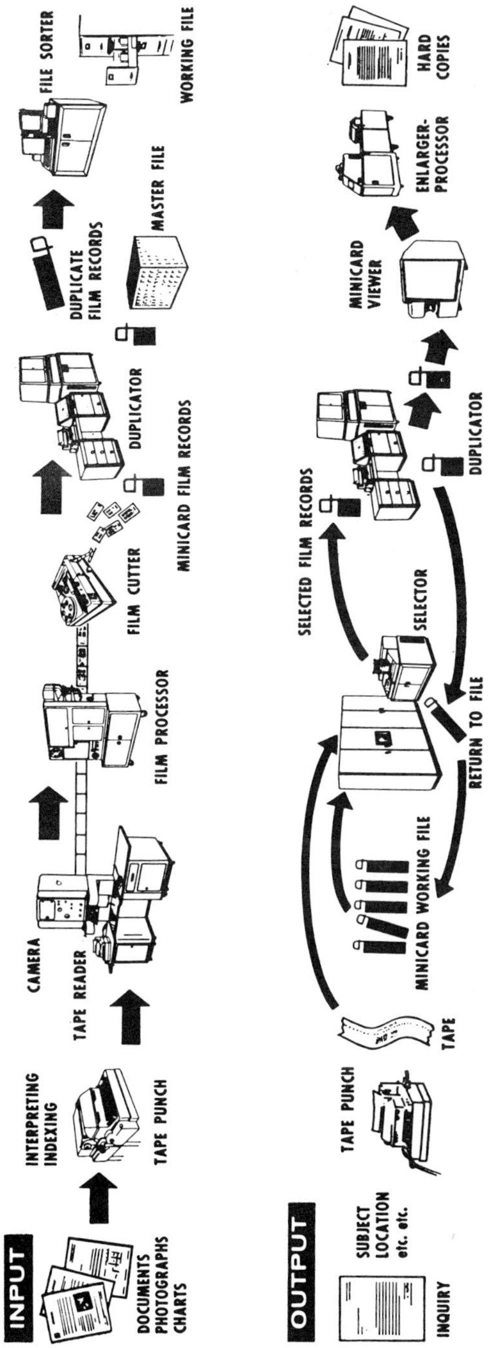

FIG. 61. Minicard equipment system. Courtesy Eastman Kodak Co., Rochester, N.Y.

microfilm fashion. This results in a string of Minicards arranged on an exposed spool of film. The film is developed, examined, and coated to protect the emulsion in subsequent handling operations. The spool is then chopped up into the exact prescribed Minicard dimensions. The cards are automatically placed on a skewer or stick, 15 inches long, which can contain 2000 Minicards. If there were 12 pages per Minicard, each stick would hold 24,000 pages or the equivalent of one four-drawer filing cabinet.

The Minicards are then taken to the Duplicator, which photographically creates multiple copies as cross reference Minicards for the different files in the system. Once the cards are duplicated, they are taken to the Sorter, which electronically reads the dot patterns and sorts the Minicards to a predetermined location, at rates up to 20 cards per second, in the same way that punched cards are sorted. The last step in the sorting operation places the Minicards into 100 different stations in the file; they are then ready to be stored in the Minicard filing bins.

The last item in the Minicard family of equipment is the "Selector," which we have described previously as the machine used for retrieving sorted and filed Minicards. For a given search, appropriate sticks are removed from the Minicard files. A coded punched paper tape instruction is prepared which is fed into a computer memory. The Minicards are then run past a reading station at 10 cards per second. Whenever any group of code combinations coincides with the instruction stored in the memory of the machine, the Minicard in question is transported to a special stick. Minicards thus selected are then available for viewing or enlarging according to customer demands.

In virtually every respect Minicard has represented an extension of the state of the art—high photographic reduction, unitized cards, high transport rates, complex logical processing, high densities of coded data. Its capabilities still have not been fully exploited; it has unusual potential for records management and library work, but it can only be judged after much more experimentation. Eastman Kodak Company points out that the equipment is still strictly experimental and will not be available commercially for some time to come.

A similar but far less complicated system is Filmorex.[25] This system, developed by J. Semaine of France, also stores both the image and code in microphotographic form and it also is a family of equip-

---

[25] J. Semaine, Documentation by the FILMOREX Technique, in J. H. Shera, *Information Systems in Documentation,* New York, Interscience, 1957, pp. 478–487.

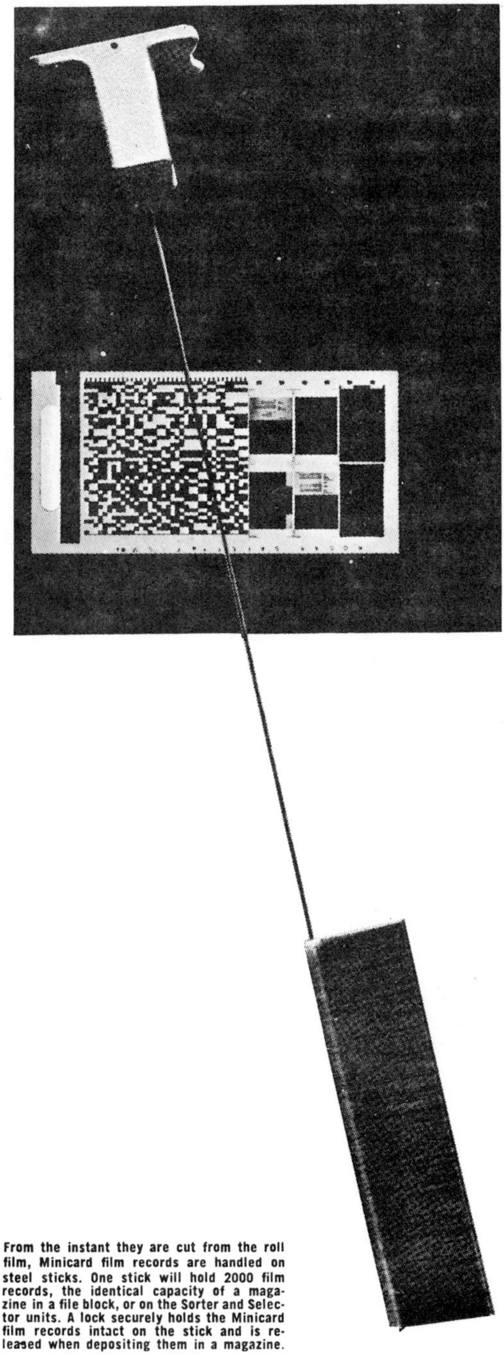

From the instant they are cut from the roll film, Minicard film records are handled on steel sticks. One stick will hold 2000 film records, the identical capacity of a magazine in a file block, or on the Sorter and Selector units. A lock securely holds the Minicard film records intact on the stick and is released when depositing them in a magazine.

FIG. 62. Minicard film stick. Courtesy Eastman Kodak Co., Rochester, N.Y.

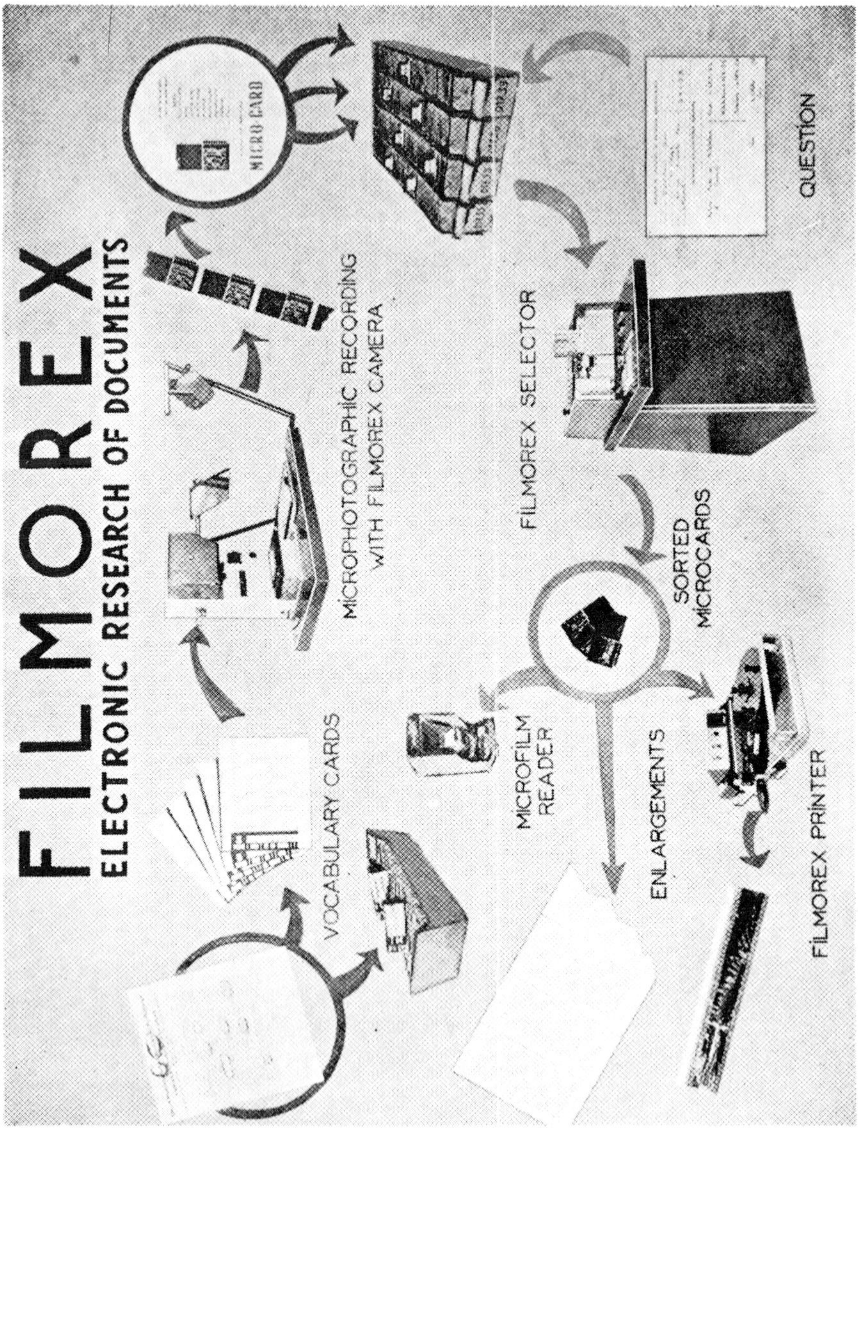
FILMOREX
ELECTRONIC RESEARCH OF DOCUMENTS
VOCABULARY CARDS
MİCROPHOTOGRAPHİC RECORDİNG
WITH FİLMOREX CAMERA
MICRO CARD
FİLMOREX SELECTOR
QUESTİON
MİCROFİLM
READER
SORTED
MİCROCARDS
ENLARGEMENTS
FİLMOREX PRİNTER

FILMOREX is a real "artificial memory" which enables to store thousands of documents under their numerous aspects and to retrieve all those that apply to a given subject matter. This system has been developed by Dr Samain in 1950.

The basic principle of the FILMOREX SYSTEM is to photograph on a micro-card each document with its relevant data. These micro-cards may then be scanned at any time by an electronic selector that retrieves and sorts all those that refer to a given topic.

THE FILMOREX MICRO-CARD

The micro-card consists of a photographic film measuring 35 x 60 mm, divided in two areas, A and B.

— In area A the text or abstract of the document is micro-filmed; this area holds two full pages including figures, charts, drawings, etc.

In area B are photographed the data relevant to the document such as characteristics, values, notions, ideas...

These data are translated into code numbers and are recorded in any sequence on the micro-card in the form of black and transparent spots. The micro-card comprises 16 rows of spots upon any of which may be recorded any code-number from O to 180,000.

The micro-card is highly wear-resistant, much more so than paper or punched cards. It lasts indefinitely and may be passed through the Selector hundreds of times without any impairment. Despite the large amount of information it contains, its size is inconsiderable thus enabling to store millions of them under a small bulk and to minimise comings and goings, and handling operations as well.

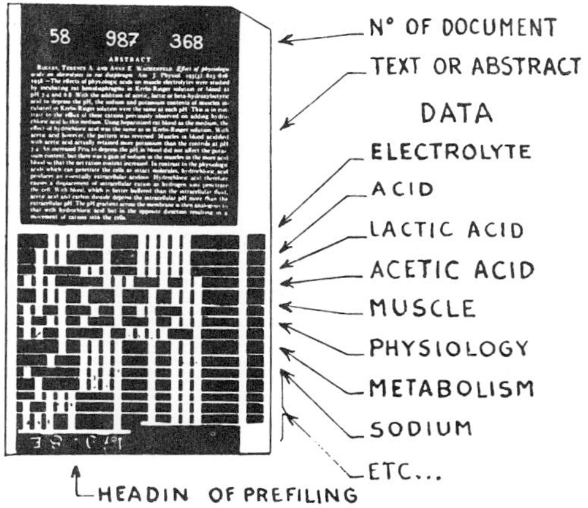

FIG. 63. Filmorex microcard.

ment. However, Semaine's approach is to provide the barest minimum of capability rather than such extreme extensions as did Minicard. The reduction ratio used for document image storage is only ten to one; the cards are handled by standard techniques at rates of 100 cards per minute; only the simplest of logical processing is provided; only a limited amount of coded data is stored. The Filmorex card measures 35 mm x 60 mm and is divided into two areas, in one of which appears two document pages and in the other up to 256 bits arranged in 16 channels.

Two pieces of equipment are provided: the "Camera" to produce the cards and the "Selector," which matches requests against the index data stored on each Filmorex card. The camera photographs the document pages at the same time that it photographs the coded information. The coded data are preprinted as black and white strips on the edges of cards assigned to each term associated with the document. To prepare material for photographing, the term cards are selected from the file of such cards and stacked one on top of the other in such a way that the preprinted coded data are visible from each card. The topmost card will also show the corresponding identification of the first subject code in readable alphabetic form. After the document and code set is photographed, a similar copy but with a different subject code uppermost, and thus with the corresponding readable data visible, can be prepared by simply rearranging the term code cards. The selector transports the cards at a rate of approximately 100 per minute and compares the stored coded patterns with request terms. The unit provides for various logical combinations of the request terms—the usual "and," "or," and "not."

A somewhat similar approach has been adopted by the Magnavox Company based on their experiences as subcontractor on Minicard. Their Media development similarly produces the coded data on the cards by a process of photographing the code at the same time as photographing the documents. This system utilizes a card of the same dimensions as the Minicard but with the code stored along the edge and consisting of less than 80 bits. The code pattern is established from a manual keyboard and appears as a set of code bars and associated readable numbers on the side of the cradle in which the document pages are placed for photographing. The Media system utilizes manual filing of the cards in small cartridges, each containing up to 200 cards, based on visual reading of the numeric data shown. The Media development provides a selector, which simply matches the 15 to 20 decimal digits of the code with a single document number

FIG. 64. Media card. Courtesy Magnavox, Ft. Wayne, Ind.

and which represents a system for retrieval on the basis of document number and not on the basis of content.

Houston Fearless Company of Los Angeles has under development an automatic unit record document file and retrieval device. For its first experimental machine this company has chosen a film chip size of 2.75″ x 4.00″ as the unit record, and each record has its own identification number. Film chips are inserted in a "cassette" to prevent

FIG. 65. Media cartridge filing system. Courtesy Magnavox, Ft. Wayne, Ind.

chip-to-chip abrasion and provide a rigid carrier for moving the records through the system. Filing and selection are performed automatically on the basis of the unit record identification number. The machine can be operated on-line with an associated digital computer serving as the index or off-line under the control of a punched paper tape or a manual keyboard. Access time to a single record is approximately 8 seconds. An especially interesting feature of the machine is its random filing. Cassettes entering the machine are sent to the first available position for filing and the machine uses a magnetic drum to keep track of the precise location of each unit record at any given time. The ability of the machine to do this "bookkeeping" automatically is an unusual advantage because in most active, fast-growing file systems that use dedicated positions for storage, the operational requirements for simply updating and controlling the unit records are usually excessive.

An entirely different approach to unitized microphotographic storage is that taken by IBM in their development of a film strip technique. Although this development is not yet commercially available, it is important to recognize that the use of strips in highly mechanized systems is as possible with microphotographic storage as it is with magnetic tape storage. The development was first begun in 1958 and was described in July 1961 along the following lines: [26,27] Walnut, as it is called, consists of a specially designed machine which stores photographic images on strips. Documents entering the system travel through a two-stage reduction in size. They are microfilmed on 35 mm film and placed in an image converter which then optically reduces the image further and transfers it to the strip. Each strip contains as many as 99 images of an 8″ x 14″ page size, at a reduction to about 1/1000th the original size. The strips are stored in a plastic cell with 50 strips to the cell and 200 cells to the machine. The machine can therefore store a total of 990,000 images.

Any one of the images can be found in a maximum access time of 5 seconds. Once the document number is addressed, a pickup mechanism locates the appropriate cell, withdraws the pertinent strip, and the image of the document is photographically transferred to an

---

[26] Prototype Information System Evolved by IBM Division for CIA, *Electronic News,* Monday, July 17, 1961.

[27] P. D. Bradshaw, The Walnut System: A Large Capacity Document Storage and Retrieval System, *American Documentation,* July 1962, v. 13, No. 3, pp. 270–275.

IBM aperture card. The selected images can then be viewed on a screen by the user or enlarged for hard-copy reproduction.

Walnut refers to the file storage mechanism only. In a total systems environment it is necessary to have associated index equipment to locate the pertinent addresses.

AVCO Corporation is another company that has experimented with mechanized files for microimage storage. With a grant from the Council on Library Resources, AVCO refined the specifications of a machine it calls Verac, which stores microimages in coordinate fashion on the face of a sheet of film. A special camera mechanism transports the film to a prescribed exposure location where the image is optically transferred onto the face of the sheet directly from the original document. Inasmuch as the reduction ratio used is 140:1, the pinhead images are meticulously positioned in such a way that each exposure precisely registers an image into a row and column corresponding to a particular location address in the memory plane.

The sheet film or memory plane used in the prototype machine is 8½" x 8½" and holds 10,000 images. A stack of 100 plates, occupying about 1 cubic foot, can therefore store one million document images.

By machine electronic addressing—dialing in the number of the desired document—one can command the machine to enter the file, raise the proper sheet in the stack, and with three orthogonal motions locate a specific microimage for readout. A TV camera then centers on this image and displays it for remote examination on a TV monitor. This output video system incorporates an electronic buffer so that the machine is able to display one image while simultaneously searching for another. Hard-copy print-out is done by enlarging the image to its original size on a Litton Printa-a-Pix tube.

Photochromic Microimages

While most microfilm or microimage applications now in use employ either silver halide or diazo film as the recording medium, the National Cash Register Company has announced a new process called Photochromics which also provides high density storage of textual and graphic images.[28]

---

[28] C. O. Carlson, D. A. Grafton, and A. S. Tauber, The Photochromic Micro-Image Memory, presented at the Symposium on Large Capacity Memory Techniques for Computing Systems, Office of Naval Research, May 1961.

NCR photochromic coatings are similar to photographic emulsions in appearance and other properties. They can be coated on the same type of surfaces as photographic emulsions and exhibit excellent resolution capabilities. The basic principle behind the photochromic process is the ability of the individual molecules in the coating to switch from a colored to a colorless state. The materials switch when subjected to near ultraviolet radiation and back to the colorless state when subjected either to heat or visible light.

Thus, by using optical techniques and ultraviolet light, documents can be exposed at microimage dimensions. The same optics and visible light make it possible to "erase" a part of, as well as the whole, microimage field and then, repeating the process, to "write" again into the erased portion of what was previously written.

With the availability of material possessing the above characteristics there arises a new capability for the erasable storage of document images at very high packing densities. This capability is primarily based on the following properties of the photochromic coatings: (1) high resolution with no grain, (2) image visible on exposure, and (3) erasure and rewrite capabilities. The latter capability brings to document image manipulation some of the same power which digital computers enjoy with respect to magnetic tape recording.[29]

---

[29] A. S. Tauber and W. C. Myers, Photochromic Micro-Images, A Key to Practical Microdocument Storage and Dissemination, *American Documentation,* October 1962, v. 13, No. 4, pp. 403–409.

SECTION II

Elements

8

Interdisciplinary character of information systems

As the previous chapters should have made evident, many individuals from diverse technical backgrounds have been contributing techniques and ideas to the solution of information system problems. Investigators have included scientific groups, librarians, documentalists, engineers, and mathematicians. Each technical background has provided a body of available knowledge applicable to some aspect of the problem. It is important, therefore, to recognize clearly where each individual can best contribute and to provide a vehicle by which they can effectively communicate with each other.

Unfortunately, with such a diverse array of backgrounds, capabilities, and interests, problems in communication and understanding are almost certain to arise. Each man is, to some extent, unfamiliar with the language of others; he lacks facility with their techniques, and he is unacquainted with their problems. Each individual approaches an information system from a more or less limited standpoint and is relatively unsophisticated with respect to other aspects of the problem. The almost inherent bias produced by specialized training makes it difficult to overcome this; each man continues to filter the problem through the screen of his own background and interests.

Lack of recognition of the importance of background and experience has led many into the fallacy of the "new approach" represented by the following fairly typical statement. It contains sufficient truth to appear valid, and yet it obscures the basic nature of what is required to solve the problem.

> Preliminary efforts toward adapting machines to the library problem indicate that specialists in the use and processing of literature are not particularly qualified to consider the problem of automation of the information center. They have a tendency to attempt to "mechanize" their present operation rather than analyze the characteristics and requirements of the system. It would probably be profitable to assign to this general problem a group of fresh minds, free of preconception but including an appropriate spread of talents in system analysis, electronic and mechanical design, and logical analysis. . . . There are strong indications that the solution of the problem will require a profound and imaginative approach. . . .[1]

The tendency, by those with operating experience, to mechanize present operation is well recognized, but it should point to the need for cooperation, not to the need to assign the problem to "fresh minds" without such experience.

The difficulties in communication caused by lack of background and experience are further compounded by the interactions among the people involved, which cannot be resolved by merely improved appreciation of language and interests. In fact, one of the sources of difficulty—the tendency to step outside one's area of competence—seems to become more significant as knowledge grows concerning the techniques of other groups. However, a far more serious consideration lies in the fact that different individuals are each concerned with a common area of overlapping responsibility, where they seem to be using the same language and talking about the same thing. Thus similar words all too frequently are used to represent superficially similar concepts which are, in fact, fundamentally different. In such cases the attempt to resolve the consequent confusion introduces yet another complicating factor—the apparently natural human tendency to become more abstract rather than more concrete when communication becomes difficult.

Finally, it has also been apparent that terminology in this field has had a role to play in addition to that of communication. John Henry Merryman phrased it this way:

> It has become clear that when talking to people in the field one should be careful to use the appropriate terms, not so much to facilitate communication as to establish status. Use of the right words in the right way early in a conversation can mean the difference between being one up or one down. . . . In any conversation in the information retrieval field one must regard the person to whom one speaks as an adversary and the conversation as a

---

[1] Automation in the Organization of Knowledge, *SRI Journal*, 1957, v. I, No. 1, 1st Qtr.

contest in which, inevitably, one will gain prestige at the expense of the other. . . . The important thing is not the *meaning* of the term. Indeed, nothing could be less relevant. What one needs to keep a firm grasp on is the *use* of the term, its prestige value and the like. Obviously the meaning depends on who is using the term and for what purpose. . . .[2]

ANALYSIS OF INFORMATION SYSTEMS

The approach of this book is that to establish effective communication requires a positive recognition of the fact that, in its present stage of development, information retrieval does represent an interdisciplinary effort. This has led to an analysis of information systems based on the assignment of individual problems to distinct areas of responsibility with the particular applicable experience and available techniques. In this way the requirements and capabilities in each area can be developed by those with the training and knowledge to do so; significant questions and problems will not be ignored or left to the untrained amateur; and the frequently unsuccessful excursions by individuals outside their field of past experience may be avoided.

In a sense this view of an interdisciplinary problem compares it to a judicial process where each of a set of interested parties is represented by an advocate presenting the needs of his area of responsibility as effectively as he can and yet willing to compromise where the direct interests of his client require it. It means that, although a highly competent individual could reasonably perform excellent work in each of the several areas, at any given time he should work only in a single area of responsibility. Furthermore, in order to perform successfully in any area, experience with its problems and familiarity with its tools must have been developed; the experience and capability in one area cannot be expected to carry over to others.

Failure to recognize this has led to confusion in many situations in the past about whether the degree of success of a given system was due to the special features of the given storage medium, the unique advantages of the file organization, the broad flexibility of the logical equipment, or the efficiency of the user's own system of operation. It is therefore essential that each of these aspects be analyzed and its separate contribution determined before the enormously more complicated problem of system synthesis can be approached. In

[2] John Henry Merryman, Tactics and Terminology in Information Retrieval: A Summary of Recent Work, *College and Research Libraries,* January 1958, v. 1a, pp. 33–37.

limiting the considerations in this way, it must be acknowledged that a simplification is being made. There is no question that the equipment, the system organization, and the requirements of the eventual user are all very much interrelated. However, it is felt that the sources of requirements and capability must be clearly understood and differentiated before the interactions can be examined.

In summary, in this view, the resolution of the communication problem in the design of an information system and, ultimately, the general problem of synthesizing an information system require analysis of what the areas of responsibility are and what the problems are when these areas of responsibility overlap. From an examination of the qualifications of present workers in the field of information systems it would seem that four distinct areas of responsibility can be defined: the user, the operator, the designer, and the equipment supplier. Each of the four areas of responsibility is concerned with the satisfaction of particular aspects of the total information problem. Most of the problems in the field seem either to fall completely within single such areas or, as we will try to show, are of overlapping interest between two of them.

In carrying out his functions the specialist in any given area operates within the boundary conditions of requirements on the one hand and capabilities on the other. The operator, for example, is provided a set of requirements by the user and a set of capabilities in the organization established by the designer. Similarly, the designer is provided a set of requirements by the operational people and a set of capabilities existing in the equipment. Overlapping interest and

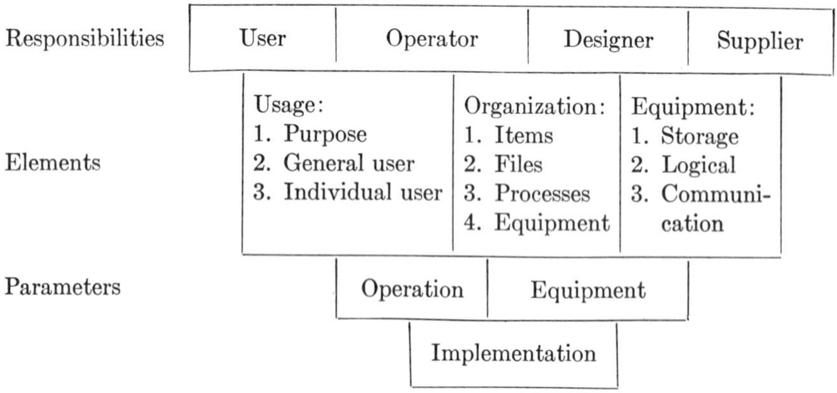

FIG. 66. Analysis of information systems.

conflict occur precisely because the capabilities required by one area are the requirements placed on another; the same fundamental elements by their very nature are thus viewed from two conflicting standpoints.

Our approach is summarized by the following chart, which also serves as a kind of index to this and the next several chapters. The present chapter has the purpose of presenting this concept of an interdisciplinary problem and, in particular, of defining the various areas of responsibilities. Later chapters will use this framework as a means of classifying the elements which characterize an information system problem.

RESPONSIBILITY OF THE USER

Perhaps the most important aspects of an information system are those which reflect the requirements of the user. Users are unquestionably the principal figures in the information storage and retrieval picture. Their needs are paramount, and the success of any system depends on how efficiently and thoroughly it serves their needs, how well they like it, and how well they adapt to it. If user needs are to be effectively met, they must be well defined and some measure of their relative importance must be provided. This, then, can be considered the area of *responsibility of the user.* Unfortunately, however, this area is not only the most important of the four defined here, it also apparently is the most difficult.

Difficulty is involved in the very definition of the user himself. Thus the user might well be considered as the management of the organization served by the information system. On the other hand, the user can be considered as an abstraction, representative of the class of users whose needs are to be met in general; with this view, the tendency is to think of the user as a constant, the typical user. Finally, the user can be considered as the individual whose particular requests must be met and who therefore cannot be considered as an average or typical person. Perhaps, with respect to the user, rather than speaking of his responsibility we should speak of a class of responsibilities: that of the individual user himself for establishing his own needs, that of some representative for establishing the needs of the class of users, and that of management for establishing the basic purpose and operating boundary conditions, such as the criteria by which usage will be judged and by which the class of customers will be defined.

Further difficulties result from the fact that a pattern or framework within which to formulate user needs does not generally exist. One is thus faced with the unhappy task of precisely formulating needs without really knowing what must be made precise. This is combined with an understandable reluctance on the part of the user himself to place any limits on needs—not only is the future uncertain but something vital might have been overlooked.

Hence there is an overwhelming tendency by the user either to ignore his responsibility to define his requirements or to rely on intuition rather than precisely formulated knowledge. The first alternative by default leaves this area of responsibility to hands other than those of the user, with a resulting distortion of user needs by other considerations, such as equipment limitations. The second alternative leads the user, since he cannot effectively communicate his intuitive knowledge, to step outside his area of experience—to attempt to specify equipment and systems of operation himself.

Fundamentally, however, the difficulties in this area stem from the fact that it is here that the questions of value arise. The determination of criteria for judging value, not only for individual questions but also for the total operation, is difficult; the design of an information system to optimize its value in meeting user needs is equally difficult. Each user has a different point of view, different needs, and different criteria of value. To serve all users with equal proficiency would mean the creation of a universal system consisting of subsystems for each known user, whether present or future. Clearly such an approach is impractical if not impossible, and some compromise must be made between value and cost. It should be recognized that the user will adapt himself to almost any reasonable system; the only question is whether it is worth the effort for him to do so.

RESPONSIBILITY OF THE OPERATOR

An information system exists as a dynamic organism responsive to its environment—it must be used, added to, and modified if its existence is to be justified. The requirements of operation are those aspects of an information system which reflect this dynamic nature. The effectiveness with which the information system responds to the user needs ultimately can be measured only in terms of operational effectiveness—the degree to which it continues to meet the requirements of operation. This means that since user interests are constantly changing, the system must be dynamic and capable of continually reorganizing according to changes in subject concepts and user requirements. Herner [3] states

> One other important attribute of systems is dynamicism. The operators of the system are keenly sensitive to changes in user-requirements: changes arising from shifting subject interests and from a growing awareness of the user-group as to the capabilities of the system. By keeping aware of shifting search demands and interests, the operators of the system are able to ensure that it meets the real needs of the group for which it is designed and thus retains its vitality. . . .

This then can be considered the area of *responsibility of the operator*. It is he who ensures that, as a dynamic organism, the information system continues to justify its existence effectively. Fortunately for most information systems, this responsibility is well defined, well understood, and well executed. The librarian, the manager of an accounting system, the information specialist—each has been faced with the day-to-day problems of providing information to the user, scheduling functions, maintaining the file, assigning personnel, controlling operations. In effect, he has been forced to meet these problems because he is the man on the spot. If failures or inadequacies become evident, he is there and obviously responsible.

It is important to distinguish carefully the operator from the "user" and from the "management." Thus the librarian, as the man responsible for the operation of an information system, may well be part of the management of the organization, but his management responsibilities are in a real sense separate from his operational responsibilities. On the other hand, he may also be a user of the system as other users are, but this is significant to his role as operator only to the extent that he finds such usage necessary in order to operate the system.

The responsibility of the operator is a two-fold one: First, he must meet the operational problems in providing the service—scheduling, maintaining the file, assigning personnel—all of the jobs involved in running an organization. Second, he must not only ensure the effectiveness of the system operation, but he must also interpret the immediate needs of the user in terms of the system operation and thus provide the communication link between the user and the system. He must understand the nature of the information the system

---

[3] Saul Herner, The Relationship of Information-Use Studies and the Design of Information Storage and Retrieval Systems, RADC Contract AF 30(602)-1857, December 8, 1958.

can provide and assist the user in translating his request into a form most suitable for the system to handle. Conversely, he must understand the user's requirements; he must interpret the file in terms of what the user is requesting. This role of intermediary is almost certainly of far greater importance in the over-all picture than is the management aspect of running an installation.

Mary Francillon [4] stated this very clearly when she said

> The requester cannot be expected to translate his own question: he is rightly bound to express it in terms of his own particular line of inquiry. Questions must be interpreted for the same reason that books and articles, already titled by their authors, must also be indexed in other ways to make the maximum amount of content retrievable. Some authors and some questioners come closer than others to providing a concise and complete description, in title and question respectively. But a gap always exists and the librarian must bridge it, indexing the answers to fit the pattern of probable request and search, interpreting the questions to fit the established organization of information. As C. L. Bernier has written: a "way of helping to bring the vocabularies of searchers and document system into coincidence or correlation . . . is the crucial problem in all systems."
>
> But we are convinced that the chief responsibility for adjustment continues to lie with the interpreter, leaving the inquirer free to ask his questions in his own terms. The very characteristics which make success in information retrieval so far from automatic, and so varied as to cause, seem to be the characteristics which permit man to find new meanings, to make new connections through old patterns and relationships.
>
> Therefore, this study leads us to emphasize that the role of the interpreter serving as liaison between the inquirer and the retrieval system, is a vital part of the continuing growth of knowledge. The burden of proof, so to speak, must lie with the librarian; the information sought may or may not exist, and it may be available only in documents entirely different in name and data from those requested. But there is the challenge and the opportunity.

Effective though he may be in carrying out these responsibilities, the operator usually is faced with one serious difficulty. This is the general lack of what might be called a "charter," or explicit definition of exactly what the requirements on the operation are. This difficulty manifests itself in the problems arising when the operator may be suddenly faced with conflicting requirements. It is most evident in the frequently anomalous position of the information center in the organization.

---

[4] Mary Francillon, Information Retrieval: A View from the Reference Desk, *The Journal of Documentation,* December 1959, v. 15, No. 4.

RESPONSIBILITY OF THE DESIGNER

An information system must exist as a *structure* before it can respond to needs. This structure must organize stored information, operations, men, and machinery so as to meet the operational needs most effectively. Developing the structure then can be considered the area of *responsibility of the designer.* The designer is concerned with the mechanics of organization and procedure; he is concerned with clarification, definition, efficiency of operation. Mechanized systems require great precision in the definition of their operation; otherwise they can't work. In addition, because of their substantial cost, mechanized systems must be organized for efficiency. It is the role of the systems designer to provide this precision and efficient design.

System design is a difficult area, as is that of the user, but for different reasons. In contrast with the definition of user requirements, which is a somewhat neglected area, system design is of almost universal interest. It so vitally affects all other areas that the problems of organization and structure are continually under investigation.

Conferences concerned with the information system problem, such as the International Conference on Scientific Information in November 1958, have examined various aspects of these different areas of interest. Usually they have been concerned with detailed results, such as specific "user studies," or details of different techniques for the organization of information, or the detailed characteristics of different types of devices. Unfortunately this great activity in system design has not been as fruitful as it should have been, precisely because the investigations have typically emphasized the specialized needs of particular interests. As a result, either day-to-day operating needs are subordinated to the optimum usage of ideal equipment systems or vice versa.

From all of this specialized work, however, there has resulted a large and ever growing set of techniques and approaches applicable to implementation of individual, discrete areas of the information system problem. These include the great variety of indexing schemes, classification schedules, data handling programs and procedures, complements of equipment, etc. On the other hand, the application of these techniques and approaches to information systems problems is still an extremely difficult and ill-defined task. There is no well-defined set of tools for selecting which of the potential answers should be combined for the optimal solution of any specific complex problem.[5]

In part, this deficiency is a result of the lack of recognition of system design as a major area of responsibility. The failure to identify the nature and even, in some cases, the existence of the problem facing the information system designer has meant there has been little or no orderly development of generally agreed-on systems methodology. There is a tendency to identify system design either with supplying the equipment or with running the installation. What is required, it would appear, is a recognition of system design as a problem distinct from operational and equipment interests as such, with the basic purpose of matching the two for the most effective total system. This recognition has been made in many specialized information problems, such as business accounting, where "systems and procedures" groups have been established independent of the operating personnel. It has not, however, yet been generally recognized in the total field of information systems.

A more basic, though related, problem affecting the area of system organization is the lack of either a general theory for design or, in lieu of such a theory, a broad base of qualified experience. In large part, the documentalists, the data processing system designers, the information scientists in general are concerned with an analytical process which must result in an operable system meeting the needs of all parties concerned in an optimal manner. Eventually some objective, quantitative measure for efficiency will be available, but at the present time one does not exist, and most system design is based solely on the intuition and experience of the systems man. Unfortunately the concept of integrated system design itself is a new one, and there is no reservoir of personnel trained in this type of work.

It has been claimed that system design represents a professional activity of extreme complexity and importance.

> No one actually planned it that way, but a new and specialized professional area has, in the space of a few years, come into being. You find systems design recognized in a number of fields [communications and space exploration, for instance]; but the largest and fastest-growing concentration is in connection with data processing activities.
>
> If the name of the profession did not spring from work with computer systems, it has already centered on such endeavors. And here the emphasis is on *concepts and methods,* rather than machines. Systems engineering (in data processing) implies *operational and procedural problem-solving,* rather

---

[5] *Information Systems Workshop: The Designer's Responsibility and His Methodology,* An ADI Publication, Spartan Books, Washington, 1962.

> than equipment development, adaptation, or maintenance. A systems engineer deals with *systems behavior* (*how procedures and functional components fit together*), rather than with the pieces themselves.
>
> In the "pure" systems approach . . . hardware considerations are apt to come into the picture last. By and large, this is a new concept. It is a shift in thinking induced by advancing technology and the same changing times and situations that favored emergence of the systems engineering profession itself.[6]

On the other hand, it might seriously be questioned whether this is in fact professional work. A survey of some of the literature in an attempt to answer this question reveals that the promulgation of a satisfactory definition of "profession" has progressed little beyond the six criteria proposed by Abraham Flexner[7] in 1915:

> (1) intellectual operations coupled with large individual responsibilities, (2) raw materials drawn from science and learning, (3) practical application, (4) an educationally communicable technique, (5) tendency toward self-organization, and (6) increasingly altruistic motivation.[8]

These criteria fail to emphasize the real role of the responsibility of the individual. It seems as though a profession is essential where the degree of individual responsibility is so great that the client cannot rely on the usual mechanisms of financial liability to guarantee performance. Educational and ethical standards then represent the only means by which the client has any measure of assurance that the work will meet his needs. Conversely, only the protection of professional position allows the practitioner to assume individual responsibility without the fear of financial destruction.

A profession, accordingly, is a vocation whose practice is founded on high individual responsibility, on an understanding of the theoretical structure of some department of learning or science, and on the abilities accompanying such understanding. This understanding and these abilities are applied to the vital practical affairs of mankind. After such a first-level statement has been formulated, the problem of defining a *specific* profession then becomes the concern of the practitioners in terms of the unique conditions of their area of specialization.

If system design is to be a profession, it will demand arduous training and personal commitment to an exacting ethical code. Both

---

[6] IBM Data Processing Information, January 25, 1961.

[7] Abraham Flexner, Is Social Work a Profession? *School and Society,* June 26, 1915, v. 1, p. 904.

[8] Ethical Standards and Professional Conduct, *Annals of the American Academy of Political and Social Science,* January 1955, v. 297.

attributes are required, and a failure in either is a failure of profession. Ethical conduct as such has received more or less general sanction. It implies, for example, rules to mediate the system designer's relations to his client, to his colleagues, to the public, to his association. It implies specific criteria for the professional, requirements for admission to practice, standards for competent service. These standards for the profession of system design certainly do not exist in well-defined form. In fact, there does not even exist an acknowledged professional organization.

Furthermore, the problem of defining adequate educational standards for system design remains. The manufacturers have supplied little or no training assistance in this area except to their own personnel, nor should they feel an obligation to do so. The colleges, universities, and management societies and associations of the country have not yet met the need for the kinds of technical training needed for systems analysis. A curriculum that would train students in the process of problem solving through the management of information would need to cover an exceedingly broad subject range—survey techniques, statistics, econometrics, projective psychological research, theory and practice of experimentation, operations research, computing machine techniques, combinatorial mathematics, analysis of administrative data, library techniques, symbolic logic, linguistics. It is difficult to visualize how such a program would fit into the normal academic structure.

Because of the lack of a well-defined "systems education," specialists in system design have been drawn from the ranks of engineers, mathematicians, librarians, and accountants.

> One remarkable thing about members of the new profession [of system design] is the dissimilarity of their academic training and experience background. Many are accountants or auditors who got ready to explore the big stream while fishing some of its tributaries. Some are graduate engineers or scientists [particularly mathematicians] who found themselves wholly new opportunities while harnessing computers to their disciplines and thorny problems. Quite a few are consultants strong in management and business administration [some consulting firms are already specialising in systems engineering], or expert in the ins-and-outs of a particular organization, industry, or field of endeavor. Still others grew up smack-dab in the middle of the ferment—methods analysts, programmers, "tab room" supervisors, data processing specialists.[9]

---

[9] IBM Data Processing Information, January 25, 1961.

The resulting "profession" is an amorphous one, at best. We can only say that the needs are evident: (1) to identify this problem area and its responsibilities, professional or not, (2) to structure it, pointing the way for further development effort in system design itself, and (3) to define the educational needs.

RESPONSIBILITY OF EQUIPMENT SUPPLIER

Modern information retrieval systems are increasingly dependent on automation. The need for precision and economic utilization which mechanization requires has probably been the real force behind all the developments discussed in the previous chapters. Another problem is how to develop equipment with characteristics and price sufficiently attractive to provide a broad enough market for economic feasibility. Meeting this problem is the area of *responsibility of the equipment supplier.* It requires good equipment design and development, economic manufacture, and superior salesmanship.

Typically the product development group or the market research group in the organization of an equipment supplier will determine the functional specifications on equipment in terms of what are called over-all market requirements. They attempt to define a total market and to fit the maximum number of customers with the minimum number of modifications. When functional specifications cannot be met with existing technology, the engineer in the manufacturer's organization must develop new technology.

When the product has finally been developed and manufactured, it must be sold. Selling systems automation is one of the most complex tasks ever assigned American business. The companies concerned with the manufacture of the components of automation are, of course, convinced of the feasibility, and in fact the inevitability, of automating countless operations which are today largely accomplished manually. On the other hand, the rapid conversion to automation is retarded because many of the managers of companies and organizations which will be the principal users of automation systems are not as completely convinced of the advantages.

Here is the crux of the selling problem. The principles involved in selling automation systems to business and government are somewhat similar to those used in what has been called "industrial selling." The industrial salesman requires the combination of technical knowledge of equipment, knowledge of the customers' operations, and pure sales ability. An important aspect of this type of selling is the creation of a dependence by the customer on the supplier. There is a tendency—because the supplier does such a good job—to rely on him to do the job of other areas of responsibility. It must be recognized that, good a job though he may do, the advice of the supplier will be legitimately prejudiced, and the results may be best for the manufacturer but not for the user.

9

Elements of usage

The fundamental aim of the user of an information system generally is to make decisions. Presumably the data obtained from the system will in some way contribute to his decision making process. The adequate specification of his requirements in this respect is, as has been pointed out, critically important to the functioning of the information system. Of more immediate interest, however, is the vital effect of this specification, by the user, on the job of the operator. The capability which the user demands of the system is the requirement which the operator of the system must meet.

In this area of overlap there are some substantial differences in view between the problem-oriented approach of the user and the file-oriented approach of the operator. The user formulates his needs for information in the context of his particular interests, involving a broad frame of reference in which information recovery occupies a fairly minor role. On the other hand, for the operator, the information process is of prime importance; he is there to provide information; what is done with it is really outside his problem. From his standpoint, the request of the particular user is just one among a great volume and variety. Its relative importance must be evaluated in terms of the operation of a total system.

To bring these two purposes into some degree of agreement, communication and understanding are of prime importance. Mary Francillon[1] phrased it this way:

---

[1] Mary Francillon, Information Retrieval: A View from the Reference Desk, *The Journal of Documentation,* December 1959, v. 15, No. 4.

The crucial point seems almost always to be the original clear definition and understanding of the question. Now on what does this depend? Principally, it seems on the recognition, by both, that differences in purpose and training equip the inquirer for one role and the reference librarian for another. The former is primarily responsible for his subject field; the latter for the tools of information retrieval—the documents and their organization. While misdirected effort and subsequent dissatisfaction can doubtless be reduced by further education of requester and searcher, the making of an expert in any field requires such specialization that this remedy has distinct limitation.

There has been, in much of the work of the documentalists, emphasis on the role of meaning, or semantics, in the operation of an information system. Discussion of semantics relates solely to the communication overlap between the user and the operator. It is unfortunate that this fact is not explicitly recognized more often; in many discussions of a more "philosophical" nature the general impression is made that semantics has relevance to mechanization. This is not valid. Meaning, in the sense of semantics, has no relevance to machinery. The question of meaning and of how items related by some concept of similarity should be retrieved is relevant to machine usage or to system design only when the concept of similarity has been expressed quantitatively for the particular situation.

Now, to define what is meant by "usage" we must distinguish among the several meanings of the term. The first is the view of management as defining the purpose of usage; the second is the view of the operator in his need for criteria of value; the third is the view of the class of customers as a whole; and the fourth is the view of the individual customer in his own individual requests.

DEFINING PURPOSE

In some way, purpose must be defined in terms of the totality of users, since this provides the very reason for the existence of the information system. Purpose, more than anything else, determines the character of the information system—the type of information stored, the nature of the requests, the class of customers. Purpose specifies not only why information is needed, but to a large extent the form in which it is needed.

Admittedly the purpose of any information system is generally, but not necessarily, to aid decision making processes. Within this general framework, though, different types of purpose can be distinguished. The simplest probably is record keeping—business records, vital documents, legal records—archival storage of one type or another. In such record keeping, generally speaking, the individual item itself is significant in the sense that a first edition of Shakespeare is valuable. The purpose of record keeping, then, is to ensure the recovery of the individual document for its own value. A second type of purpose one might distinguish is "fact recovery." This is the purpose in the typical technical information service or the customer interrogation service. The individual item is not of great importance; what is valuable is the information extracted from it. A third type of purpose which one might distinguish is research and analysis, wherein it is not the individual fact that is important but some analytic combination of facts. Scientific research files usually fall in this general category.

The importance of these distinctions was emphasized by Herner: [2]

The foregoing hypothesis (concerning the differences between the engineer and the scientist) simple as it is, gives rise to a number of broad implications relating to the design of storage and retrieval systems. One implication is that the intellectual demands on the operator of a system serving pure scientists are significantly lighter than those placed on the operator of a system serving applied scientists. In the first instance, all that is required of the system is a list of references, and nothing more. In the second instance, specific answers to specific questions are required. Producing actual answers to questions implies a far more complicated input and output mechanism than does the production of mere references.

By contrast, a two-stage system serving pure scientists has a much easier job to do. The reason for this relative simplicity is a negative one: owing to the high level of sophistication and the narrow fields of specialization in pure science, it is extremely difficult for anyone but the requester himself to perform the selection and interpretation phases of a search. Literature selection and interpretation, and the subsequent process of synthesis, constitute, for the pure scientist, the very essence of creativity. This is a hard thing to have done by proxy.

Thus, the person putting information into a storage and retrieval system serving pure scientists, must, more or less by default, do his encoding in only the most general terms; he must describe whole published units, such as books, papers, articles, etc., rather than the specific information contained in these units. This means a storage and retrieval system in which the primary job of the operator is not to exploit a collection of information on

[2] Saul Herner, The Relationship of Information-Use Studies and the Design of Information Storage and Retrieval Systems, RADC Contract AF 30(602)-1857, December 8, 1958.

behalf of a user group but to arrange the collection in such a way that the user can find what he wants by himself. This logically connotes a conventional library in which publications are arranged according to their subject content.

Because of the importance which these distinctions have, it is vital that an information system operate under some kind of charter which will establish its organization and its mission. This charter should definitely assign responsibility for the efficiency and operation of the information system. It should define how the system will be supported, what the scope and nature of the material should be, and what the class of customers should be.

DEFINING CRITERIA OF VALUE

Definition of purpose is not necessarily a clear-cut problem. In the first place, purpose for the system as a whole may vary from highly specialized to highly general. On the other hand, the purpose of individual users may also vary over a similar range but may not necessarily coincide with the over-all interests. Thus the operator of a highly specialized system may be faced with a highly generalized request and vice versa.

Hence, the establishment of criteria—unfortunately usually implicit rather than explicit—by which the relative importance of individual requests and other operations can be weighed is basic to the definition of purpose. For example, if two requests come in almost simultaneously, which is to be handled first? The criterion may be very simple, such as time order or perhaps customer number. Perhaps it will be an assigned priority; thus a request from management is treated very differently from a request from an individual user of another type. In inventory control it is very typical to have priority requests which are handled immediately, other types of requests which are handled on a two-hour basis, and then the great routine volume of requests which are handled on a daily or even a weekly basis. Similarly, different types of usage are handled with different priority. In the utility business a customer bill is not handled in the same way as a customer request for information; a priority is given to "requests for information" which will be handled immediately, with perhaps a two-minute service. A priority may be given to certain types of reports, which will be produced before anything else. In any event there must be some criteria available for weighing the relative importance among the set of requests against the file. These criteria provide the operator of the information system with the framework of purpose within which he controls the operation.

In part these criteria are a function of the needs of the typical user —as we discuss below—and, in part, a function of the needs in the individual request. Fundamentally, however, the criteria must be economic ones and must reduce to the basic issues of value and cost.

Much attention has been given in recent years to attempts to assess the value of information to a researcher. Although this kind of inquiry may lead to some interesting theories of value, it will not lead to an ability to establish the desirable level of support for, say, an information center. First, to be at all accurate the theories of value must of necessity operate on the micro level—determining the value of discrete responses to individual requesters. The difficulties involved in aggregating a large number of these microanalyses into a gross value support level for any system of interest would be large. Second, the value support level of a service cannot be divorced from the costs of providing it.

A mechanism for relating the discrete responses to the service costs of providing them is required. In economics, the market is considered as the mechanism which adjusts the prices of goods and services to reflect their relative value. The relation of these prices to the costs of production in turn determines the amount of productive capacity which will be allocated to the various commodities. Repetitive operations in the market adjust the supplies and prices until they are in line with the demands and costs. Essentially, by providing circumstances in which commodities are sold in competition with others, the market serves to accumulate the microdecisions concerning the value of a commodity to a buyer and its cost to a seller. Although there are both theoretical and practical limitations to the market mechanism, it remains one of the most satisfactory techniques available for determining prices.

In addition to these "open" markets there are numerous "closed" systems, in which techniques have been developed to resolve some of the difficulties encountered in allocating scarce resources to competitive productive factors. Much of internal cost accounting is intended to provide information on allocation and utilization of resources which cannot be bought and sold in small increments. For example, facility purchase costs may be allocated to departments (or projects) on the basis of usage, though the facility is provided in advance and its cost is independent of actual usage.

Information services, in general, are not provided through a market, that is, those who consume the services on a daily basis do not pay for them. Furthermore, these consumers are but remotely associated with the people who make the support decisions, that is, those who decide how much information service will be available. While the lack of feedback between the consumers and the information suppliers has received extensive publicity, none has been given to the lack of communication between the consumers and those paying for the services. There is also no reason to believe that the suppliers and those paying them are any more closely coupled. The poor communication and long delay times render such a system useless as a market mechanism.

The tremendous operating success that market and cost accounting mechanisms have had throughout our economy makes it desirable that careful attention be given to the possibilities of developing and applying such a mechanism to the information services. The costs of information services would no longer be hidden in a gross overhead percentage and thus they would no longer be considered as free goods. In such a case the project manager would become concerned with the use of information services as a productive factor in his project performance. On the policy level, data would be provided on the total utilization of information services and the comparison used to adjust the criteria on service.

Those who provide the information services would work in a changed context, because management and consumers pay greater attention to the service when it is evident that the service costs money. A corollary of the economist's dictum, "cost equals value," is that "free goods are worth their cost." Thus information services would be given their correct status as one of a set of available productive factors.

The costing data would also provide knowledge of differing approaches to information utilization. Over a period of time, guidelines may be established which would indicate when a proposed usage appeared radically out of line. Also, this knowledge could be made public and would promote quantitative knowledge and experience in the field. Individuals within the field have limited means of discovering the operating methods and results of others. Increased stimulation can be expected to lead to improved information systems on a nationwide basis. To the extent that information is indeed a productive factor, this would lead to improved research and development.

What must be done in order to determine the feasibility of establishing such a market mechanism? Two general questions must be answered. How much does it cost to have such a system operating? What are the benefits obtained? In a real sense these are themselves economic questions. The foregoing discussion has been concerned with the potential benefits of such a mechanism. In order to establish the costs, the mechanism must be specified in detail. Only then can the question be resolved whether the benefits of a cost accounting system warrant the cost of establishing and running it.

A cost accounting system for a library would require definition of the unit of information service. A single system normally provides numerous kinds of service. If a total budget constraint is to be useful to the service, the way in which these individual "products" contribute to the aggregate cost and service must be explored. To begin, one would want to classify these services and obtain a "standard" cost for each of them. The purpose of a standard cost system is to charge the same amount for services which are identical. This is attained by charging to individual services the costs which should have been incurred in their performance.

In the development of these costs, both job costing and process costing are likely to be helpful. A pure job cost system is one in which the costs are collected for each individual item of service provided. A pure process cost system does not attempt to collect costs for the individual units of a discrete service operation; instead, all costs incurred on parts of the process in a given time period, such as a month, are collected. A mixed system may well be the most suitable for information systems. It is in mixing the two to arrive at a standard system that one would answer such questions as whether to base charges on total search time or on some other basis.

There are other costs to be allocated on a rational basis to the services provided. These are primarily related to the initial costs of providing the facility—the building, the equipment, the documents, etc. How rapidly the costs of these items should be charged off against operations is an open question. In the general area of buildings and equipment, standard practices from industry provide adequate guidelines. The guidelines for writing off documents are less conspicuous. Some work on the relation of document usage to document age does exist. In the technical area, particularly, this relation is dependable enough to serve as a basis for amortizing the cost of placing the documents in the system.

In summary, the determination of the value and cost of information services does not call for research; rather, it requires the implementation of operating cost accounting systems for existing information services. Work measurement is not theoretical; it is an accomplished industrial fact. Its usefulness lies in providing quantitative data about real, continuing operations.

To be sure, there are questions to be answered before such a requirement is imposed. Answering such questions may well require research. However, such research is only secondarily related to research in information retrieval.

As we have indicated, many of these questions will resolve to the fundamental one of, Do the benefits from a cost accounting system justify its costs? On the surface, it would certainly seem that the answer is highly dependent on the environment within which the information system itself operates. To a large extent, if the needs for information are sufficiently immediate and of sufficiently high importance to warrant the installation of a complex automated information system, then almost certainly a cost accounting system is completely justified. On the other hand, if the immediacy of the needs for information or the importance of those needs are not sufficient to justify an automated system, it is unlikely that cost accounting procedures would be wise. In particular, because of the character of scientific *research*, as opposed to engineering and technology, the needs for information rarely are immediate and, therefore, cost accounting systems would probably not be of significant value in a university research environment, for example. In fact, it is debatable whether any complex retrieval system is required in scientific research (again, as opposed to engineering and technology). Such research is rarely "immediate" in its need for information; the arguments concerning eliminating duplication have far less significance than they do in the industrial environment, since duplication in scientific research is not redundant; and perhaps most important it is the process of research which is significant to the scientist and not so much the specific data which may result.

DEFINING THE TYPICAL USER

Recognizing the importance of a defined purpose and of criteria based on value and cost is one thing; actually determining what the purpose and criteria should be in a particular situation is another. In principle, the purpose should be established in terms of total organizational interests and should be expressed in the form of a written charter. All too frequently, however, it is actually determined by the organizational position of the information center, or by the needs of particular individual users, or by the personalities of certain administrative personnel.

If the purpose is to be well defined in terms of total organizational interests, how is this to be done? Presumably it should, at the very least, specify the needs of the typical users and how they are to be met. Until recently the role of the user was largely unexplored, with few documented studies to support speculation about his needs. Now, however, several studies are available, including the early reports of Shaw,[3] Herner,[4] Henkle and Egan,[5] the valuable papers presented at the International Conference on Scientific Information in November 1958, and the recent paper by Bourne et al.[6]

These studies show that, though perhaps less predictable and less open to investigation than other elements of the information system problem, the user does have pertinent habits which can be observed, counted, and analyzed. Herner[7] summarized previous work and indicated that:

> The majority of these studies have produced results, in the sense that they have furnished operators of information programs insight as to how programs are used or are likely to be used. A striking characteristic of these results is that despite the fact that they have been derived by a variety of means they have corroborated one another in a number of important respects.

Among the questions involved in the attempts to define more clearly the role of the user in information retrieval are: What does he ask for and how does he ask? Does he prefer answers in the form of full copies, abstracts, title lists? What factors affect his question and his satisfaction with the answer? Answering these and similar

---

[3] Ralph R. Shaw, Pilot Study on the Use of Scientific Literature by Scientists, 21 November 1956, Report on Study for the National Science Foundation.

[4] Saul Herner, Information Gathering Habits of Workers in Pure and Applied Science, *Industrial & Engineering Chemistry,* January 1954, v. 46, pp. 228–236.

[5] H. H. Henkle and M. Egan, Ways and Means in Which Research Workers, Executives and Others Use Information, in *Documentation in Action,* by J. H. Shera, Allen Kent, and J. W. Perry, New York, Reinhold, 1956.

[6] C. P. Bourne, G. D. Peterson, B. Lefkowitz, and D. Ford, *Requirements, Criteria, and Measures of Performance of Information Storage and Retrieval Systems,* Stanford Research Institute, December 1961, Final Report on Study for National Science Foundation.

[7] Saul Herner, Information Gathering Habits of Workers in Pure and Applied Science, *Industrial & Engineering Chemistry,* January 1954, v. 46, pp. 228–236.

questions is extremely difficult. Bourne [8] attempted to evaluate the relative importance of several such factors and reported:

Unfortunately, information about the user is extremely difficult to obtain. Measurements are difficult, if not impossible, and most studies resort to judgments or opinions. The user himself is frequently a poor source for direct comment on his needs; he is usually influenced by the tools and facilities that he is familiar with, and he usually cannot discriminate between his actual needs and his way of performing work. After interviewing over 90 researchers in electronics and 11 metallurgists, it was found that, to a limited degree, information requirements could be measured quantitatively, and measures could be formulated of the relative importance of each of these requirements. The interviews did provide a composite or over-all agreement on the relative importance of seven different factors; the most important of which was agreed to be the response time, the time involved between the request and the receipt of the major group of relevant references. However, there was no strong agreement as to the relative importance of the other six factors.

The problem, in summary, is how to gather and interpret facts about the user so as to give them meaning. The techniques available include (1) the study of existing records, (2) the use of interviews, (3) the use of questionnaires and information request forms, and (4) personal participation and experimentation. If the organization has any type of systems department established, there will be manuals of instruction, published procedures, organization charts, etc. These will be very useful, for they provide the description and basic authority for certain of the functions performed. Existing reports will provide statistical data, which can be studied away from the problem. The other three techniques, however, are not homework. These are where the work really lies: the techniques of interviews, questionnaires, and personal observation.

Herner [9] said:

The method used to determine needs varies with the organization activity, the size of the user group, organizational policy, and other factors. In some cases, the method consists of group discussions between the designers and users of the program or system; sometimes a simple questionnaire is

---

[8] C. P. Bourne, G. D. Peterson, B. Lefkowitz, and D. Ford, *Requirements, Criteria, and Measures of Performance of Information Storage and Retrieval Systems,* Stanford Research Institute, December 1961, Final Report on Study for National Science Foundation.

[9] Saul Herner, Information Gathering Habits of Workers in Pure and Applied Science, *Industrial & Engineering Chemistry,* January 1954, v. 46, pp. 228–236.

used; in other cases, face-to-face interviews are used; in still other cases, the analysis is done by examining circulation files and other records of literature use.

Bourne [10] summarized in somewhat more detail by distinguishing different approaches in these techniques.

Any of the following methods, or combinations of them, might be used to obtain information about the user's requirements:

(1) Ask the users specific questions about what they think their requirements are [e.g., tolerable delay, form of resulting product, types of service preferred].

(2) Analyze recent information requests. Probe the circumstances that motivated the request for information. Determine the parameters—such as response and error rates—that would have been tolerable in a particular situation. Find out the nature of any disappointments or unsatisfactory results. Taking advantage of the user's hindsight, find out what he would like to have obtained in the way of specific products or services.

(3) Monitor the establishment and fulfillment of a research project or experiment, and note the specific needs and requirements as they occur. Although realistic data may be obtained in this way, the method has the disadvantages of interfering with the working group, requiring a relatively long lag time for completion of the data gathering through a complete project schedule, and probably requiring a relatively large amount of observer's time for a number of different projects in order to obtain statistically significant data.

(4) Postulate a "perfect" retrieval system; then allow people to pose questions to the system.

(5) Determine the functions [e.g., preparation to learn new techniques, to learn experimental results, to plan new research, to prepare lectures, to keep abreast, etc.] of the various portions of the information services and find out how well each of these functions is being met. The dual of this method is to examine the various portions or channels of the information system [e.g., abstracts, books, journals, advertisements, etc.] and find out the functions that each of these channels serves.

(6) Measure the result that a user usually obtains [by performing his regular type of search] and compare it to the result that can be achieved by an exhaustive search of all available resources. This would give some indication of the amount of overlooked material he could tolerate.

(7) Perform a controlled experiment in which identical or comparable tasks are performed by groups with different information resources. This

---

[10] C. P. Bourne, G. D. Peterson, B. Lefkowitz, and D. Ford, *Requirements, Criteria, and Measures of Performance of Information Storage and Retrieval Systems,* Stanford Research Institute, December 1961, Final Report on Study for National Science Foundation.

would give some indication of the relationship between user productivity and the availability of information.

(8) Record, in some uniform measure, the amount of information that is normally available to the individual in his own office. This would give an estimate of the scope of interest or range of coverage of the individual user, and would show how large a file of information he considers sufficiently important to warrant the expenditure of his own time and money.

(9) Determine the circumstances surrounding the *critical* requirements for information [that is, those requests for information that are critical or fundamental to the solution of a given technical problem].

Perhaps the most important results of Bourne's work lies in his definition of an interview framework—admittedly a preliminary one, but still a step—for the formalized statement of general user needs. He states:

A survey technique, using personal interviews among a specific user population, was selected for determining user requirements in this study. A preliminary guide, incorporating the so-called *critical-incident* approach as well as direct questions, was developed after some intensive interviews and after discussions among members of the project team. The preliminary guide was pre-tested among nine electrical engineers on the Institute staff.

The final interview guide was designed to obtain four kinds of information.

(1) A list of critical requirements, using the critical incident technique.

(2) Measurements of selected requirements that were considered both important and susceptible to measurement. [Some requirements known to be important were unavoidably omitted because of the preliminary nature of this project.]

(3) Rank order of the importance of seven factors that were believed to be important to users and were amenable to ranking.

(4) Background variables that might influence the user needs [company, age, academic degree, specialty field, type of search, and the like].

Sometimes the interview, as selected and defined by Bourne, is the only available method. One cannot distribute questionnaires and cannot experiment or personally participate in the operation. Furthermore, interviews are stimulating, for the ideas developed by people working on the problem are often excellent. There are some cautions, however. The accuracy of interviews is questionable in two respects. The interviewer is frequently inaccurate and the person interviewed is usually inaccurate. There is a tendency to emphasize the exceptions, to use the extreme situations for examples. The exceptions are important, but they are not that all important; they should occupy their relative role.

Some of this can be avoided by accurate record keeping and by interviewing only after adequate preparation. The interviewed person should have been selected very carefully for the information he can give, and the information desired from him should have been defined with similar care, perhaps in a prebriefing of the interviewed person. Finally, it is important to verify the accuracy of everything done. Let the interviewed person check the notes; be sure to get samples of any existing forms or examples of questions, etc.

The technique of questionnaires is of debatable accuracy, but they do have value, particularly when used to supplement interviews. Since the specialized situation is obtained from the interview, the questionnaire may well give the total picture. If the total picture supports what the interview has brought out, fine; if it contradicts, this may mean it will be necessary to investigate more closely. Questionnaires may also be useful to recover objective data which can then be tabulated or subjected to statistical analysis, although there are cautions here, too. There is a great likelihood of misinterpreting both the questions and the answers. Also, there is a great possibility for statistical bias, for the people who do not answer the questionnaire are probably the ones who should have been talked to.

The technique of personal participation and experimentation, where one really gets into the operation itself and finds out by work what is going on, is certainly the most illuminating. It ensures dependability, since the information gathered is now dependent only on oneself. Furthermore, it develops know-how; one has learned from actually carrying out the work itself. This develops an understanding of the problem which could not possibly have been gotten otherwise. It is, of course, expensive, the most costly of the three techniques.

DEFINITION OF THE INDIVIDUAL REQUEST

All of this discussion of the typical user, however, serves to emphasize one factor that has seriously hampered the development and use of advanced information storage and retrieval systems. This has been the tendency of the designers to think of the user as a constant. Most of the research about the user has emphasized the problem of determining the requirements of the general user. Of course, the smaller and more specialized the population of users, the more possible it is to do this effectively. But, frequently, the problem of defining this "general user" is solved by the designer assigning to himself the role of typical user and extrapolating from his own information requirements and experience in developing his system. The usual result in such cases is that the system suits the designer's needs but not those for whom it is designed.

Herner[11] points out:

> . . . the common shortcomings of most storage and retrieval systems; they treat the user as a constant; their structure and design are based on the content of the literature, rather than on the way that the literature is used. As a result, the literature in a given special library is likely to be arranged in the interests or viewpoints of the clientele of the given library. This is actually no more realistic than using the same type of facilities to house organic chemists and theoretical physicists.

Therefore, basic to the definition of purpose, but related to the treatment of the individual request, is some measure of value or significance of particular information obtained. With such a measure, the operator can evaluate the stored data and screen them for their relevancy to the needs. This also implies criteria by which specific needs within a request can be evaluated for their relative importance. These criteria may well be implicit; on the other hand, it would be very desirable if they were explicit, and it would be even more desirable if they could be quantified.

The elements of usage constitute the framework in which the individual user will state his requirements and the operator will evaluate how to treat them. For the purposes of this discussion, the elements have been divided into two groups, precision and complexity.

Precision

Now, let us examine the question of precision. One can distinguish between the precision of the request and the precision of the recovered information. There is a well-known variation in the precision with which requests are given. To a large extent it is dependent on the knowledge by the user of his own needs; if he understands them, he will generally be able to specify his information requirements with a good degree of precision.

One cause for lack of precision is unfamiliarity with the file. This is almost certainly undesirable and should be avoided. The individual user should be informed of the nature of the file, of what he

---

[11] Saul Herner, The Relationship of Information—Use Studies and the Design of Information Storage and Retrieval Systems, RADC Contract AF 30(602)-1857, December 8, 1958.

can get from it, of how precisely he should define his questions in order to achieve maximum effectiveness, and so on.

For example, the user manually searching in a card catalog is uncertain of the proper subject headings to look under and also ignorant of the historical growth and development of the catalogs' basic structure. In consequence, while he may believe his search is comprehensive, in reality it may not be. Unaware of this, the researcher considers his work complete when he personally looks under headings which occur to him or to which he is referred by cross-reference. In this respect, mechanized systems may well provide a substantial aid in defining the character of the file to the user. In a machine system, alternative headings, synonyms, related headings, etc., can be stored internally in a manner which ensures that a given search will result in truly comprehensive coverage. In turn, the researcher will get more references than he is accustomed to receiving in a manual system. Correctly or not, the researcher usually interprets this abundance as a machine weakness. Since it is not possible to measure accurately what a researcher "overlooks" in a manual card catalog when he uses it, no reliable standards are yet available for making worthwhile comparison. The machine is able to generate *all* of the same responses for each and every equivalent request.

In visualizing the future Doyle imagines the user sitting at a TV console directly connected to the machine system.[12] With each search the user is first exposed to a master framework or "semantic road map," computer generated, to give him "a good mental picture of the library structure," before he formulates his questions. This form of man-machine feedback is to make it easy for the searcher to discover crossconnections among subjects in the particular library structure within which he is working that might not otherwise have occurred to him.

While studying the theoretical design considerations affecting the development of a special purpose centralized machine system for information retrieval, the Stanford Research Institute undertook considerable research work to determine the feasibility of rapid-feedback, man-machine relationships in which the user could choose from several levels of response from a data file. SRI refers to the proposed file as MIRF, Multiple Instantaneous Response File, and has this to say about the role of the user:

---

[12] Lauren B. Doyle, Semantic Road Maps for Literature Searchers, *Journal of the Association for Computing Machinery,* October 1961, v. 8, No. 4, pp. 553–578.

The user must communicate his interrogation to the machine, and once again, there are very many ways of accomplishing this communication, ranging from one extreme, the spoken word, to the other, a string of symbols in machine language. A given choice requires a compromise between user's convenience and machine costs.[13]

The physical system that would demonstrate new man-machine retrieval operation modes is described briefly as follows:

. . . Access to the file would be from an operator's console, with automatic control equipment to facilitate various detailed steps of searching. Responses to interrogations could be available on several levels of detail, enabling searches to be made roughly or precisely, as needed. For searching purposes, the descriptors would be encoded by single-field superposition. For display of descriptor lists to the user, two alternative forms of storage were proposed. The first was digital storage, by expanding the search memory; the second was photographic storage, in which the information content would be minimized, in order to simplify mechanical design. The machine would be capable of serving several inquiry stations.[14]

On the other hand, lack of precision may be due to the fact that the user does not understand his own problem. This should not be considered a bad situation. Frequently a file is used as a tool for developing understanding, and the file should be responsive to this type of need. In fact, the files may have been established precisely for the purpose of providing this kind of service, to aid in the understanding and definition of a problem. There seems to be little doubt that in certain research situations there is heuristic benefit in the very process of searching for information. As a researcher uses a central system, say a card catalog in a library, new thoughts constantly impinge on his mind which cause him to follow new leads, alter his original approach, and evolve new combinations of ideas which may not have occurred to him when he started. The searching process is essentially a form of feedback which enables the researcher to change his strategy in accordance with the kinds of information that he sees. The librarian calls this process browsing, and books may be deliberately arranged on shelves to facilitate the process.

Lauren B. Doyle points out that literature searchers find and value both the unexpected and the expected.

---

[13] Multiple Instantaneous Response File, SRI Project 3101, Stanford Research Institute, Menlo Park, Calif., August 1961, p. 12.
[14] *Ibid.*, p. 6.

When something unexpected is found, one thereby obtains information; when the expected is found, one obtains confirmation. However, when one formulates a search, the unexpected is hardly ever involved. Search requests are practically always constructed out of familiar combinations of terms. If a searcher tries to be "cute" and choose an unusual combination of terms, the result of his search will hardly ever be satisfactory. Either there will be no documents satisfying his request, or else the ones that do will have either an incidental or inappropriate relationship between the terms of his request.[15]

Little is known about the precise degree of heuristic value which accrues to a researcher during searching, nor of the search situations which are characterized by it. However, it seems logical to assume that heuristic benefits are more the handmaiden of generality than of specificity. Machine systems cannot discount this as a problem but must find some satisfactory substitute to preserve the advantage.

The other aspect of the demands with respect to precision relates to the information recovered from the file and its degree of logical agreement with the requested information. Such agreement may be complete, fragmentary, uncertain; items may be missed or irrelevant items may be recovered; too many or too few items may be presented to the requester. Each of these considerations—logical agreement, coverage, volume—must be specified in some way.

Users will at one time want a central system to provide great specificity of detail, whereas at other times they will expect and need generality and scope. The requirement for generality is based on the necessity for the system to meet changing conditions. In general searches the researcher must expect to work harder and spend more time at the process. However, during just such times he is likely to obtain the heuristic advantages enumerated above. If the information furnished to him is abundant, then his problem is temporal. When he cannot afford to spend the required time, he will want the central system to highlight only the "most relevant" items for him.

Let us look more closely at the precision of the recovered information. First of all, what does precision in logical agreement with the request mean? For example, the request may demand complete agreement. A transaction against an inventory item would require absolute agreement with that inventory part number; otherwise, the system should indicate an error. On the other hand, the requester

---

[15] Lauren B. Doyle, Semantic Road Maps for Literature Searchers, *Journal of the Association for Computing Machinery,* October 1961, v. 8, No. 4, pp. 553–578.

may accept fragmentary agreement. The requester may say, "I will accept a document satisfying characteristics A, B, and C, although I really want A, B, and D." This will require some criteria for weighing whether to accept an item as matching the request or not. An example might be credit files or dossiers, where the information provided in a request may be name, address, age, occupation, and so on; but items in the file may have only name and age, name and address, or other combinations.

A further step in this direction might allow some uncertainty. In such a dossier file, a name in the file might be A. M. Jones and the request calls for A. N. Jones. Are these the same people? It is uncertain, and the system might judge on a probabilistic basis. In this case, the system must provide some means of measuring the probability of whether or not agreement between the request and an item is sufficiently certain. This problem is very clearly illustrated by the difficulties in handling agreement between names, since many names which sound similar are spelled quite differently.[16] For this reason, the Soundex coding system for names (see page 143) has been designed to group together names which sound the same or tend to be confused when communication is blurred.

Another aspect of the precision of the recovered information is that of required coverage. Very frequently a requester is willing not to get every item relevant to a given subject; it may be that a single document would be completely adequate. Conversely, he may well be willing to accept irrelevant documents. It may be, however, that he has insisted on nothing but items immediately relevant to this subject or that all relevant items must be recovered. Typically in credit and dossier files, for example, it is essential not to miss anything. That is the whole purpose of the file—to indicate that there is a record.

A third aspect of precision is volume. How many items is the requester willing to accept: What will be too many or too few? The request should either implicitly or explicitly give some criterion for judging. If the system produces twenty thousand items, they probably are not going to be sent to him. If it comes out with just one, this may be too few. In any event, the question of volume is highly relevant and arises continually. Furthermore, there is certainly interplay among these. Let us take the question of coverage. Would

---

[16] William Phillips, Jr., Anita K. Bahn, Mabel Miyasaki, Person-Matching by Electronic Methods, *Communications of the ACM,* July 1962, v. 5, No. 7, pp. 404–406.

the requester be willing to have 50% irrelevant documents or "false drops"? There are times when he might, say if the file search recovers only two documents, one of them irrelevant. On the other hand, if the system recovers two thousand documents, one thousand of which are irrelevant, something is wrong.

The Western Reserve group was very concerned about the entire question of the precision and volume of coverage. They defined several measures of "retrieval effectiveness" to characterize the problem numerically.[17] They related the total number (C) of documents in the system, the number (M) of retrieved documents, the number (X) of relevant documents, and the number (W) of relevant documents retrieved. These measures included:

1. The "resolution" factor (M/C).
2. The "elimination" factor ((C-M)/C).
3. The "pertinency" factor (W/M).
4. The "noise" factor ((M-W)/M).
5. The "recall" factor (W/X).
6. The "omission" factor ((X-W)/X).

These certainly represent all of the factors which can reasonably be derived from the parameters C, M, X, and W. The question is, Where do we go from here? Some means must be developed to relate these factors to the needs of the requester. WRU, by defining these factors, has taken an important step in this direction, but additional work is clearly required.

Complexity

The aspects of precision are very closely related to those of complexity—although they are by no means identical with each other. Thus requests may be well-formulated, though complex, or very ill-defined but simple. Like precision, complexity also has two aspects—of the request and of the information recovered.

The spectrum of complexity of requests in a sense reflects the spectrum of development of scientific theory; to the extent that a field can be given a good theoretical structure, requests for information will be similarly well structured. At one end of the spectrum, requests can be formulated in terms of a completely structured universe. In other words, the system could conceivably receive a request

[17] J. W. Perry and Allen Kent, *Documentation and Information Retrieval,* New York, Interscience, 1957, p. 27.

stated in terms of a classification system, such as a request for all documents relating to a well-defined category in the classification. A bit away on this spectrum from the completely structured requests would be requests each expressed in terms of its own complete structure. For example, the OASD (Office of the Assistant Secretary of Defense) catalog problem involves requests against the cataloging file in the form of "signals" which are completely structured within defined patterns; there has not been any "order of the universe" established among the inventory items themselves. Next more complex would be the coordination of well-defined ideas, as in the Uniterm system, in the Minicard system, or in other systems of the same general nature.

A request problem of this type really begins to get difficult when the researcher, for example, asks for a list of all reports which have been published in the past year, from any source, and which deal with a certain subject. In this request category the researcher has the option of also imposing other form limitations like publisher, language of the text, certain authors' works only, etc., each of which would help to narrow the request down further.

Next would be requests in terms of natural phenomena, phrased with no obvious structure although implicitly there will be some hidden structure. At the far end of the spectrum would be completely free associations of ideas, the least structured requests of all.

Similarly, the information requested will fall within an entire spectrum of complexity, similarly related to the status of a theory of the scientific discipline—the better the theoretical foundation of the stored information, the easier it is to obtain complex relations among facts. For example, we may attempt to recover only simple facts. The identification number of a physical item which fits a given description is one example of such information. Another would be the provision of factual answers, such as "the rainfall in Cleveland, Ohio, on a given date." The request might be expressed in a very complex fashion, but the answer comes out with simple facts.

Moving along the spectrum of complexity, the request might desire relationships among facts. For example, the request might want a statistical analysis of the population of a certain class of city. Or this type of request may come from a researcher who has been directed to prepare a comprehensive, full-length study on a special subject. He perhaps asks for a list or bibliography of all available literature which touch on his field of interest. He would like, if possible, to have brief descriptions of abstracts of the more important documents on the list in order that he may decide, without much time-consuming research, which are most likely to be of value for his particular purpose. Not only is the central system asked in this instance to interpret its resources in the light of the researcher's subject need, but it is also made responsible for evaluating what it finds and for preparing a synopsis of content.

In academic life, where time is not usually a significant factor, the researcher usually performs this service for himself. He gets from the library's card catalog a list of the volumes which deal with his problem. Then he consults the bibliographies given in each of them for additional titles. Little by little he builds up an imposing bibliography for his own study, and over a period of months he sifts the books one by one for the chapters, sections, and statistical tables which have a specific bearing on his job. In business and industry, however, research cannot always be handled in this leisurely way; deadlines must be met and "time means money." Hence a central system that meets the various demands for service in an efficient and effective manner performs a service of value which can scarcely be overestimated.

The request might ask for recognition of patterns or laws relating groups of facts. For example, the request might ask the information system to provide a classification schedule of its file tailored to the requester's needs and based on an analysis of the contents of the documents or the information stored. In this respect, the researcher uses the central system to satisfy his needs with the same degree of specificity and the same detailed patterns as his personalized file may provide. This may not always be possible, for no central system can cater completely to the specific needs of each of its potential customers and still remain within a single over-all indexing scheme. However, the researcher has already invested much of his time in the maintenance of his own desk file and he may not be prepared to invest more in reorganizing the more general population of facts in the central system. When the central system is not structured in an analogous way to the researcher's private indexing scheme, it does not serve him with highly relevant responses, and he therefore becomes dissatisfied with it. Research is recognized as a dynamic process, subject areas change with time, and new subjects evolve. A researcher is often faced with the problem of creating new files on subjects not anticipated by his own filing scheme. In this case he expects the central system to be more general, he is more willing to review all the information available on the subject, and consequently he is prepared to spend the time at work in isolating pertinent facts from among the general population in the central system.

Finally, the request might call for the exercise of human judgment, probably the most complex recovery of information.

Now, it should be recognized that the complexity of the information recovered is not necessarily a reflection of the complexity with which the request is phrased. In fact, as we pointed out, there is a very close relationship between these two aspects of complexity and the existence of a theory in the discipline of the stored information. In general, the better the theory, the simpler the question which can be asked and the more complex the possible answer. If a very good theory exists, as in physics, then very simple questions can be asked and very complex answers recovered. On the other hand, with a poor theory, one must ask very complex questions in order to recover even simple answers. There is thus an inverse relationship between the complexity of the request and the complexity of the recovered information, which depends on the theoretical foundation of the information stored.

For example, regard a total scientific discipline as analogous to an information system. One can ask extremely simple questions in physics—stating a few simple facts—and from the available equations derive extremely complex results. Thus the boundary conditions of a physical problem are a fairly simple sort of thing to specify; from the information system—the system being physical theory—one can recover a very complex description of the resulting extremely complex phenomena. A file with a good theoretical foundation to explain its contents can be organized by a classification scheme based on that theory. This means that an extremely simple request for all the contents in a certain category of the classification yields a very complex set of information as an answer. It can be recovered precisely because the file has been structured in terms of a well-understood theory. Essentially the complexity is transferred from the individual requests into the theory which is controlling it; this is fine because the theory, once established, is available. On the other hand, not so well-structured files for which there is not a good theory of the file contents will require extremely complex requests in order to recover even a single item of information.

It should be made clear that this discussion has no relationship whatsoever to a theory of information storage and retrieval; it is concerned with the theory governing the content of the file. There is no means by which a good theory of information storage and retrieval will allow simple questions to get back complex results because this is dependent on the nature of the material.

10

Elements of organization

The elements of organization are those considerations of overlapping interest between the operator and the system designer. In effect, these elements have the same dual nature as do the elements of usage in that the capabilities needed by the operator become the requirements on the system designer. From the operator's standpoint, organization and structure are of prime importance to his job of understanding and communication. He must understand not only the user's needs but also the file and the way it operates. It is by imposing a structure on files that the operator most easily comprehends their contents.

The system designer views structure in a very different way—as a means of optimizing the operation of the system. He organizes not for the purpose of understanding, not for the purpose of communication, but for the purpose of saving time, or saving operations, or saving cost. The purposes of the operator and designer may frequently coincide, but this only disguises the existence of two opposing views of organization—one for the purpose of understanding, the other for the purpose of optimizing. Failure to recognize this difference in views has been the source of much confusion about systems.

Let us take a look at some specifics. Classification, for example, is an ideal tool for understanding and communication, particularly with some of the mnemonic devices wherein the individual parts of the classification terms have independent meaning. On the other hand, from the standpoint of efficiency, classification will also be useful. If somebody has a request involving mathematics, he need not look all over the library; he goes to the QA shelves (in the Library of Congress classification) and finds there nearly all of the books in which he is likely to be interested. A classification scheme is thus very useful for bringing requested items together physically, when questions are likely to be formulated in terms of a single frame of reference.

When multiple usage is involved, efficiency may require a different organization which destroys the ease of understanding implicit in a given classification. In such cases the two purposes of communication and efficiency may become diametrically opposed.

Another aspect of this problem is the logical relation of concepts. The operator is interested in logical relation of concepts because it provides a means for interpreting requests and the relation parts of a request bear to each other. The correlation of concepts is thus a means by which the operator can understand the user's requirements. On the other hand, to the system designer the logical relation of concepts is important because it is in such terms that he must program system processes (not just in the limited sense of programming a computer, but including any sequence of steps by which he will accomplish this coordination and interrelationship of concepts). These are very different ways of viewing what is apparently the same thing.

The concepts of coding also are viewed very differently by the operator and by the system designer. The operator views coding as a tool to aid in the representation of idea content, and this may be the point at which the "semantic" irrevelancy seems to enter machine considerations. A classification scheme is such a technique. The degree to which the coding is mnemonic will aid in understanding it, in easily translating from the code to the idea, and vice versa. This is usually in direct conflict with the designer's aim. He wants to code for efficiency. He wants to represent items in such a way that he can store them easily and process them cheaply. He wants efficient codes, codes which will be convenient for the machine logical processing. The system designer may well use codes, therefore, which are very different from those which would be convenient for the operator in his translation between idea and code.

In addition to the basic differences in their view of fundamental problems, one further difficulty has arisen in this area. This is the tendency on the part of both the operator and the designer to identify the library with the librarian, that is, there is an emphasis, in most of the work which has been done on information retrieval, on the logical processes, which essentially describe what the librarian does in a library, as opposed to the physical processes, which represent the library itself. Certainly, from an intellectual standpoint, the investigation of logical processes is the intriguing part of the problem. Computer-orientated people like to speculate about how they will program pattern recognition or other complex logical processes. The sheer drudge work of organizing a file for maximum physical efficiency is really rather dull and hence usually neglected.

There is some basis for this emphasis, of course. First of all, the logical processes are vitally important; they must be understood and investigated. Secondly, some logical processes are routine. They do not really involve human judgment and so can be programmed. Shaw [1] made the statement, "Analytical bibliography is the attempt to do routinely what has been a large part of so-called research in the past"; and in a sense this is the continual effort—to take things which are not well defined, which cannot be easily programmed, and to define them and make them programmable and, therefore, routine. Finally, and this is probably the most important consideration, whenever a machine operation is involved, it must include some logical processes. These must be built into the equipment—programmed into the equipment if this is the case—because communication is not easy between the human beings and the stored information in machine form. Certain processes have been removed from the area of human judgment, and they must be provided by the machine.

Unfortunately such emphasis is *unreasonable* to the extent that it ignores the basic problems in mechanizing the library itself. Furthermore, it leads to overstating, on the part of those who are equipment oriented, of the present capabilities for mechanizing nonroutine human judgment, and it leads to a leap, on the part of those who are usage oriented, from the statement of an information requirement to the presentation of the desired end results without consideration of all the machine steps in between. It is a natural tendency to confuse the tool with its purpose, and this appears to be the source of this particular confusion. In certain types of investigation it may be desirable to introduce this simplification, particularly if the tool is a well-defined segment of an over-all operation, since the intellectual effort can then be devoted to considerations of how to use it as a tool. This is not the case with information systems. They are usually not well defined. There is therefore a basic need for analysis to determine

---

[1] Ralph R. Shaw, *Bibliography In An Age of Science,* Urbana, University of Illinois Press, 1951.

the legitimate role of mechanization of logical processes, to understand the basic problems in mechanizing the file system itself.

Let us take a look at the elements of organization, classified here under five categories. Each of them will be discussed in turn: first, the organization of items; second, the organization of files; third, the organization of processes; fourth, the organization of responses; fifth, the organization of personnel and equipment.

ORGANIZATION OF ITEMS

In the following discussion, a distinction is made between the attempt to represent the information content of a document in some short form (this is abstracting, for example, but there are a number of other levels of abstraction which, generally speaking, do not have the term abstract applied to them) and the attempt to store such a representation in an efficient form. Furthermore, we also distinguish both aspects of document representation from the organization of groups of such representations in a file. To summarize, consider a document. That document is represented by an abstract. To store this abstract, it must be coded into some efficient form compatible with machine operation. Then the whole set of these abstracts will be organized in some way and will represent a file.

Abstracting, the representation of a document (or, in fact, of any physical item), always involves some loss of information. Even when an exact reproduction is made, such as a photographic copy, the form of the original, and therefore some information content, has been lost. This becomes particularly significant with aerial photographs, holographic copies and first editions, and similar cases where the item itself has special value. Thus in some types of research, where the concern is with original source material, recovery of the original document is significant. A photographic copy, a microfilm copy, or a magnetic tape copy would not be adequate. For this usage, any representation of the document involves loss of vital information.

The problem then is how to compromise with this loss of information, how to provide that amount of information sufficient for the logical recovery process. Shaw [2] provided a start on an answer when he said:

---

[2] Ralph R. Shaw, *Bibliography In An Age of Science,* Urbana, University of Illinois Press, 1951.

The extent to which we are justified in completely organizing the ideas contained in the written record depends upon a great complex of factors. The first of these is the purpose of the group served, the second is the volume of material to be handled.

There are obviously a great many other factors which must and will be discussed. In any event, the compromise is between the amount of information that is lost and the amount of information that must be stored.

Several levels of abstraction are possible. The first is the storage of the complete document itself—the physical document or some copy of it completely sufficient for all usage, for example, recording the whole contents of the book. This might be a punched tape, such as an original monotype tape, or a microfilm copy. The second level of abstraction is a reduced document, generally called an abstract, which attempts to convey the complete meaning but not necessarily all of the information. The next level of abstraction is the use of key words from the document. Such key words do not really identify the information content but merely the areas in which it occurs. The fourth level of abstraction is a classification of the document. Any classification, in this sense, represents an attempt to convey an area of meaning of the document, but it is a fairly limited way, and the individual item, in effect, completely loses its identity by losing those characteristics which do not fit the classification pattern. Classification, in fact, is primarily an aid to pattern recognition; it attempts to represent an entire complex of relationships in a compact form. At this level of abstraction there has been quite a loss of information, but it must be re-emphasized that at each level there is such a loss of information.

The National Bureau of Standards [3] described this as follows:

> The item analysis records, or set of search entries . . . represent to some degree the information items that are stored, and may be used at and for different levels of storage. In fact, the information item stored at some one level may itself serve as the guidon for an item at another level.
>
> At still another level, copies of the original papers in question may themselves serve as guidons to the information item(s) recorded in and communicated by these papers. This latter possibility may involve automatic systems of the future where selections of items meeting the conditions of an inquiry might be made by machine search of the full text of items as re-

---

[3] General Aspects of Storage of Scientific Information, National Bureau of Standards Report NBS 6675, February 15, 1960.

corded in either natural or machine language, but it is already realized, in a sense, whenever a human searcher reads every word of the complete text of some document in order to determine whether or not it is relevant to his intended usage. Finally, the [representation] might consist not only of the complete recorded text of an information item, but also of pre-deposited records of an analysis of the conveyed meaning(s) of the item that relate to the meaning of other items, of the results of evaluation of the conveyed meaning(s) of the item that have previously been found useful and for what purposes. In this last category would be included, for example, documents bearing marginal annotations, pencilled-in-citations and cross-references and evaluative comments by a prior user.

Since [these] represent the items to which they refer with varying degrees of completeness, information selection and retrieval systems are sometimes distinguished by the extent to which the [representations] used . . . conserve or reduce the information presumably conveyed by the original items received into the system.

Vocabulary

Having distinguished among levels of abstraction, the problem arises of "item representation," whatever level of abstraction may be involved. Item representation essentially involves two aspects: vocabulary, which provides the words or symbols that might be chosen to represent the abstracted information, and syntax, which defines the structural relationship among the words as they are used in the representation.

For example, given an original document, the resulting item, or reduced form of the document, must be described in terms of words and symbols chosen from a vocabulary. The vocabulary can be natural language itself, perhaps the language from the document. On the other hand, some degree of standardization can be imposed. For example, even when using natural language, perhaps only one form of the word may be allowed. The use of Uniterms or descriptors is a further step in standardization. In this case the words of the document are then forced to fit the standard words which will be used to represent it.

As a further step, it is possible to organize the standardized words so that synonymity, antonymity, and other *a priori* relationships among them are indicated. The concept of grouping by classes, to aid in generic recovery at some later time, would be one such organization. In this way the standard word would convey not only the content of the specific term but also relations of it to other terms.

The National Bureau of Standards [4] gave the following example:

For example, a patent application might state that a medicine was to be compounded of several specifically named ingredients and, in addition, the pulverized bark of a certain tree.

(a) Gin; Aspirin; Cinchona; Bark; Fever—Document No. 1234.
(b) COAEG; CO95A; . . .
    . . . Document 1234.
(c) Alcohol; Acetyl-Salicylic Acid; Cinchona Bark—DuBious, I. M.; Patent 2,810,000.
(d) 69; 28; 235—DuBious, I. M.; Patent 2,810,000.
(e) Alcohol, aspirin, pulverized cinchona bark; in admixture—Patent 2,810,000.
(f) Compounds containing alcohol . . .
(g) Compound—1; Ingredients—3; C_2H_5OH—1.1; $C_9H_8O_4$—2.1; . . .
(h) Process-Admixture; . . . Use—Medicinal; Specific-Antipyretic; . . .
(i) C_2H_5OH—SM; . . .
    Antipyretic—U . . .
(j) Patent Medicines—Q91 × P. 1878.
(k) Peruvian Bark . . .
    (*Cf. also,* Jesuits' Bark) . . .
      Medicinal uses of . . .
(l) South America . . .
    Peru . . .
      Exports . . .
        Agricultural Products . . .
(m) Rubiaceiae
(n) Alkaloids derived from *Rubiaceiae:*
    esp. C. ledgeriana or C. succiruba, used in antipyretics . . .
      Pulverized cinchona bark is mixed with acetyl-salicylic acid (as a fine crystalline powder) and ethyl alcohol as 80 proof Holland gin to provide a stomachic, also used as an antipyretic . . .
        U.S. Patent 2,810,000, Issued to I. M. DuBious, August 21, 1878.
(o) Alkaloids: . . . 0139 . . . 0605 . . . 1234 . . . 2111 . . ., Rubiaceiae; . . . 0028 . . . 0888 . . . 1234 . . .; Medicine: . . .
    . . . 0899 . . . 1234 . . ., Alcohol; . . . 0019 . . . 0137 . . . 0899 . . . 1234 . . .; Acetyl-Salicylic Acid (Aspirin); . . . 1234, 1235 . . .;
(p) Document 1234. [Accessioned November 17, 1959.] *DuBious, I. M.* [U.S. Patent 2,810,000]. [1878]. One of a series of patent medicines patented by DuBious in the 1870's, making use of an early crystalline form of acetyl-salicylic acid [see *Aspirin, history of*]. Principally recommended as a stomachic and as a tonic in mild fevers, other ingredients include alcohol (Holland Gin) and a form of quinine.

---

[4] General Aspects of Storage of Scientific Information, National Bureau of Standards Report NBS 6675, February 15, 1960.

Alcohol.
Aspirin.
Cinchona bark.

(q) DuBious, I. M., A Stomachic Tonic, U.S. 2,810,000. Received Nov. 17, 1959. 1234.

The above examples of possible representations obviously contain various search entries of different types. Examples (a) and (b) may differ from each other only with respect to the fact that the entries of (a) are immediately legible to the human reader [i.e., in natural or abbreviated natural language], while those in example (b) might be precisely the same entries encoded in accordance with a specific coding scheme.

Example (d) again illustrated a possible encoding on the same search entries as are given in guidon (c). In these cases a vocabulary of permissible search entries has been established. The information item [patent 2,810,000] describes, among other matters, the use of Holland Gin as an ingredient. In the identificatory-analytic operations, the gin is equated with the permitted search entry, "alcohol." This term, "alcohol," has the serial number identification, "69," in an alphabetically-ordered list of terms permissible to use as search entries. It is obviously much more generic in scope of connotation than is the word "gin" appearing in the original document. On the other hand, "acetyl-salicylic acid" [number 28 in the same vocabulary list] is quite commonly to be considered as synonymous with "aspirin." Thus the effect of reductive representation may be (1) to select only the "main" or "principal" subjects and to ignore less significant concepts and details; (2) to utilize tropes to subsume specific concepts mentioned under a more general concept or under a concept more useful for search; and/or (3) to substitute for any of a number of synonymous expressions of a concept some single, standardized term to represent that concept.

Syntax

Syntax essentially defines the relationship, within the context of the document, among the words chosen from the vocabulary. Again, as with the vocabulary, the syntax can be that of the natural language itself. This is the case in a normal abstract written in normal English. It is possible, however, to describe specifically the context for each word (essentially, this is what the Western Reserve System provides). This attempts to convey the context of each term, as it fits into the total picture, by a part of the term word itself. Inflexional natural languages, like Latin, represent syntax in much the same way. On the other hand, it is possible to describe interword relationships on a much more limited scale. The classic "man bites dog, dog bites man" example can be described by defining permutation within a phrase, indicating which is the first word in the phrase, which is the second word, etc. The extreme step in this direction is to establish standard syntactic patterns, such as the descriptive patterns in the cataloging system, which provide a standard syntactical relationship among the successive "words" used.

Coding

An abstract, having been chosen and represented in some vocabulary and syntax, must be stored. This means that it must be coded and the codes arranged in a format. Codes must be provided for both vocabulary and syntax, although the format can sometimes be used to indicate syntax, as with the sequence in descriptive patterns, for example, or with fixed field punched card coding.

What kind of codes can be used? Again, it is possible to use uncoded natural language. This is the situation in books, records, and film. For the material usually stored in a mechanized system, this type of coding is likely to be machine coded natural language, as in the machine code obtained from monotype tape. Essentially, of course, this is equivalent to representation in normal printed language.

One can use a classified coding, which is to some extent mnemonic. In this case the vocabulary is represented in such a way that it will convey meaning easily, although not necessarily as easily as natural language. At the opposite extreme, randomized coding deliberately forces the code not to convey any mnemonic significance.

Format

The other aspect of item storage is that of format. When an item is stored, not only must the words and the syntax be coded, but they also must be stored in some type of physical arrangement. Format is concerned with this physical arrangement. The natural language arrangement uses as typical format control features the period, the paragraph, the capital letter at the beginning of a sentence, and so on. Thus even in relatively unformalized natural language, there are a good many controls implicit in the format. As a next step in formalization, one can introduce the concept called the "open field." This is used in the open field of Minicard which does not assign any particular card position to any particular meaning. The codes involved in the representation of the item are stored in arbitrary locations. In doing so, however, the meaning of each code must be identified by a code identification.

The next type of format is "dedicated space," or *fixed field,* wherein each physical unit has a pre-established significance and associates a meaning with the characters stored in it. For the fixed field, logical operations are the simplest. As soon as the flexibility of format increases from the fixed field to the open field (sequence-identified and code-identified), logical operations become more complex, since the equipment must time events or make other logical decisions.

Data Type

Finally, in the organization of items, it is desirable to distinguish possible item subdivisions into data type. The information stored in an item is not necessarily all stored for the same usage. Three types of usage can be distinguished: (1) display data, which are intended for output or control of subsequent operations; (2) processing data, which are stored in the item for the purposes of the immediate operation; and (3) identification data, which are intended for the identification of the item.

These three should be distinguished because they do not need to be stored in the same form, and very frequently they are stored in completely different forms. For a concrete example, consider the aperture card. It contains a microfilm image of the document page; there may be some punched information to represent the area of subject matter of the document; there may be an abstract in printed form on the card; and, finally, across the top of the card may be typed a number, or a name, or other identification.

Notice, and this is the point of interest in this example, that the three types of data—the identification data, the processing data, and the output or display data—have three different representations, three different forms of storage. This may not be the typical situation, but it is a possible one. The typical situation, of course, is where some of these types of data are combined; where, for example, the display information and the processing information are the same. When a utility customer's record is interrogated, the customer's account total is processing information, but it is supplied as an output.

The importance of all these considerations of coding, format, and data type was particularly evident in the development, by Advanced Information Systems Company, of computer programs to retrieve and produce reports from a multiplicity of magnetic tape files.[5] Typically this task is accomplished by writing special report prepara-

---

[5] J. A. Postley and T. D. Buetell, Generalized Information Retrieval and Listing System, *Datamation,* December 1962, v. 8, No. 12, pp. 22–25.

tion routines, each tailored to a particular data file and reporting requirement. Producing a report consolidating data from separate files is much more complicated, requiring the treatment of each of the different formats encountered.

Recognizing this problem, AIS has produced a generalized retrieval and report preparation system to prepare reports in any format, according to any request criteria, from any defined file or group of files. The heart of the system is a dictionary, maintained on magnetic tape, which defines for each file details about the item codes, formats, and data types.

ORGANIZATION OF FILES

To this point in our discussion we have been concerned solely with the organization of items—the representation of an abstract, of a document, or of any other piece of information, and its storage in some form. It is on the representation of items, and almost solely on this consideration, that the intellectual questions arise. Logical processing is related primarily to the organization of items, not to the organization of files. The problems of logical decision making have therefore essentially been resolved in the way items are organized, in the way they are coded, and in the format in which they are stored. But the way in which a *file* is organized depends on physical considerations, physical indexing speeds, physical scanning speeds.

The purpose of file organization is to bring together the items "likely" to be considered together (and the word "likely" is in quotes in order to raise some question about what is meant by "likely," but let us leave it as intuitive for the moment and merely raise it as an issue). This fact has frequently been obscured in investigations of the problems in file organization, particularly where the usage of the system is well defined and predictable. Under such well-structured conditions, requests for information and the stored information itself both can be identified in terms of some classification scheme which will, under these circumstances, fit the needs of both logical processing (handling information in terms of this classification scheme) and physical access by bringing together those items which are related in the classification scheme.

Where usage is not well defined, or where multiple usage prevents organization in terms of particular predictable needs, file organization must become a complex of structures. The aim of each substructure in the complex is to provide access under some type of entry, for which the substructure is organized to respond optimally—to bring items together which should be considered together under that particular type of access. Thus, in the typical library, the books are arranged in a classification and the card catalog by subject headings. The card catalog is used for subject heading entry, and the references which the user wants to consider together under a subject are found together. On the other hand, the classification of the books answers requests phrased in terms of the classification scheme by bringing the books together which fit within a particular category.

As a gross organization, a file consists of a multiplicity of stages. Any subdivision of a file into a set of defined subfiles implies the existence of another file—an index file to identify the location of each subfile. The existence of these index files may be explicitly recognized at times; it is frequently implicit and quite subtly hidden. For example, in the card catalog, the tags that fit into the front of the trays actually represent an index to the trays; when the user walks up to the card catalog trays, he can scan through this index to find the particular tray that he wants. The user may not even recognize what he is doing; and yet the fact is, of course, that he is using this index to locate the particular block of interest to him.

In general, the purpose of file organization is to provide in this way a means of physically addressing sections of a file. The analytical searching, the information scanning, and the logical processing are reduced and replaced by physical indexing and "coordinate" searching. This is important, for the operation of linear scanning through a file is expensive. For example, to read every book in the library to find the one wanted would be time consuming and would use a very expensive instrument to make the logical decisions. On the other hand, if the relevant physical location can be pinpointed and then only a small section of the file scanned, much of the reading has been replaced with a physical indexing. Therefore it appears that the purpose of file organization is to replace linear scan and decision making by physical indexing to a specified coordinate, reducing the size of the unit which will be scanned.

Frequently the result of such a search at one level is referenced to another index location at another level. This process is thus the characterizing process for each stage in an information system. Individual stages are differentiated by the decision criteria used in the searching task, by the size of the task in terms of how many items must be scanned on the average, by the complexity of the logical processes.

In the organization of individual stages in the file, certain physical organization problems must be recognized. For example, it is necessary to distinguish between the *record,* which is a physical unit, and the *item,* which is a logical unit. Very frequently it is necessary to have multiple item records, where several items are stored in a single physical record. A single physical record, for example, would be a reel of magnetic tape; it is typical to store multiple items on a reel of magnetic tape. On the other hand, it is also possible to be concerned with multiple record items. This is very standard in punched card installations in the accounting field, where a single punched card is inadequate to contain all of the information concerning a given logical item, and one must therefore use multiple cards for a single item.

In either case, whether multiple item records or multiple record items are involved, logical complexity is introduced. One attempts to avoid such multiplicity problems if possible because of the serious procedural problems they cause; however, there are many cases where circumstances force these multiplicity problems usually because of the limitations of the physical storage media.

ORGANIZATION OF PROCESSES

Various types of processes are involved in the operation of an information system, as will be seen from the following material. These processes can be organized in many ways. Some can be combined into single logical steps; two such processes may occur simultaneously; and the sequence of processes in otherwise equivalent sytems may be completely different.

To illustrate, consider the following example. Compare an accounting operation based on a punched card system with one based on key-operated accounting machines. In punched card systems it is very typical to perform a key punching operation, and then a sorting operation which sorts the input items into sequence by, say, account number, then a matching of the transactions against the file, and, finally, a posting against the affected file items. This completes the processing, for the purpose of this example. Now, contrast this sequence of steps—an input step, a sorting step, a file matching step, and a posting step—with the equivalent processes for the same problem in a key-operated accounting machine. Typically the operator will take the incoming sales slips or other physical documents and sort them into order. They then will be matched against the file by the operator of the key-operated accounting machine, who will perform the input operation and the posting operation as part of one operation. In effect, the two steps of input and posting are combined as the key-operated accounting machine, and the sequence has changed from input-sort-match-post to sort-match-input-post. This is a rather simple example, but it illustrates the basic principle that with different pieces of equipment the same job will be done with different sequences of processes, performing them in different ways and yet arriving at essentially the same ultimate result.

The organization of processes is separate from logical considerations, except as they may relate to the actual programming, that is, the organization of processes relates primarily to the nature of information handling and not to the nature of the information itself. In particular, even the logical or arithmetical processes are independent of the information itself, even though the selection among alternative processing paths may be determined by the information. The distinction made relates to the pre-existing organization of processes in an information system as opposed to their functioning under particular situations. In general, the differences between two types of files are determined by the organization of processes and not by the stored information itself.

This can be said in the following way. When a file is established, it is based on an organization, which is thus pre-existing. The information and its handling, then, fit into this organization. Although the information may force the system to choose alternative processing paths, these must have been pre-established. The information merely determines which of the available alternative paths is chosen but does not determine the structure.

Of course, the machine oriented will immediately think about the concepts of learning machines, self-modifying machines, and self-organizing machines. To the extent that such devices can be built, their organization will reflect the nature of the information and not the nature of a pre-existing structure. This possibility must be admitted, but for most practical situations, the information will fit into a pre-existing structure.

Processes will be classified into the following groups: input, posting, repetitive handling of nonfile items, repetitive handling of the file, file item access, computing, special situation handling, and system output.

The Input Processes

One can distinguish between the external characteristics of input and the logical characteristics of input. For example, collection of the input data is usually external to the processing of the system itself. The physical input creation (which is usually by key punching but may involve character reading machines) is the point at which the system and the external world interact. In the creation of the input, key punching equipment occupies a unique position. A human being has the capability of reading documents and recognizing the information contained in them, which cannot be equalled by any other device. The human being is the pattern recognition machine *par excellence*. The Flexowriter, the punched card key punch, the key-operated accounting machine with a punch tape attachment —all of these devices are essentially key-operated devices depending on the human being to punch the appropriate keys.

Another way of creating the input, most useful where it can be implemented, is by what are called "re-entry documents." In this case the document is created in machine form and sent out with the hope and expectation that it will be returned in unmutilated form.[6] Prepunched and preprinted cards are very useful where they can be implemented. The utility industry, of course, has gone a long way in this direction.

Also connected with input are logical processes which must be recognized. The first of these is the requirement for verification to ensure the accuracy of the input information. Mechanized means of verification usually reduce to some form of "punch twice and compare." Visual verification amounts to proofreading. The use of control totals and other types of redundancy, such as parity checks, provides another means of verification. The numbers on most credit cards are redundant numbers in the sense that they include extra digits to provide a redundancy check.

Another logical process involved in input is code conversion. It is very typical to convert one code to another, to change a six-bit code, for example, into a twelve-bit representation, or an alphabetical code into an alpha-numeric code, etc. Related to this is another type of code conversion which causes a great deal of trouble—the conversion from one format to another. For example, a typical punched card is

---

[6] This appeared in "The Phoenix Nest," edited by Martin Levin, *Saturday Review,* September 19, 1959.

EPITAPH

Here he lies moulding
His dying was hard—
They shot him for folding
An IBM card.
Leslie Mellichamp

arranged in 80 columns and 12 rows. The cards are transported by most of the punched card handling machinery so that the 80 columns are scanned in parallel. The only generally available device which scans the cards the other way, and thus provides the characters serially, operates at only 10 characters per second; that is the key punch itself. Manufacturers, in designing peripheral equipment, have been continually plagued with this problem of the parallel-to-serial format conversion.

Finally, *handling* processes are involved in input. In part, these handling processes involve some logical considerations—in particular, the definition of items. What is an item? Where does one item end and the next one begin? Should an item be duplicated and how many duplicates should be provided? (In the Minicard system, a whole machine has been built specifically for this purpose of handling input items, defining items, and "exploding" the input items to create a multiplicity of copies.) The item is not necessarily a predefined thing but may actually be created from input data. In other words, a piece of information is pulled from here, a piece from there, and so on, and put together to form an item.

The Posting Processes

The next class of processes are "posting" processes which involve the addition of new information to existing records. Some areas where these posting operations are involved have been discussed already. In the coordinate indexing scheme, for example, there is a substantial posting problem, for the file aspect card must have the new document number posted to it. In accounting systems, of course, posting is a standard operation; for example, in bank commercial checking accounts, each check that is issued and returned to the bank must be posted to the account record. In fact, posting is particularly important in accounting because of the concept of "the chain of recordings," the accounting trail to provide for accuracy, control, and tracing of what happens to particular transactions.

Handling of Nonfile Items

The third type of process is repetitive handling of nonfile items—the sorting and collating of requests, new items, transactions against the file, and so on. In this respect, the concept of batching, sorting, and merging groups of sorted items together—accumulating them until there is a large enough group to process or until some time interval has elapsed, batching them together, and treating them as a unit in this repetitive handling—is fundamental. The idea is to produce an arrangement of the transactions which will most effectively match the master file and make file searching more efficient.

Batching introduces difficulties, particularly in large volume problems, in the growth of intermediate files and the handling of them. Of particular difficulty in the documentation field is the handling of requests against not only the master file but these intermediate files. To make this clear, assume that there is a basic file in the information system. There are nonfile items which relate to the file. These include, for example, requests for information; they include new items, which will become part of the file; there are transactions, which affect items in the file and will modify them; there are file items which have been removed from the file and which must be treated just like new items. All of these are encompassed by the term *nonfile items* and may be significant in answering requests, which must therefore be matched against the intermediate files of these nonfile items.

Although a system handles nonfile items for the purpose of batching them for efficient matching of them against the file, there is another reason for handling nonfile items. This is the reporting function—arrangement and rearrangement of the nonfile items for reports of various types. Dissemination, in a sense, has this characteristic. The new items coming into the file, before they enter the file, may be processed for the purpose of dissemination. This, then, would come under the classification of repetitive handling of nonfile items. There is also handling of nonfile items caused by external requirements; in particular, preparation of an invoice comes under this classification. It is a standard procedure to sort invoice line items, separating them away from the invoice and merging them with those from other invoices for matching against the file. Pricing information is obtained from the file and extended for the line item. Then the system must rehandle the line items to break them apart into invoice grouping again.

Batch processing has been a particularly important tool in business data processing problems. On the other hand, it is probably characteristic of low density and interrogation problems, such as those involving very large files, that batching and sequential processing—even if permitted by time limitations—would not necessarily improve access times and overall operation to a significant extent. This appears to be true because relatively few of the requests will fall into a single selected file unit in which sequential search will take place;

the situation becomes virtually a random search even when a sequential processing is utilized. Furthermore, because of the size of these files, it is usually economically impossible to provide automatic availability of all file items, and manual selection is necessary under any circumstances.

Handling of the File

The next type of process is repetitive handling of the file. In certain respects this is the area of greatest potential and yet the most neglected area of investigation. For example, file reorganization for improved efficiency in new situations is a very powerful tool. In particular, a consideration which is highly relevant to file operation, though frequently neglected, is its responsiveness to a changing situation. As growth in isolated sections of the file or an increased interest in new specific interrelationships occurs, the information system should be easily capable of providing high-speed response. This implies the need for a continual reorganization of the file in the light of changing environment.

To illustrate this with a very simple example which carries some of the principles relevant here, consider an inventory control file. It is very typical for a very small percentage (say 10, 15, 20% of the file) to carry the great volume of activity (say 80% of the activity). One might visualize a system such that whenever an item is active, it is brought to the most easily accessible section of the file. Then each time a transaction is searched against the file, the search starts at the most accessible item and continues until the active item is reached. Items in the file will gradually become activity organized: the highly active items are going to be pulled to the "front of the file"; the inactive ones will gradually drift back into the file. In fact, the file will divide into two sections, a "front" section which has been active during some period of time and those behind which have been completely inactive with no transactions on them whatsoever. The ones in the front, the active ones, will be essentially organized in a statistical distribution related to activity. The more active the item, the more probable it is to be toward the front of the file.

This kind of an activity-organized distribution then carries some of the characteristics of responsiveness to environment. It is a very simple sort of "self-organization." Thus, suppose that the environment now changes and that the center of activity, instead of being centered on one set of inventory items, switches to another set. What is going to happen? Given a sufficiently long period of time under this changed environment, the organization of the file is going to completely change, and the new area of activity will be brought to the front of the file, the old area gradually drifting back.

However it may be implemented, this capability for reorganization of the file, which a mechanized system implies, should be utilized. It is one way in which a mechanized system can pay for itself. If file reorganization is a fundamental part of the system procedure, the system gains enormously because it thus utilizes equipment to its fullest capability.

Repetitive handling of the file is also used for more mundane purposes, such as reporting. It may well be necessary to take file items out of the file and to sort them into a different order for the purposes of a report, then to sort them back into the original order and collate them back into the file. Similar repetitive handling of the file is used for insertion of new items by a collating operation of them with the file.

One type of repetitive handling of the file which is worthy of being viewed independently is *file item access.* This is particularly of interest in terms of what is called *random access,* or access without repetitive handling of the transactions. The single transaction is handled as a unit and is individually matched against the file to look for that particular active item. Some pieces of equipment, as we have discussed, have been especially designed to facilitate this type of operation.

The term "random access" has been used in a number of ways (depending usually on the kind of machine being sold). Random access has been used to represent the situation where the access is random only because of the usage, with the sequence of transactions randomly distributed in the file. The term has also been used as synonymous with "coordinate access" and in this sense is contrasted with scan access; this usage implies a well-organized file so that one can identify exactly the location of an item in the file and go to that position. The term has also been used to mean "immediate access" in contrast to delayed access. In each of the three types of usage, the term conveys the implication that batching has been avoided.

Now, it might be asked why one should be interested in random access. There seem to be a number of reasons; one of them is an emotional one. Many users never can quite understand what is going on in a mass of sorting operations, collating operations, matching against the file, sorting back into original order, etc. But what happens! The equipment salesman says, "We make it simple for you. One transaction goes all the way through, and you see exactly what happens at every step of the way." What an appealing concept! Finally, we can understand what is going on in this mysterious machine room.

This emotional aspect of what is called "in-line processing" may help explain the extent to which random access devices have been sold. But, aside from this emotional response to in-line processing, why would one want to have random access? There seem to be more critical reasons for it: A user asks for information and wants it *now,* or a priority transaction must be processed immediately. For such functions, batching just cannot be considered. One cannot afford to include priority requests with the routine processing, batch them, sort them, and then produce the answer two hours later, or a day later, or whatever the batch handling time is. They must be handled *now,* and this is what a random access capability provides.

A somewhat more subtle reason for random access capability is multiple access for the single transaction. To illustrate, consider the situation where, in an inventory file, there is a requirement for substitution. In other words, there is none of the item requested, but there is a substitutable item which can be sent to the customer. Having discovered that there is a substitutable item, what should be done? The request could be added to the next batch and treated as a new request against the other item in the file. This is all very well, but the delay becomes more critical. It therefore may be that where multiple access to the file is required, as is in the substitution situation, the random access capability is desirable.

Computing Processes

The next type of process is *computing.* To review what we have said in Chapter 6, the term "computing" should not be identified with arithmetic calculation, as it is by many people. The general purpose computer is a device with a built-in set of capabilities and a stored program. The fact that the built-in set of capabilities may, or may not, include arithmetic capabilities is irrevelant. As a matter of fact, given a certain minimum set of capabilities, all the arithmetic operations can be programmed. All that is required is that there be logical operations available—extracts, comparisons—in other words, that one be able to make a certain minimum number of decisions. The more built-in commands given, of course, the simpler operations are.

Therefore within the term "computing" both logical processes and arithmetic processes are encompassed.

Incidentally, this usage of the terms *computer* and *computing* is fairly standard. In fact, it coincides with the usage of logicians when they refer to computability as a subject related to recursive function theory. There is nothing in the concept of computability which necessarily implies arithmetic operation.

These logical or computing operations, as is evident from what has been said before, occur as part of other processes. They are important during input to determine, for example, "Is this an item, and if so, what is done with it?" Similarly, in the repetitive handling processes, decision making is a functional part of sorting and of collating.

However, it is essential to describe it separately at this point because computing is critical in the logical processing in information retrieval, the matching of a request against a stored item. Such computing is really pattern recognition of some degree of complexity. It may be very simple. Do these two patterns of request and document match exactly? Or it may be quite complex and involve the recognition of a pattern with something comparable to human judgment. In this respect, pattern recognition, as a particular type of computing, is of great interest. The computer-orientated people continually investigate this type of logical process. "Learning machines," in effect, have the aim to develop a means of recognizing certain patterns and of responding to them.

Another type of computing is also particularly important—*special situation recognition.* A special situation can be defined as a situation for which no standard procedure has been established. Certainly the mechanized information system is not going to be able to handle it then, but one of two things can happen. Either the information system does not recognize the existence of the special situation—in which case it does handle it, but invalidly—or it does recognize the existence of a special situation.

There is a great difference between recognizing that something is wrong and knowing what to do about it. The system designer must realize that special situations are going to arise and must provide capability for recognizing their existence. Under such recognized special situations, the human being is called on to use his judgment and to define what should be done. One can also build in the concept of feedback or learning, so that when a special situation arises, a procedure can be added to modify the programmed behavior to include the new approach.

ORGANIZATION OF RESPONSES

So far the following have been discussed: the organization of items, the organization of files, and the organization of processes. The next element of organization concerns "responding" as an operational procedure. For example, supplying documents in answer to a request is a response of the system. Response can also be generated as a result of prescheduled, routine listings and reports. An accessions list, for example, is such an output; similarly, a summary report of the status of inventory items. Typical accounting reports fall within this class.

In some organizations the researcher may make use of a central dissemination service which reads and routes incoming printed materials in accordance with his expressed subject interests. While this may delay somewhat the receipt of the material, it does restrict the volume of material which might otherwise reach the researcher's desk. Greater selectivity can be achieved only by refinement and by a narrowing down of the requirements placed on the disseminators. Continuing effort is made to achieve this refinement by means of discussion and agreement with the researchers.

Dissemination, as a response to a certain set of pre-established requests, is a system response. Dissemination of printed information is the chief way in which the researcher is kept informed of new information in his field. The exact form which this initial dissemination takes can usually be of the man's own choosing. He can receive an abstract, an accessions list, a reproduction of the original source material, or a copy of the original material. The source material may vary from a confidential company working paper to a printed and published journal, article, or report. The researcher will generally favor seeing full-length material, and to nourish his wider interests he will subscribe and regularly receive complete issues of periodicals and journals published in his sphere of interest. This is the safest method, so far as he is concerned, and the only one which assures him of seeing all of the pertinent details contained in new printed material. He will argue that this detail would otherwise be lost in someone else's condensation or summary and that only *he* really knows what it is that is worth his current attention and time.

His logic may be valid, of course, but sooner or later conflicts arise when the volume of material pouring across his desk exceeds his capacity to read it all and still have time to perform research work. There appears to be little doubt, however, that a researcher considers his right to inspect the *total* flow of documentary material in his chosen field as a sacred prerogative.

If a researcher became assured that he could obtain from a central system, at any time, all the documents which bear on a given subject, he might place less insistence on receiving a heavy volume of daily material to winnow himself.

ORGANIZATION OF EQUIPMENT AND PERSONNEL

The next element is the organization of equipment and personnel. In summary, the functions involved in organization of equipment and personnel are the assignment of tasks to particular men and machines, the programming of the machines, the assignment of the interrelationships among them, and the definition of the flow of information from one part of the system to another. The next several chapters will present the tools for executing these functions.

Before discussing the organization of equipment and personnel in detail, it is important to recognize the relationship between men and machines in their performance of system processes. The human being can be utilized either for his judgment capability or his mechanical abilities. In the latter case, the role of the human being in the organization of processes is somewhat unique, since, on the one hand, he should be utilized as a machine with certain capabilities and limitations, but, on the other hand, he is subject to influences of a more complex nature than those affecting other machines. Specifically, he has the characteristic of frequently doing either more or less than he is supposed to. (And not in the same sense of failure which one would associate with machines. For example, if a machine did something more than it was supposed to, one would say that it had failed; something went wrong. If the human being does more than he is supposed to, one does not say that the human being has failed. One merely says that he did not quite understand what he was told or that he saw a better path by which to go.) Typically, for example, in manual systems the individual will introduce his own specialized tools; he remembers something and he may mark down the fact that he remembers it to aid him. If he is doing this, he is operating outside of the system.

In his role as a machine-like component, however, it must be assumed that the human is a well-operating machine and that he does what he is supposed to do. If he fails, it is in the same way that a machine fails; in this sense, he may make a mistake, a blunder, and therefore will have to be controlled in the same way that a machine will be controlled.

Human beings have three roles in an information system: this first is the "machinomorphic" type of role, wherein the human being is strictly a cog in a machine. A key punch operator serves exactly this type of function. People who believe in the "human use of human beings"[7] would like to mechanize such tasks with equipment rather than with human beings. However, there is a good deal of doubt as to the desirability of such complete automation because the human being turns out to be a very effective machine for certain functions.

The types of tasks which fall in this class are equipment operation ("pushing the button"), manual file handling, key punching operations involving interpretation of information, various types of clerical functions, such as picking up paper as it comes out of the tabulator or putting paper into envelopes and sealing them, and so on. These are essentially jobs which can be, and in fact have been, mechanized and done by machines.

The second major role of the human being in the information system is somewhat closer to the "human use of human beings," namely, the role of a communication link. The human being has a vital role in this respect. It is unlikely that human operation as a communications device could be effectively mechanized. There are many reasons for this. The psychological aspects are particularly important. The customer does not want to talk to a machine, he wants to talk to a lovely lady with a lovely voice—and she very frequently calms ruffled nerves. It appears that only the human being can handle this effectively. Another aspect is communication with the machine to ensure that it is operating properly. In effect, the human being is using his judgment as to correctness of machine performance in terms of ill-defined criteria. In this connection, the problem of display is vital; it is extremely important to provide an easy means for communication between the human being and the machine.

This particular aspect of communication relates to the third role of the human being, the real human use of human beings—*judgment*. In the handling of special situations, or in browsing, the use of judgment in a file search is the key capability.

The general role of machines is also worthy of some preliminary discussion. It appears that machines are useful: first, for large

---

[7] Norbert Wiener, *The Human Use of Human Beings; Cybernetics and Society*, Houghton Mifflin, Boston, 1950.

volume file maintenance, and the emphasis is on the *large;* second, for *routine* analytical work including computation. As a result, routine data handling (such as sorting, collating, matching, organization, and reorganization) and responsiveness generated from the file (such as preparation of reports) are natural tasks for mechanized systems.

In each of these areas the human suffers seriously in some respect. Where large volume file maintenance is involved, the human being quickly reaches his capacity; he has certain built-in limitations as to how fast he can operate, how much he can handle, and so on. Where analytical work which is well defined is involved, the human being actually is very poor; he is slow and he is highly susceptible to errors. He forgets things; he does not combine them in the proper, well-defined way, and so on. The well-functioning machine will never make such mistakes.

On the other hand, it must be recognized that the human being does very well in certain other types of problems. Thus manual systems will handle posting, interrogation, and special, ill-defined situations very well precisely because the system has been set up for the human being.

Incidentally, where random access capability is involved, the human being has some unique advantages, since frequently, as with interrogations, for example, he must be involved. He must talk with the customer on the telephone; he must interpret the question and understand completely what is requested. If a machine is now introduced between the person at the telephone and the file, the request must be communicated to and from the machine. It seems that it would be simpler in such situations for the human being to bypass the machine. To allow this, it would be essential in such interrogation-type problems to provide a file record which is simultaneously accessible to the machine and to the human being. Thus the machine would handle the routine processing, the great volume processing, and the human being would handle the random interrogation situation.

11

Elements of equipment

In developing the optimum system for a given information problem, the designer must provide the best possible organization of men, machines, and procedures to meet the operational requirements. In doing so he must either work within the limitations of the equipment available or specify the functional capabilities he requires. A major part of the organizer's responsibility is therefore the communication of the equipment needs to the engineer and the supplier of equipment. Again we have an area of overlapping interest—the specification of equipment characteristics—which is viewed in very different light by the system man and the engineer. The one is concerned with how the equipment will be used, the other with how it will be built.

For example, consider functional specification. In this area of overlap, the designer thinks in terms of processes to be performed, the engineer in terms of hardware limitations. The designer wants generalized capabilities so that he can specialize them as they may be needed. The engineer wants specific functions because they are simpler to mechanize. The designer wants modular units which can then be combined into any size or arrangement of system to do the job. The engineer wants complete packages because they represent efficient utilization of the whole set of components. In one sense, it is these differences which have really made the general purpose computer the ideal component in system design.

The elements of equipment, then, constitute the framework within which the designer will state his functional requirements and the engineer will evaluate how they shall be mechanized. Ultimately these decisions by both the designer and the engineer must be based on quantitative parameters, which we will discuss later. But quantitative data are not always available, particularly during the early engineering stages in the development of equipment, where cost figures and detailed specifications are simply not possible. It is precisely at these early stages of development that specification and comparison are perhaps most important, however. Proposed developments must be compared with existing mechanizations, as they might be improved with a similar investment. The potential user of equipment must evaluate alternative equipment proposals for the solution of his problem, and, although cost quotes and specifications are very often submitted with these proposed equipment solutions, such data (particularly on cost plus fixed-fee contracts) are frequently not representative of the final results. Finally, the manufacturer of equipment must develop his competitive position and choose satisfactory equipment lines and yet do this without really adequate specifications on operative characteristics and cost.

In Chapters 5, 6, and 7 we covered most of the specific "elements of equipment" of interest in information system design. There are, however, some general considerations which should be raised here, for they relate precisely to the more analytical problems in comparing and specifying equipment. They represent those essentially qualitative factors by which the designer can evaluate utility in operation and the engineer can evaluate complexity in design.

STORAGE MEDIA

Storage media are fundamental to the problems of information storage and retrieval, although they are not critical for more prosaic information processing systems. Certainly in scientific computation, for example, the role of the external storage medium is relatively minor. On the other hand, as soon as even business data processing is involved, the storage medium becomes possibly the predominant element in the processing system. The considerations relevant to the storage medium include its physical structure, the methods of reading and recording, its handling equipment, and its filing equipment.

Physical Structure

The elements relating to the physical nature of the storage medium include its physical dimensions, its form, its inherent resolution, its stability and life. These are factors which the designer of a system utilizing a storage medium must critically examine. Its physical dimensions will determine possible handling speeds, storage capacities, information rates; its form will determine ease of handling, ease of performing certain types of operation; its inherent resolution will determine the reliability of the recording methods which may be used; and, finally, its stability and life will determine the operational problems in using it.

The form of the storage medium, for example, is concerned with structure independent of measurement. Thus a tray of cards is in form quite different from a reel of tape. Each of these, in turn, differs from the drum and from the disk. These topological differences are quite significant. For example, the ability to handle cards as single unit records and collate or merge them together easily is operationally important. In this way information handling operations can be performed without handling the information itself but simply by handling the storage medium.

Another consideration relevant to physical structure is the stability and life of the storage medium. The wear on the storage medium during handling is very important. Punched cards normally have a life of perhaps 200 passes; at the end of this time, the "picker knife" in the feed, by continually hitting the edge of the card, has begun to spread it to the point that it will not feed properly. Minicard, because of the physical properties of its emulsion, is perhaps an extreme case in respect to its life in handling, and Minicard equipment had to be designed around the problems of the life of the medium. Specifically, the card has a very thin photographic emulsion. If it is subjected to frictional forces, by one card rubbing against another, the resulting scratches, at the 60 to 1 reduction, will completely destroy the value of, say, an aerial photograph. In order to prevent handling the cards in a way which would damage them and reduce their effective life, the entire set of Minicard equipment was designed so that the cards always move normally, or perpendicular, to each other. This very interesting limitation was a predominant factor in the design of Minicard equipment.

The life of the storage medium, then, under wear in handling equipment, is an important factor. Similarly, the life and stability of the medium under environmental conditions are other considerations to which a great deal of attention must be paid. How long will the medium last? How stable will it be under heat and humidity changes? Six to eight years ago, when magnetic tape was first utilized as a storage medium, the question of how long it would last was important. There is now sufficient experience with magnetic tape to answer that question positively. Newer media must similarly be evaluated.

Reading and Recording

The consideration, with respect to the storage medium, of major system design significance is the nature of the reading and recording. The qualitative characteristics of interest are "erasability" and "storage of an image."

The importance of erasability lies in the resulting ease of manipulating, adding, and changing individual items of data. Contrast magnetic tape with microfilm: the one can easily be used for complex data handling and processing; the other is almost static and completely inflexible. Of course it must be recognized that there is a penalty paid for erasability in the loss of resolution, that is, a requirement for selective change imposes severe limitations on the possible density of storage.

This loss of resolution is further exemplified in the difficulties in storing images in erasable media. Only recently—in the Photochromic development of National Cash Register and the Thermoplastic development of General Electric—have erasable high resolution photographic emulsions become at all feasible. These developments seem to provide a quantum jump of technology, in comparison with, say, video magnetic tape, which is severely limited in the possible resolutions in image storage.

The storing of images is of vital importance: the image is directly usable by the human being. It may require a viewer to do so, but it does not require complex information processing equipment to translate an image from magnetic form into usable form. Thus a great drawback with magnetic tape, or any magnetic recording medium, has always been the feeling in the user that he cannot see it. Usability by the human being is a factor of tremendous operational significance; it results in a file which can be handled both by the machine and by the human being. In this respect, punched cards occupy an intermediate position. It is conceivable, in an operational job, to read the contents of a punched card; therefore, one can easily correct errors, recover the information from damaged cards, etc.

The characteristics of erasability and image storage are essentially qualitative. The information rate provided from the storage medium is one of the quantitative characteristics with significant qualitative effects. Data rate is partly a function of the storage medium and partly a function of the handling equipment. There are very high-speed information rate devices—magnetic tape, 60,000 characters per second; magnetic cards, 100,000 characters per second; photoscopic disks. For most purposes, one can classify storage media into (1) extremely high speed—greater than about 30,000 characters per second, (2) high speed—greater than 5,000 characters per second, (3) medium speed—500 to 5,000, and (4) slow speed—less than 500 characters per second. This breakdown fairly well divides the field of available equipment and relates well with the technology in each case.

Various storage media exhibit different relationships among form, erasability, image storage, and information rate. Normal tabulating punch cards do not have an image stored in them, are nonerasable, and provide a relatively slow information rate of 500 to 1000 characters per second. Similarly, reel and strip punched paper tape provides information rates up to 1000 or 2000 characters per second. An erasable card with a slow information rate was a magnetic card development of Sears-Roebuck which involved the storage in magnetic form of descriptive information concerning inventory items. The operator would manually select the card and put it into the reader, which would automatically read the information from the card, and convert it for the processing system. Bendix, with their G15, has a magnetic tape which provides about 400 characters per second; thus it is a slow-speed erasable reel storage medium. Minicard provides a high-speed nonerasable media. The maximum capacity of 3000 bits, or about 500 characters, per card handled at the rate of 10 to 25 cards per second provides somewhere between 5000 to 15,000 characters per second. This is a reasonably high rate for an input device. Any of the more recent magnetic tape or card developments provides an erasable medium with information rates up to 100,000 characters and more per second.

Unit record capacity is another operationally significant quantitative characteristic. The capacity of a punch card, using its normal recording, is 80 to 90 characters. The actual capacity is greater than that, with optimal coding—500 to 1000 bits, which with a 5-bit coding would be about 100 to 200 characters. There have been times when cards with this type of coding have been used, particularly as a means of high-speed input to a computer.

One very significant set of quantitative parameters with respect to reading and recording is the set of tolerances required. Tolerance problems, such as "skew" and "lateral positioning," are best exemplified in magnetic tape as we have illustrated, but they exist in other types of storage media. Skew can represent a very significant problem. To define it, consider magnetic tape. Information is recorded on magnetic tape in a set of, say, five channels. When recording at high density, a misalignment of the character column produces a timing problem in the difference in timing between the two edges of the tape. This becomes more critical at higher and higher densities and higher and higher transport rates. Storing a thousand bits to the inch, for example, requires skew tolerances of far better than one-thousandth of an inch; this means expensive equipment and operational difficulties.

Handling Equipment

For any storage medium there is at least the potential of several different types of handling equipment. Particularly for cards there can be a variety of sorters, collators, tabulators, and the like. Each may be structurally a very different device from the others. They may each use a very different way of feeding, transporting, and handling the cards. They may have different types of elements and different capabilities.

It is important to know the structure of the handling device and therefore the operations which it will physically permit, as contrasted with what it will logically permit. For example, physically the collator will permit a much greater variety of operations than the sorter. The flexibility which the machine has must be examined very closely when deciding on the handling equipment for a storage medium. In this respect, form again arises, this time in respect to the handling device. Thus, in order to utilize the information again, magnetic tape usually must have a runback to get the reel into the original sequence; some tape units, on the other hand, can read on the reverse run.

The possibility of a reversal in stacking a set of cards is a similar topological problem, raised by the handling equipment, which can have a significant operational effect. A normal punch card sorter stacks cards in the same sequence as the sequence of feeding. With Minicard, on the other hand, the cards are successively stacked in reverse sequence. Whereas the original sequence might have been 1, 2, 3, 4, as a result of operation it ends up 4, 3, 2, 1. To get around this, Minicard introduced an intermediate hopper; the cards are put into this hopper by the machine and then brought out and sent to the place they are to go in. Minicard equipment is designed to deal with groups of cards, representing all the pages in a document, as a unit. Thus, if two cards are the group for a document, these two are run into the collecting hopper and then, at the end of the document, they are run out. As a result, the cards in a document group will be in sequence, but the documents will not be. The approach in Minicard is that document sequence on a stick is not important, for everything on a stick will be scanned through every time anyway. That is fine, but it must be recognized that, even though one can make a virtue out of necessity, one is forced into a procedure which one may not want and which may have certain disadvantages. The important thing is there are certain types of systems on which one cannot utilize Minicard without introducing procedural changes. For example, there are many times when document sequence is relevant and the procedure of running the document through the machine becomes very difficult. If the system for which Minicards were used depended on the preservation of document order, it would be necessary to introduce procedural changes.

The transport speed is important. There are limits to how fast a physical medium can be moved. Those limits are amazingly high, but they exist. A mass production printing press, as used for a newspaper, moves the paper at several hundred feet per minute. In the Magnacard system, the cards are moved at 300 inches per second. The latest punch card sorters, operating at 2000 cards per minute, move the medium at speeds better than 100 inches per second.

The tolerances in the handling equipment are related to the tolerances in the storage medium itself but include, in addition, their own physical limits. How closely can tolerances be held during the manufacture of physical parts? The more tolerance requirements placed on the machine, the more expensive its manufacture. Some machine tolerances may be less than a mil (a thousandth of an inch); in manufacture, these are quite critical.

Filing Equipment

Handling equipment, as we have discussed it, generally involves a method for transporting and scanning the storage medium. The logical equipment may make a decision which is then carried out by the mechanical handling equipment, but it makes this decision on the basis of information which is read.

Scanning, however, is generally an expensive and time-consuming operation. The purpose of filing mechanisms is to provide a means for replacing scanning by physical indexing. They usually imply the multiplexed use of a single handler for several groups of storage media. They involve some mechanism for locating a particular such group and either bringing it to the scanning unit or vice versa. They thus provide the significant functional capabilities of large files with some degree of indexed rather than scanned access. To the extent that the index unit can be made small, it can be scanned quickly. Thus the total access time to a given item is improved. On the other hand, the smaller the physically indexed unit, the more difficult are the problems of file organization and logical accessibility. Hence it is in this way, when file mechanisms are introduced, that the problems of physical access and logical organization arise.

It is essential to examine very carefully the equipment available for filing, the types of access that it provides, the physical steps involved in locating, and so on. How long a time does it take from placing a request to the file until the physical indexing process recovers every index unit involved and brings it to the handling unit for scanning? The capacity of the selected unit, how large is it? Is it a Minicard stick of 2000 cards, each with a large number of bits, or a much smaller unit like a sector on a Ramac disk with just 100 characters? The resulting index ratio is a very significant parameter; in the case of the Ramac, it is 60,000 units to 6,000,000 characters total capacity.

LOGICAL EQUIPMENT

The basis of logical equipment is the concept of built-in capability, that is, logical equipment provides a defined set of operations which can be performed on data. These operations can be simple or complex in terms of some intuitive understanding of the concept of complexity. For example, a command which results in the addition of two numbers is a fairly simple command; a command which results in a sort of 10,000 items into prescribed order is a quite complex command. In using the logical equipment, these built-in capabilities are usually considered as elementary operations. In a sense, they are all trivial: they are each called on by a simple command.

The complexity of the built-in capabilities for data handling provided by the logical equipment is one of the significant qualitative considerations. For example, in comparing computers it is important to recognize the difference between alternative order codes. One may be simple and limited; the other may provide a great variety of decision operations, special commands compatible with alpha-numeric codes, special operations oriented to data manipulation, special input-output controls. One may allow for handling only single items of data at a time; the other may handle whole masses of data with a single command. One may provide no tools to assist the programming itself; the other may provide index registers, monitor codes, check digits, break-points. One may be essentially sequential in its operation; the other may allow a large degree of parallel functioning.

In each case the difference may well imply difficulty versus ease in application to a problem of interest. In addition, there may be a particular affinity between the order code of one machine and the problem of information retrieval. There may be exceptional compatibility between the logical equipment and the storage media of maximum value. These considerations of ease of programming, affinity with the problem, and compatibility between devices must therefore also be recognized.

Finally, the flexibility of the logical equipment must be considered. Is it special purpose, difficult to change? Some of the built-in capabilities may be built-in as hardware; some of them, and this is the more recent concept, can be considered as built-in by the program. In such cases the flexibility is vastly increased. This has been the source of the power of the general purpose computer.

12

Parameters and implementation

The elements which have been discussed in the preceding chapters in a sense represent a qualitative description of the characterizing features of an information system. To design, organize, operate, and use a system, each set of elements must be effectively communicated between the individuals responsible for the areas concerned and the resulting specifications implemented. The user must effectively communicate his needs to the operational people to result in answers to his requirements; the engineer must effectively communicate the capabilities of his equipment to the system man to ensure that they are fully utilized, etc.

If good understanding has been established between individuals through long working relationship, this communication can be easy and sometimes congenial, and it may even be successful at the qualitative level covered in our discussion of the elements of an information system. In such cases the systems man, for example, may provide the engineer with a qualitative description of what he wants, and the engineer may understand completely what characteristics the machine should have and how to design it.

Such rapport is rare, however, and even when it exists, the qualitative description is usually not satisfactory. It is almost always necessary to specify well-defined quantitative characteristics which will describe the particular information systems as a reality rather than as the abstraction discussed up to now. These "parameters" are basic. Unfortunately there is an almost universal tendency for human beings, when faced with a problem, to become more abstract rather than less so, to avoid—almost like the plague—being concrete in their handling of a problem. Part of this tendency is the lack of a defined set of parameters to be determined. Thus a basic problem which must be resolved in this field is to develop such a set of parameters. As a first step in doing so, those quantities relevant to design and implementation of an information system might be grouped into two classes.

The first consists of those "parameters of operation" which define in concrete terms the requirements posed by usage and the capabilities which must be provided by the organization. The second set, the "parameters of equipment," similarly relates the requirements placed by the organization with the corresponding capabilities of the equipment. In each case these parameters represent not only the means for defining the system but also the means for resolving the differences in terminology, interest, and approach. Thus, if it is not possible to resolve differences on a qualitative level, it is essential to do so at the parametric level in terms of the actual numbers involved.

PARAMETERS OF OPERATION

Some of the parameters of operation may be phrased in terms of the existing situation, some in terms of the anticipated one. This reflects the ambiguous position in which system design must be formulated. One does not know exactly how the system will actually function. Therefore it is hoped that present needs will reflect to a large extent what future needs will be. On the other hand, it must be recognized that they also reflect the limitations of the existing system.

In either event—whether they reflect present needs or anticipated ones—these parameters are so important that a concerted effort should be made by workers in this field to develop a complete list organized according to some reasonable scheme. Much work of this type has been done already for specific problems, particularly in the accounting area. Experts in systems and procedures have developed check lists, standard interview forms, questionnaires, and so on. All such material should be brought together and consolidated into documents usable for specifying the characteristics of any type of system in a uniform manner. The development of standardized listing, both of operation and of equipment, is a task which has been delayed too long. It requires a cooperative effort of individuals from all four areas of responsibility. When the list has been developed, it should be checked against existing systems to ensure that it is complete and adequate. Once these parameters have been defined, they can represent, then, the starting point for discussion of specific mechanization and theoretical work. Until they are identified, all such effort will remain at a rarified level of discussion.

Let us take a look at some specific parameters to illustrate the needs. This can best be done in the form of an outline, or check list, as follows:

I. Parameters related to data storage
   A. Number of files
      (Recall that an information system is really a hierarchy of files, each organized for particular access.)
      1. What are the required number of diverse entry points in the system?
         a. How many types of usage are there?
         b. What is the pattern, or distribution, of usage among them?
      2. What is the quantitative extent of overlap among the files?
   B. Size of each file
      (Recall that this will determine what capacity must be provided and what type of storage units will be needed.)
      1. How many items are stored in each?
      2. What are the sizes of individual items?
         a. How much is descriptive data?
         b. How much is identification data?
         c. How much is for display or output?
      3. How are the file sizes determined?
         a. By users' need?
         b. By file storage limits?
   C. What is the growth of the file?
      1. Are certain areas highly active?
      2. What is the rate of growth?
II. Parameters related to data input
   A. Number of terms related to an individual input item
      (This will determine the character of the analytical problem in file searching.)
      1. Are certain terms highly used?
      2. How are terms distributed among types of data?
   B. Number of separate file items generated or affected by a single input item
      (This will most seriously affect the rate of growth of the file itself.)

C. Volume of activity
(This will similarly affect the rate of growth of the file.)
1. Are there seasonal trends or other characteristics of significant maxima or minima?

III. Parameters related to usage
A. Parameters defining the character of the individual request
(These parameters relate primarily to the elements of usage in the definition of individual requests.)
1. How many terms are involved?
2. Can a quantitative measure of logical complexity (such as number of levels of disjunction) be defined?
3. Are there numeric criteria for the relative importance of parts of a request?
4. Is there a measure for precision of logical agreement in recovery?
5. Is there a measure for precision in volume of recovery?

B. Volume of requests
(These parameters are most particularly concerned with the definition of the general user.)
1. Is there a seasonal distribution?
2. What is the number of requesters, and how are the requests distributed among them?
3. What are the criteria for assignment of priority?

C. Relationship between usage and the file itself
(These parameters similarly relate to the definition of the general user but are more concerned with the effect upon file operation.)
1. What is the ratio between the volume of requests in a day and the size of the file?
2. What is the distribution of requests in the file?

D. The character of file usage in reporting and other routine responses
(These parameters will describe the requirements for organization of response.)
1. What is the volume of dissemination?
   a. How many customers are there?
   b. How many standing requests are there?
   c. How many items are distributed as a result?
2. What are the periodic reporting needs?
   a. How many reports are there?
   b. What period is covered by each, and how frequent are they?

c. How many copies are distributed and what is the size of each?

IV. Parameters related to time and cost

A. Time limitations

(These parameters will determine the particular organization of processes required to meet the time limitations in operation.)

1. For the individual request, what is the interrogation response limit?
2. What is the relation between average activity and processing rate?
3. What are the limits on "pipeline" time—the time from initiation to completion of an operation?
4. Can a "unit-of-work" measure of processing time be defined?

B. Cost limits

(These parameters will affect what type of equipment can be utilized.)

1. Is there a required distribution of costs?
2. How is overhead handled?
3. How is fixed investment amortized?
4. How are premium costs for overtime and second-shift operation handled?
5. How are equipment costs—rental, maintenance, repairs, parts replacement, etc.—handled?

PARAMETERS OF EQUIPMENT [1]

To illustrate the extent to which parameters of equipment may be developed, we have chosen three parameters for each type of equipment, cost C, operating time T, and unit of operation N. These provide a measure CT/N for evaluation of the "efficiency" of single components viewed in the context of defined operations with no other system considerations involved. The components which have been compared in this way include the following:

1. Computer arithmetical and control units.
2. Output printing and composition devices.

---

[1] Advanced Information Systems Company, Mathematical Models for Information Systems Design and A Calculus of Operations, Report to Rome Air Development Center, Contract AF 30(602)-2111, ASTIA Document No. AD266577, 1961.

3. Other types of input and output devices.
4. File units.
5. Combined image and coded storage.

In Chapter 15 we discuss the theoretical basis for this measure of efficiency and its use in evaluating or designing systems.

Computer Arithmetical and Control Units

Attempts have been made by several people [2] to provide some criterion for evaluating the performance of computer arithmetical and control units. Usually these have involved a selection of some unit of work and an evaluation of the time required by the computer for performance of the defined task. This approach is complicated by several considerations, the most significant of which is the lack of a general theoretical model within which the unit of work measure could be viewed. It is hoped that the model presented in Chapter 15 provides an answer to this difficulty. However, there are still other problems. First is the problem of adequately defining a unit of work which will effectively measure the capabilities of the arithmetical and control unit. The second is the wide disparity of memory devices associated with different computers, in terms of both their size and operating speed. These problems are reflected in the corresponding difficulties in determining the three parameters, C, T, and N, in the measure of component efficiency. For example, should the cost C include the costs of associated peripheral equipment, such as the memory unit, and, if not, then how is the cost of the memory unit to be determined and eliminated from consideration? Similarly, is the time T to include the time required to obtain data from the memory, and, if not, then how is the time T to be estimated? What measure is to be used for problem size N, since no really adequate measure of operation complexity has yet been defined? The purpose of this illustration is to show how these questions can be resolved.

The problem of operation definition is probably the simplest to resolve since it is mainly a matter of defining a unit of work which adequately tests the capability of the arithmetical and control unit. The particular test operation should be chosen in terms of the general class of problems for which evaluation is being made. Thus, for example, if the class of problems itself involves a high percentage of

---

[2] *A Third Survey of Domestic Electronic Digital Computing Systems,* U.S. Dept. of Commerce, Office of Technical Services (PB171265), March 1961.

add-type commands as opposed to multiply-type commands, a problem will be defined with a high ratio of adds to multiplies. If decision processes are a major factor, another class of operations reflecting this significance will be used. Similarly, if the class of problems involves a preponderance of multiplications and divisions, then the operation selected will emphasize the effects of these commands. Thus the choice of operation on which to base comparison of efficiency is determined primarily by problem-oriented considerations.

For the purposes of this example we have arbitrarily chosen an operation which consists of one hundred add commands and a multiply command. It is thus an operation which is relatively weighted in favor of the add-type commands. It must be recognized that this is merely for the purpose of illustration and that other operations could be defined which would reflect other types of problems. Furthermore, it must be recognized that this rather arbitrary choice of operation does not in any way allow for reflecting the capabilities which particular computers might have, since we have made no attempt to program such an operation for each computer.

The second problem—the different sizes, mechanisms, and operating characteristics of memory devices and other associated peripheral equipment—is far more difficult to handle. Thus computer memories range in size from several thousand bits to several million bits and are available as disks, drums, cores, etc., with access times ranging from several seconds to several microseconds. In evaluating arithmetical and control units, their memory characteristics must be reduced to a common denominator. In this example, an attempt has been made to eliminate the effects of both memory costs and memory characteristics from the efficiency calculations. This is an arbitrary choice; others could have been made. It has been difficult to carry out even this, for in many cases it has involved breaking the instruction cycle into its component parts to make them comparable among the various computers.

It has been particularly difficult to determine how much of the computer's cost is attributable only to the arithmetical and control unit, for different manufacturers quote prices in different ways. Cost data were gathered from the different manufacturers toward the aim of elimination of memory costs from the calculations in this example. These data fall into two classes: those memories which appear to include the circuitry for addressing and memory control and those memories which do not. Fortunately some of the manufacturers have memories in each category and thus provide calibration points for evaluating other manufacturers' comparable costs. In this way estimates can be derived of the probable cost of any manufacturer's memory, either directly from his quoted prices or by calibration from the costs for his memories with addressed circuitry.

Figure 67 depicts these data in a logarithmic plot of the number of bits in various commercially available core memories which do not apparently include addressing circuitry. Figure 68 is a comparable set of data for those memories which apparently include such circuitry. Similar data have been gathered on drum memory costs. "Raw costs" are defined as the physical memory costs, separated from the costs of the arithmetical and control unit and addressing costs. These

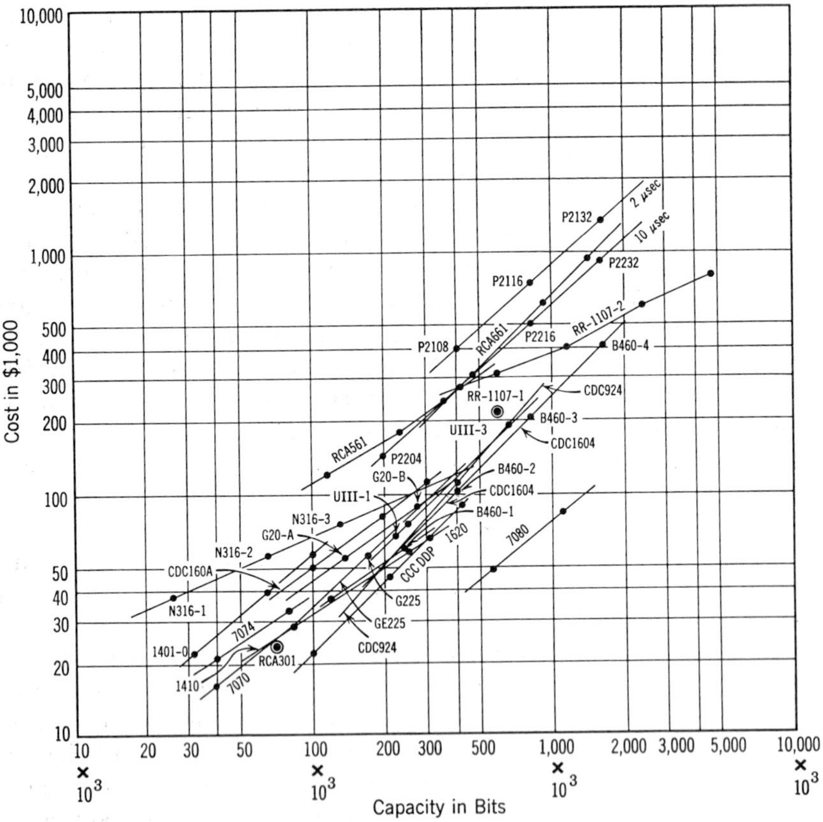

FIG. 67. Core memory costs, without addressing. Advanced Information Systems Company, Mathematical Models for Information Systems Design and A Calculus of Operations, Report to Rome Air Development Center, Contract AF 30(602)–2111, ASTIA Document No. AD266577, 1961.

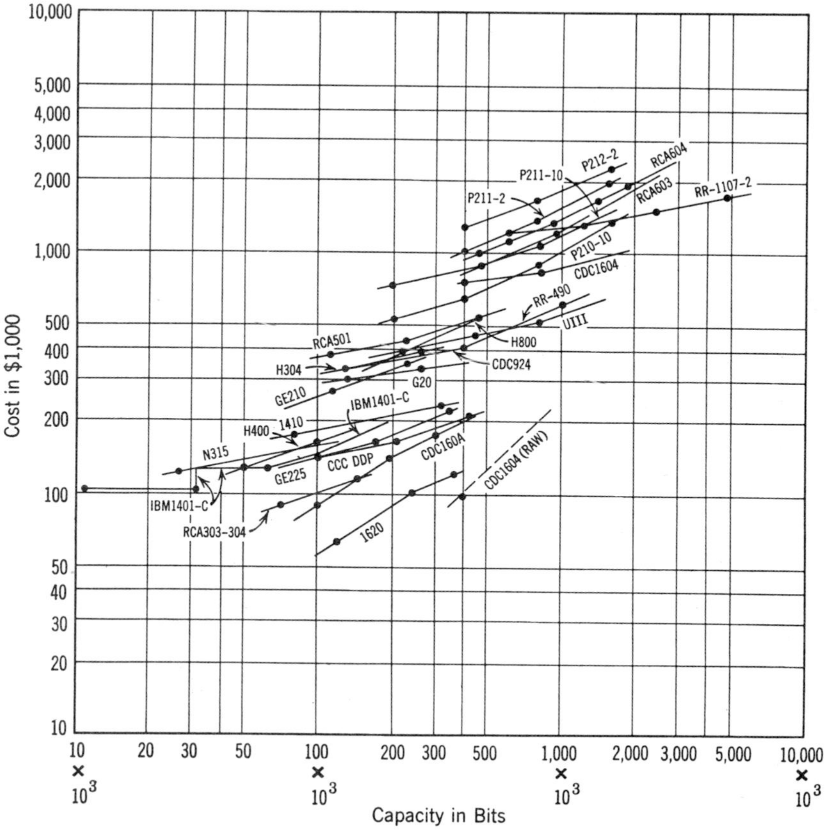

FIG. 68. Core memory costs, with addressing. Advanced Information Systems Company, Mathematical Models for Information Systems Design and A Calculus of Operations, Report to Rome Aid Development Center, Contract AF 30(602)–2111, ASTIA Document No. AD266577, 1961.

costs have been estimated either from the manufacturers' quotes for memory costs or from subjective criteria. Where a subjective decision for a particular computer's memory costs needed to be made, a memory of known raw cost, as closely parallel as possible in size, mechanization, and operating speed to the memory of unknown raw cost, was selected as an approximation. No attempt has been made to reckon with marketing decisions that may have been necessary to bring a product within a certain competitive cost range.

Finally, the problem of measuring operation complexity is complicated by the lack of any standard criterion for such measurement,

TABLE 10

Character and Efficiency of Selected Arithmetical and Control Units

Efficiency $\sigma = n/tCa$	n *	Add Time, in micro-seconds (a)	Multiply Time, in micro-seconds (m)	$t = a + 0.01m$, in micro-seconds †	Cost of Total Processor, 000's omitted	Memory Size, in bits ($\times 10^3$) ‡	Cost of Memory, 000's omitted	Cost of Arithmetical and Control Units, 000's omitted (Ca) §
62.85	56	1.05	4.8	1.1				810
48.50	24	15	279	18	39.5	C55.68	12	27.5
24.13	48	3.5	44.8	3.95				504
23.67	33	6	30	6.3	300	C135.2	0.55	221.3
23.54	25	9.5	47.5	10	140	C102.4	22	106.2
19.6	49	10	42	10.42	265.6			240
18.9	18	10	325	13.25	120	C73.73	48	72
18	48	2	60	2.6	1000	C150	160	840
15.69	53	10	60	10.6		C40	208.6	320
13.6	53	12	64	12.6				310
11.48	54	24	162	25.62	384	C221.2	180	183.6
10.74	48	7.2	44	7.64	750	C393.2	100	585
10.12	30	12	19.2	12.2	450	C491.5	180	243
10.06	56	6	10	6.1	998.6	C458.75	130	795
9.31	48	15	91	15.91				324
8.01	36	4.36	17.44	5.53				817.5
7.5	27	12	40	12.4	390	C220.9	100	290.7
7.5	24	12	60	12.6	362	C196.6	50	250
6.14	48	15	52	15.52				504
6.08	56	13.1	74.2 (11 × 11)	13.84	869.7	C458.75	130	666
5.51	36	4	12.7	4.13	8			800
5	26	48	1635	64	127.5	C26		81
4.81	50	120	2160	141.6	132	C51.2	50	73.8
4.4	53	72	1008	82.1		C40	160	145.5

3.8	54	51	1780	68.8	250	*D*300	20	207
3.5	21	54	540	59.4	135	*C*86	30	94.5
3.26	35	13	265	15.65		*C*560	480	685
3.1	62	224 (6+6)	13,860 (6×6)	363				55.5
3.03	36	24	240	26.4				450
2.84	70	329	8600	415	89.4	*C*70	23.5	59.31
2.83	36	24	132	25.32				500
2.8	72	960	17,700	1037	64	*C*120	37.1	24.21
2.7	36	24	180	25.8	760	*C*160	160	508.5
2.3	72	167	3506	202	174.5	*C*80	28	155.8
2.1	36	28		30	1000	*D*1000	120	580
2	29	300	16,000	460	50	*D*60	20	30
2	16	250	16,000	410	40	*D*65	20	20
2	48	4	8	4.1				6000
1.9	40	85	2000	105	250	*D*200	40	210
1.7	28	96	512	101.1	268.8	*C*114.7	85	165.4
1.6	20	520	14,000	660	30			19
1.5	45	345	6785	413				73.2
1.5	18	48	444	52				230
1.5	40	440	20,000	640	79	*D*160	37	42
1.2	41	2500	10,800	2608	135	*D*160	40	95
1.1	84	1512	22,711	1739	66			45
1	45	345	6785	413	105.4	*C*11.2	6	112.5
1	36	220	11,000	330	90			90
0.9	51	672	10,660	778	170	*D*100	25	72

* n = the number of bits in a word or an average instruction, whichever is greater.

† This represents the time for a particularly defined class of problems. Defining another class of problems may result in another time.

‡ C = core; D = drum; A/D = acoustic delay.

§ An additional 10% was deducted from the difference between total processor cost and memory cost for operator's console costs, where an estimate was necessary.

TABLE 10 (*Continued*)

Efficiency $\sigma = n/tCa$	n *	Add Time, in micro-seconds (a)	Multiply Time, in micro-seconds (m)	$t = a + 0.01m$, in micro-seconds †	Cost of Total Processor, 000's omitted	Memory Size, in bits ($\times 10^3$) ‡	Cost of Memory, 000's omitted	Cost of Arithmetical and Control Units, 000's omitted (Ca) §
0.9	48	500	16,000	660	100	*D*120	28	72
0.9	41	185	2095	206	320	*C*200	100	220
0.8	33	330	18,300	513	97	*D*33	12	85
0.8	20	520	14,000	660	40			40
0.73	33	1000	17,000	1170	56.8	*D*275	18 est.	38.8
0.7	48	11,000	85,000	11,850	75	*C*9.6	25	56.3
0.65	41	330	18,300	513	155	*D*130	30	125
0.6	36	910	2990	940	100	*D*135	34	66
0.6	72	900	3260	933	258		126	130
0.5	72	700	20,000	900				150
0.5	66	600	1020	610	366.6	*C*132	130	212.9
0.4	72	200	1900	219	970	*C*100	130	873
0.35	12	800	20,000	1000	60	*C*49.15	20	35
0.31	35	204	2414	228				500
0.31	56	540	22,950	770				231.3
0.3	72	323	1948	342				675
0.30	35	133	1618	149				788
0.30	12	800	20,000	1000	90	*C*98.3	50	40
0.2	42	4000	15,000	4150	65	*D*43	16	49
0.2	20	230	3358	260	400			358.8
0.12	41	5000	25,000	5250				67.5
0.09	41	5000	25,000	5250	97.5	*T*1	20	87.8
0.05	50	50,000	250,000	52,500	30	*D*10	6	24

0.03	70			30	100	{C.6, D8}	{3, 4}	68
0.03	40			70	20	D4	3	17
0.003	32			300	55	D3	3	52
0.002	72	10,000	20,000	10,200				30
0.001	72	10,000	20,000	10,200				102.9
0.001	40	22,500	5×10^6	27,500	50	C350	1.5	3.5
Not available	40	1040	20,800	1248	95	164.5 Disk	Not available	Not available
Not available	40	540	10,800	648	65	164.5 Disk	Not available	Not available
Not available	72				15	D3	3	12
Not available	60	0.3	3	0.33	Not available	Not available	Not available	Not available
Not available	28	25	70	25.7		C29	Not available	Not available
Not available	44				5		Not available	Not available
Not available	33	3650	28,470	3934.7	24.5	D338	15	9.5

* n = the number of bits in a word or an average instruction, whichever is greater.

† This represents the time for a particularly defined class of problems. Defining another class of problems may result in another time.

‡ C = core; D = drum; A/D = acoustic delay.

§ An additional 10% was deducted from the difference between total processor cost and memory cost for operator's console costs, where an estimate was necessary.

Source: Advanced Information Systems Company, Mathematical Models for Information Systems Design and A Calculus of Operations, Report to Rome Air Development Center, Contract AF 30(602)–2111, ASTIA Document No. AD266577, 1961.

which is invariant with respect to choice of computer. The number of words in a program to perform the operation might be utilized as a measure of such operation complexity but, unfortunately, the characteristics of computers vary so widely in terms of the number of words required to perform a specified operation that this measure is relatively useless. In a sense, this results from the variation in component sophistication, which is difficult to handle. For arithmetical and control units, one needs to somehow measure the effect of such things as the power of command structure, addressing and indexing problems, number of registers, etc. It would seem that this is closely related to the number of bits in an instruction word. Therefore, in this example, the number of bits in the program required to perform the operation is utilized as a measure of operation complexity. It is arbitrarily assumed that, for all units selected, this is the number of bits in 100 instruction words. In actual practice, the operation would be optimally programmed for each unit to get a dynamic bit count.

It is important to recognize that the foregoing decisions are completely arbitrary. If a detailed comparison of arithmetical and control units were desired for a specific purpose, then a far more careful analysis would certainly be needed. For example, the problem on which two different arithmetical and control units are to be evaluated should be completely programmed for the relevant computers. The two resultant programs would then represent the operation on which computation times would be based. The effects of the memory might be better expressed by considering the computers with an identical but not necessarily zero memory, if this is possible. Finally, the actual number of bits required for the two programs should be used as a measure of their respective complexity. However, for the purposes of this illustration, the foregoing assumptions have been made and result in Table 10.

Output Printing and Composition Devices

Counterparts of the same considerations of operation definition and complexity, of component definition and sophistication arise in the evaluation of efficiency of output printing and composition devices. Thus the effectiveness of a given device is certainly highly dependent on the type of printing operation which is defined. For example, printers with high-speed skips would perform better on printing jobs requiring such a capability than would printers without this feature.

With respect to component definition, some printers require a controller when connected to a computer while others do not; some are buffered while others are not; some supply their own format control while others have this provided by the computer, etc. This disparity in component characteristics is extremely difficult to measure. In this example, output devices have been defined according to the manufacturers' specifications.

The sophistication of output components, as with arithmetical and control units, is similarly difficult. No criterion exists to measure the value of such things as the quality and registration of print, number of producible copies, number of intermediate steps required to produce the finished product, etc. In this example, output component sophistication is assumed to be a function of the size of the character set available for printing at a given time.

In summary, for the purposes of this example, we have made some arbitrary assumptions concerning these considerations.

1. We assume that a printing job is simply that of line-by-line printing with full character capacity per line. This type of printing task means that the printing job is simply that of printing characters—as many of them as possible.
2. The printer, as a component, is accepted as that defined without attempting to reduce it to a common denominator.
3. The sophistication of the printing device is defined by the logarithm to the base 2 of the number of characters (size of the character group) available for printing at a given time.

The foregoing assumptions result in Table 11, which shows the efficiency of selected output printing and composition devices.

Other Input and Output Devices

Because of their general nature, other input and output devices tend to be somewhat easier to handle in terms of the three considerations discussed. Thus the operations they perform are generally limited to input and output; the component is generally well defined; and the unit of measure of the operation as a bit is standard. There are some complications, however, when the input-output unit includes buffering capability or some degree of off-line function. In most cases these considerations can be relatively easily separated out. Table 12 lists a set of such devices in terms of their characteristics.

TABLE 11

Selected Output Devices

Efficiency ($\sigma = n \cdot 10^{-3}/tc$) *	Category	Different Characters Available (a)	$n = \log_2 a$	Characters per second ($1/t$)	n/t	Purchase Cost, 000's omitted (c) †
592.5	Electrostatic	64	6.00	17280	103680	175.0 est.
394.0	Photographic	60	5.91	15000	88650	225.0
384.0	Electrostatic	64	6.00	6400	38400	100.0
360.0	Mechanical	64	6.00	300	1800	15.0 est.
285.7	Photographic	64	6.00	15000	90000 on-line	315.0 est.
282.5	Mechanical	63	5.98	3000	17940	63.5
250.0	Photographic	64	6.00	15000	90000 off-line	360.0 est.
239.6	Mechanical	48	5.59	1320	7379	30.8
211.3	Mechanical	51	5.67	1200	6804	32.2
184.5	Mechanical	48	5.59	1000	5590	30.3
181.1	Mechanical	64	6.00	2400	14400	79.5 est.
174.9	Electrostatic	64	6.00	8747	52482	300.0
163.2	Mechanical	64	6.00	2000	12000	73.5
156.1	Mechanical	63	5.98	1300	7774	49.8
154.1	Mechanical	63	5.98	1080	6548	42.5
149.5	Mechanical	51	5.67	1300	7371	49.3
140.4	Mechanical	47	5.55	2783	15446	110.0 est.
138.4	Mechanical	66	6.04	2200	13288	96.0 est.
137.4	Mechanical	44	5.46	1800	9828	71.5
134.3	Mechanical	64	6.00	1600	9600	71.5 est.
134.2	Mechanical	66	6.04	2000	12080	90.0 est.
132.9	Mechanical	64	6.00	1440	8640	65.0 est.
131.1	Mechanical	56	5.81	1800	10458	79.8

112.5	Mechanical	51	5.67	1200	6804	60.5
109.0	Mechanical	56	5.81	1360	7902	72.5
107.2	Mechanical	51	5.67	1493	8465	79.0
105.1	Mechanical	55	5.78	2000	11560	110.0
86.7	Mechanical	44	5.46	1080	5897	68.0
78.3	Mechanical	64	6.00	1800	10800	138.0
75.2	Mechanical	51	5.67	1493	8465	112.5
72.5	Mechanical	96	6.59	1100	7249	100.0 est.
71.5	Mechanical	56	5.81	1700	9877	138.1
66.7	Mechanical	61	5.93	1800	10674	160.0
63.1	Mechanical	44	5.46	720	3931	62.3
60.4	Mechanical	49	5.62	1000	5620	93.0
53.5	Mechanical	49	5.62	11240	11240	210.5
39.9	Mechanical	63	5.98	400	2392	60.0
32.0	Mechanical	47	5.55	300	1665	52.0
29.9	Mechanical	40	5.32	118	628	21.0
26.4	Mechanical	100	6.64	10	66	2.5
22.2	Mechanical	47	5.55	300	1665	75.0
14.0	Mechanical	48	5.59	150	839	60.0
13.2	Mechanical	100	6.64	10	66	5.0
3.0	Photographic (cold type)	1400	10.45	0.33	3	1.0
2.3	Photographic	15,000	13.87	10	139	60.0
1.6	Hot-type mechanical caster	256	8.00	3	24	15.0
1.6	Photomechanical caster	256	8.00	5	40	25.0
Not available	Photographic	256	8.00	667	5336	Not available
Not available	Hot-type mechanical caster	324	8.34	6	50	Not available
Not available	Photographic	1500 est.	10.55	30	317	Not available

* The higher the efficiency number, the more efficient is the output device.

† Only the cost of the output device is considered; the cost of mandatory auxiliary equipment, such as a printer controller, is omitted.

Source: same as for Table 10.

TABLE 12

Other Input/Output Devices

Type of Device	Efficiency $\sigma = n/tc$	Bits per "block" (n)	Time per "block" in seconds (t)	Purchase Cost (c)	Comments
a. Card Readers					
	0.77	960	0.075	16,600	
	0.7	960	½	2750	
	0.67	960	0.03	48,000	
	0.62	960	0.100	15,750	
	0.56	960	½	2900	
	0.53	960	0.03	60,000	
	0.52	960	0.075	24,800	Cost is for combined read-punch unit
	0.5	540	½	2200	
	0.50	960	0.086	22,500	
	0.47	960	0.075	27,050	Cost is for combined read-punch unit
	0.47	960	0.133	15,290	
	0.44	960	0.12	18,000	
	0.38	960	0.100	25,290	
	0.35	960	0.3	9130	
	0.34	960	0.2	14,000	
	0.32	960	0.15	20,000	
	0.27	960	0.24	14,650	
	0.26	960	1.00	3700	
	0.25	960	0.24	16,350	
	0.22	12	1/80	4000 est.	
	0.13	960	0.30	25,000	Cost is for combined read-punch unit
	0.13	960	0.24	32,000	
	0.13	960	0.24	30,000	Cost is for combined read-punch unit

	0.12	960	0.33	25,255	
	0.11	960	0.24	36,800	
	0.09	612	0.33	19,475	
	0.07	960	0.50	28,400	
	0.07	960	1.00	13,500	
	0.06	960	0.38	40,000	Cost is for combined read-punch unit
	0.06	960	0.24	64,450	
	0.05	960	0.40	51,000	Includes substantial amount of other abilities; somewhat unfair to consider strictly as a card reader
	0.05	960	0.40	52,750	Includes substantial amount of other abilities; somewhat unfair to consider strictly as a card reader
	0.049	960	0.40	48,650	Cost is for combined read-punch unit
	Not available	540	½		
	Not available	80	60/2000		
	Not available	960	0.03		
b. Card Punches					
	0.28	960	0.6	5800	
	0.20	960	0.24	20,250	
	0.16	960	0.24	24,800	Cost is for combined read-punch unit
	0.15	960	0.24	27,050	Cost is for combined read-punch unit
	0.13	960	0.6	15,000	
	0.13	960	0.60	12,250	Cost is for combined read-punch unit
	0.11	960	0.400	22,500	
	0.093	960	0.200	51,750	
	0.09	960	0.6	18,675	
	0.07	480	0.33	19,475	
	0.07	960	0.60	25,000	Cost is for combined read-punch unit
	0.07	960	0.4	36,000	Modified punches
	0.06	480	0.33	25,255	

TABLE 12 (*Continued*)

Type of Device	Efficiency $\sigma = n/tc$	Bits per "block" (n)	Time per "block" in seconds (t)	Purchase Cost (c)	Comments
	0.06	960	0.38	40,000	Cost is for combined read-punch unit
	0.06	960	0.50	30,000	Cost is for combined read-punch unit
	0.049	960	0.40	48,650	Cost is for combined read-punch unit
c. Paper Tape Readers					
	1.52	8	0.001	5280	
	1.52	7	0.0023	2000	
	1.52	8	0.0017	3100	
	1.28	8	0.0017	3665	
	1.23	8	0.001	6500	
	1.14	5	0.0017	2575	
	1.08	8	0.001	7400	
	1.03	8	0.003	2600	
	0.98	8	0.0033	2485	
	0.95	8	0.003	2800	
	0.84	8	0.001	9500	
	0.83	5	0.0017	3530	
	0.82	7	0.0045	1892	
	0.69	8	0.0167	690	
	0.57	16	$1/45$	1260	
	0.53	8	0.001	15,000	Cost is for combined read-punch unit
	0.42	16	$1/30$	1140	
	0.37	8	$1/45$	960	
	0.37	8	0.33	650	
	0.3	6	$1/1800$	32,800	
	0.29	8	$1/30$	850	
	0.28	8	0.0017	16,950	Cost is for combined read-punch unit

	0.27	80	0.167	1800	
	0.27	16	1/18	1050	
	0.20	8	0.002	20,000	
	0.2	8	1/18	740	
	0.13	8	0.007	9100	
	0.10	8	0.001	80,000	Modified reader
	0.098	8	0.001	81,600	Cost is combined for read-punch unit
	0.032	8	0.083	3000	Cost is combined for read-punch unit
	0.028	8	0.008	35,120	
	0.01	8	0.050	13,000	
	Not available	7	1/1000		
	Not available	8	1/1000		
	Not available	8	60/500		
	Not available	6	60/500		
d. Paper Tape Punches					
	1.60	8	0.01	500	
	0.48	8	0.01	1650	
	0.48	8	0.0167	1000	
	0.37	8	0.33	650	
	0.34	8	0.003	7900	
	0.31	8	0.008	3200	
	0.22	8	0.033	11,050	
	0.22	8	1240	8750	
	0.20	8	0.04	995	
	0.12	7	0.0167	3400	
	0.11	8	0.05	1500	Cost is for tape punch unit alone
	0.10	8	0.055	1400	
	0.09	8	0.067	1400	
	0.09	8	1/20	1780	
	0.082	8	0.055	1780	For use with cash registers, adding and accounting machines

TABLE 12 (Continued)

Type of Device	Efficiency $\sigma = n/tc$	Bits per "block" (n)	Time per "block" in seconds (t)	Purchase Cost (c)	Comments
	0.07	8	0.0067	16,950	Cost is for combined read-punch unit
	0.06	8	0.0083	15,000	Cost is for combined read-punch unit
	0.05	8	0.055	2900	
	0.04	5	0.055	2500	
	0.011	8	0.009	81,600	Cost is for combined read-punch unit
	0.01	6	0.33	1825	
	0.01	5	0.10	3600	
	0.008	8	1.0	985	
	0.008	8	0.333	3000	Cost is for combined read-punch unit
	0.6×10^{-3}	8	0.0167	80,000	Cost is for combined read-punch unit
	Not available	8	$1/20$		
	Not available	8	$1/20$		
	Not available	8	$1/60$	17,800	
	Not available	8	$1/15$		
	Not available	5	$60/500$		
e. Other					
	265×10^{-6}	6	0.36	63,000	n is in digits; a block can be a check; encoded with magnetically inked characters. Also has sorting abilities
	209×10^{-6}	6	0.40	71,800	
	202×10^{-6}	6	0.48	62,000	n is in digits; a block can be a check; encoded with magnetically inked characters. Also has sorting abilities
	Not available	Not available	0.15	120,300	

Source: same as for Table 10.

File Units

File units represent a class of components which should be viewed in terms of more than one operation, since they generally provide the capability not only of input and output, but of some degree of indexing. Magnetic tape units with an off-line searching capability and disk files with indexing capability are examples of such units. The operations which must be considered are therefore at least those of indexing (or searching) and input-output. The components themselves are generally well defined except in the case of those units which require a logical black box for the performance of searching functions. In these cases, the costs of the logical black box must be added to that of the file unit itself.

The obvious choice for the unit of measure of each operation is the capacity of the block of data which is of interest in the operation. Where a complete file operation is involved, such as in a scanning search, this unit of measure would be the capacity of the file unit itself. For the sake of convenience in presentation, we have chosen this unit of measure for both types of operation.

Table 13 summarizes the characteristics of several file units in terms of the two classes of operations, indexing and input-output. For a true picture of the efficiency of any one such component, it would be necessary to define the relative volumes of the two classes of operation in the form prescribed by the model. This could be done by assuming a relative density of searching requests with respect to file capacity. Such densities are characterizing features of particular classes of problems. For example, a density of 10% search requests per day is very typical of such business problems as inventory control; densities of 0.1% per day are very typical of large-scale file problems.

Combined Image and Coded Storage

Equipment very much related to the file units discussed above is that which provides capability for storage of both image and coded information. This type of equipment includes, for example, Minicard, Filmorex, Film Sort, and others. For such units, however, the unit of measure for input and output is somewhat difficult to express in the form of bits since the entire problem of resolution of the image and related considerations are difficult to handle in this way. For discussion of these units, we have therefore chosen as our unit the "page." The operations involved are essentially the same as those

TABLE 13

Selected File Units

Efficiency, $\sigma_1 = n/t_1c$	Efficiency, $\sigma_2 = n/t_2c$	Category	Capacity bits $\times 10^6$ (n)	Average Read Time/bit, in seconds $\times 10^{-6}$ (T)	Time to Read ½ file, in seconds ($t_1 = 0.5nT$)	Average Index Time, in seconds (t_2)	Purchase Cost in 000's (c)
148	1830	Drum	28.2	0.15	2.115	0.17	90
71	87.2	Drum	1.57	0.39	0.307	0.25	72
50	125	Tape	50	2	50	20	20
48.8	48.8	Tape	224.7	1.4	160	160	28.75
40	40	Magnetic card	15	2	15	15	25
35.7	5800	Tape strips	44.4	1.67	33.4	0.2	38
33.3	250	Magnetic card	150	2	150	20	30
26	26	Tape	107.4	3.2	171.9	171.9	24
23.5	23.5	Tape	312	2.2	349.6	349.6	38
20.5	6963	Disk	94	0.65	30.55	0.09	150
18.4	18.4	Tape	107.4	3.2	171.9	171.9	33.8
17.8	17.8	Tape	92.2	2.6	119.86	121	43.2
17.6	17.6	Tape	92.2	2.6	119.86	121	43.2
17.1	11,605	Disk	188	0.65	61.10	0.09	180
17	17	Tape	73.3	3.3	120	120	36
16.9	16.9	Tape	78.9	3.3	129	129	36.25
16.6	16.6	Tape	54.7	4.4	120	120	27.5

16.6	1250	Magnetic card	2250	2	2250	30	60
13.4	13.4	Tape	45.6	7.5	171	171	20
13.2	13.2	Tape	45.6	7.5	171	171	20
13	13	Tape	78.9	4.9	194	194	31
11.1	11.1	Tape	45.6	8.9	205.2	205.2	20
10.7	10.7	Tape	45.6	7.5	171	171	20
10.4	10.4	Tape	78.9	10.1	400	400	19
9.2	9.2	Tape	22.8	14.25	156.75	156.75	20
8.8	1772	Disk	144	3.5	252	0.125	65
8.5	8500	Disk	168	2	168	0.167	115.5
7.5	7.5	Tape	35	7.3	128.2	128.2	36.25
5.8	5.8	Tape	35	11.1	194.6	194.6	31
5.4	10,800	Disk	336	2	336	0.167	185.5
4.6	4.6	Tape	35	22.9	400	400	19
3.8	2950	Drum	140	3.8	266	0.34	140
1.9	8192	Disk	512	8.3	2124.8	0.500	125
0.47	2.9	Tape	10	620	3100	500	6.8
					(Indexing proceeds at 6 times reading rate)		
0.33	694.4	Disk	25	100.0×10^{-6}	1250	0.6	60
Not available	Not available	Tape	35	5	87.5	3.5	Not available
Not available	Not available	Tape loops	21	Not available	Not available	1.9	Not available

Source: same as for Table 10.

TABLE 14

Selected Image and Coded Data Storage Units

$\sigma_1 n_1/ct_1$	$\sigma_2 = n_2 \cdot 10^{-6}/ct_2$	Category	Capacity in bits $\times 10^6$ (n_1)	Average Read time/bit, in microseconds	t_1, in seconds *	Capacity, in pages or cards $\times 10^3$ (n_2)	Average Output Time per Page or Card, in seconds †	t_2, in seconds ‡	Cost, 000's omitted
3.33	3300	Film cards	1.0	100	50	12	0.1	600	6
					2000 cards per tray and 500 bits per card assumed.				
1	333.3	Film cards	4.9	20	49	4	0.06	120	100 est.
					2000 card spindles assumed.				
0.67	8	Microfilm	10.1	30	151.5	42	2.5	52,500	100 est.
0.40	16	Microfilm	2.3	100	115	72	2.5	90,000	50 est.
0.16	800	Film cards	0.4	2500	500	2	0.5	500	5 est.
					2000 cards per tray and 200 bits per card assumed.				
0.13	1000	Film cards	0.7	150	52.5	24	0.01	240	100 est.
					2000 card spindles assumed.				
Not available	Not available	Film plates				1000	2.0	1×10^6	Not available
Not available	Not available	Film strips				990	1.50	74×10^6	Not available
					Prototype approved for use by Central Intelligence Agency				
Not available	Not available	Film cards	0.1			4			Not available
					2000 card spindles assumed.				
Not available	Not available	Microfilm	17.0	10	85	36	0.30	540	Not available
Not available	Not available	Magnetic	86.4	5	216	60	0.2	6000	Not available

* t_1 = time to scan $0.5n_1$ at bit reading rate, or the time to index to a block and read half of the block, whichever is the lesser. Same built-in logical ability is implied.

† This is the time to obtain a page or card from the file in human readable form.

‡ t_2 = time to produce in human readable form half the page or card capacity of the file; the mechanical output time.

Source: same as for Table 10.

with the file units, namely: indexing (or search) and input-output. The indexing operation involves a scan of the stored coded information, while the input-output involves a reproduction of the pages. In each case, for the rate of reproduction of pages, we use the fastest rate permitted by the set of equipment in its typical operation. These results are presented in Table 14.

General Information Transfer

As a concluding illustration of the application of the model to the efficiency of single components, an analysis was made of the efficiencies of the several classes of components considered as information transfer devices under various single operations. The results of this analysis are presented in Figure 69, which plots the efficiency N/CT of these classes of components as a function of the effective information transfer rate N/T.

IMPLEMENTATION

As we indicated in the introduction in Chapter 1, the purpose of this book is not to show how to *solve* a problem—and implementation is, of course, precisely that. Several manuals and texts are available which provide details in this area.[3,4] It is desirable, however, to outline some of the considerations which are involved in implementation.

Planning and Design

The first step in any implementation is the planning and design step. It provides the answers to all of those things which we have discussed under the elements of analysis. In particular, during the planning stage, data gathering must develop the information, concerning both present operations and the anticipated future ones, on which to base design decisions about the elements of usage. Furthermore, it is in this planning stage that all of the various items of information and pieces of data must be defined and the relationships established among them. This corresponds exactly to the organization of items, files, and responses as one of the major parts of the elements of organization.

---

[3] Management of Data Processing Equipment, Air Force Manual 171–9, 1 June 1958.

[4] Good and McCall, *System Engineering,* New York, McGraw-Hill, 1957.

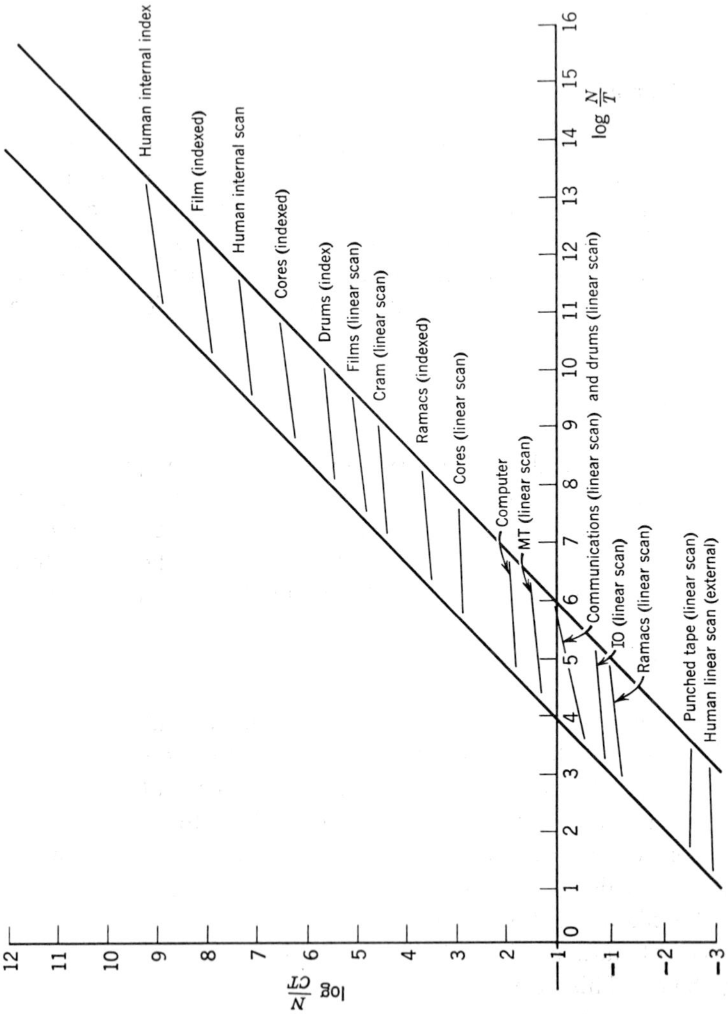

FIG. 69. General information transfer efficiency. Reference: Same as for Figure 67.

In particular, the various items of input must be established; the format of stored file items must be defined; details of items generated as a result of logical processes in system operation must be given; the structure and format of items of information output from the system must be defined. In each case the detail must define the vocabulary, the coding, the format, and the data type.

Once the items have been defined, the relationships among them must be established. There have been several methods developed for doing so. One of these pictures the relationship between items of input and items of output, such as reports, in the form of a matrix.[5] The individual columns of this matrix would correspond to the various items of input and the individual rows to the various reports or file items. The element in the matrix would then describe whether the item of input was involved in a given report and, if so, in what way. Other methods of presenting the same kind of item-to-item relationship include that shown in Figure 70 developed by G. Salton [6] and that developed by National Cash Register in their MAP procedure [7] illustrated in Figure 71. The details shown in this type of presentation are almost sufficient for the construction of logical flow diagrams, the next step in system planning and design, that is, once the items of interest to the system have been defined and their interrelationships exhibited in some useful form, the various procedures and processes for transforming data and implementing the organization of processes outlined in Chapter 10, The Elements of Organization, may be presented in several forms. The simplest is probably a set of procedural descriptions which describe, in natural language, a picture of each process, its purpose, and the method for its execution. Such procedural descriptions, however, do not make it easy to see how the processes relate to each other and how the information flows from one process to the next. It has therefore become traditional in the field of data processing to present the structure of system procedures in the form of a "flow chart" using standardized symbols to represent various types of operations, various sources of data, and various types of decision processes.

More recently, a method of presentation of the details of procedure

---

[5] Formalized Analysis Techniques—Aids to Computer Design and Computer Use, presented to the Fourth Annual Symposium on Computers and Data Processing, Denver Research Institute, August 29, 1957, Denver, Col.

[6] Gerard A. Salton, An Automatic Data Processing System for Public Utility Revenue, Harvard University, Cambridge, Mass., January 1958.

[7] Introduction to MAP, National Cash Register Company, Dayton, Ohio, 1961.

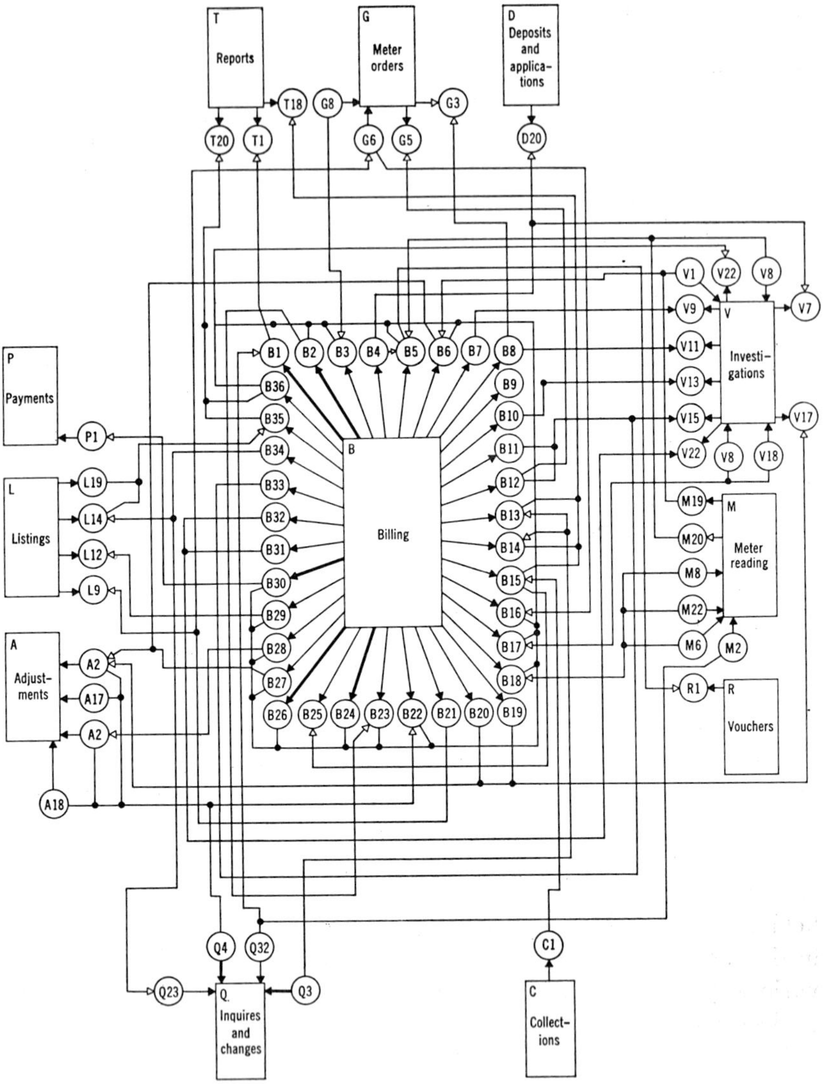

FIG. 70. Charting for interrelationships among operations. Gerard A. Salton, An Automatic Data Processing System for Public Utility Revenue, Harvard University, Cambridge, Mass., January 1958.

BILLING

Adjustments

A2: Adjustments for billing rejects
A3: Sales adjustments due to complaints
A17: Adjustments due to meter testing
A18: Rate adjustments

Billing

B1: Cycle bills issued including arrears and estimated bills
B2: Out of cycle bills for revenue protection
B3: Bills issued for advanced consumption on inactive accounts
B4: Billing rejects for advanced consumption
B5: Bills issued for unknown users
B6: Bills issued for unmetered service charges
B7: Billing rejects for insufficient consumption on active accounts
B8: Billing rejects on meters inactive for excessively long periods
B9: Billing rejects resulting from meter changes
B10: Billing rejects for low or high consumption where reading cannot be estimated
B11: Billing rejects for unusual demand readings
B12: Billing rejects for negative consumption which fail to pass test for meter turnover
B13: Out of cycle duplicate bills issued
B14: Out of cycle requests for itemized bills
B15: Duplicate bills issued with special certification
B16: Bills issued out of cycle because of missing meter change orders
B17: Out of cycle bills due to return of special read orders
B18: Out of cycle bills resulting from returned dial cards and skipped readings
B19: Billing rejects due to previous overestimates
B20: Billing rejects due to billing errors
B21: Rejects due to missing meter change orders
B22: Out of cycle corrected bills due to customer complaints or special investigations
B23: Bills requiring review after billing
B24: Bills for accounts using both alternating and direct current requiring review
B25: Bills requiring special certification
B26: Bills for governmental agencies which may require special review
B27: Minimum bills for which previous reading was estimated requiring special review
B28: Bills for customers not consuming yearly assessed minimum
B29: Bills for special minimum accounts
B30: Bills for banking plan customers
B31: Billing rejects covering excessively long service periods
B32: Bills for excessive money amounts requiring review
B33: Bills for demand accounts without billable demand for a given service period
B34: Rejects due to discrepancy with master record
B35: Out of cycle bills issued after discrepancy with master is cleared up
B36: Bills for accounts requiring collection activity and investigation

Collections

C1: Collection letters sent out

Deposits and Applications

D20: Applications sent to inactive accounts

Meter Orders

G3: Meter remove orders issued
G5: Meter change orders issued
G6: Meter change orders returned
G8: Meter connect orders returned

Listings

L9: Listing of no bill accounts
L12: Listing of special minimum rejects
L14: Listing of rejects due to master discrepancy
L19: Listing of multiple meter rejects

Meter Reading

M2: Meter reading medium returned from field
M6: Spoiled meter reading medium
M8: Dial cards returned from customers
M19: Meter reader's reports of hazards
M20: Meter reader's reports of vacant premises
M22: Out of cycle skipped meter readings

Payments

P1: Payments for banking plan accounts

Inquiries and Changes

Q3: Inquiries requiring duplicate bills
Q4: Inquiries requiring bill corrections
Q23: Changes in revenue classification
Q32: Changes in billing cost information

Vouchers

R1: Unknown user vouchers

Reports

T1: Customer record information
T18: Report of duplicate bills issued
T20: Bill register

Investigations

V1: Investigation of irregular conditions returned
V4: Special read orders returned
V7: Investigation on unknown users issued
V8: Investigation on unknown users returned
V9: Investigation on no consumption accounts
V11: Investigation of inactive accounts
V13: Investigation of high-low failures
V15: Investigation of demand or multiple meter rejects
V17: Special read orders due to complaints
V18: Special read orders (V17) returned
V22: Investigation of excess billing period
V28: Investigation of undeliverable mail

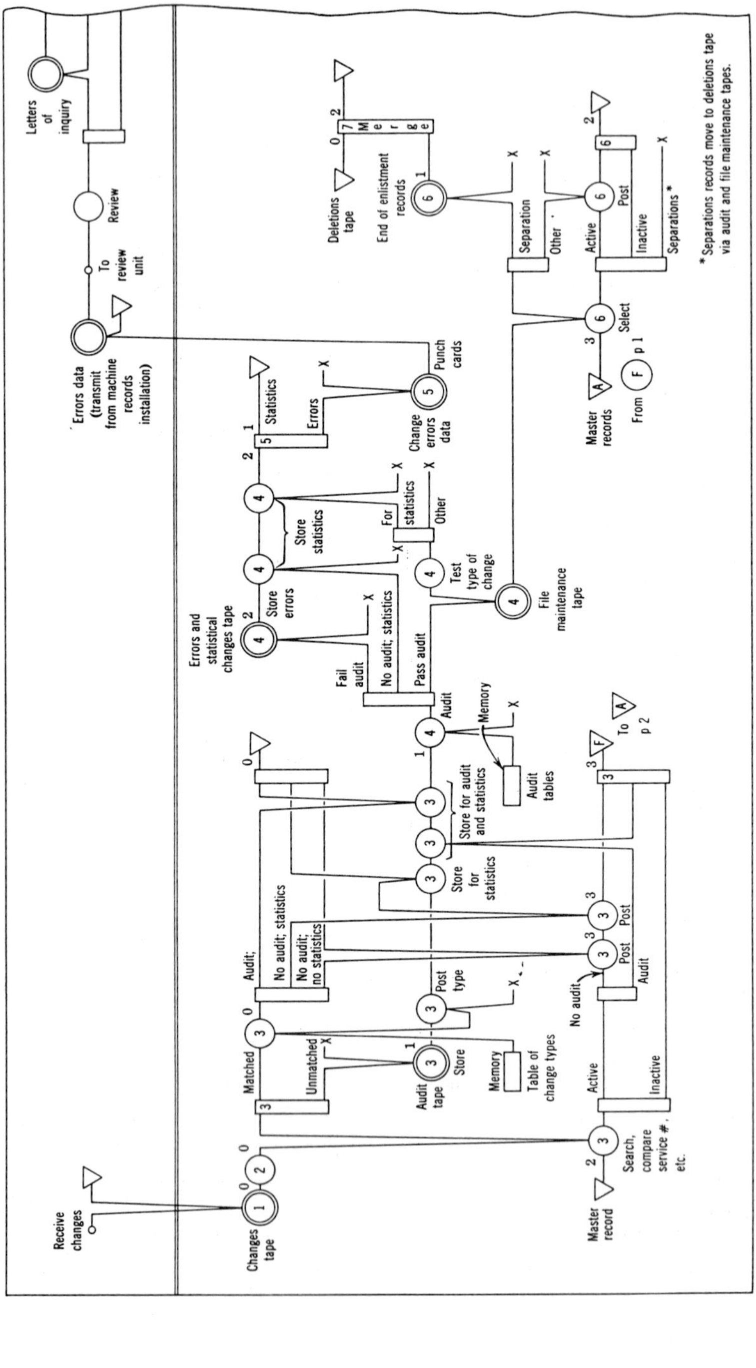

FIG. 71. NCR "MAP" description of procedures. Courtesy National Cash Register Co., Dayton, Ohio.

has been developed which is intermediate between the description and the flow chart. This method of presentation, in effect, describes the procedures as one would describe a computer program, namely as a sequence of individual steps. These steps, however, are themselves described in a "language" which is highly formalized to the point that it may even be handled by a machine. For example, one of the critical areas in the presentation of a complex procedure is the definition of the operational decisions which must be made as a part of the procedure. This is so significant in data processing and in information retrieval that a specialized language called TABSOL has been developed for description of decision steps in the form of tables. Similarly, data handling operations—sorting, merging, etc.—are so important in business data processing, and presumably also in information retrieval, that another language called COBOL has been developed to describe them.

Such programlike descriptions are valuable not only because they provide a method for procedural design in formalized language but also because of the increased understanding which they provide of the very nature of procedural description. Ultimately such languages will provide the means for defining the concept of equivalent procedures and thus increase our understanding of what we mean by the processing of data.

In the development of a procedural design, in whatever form it may be presented, the designer is faced with a choice among several alternatives. The simplest is to base the procedural design on the existing system. This is simplest largely because it involves merely a translation of present operations into a well-defined form. It is also simple, however, because it implies relatively easy conversion of files, decision processes, and personnel capabilities. At the other extreme lies the alternative of designing an "optimum" system. Such an approach attempts to understand the basic reasons for the operation of the system, independent of the way it presently functions, and to develop procedures which will perform precisely those functions. The tendency in this "ideal" approach is to use more advanced techniques of data handling and decision making and perhaps even to change policies which seem to interfere with efficient design. Such a system usually results in drastic changes in the flow of data. The approach of optimum system design is certainly more complex than that of merely mechanizing the existing operation, and it will usually result in rather drastic upheaval during the conversion to it.

Between these two extremes is a whole spectrum of compromise approaches which attempt to improve efficiency in a larger sense by including consideration not only of efficient operation itself, but also of efficient conversion to it. The attempt is to obtain improved efficiency with minimum change. For such compromise solutions to be truly effective they must include provision for continual modification and improvement of the operation with the aim of ultimately bringing it closer and closer to an optimum system. This means that the capability for gathering and evaluating statistics must be an integral part of the system design.

The final part of the planning stage is the evaluation and selection of the equipment to be used. This corresponds precisely to the Organization of Personnel and Equipment as discussed in Chapter 10 and to the Elements of Equipment of Chapter 11. It may take the form of requesting competitive proposals from the various equipment manufacturers to provide the basic data from which to derive a decision. Very frequently such requests for proposal have defined a "unit of work"—a job representative of the general character of the problem to be solved. The relative cost and time for each of the competing devices can therefore be directly compared. If the unit of work is directly representative of the over-all task, this approach can provide an extremely effective criterion for measurement.

Programming, Equipment Installation, and Conversion

Once the decisions of the planning stage have been completed, the actual work of implementation starts. This includes the tasks of programming, equipment installation, and conversion. All too frequently the time and cost for these implementation steps are drastically underestimated. They perhaps can be appreciated if it is recognized that the engineering of a piece of data processing machinery is not completed until the programs have been prepared for it and the files on which it is to operate have been converted to an appropriate form.

The work in programming is as complicated a technical task as the design of the equipment itself. It requires specialized training, experience, and hard technical work. To place the magnitude of the programming task in its proper perspective: typical computer programs will involve perhaps 10,000 to 100,000 individual machine language steps, and good programmers may develop an average of perhaps 50 program steps per day. This means that programming will involve on the order of 200 to 2000 man days of technical effort per program. Large installations may very well require perhaps 100 different programs. This can all be summarized in the following way. It has become a rule of thumb in the computing business that system design and programming costs over the estimated life of an installation will very nearly equal the costs in equipment rental during that same period.

It is outside the scope of this text to cover the details of the programming effort; however, it does seem worthwhile to outline some of the important steps involved. For example, various types of controls must be established and included in the programs to assure that processing in the operating installation is accurate or, where inaccurate, can be corrected. These include batch totals, item counts, audit trails, and similar techniques for error control.

The programmer will usually establish "utility" routines. These are routines of general usage, partaking of the nature of subroutines. They include monitor routines, assembly routines, general data handling routines, and, perhaps for the field of information retrieval, general purpose logical routines. Once these utility routines have been established, attention can be directed to the writing of the operating routines themselves. They may include special purpose routines for file establishment, including reconciliation among the original records and conversion of them into standard form.

Once routines have been written, they must be checked out to detect errors in programming and system design. Where such errors are detected, they must be removed and corrected. This processing or "debugging" may occupy as much as one third to one half of the total programming effort.

Usually programming proceeds in parallel with the schedule for delivery and installation of the equipment. All of the timing and details involved in establishing space, structural requirements for floor loading, air conditioning and power supply, storage for tape and cards, and office space for personnel can be found in manuals prepared by each of the manufacturers.

Once the equipment has been installed and the programs checked out, the next step in developing and operating an installation is the conversion to the new operation. This requires converting and consolidating the files and converting the procedures. In some cases this process of conversion has been carried out as a parallel operation so that the old system and the new one run simultaneously for some period of time. In other cases, the confidence in the correctness of the new procedure has been so great that the conversion to the new operation has been done in essentially one day.

SECTION III

Theories

— 13

Role of a theory

For some time the need for a theoretical foundation in the field of information system design has been recognized and pointed out by a number of people. Ned Chapin, of Stanford Research Institute, commented on this at the ACM Meeting in 1956 on the design of business systems for computers, and the situation that he described has not changed appreciably since then.[1]

> There is little theoretical framework upon which the analyst can draw, because as yet our knowledge and understanding of systems theory is extremely weak. The fundamental research has not been done. The fundamental theorems have not even been propounded, let alone proved. It therefore becomes imperative to derive basic principles for the guidance of the systems man, for the librarian, and for the documentalist in developing new techniques as well as in evaluating, modifying, and adapting old ones.

This type of comment has been repeated again and again. Metcalfe said in 1943, in reference to the library field, that[2] "The lack of any adequate connection with a theoretical discipline to serve as its foundation is perhaps the greatest weakness in the library school program." Another comment has been made by H. R. J. Grosch, who said:[3]

---

[1] Ned Chapin, On the Design of Business Systems for Computers, ACM Annual Meeting, August 27–29, 1956.

[2] Metcalfe, Russell, and Osborne, *The Program of Instruction in Library Schools,* Illinois Contributions to Librarianship No. 2, University of Illinois Press, Urbana, 1943.

[3] H. R. J. Grosch, Men, Information, and Now Automation in the Decision Making Process, in *Documentation in Action,* Reinhold, N.Y., 1956, Part II, ch. 10, pp. 190–196.

> Decision makers must have concrete, mathematically describable, arithmetically weighable objectives before they can make decent decisions. If we are going to talk about information handling in the large, using electronic gadgets, we have to make mathematical models of what we want. . . . [Information storage and retrieval] is *not* a science, and until recently, there has been no science back of it—no real science of classification and indexing, nothing available as a mathematical measure of the contents of a document.

The models described in the following chapters represent the work of many different groups. Each has been a significant step in the development of such a theory. Each is described in the context of a single, integrating, picture of information systems. This picture, since it is a quantified one, potentially can be a powerful tool for the analysis, comparison, and design of methods for file organization and reorganization in information systems, when placed in the hands of competent professional system designers.

This view of a model as a design tool is one of the several roles which it can play in the development of a theory for this field. In this usage, when the model is accepted as an adequate picture of a problem, the systems designer can specify the parameters of the problem in task-oriented terms and then ask a clerk or even a computer to develop the consequences as prescribed by the model. As usage and understanding of the model develops, it may be used by the less well-trained designers to solve completely problems of relatively noncomplex character. This has been the history of all such models, whether those for servomechanism design, for linear programming, for decision making, or for any other purpose. Of course, when utilized in this way, there is grave danger that it will be misapplied and used as a crutch; but despite that danger, the gains from having such a tool available are substantial.

A second, more subtle but more significant, role in the hands of the competent professional system designer is for exposing the fundamental nature of a given problem. In this role the model is again accepted as an adequate picture of the problem but is used as a means by which the system designer can evaluate hypotheses about the parameters of the particular situation. When used in this way, the system designer can postulate some particular parameters and arrive at extremely complex consequences which he can then compare with his intuitive experience or experimental results. In this way discrepancies between, on the one hand, the consequences as developed by the model from the hypothetical problem description and, on the other hand, the designer's intuition as to what the results should be will pinpoint those hypotheses about the problem which are in error.

In other words, the model, by simulating the information system, becomes a means by which to clarify the basic assumptions concerning it.

A third role, which in certain respects is the most significant, is the use of a model as a step in developing a theory for information systems. In this role the model itself is critically examined and improved. Thus, since the model provides a mechanism for deriving consequences from hypotheses, if the consequences do not match experimental evidence or intuitive experience, either the description of the problem is incorrect and must be adjusted (and this is the second role described above) or the model is incorrect and must be improved. Again, this has been the historical experience with the development of models. Effectively the system designer will be operating as a scientist utilizing the scientific method for developing a theory for this field.

Scientific Method

Scientific method—on which all of modern technology is based—essentially involves four steps in an iterative procedure. The first step can be called the "judgment step" in which the principal purpose is the formulation of the problem and the establishment of objectives and criteria of value. This step is essentially an intuitive one dependent on the experience and knowledge of the individual researcher. Based on this preliminary view, the procedure then enters the second step—the data collection step—in which information is accumulated concerning the problem. In principle this second step should be completely objective and independent of any particular formulations or objectives. In practice, however, data collection is very heavily biased, even though not deliberately so, by the objectives which have been established.

As soon as sufficient data have been accumulated to allow it, the third step—the formulation of hypotheses and models—is undertaken. This involves the establishment of measures of effectiveness with which the model is to fit the data. Having established a model which fits the available data to the required accuracy, it is then used to develop necessary consequences from the hypotheses. The model, in this usage, really acts independently of the physical world and the particular problem. This is the reason that mathematics is the principal source of models, for it is concerned with the analysis of structure, removed from the physical objective world, idealized, and independent of reality.

Therefore predictions by the model are derived without reference to the actual physical situation but merely as consequences of the hypotheses. Having developed the consequences (which cannot be avoided, since, once the hypotheses are accepted, the consequences must also be accepted), the scientist must experimentally test their validity. This process, the fourth step in the scientific method, is the experimental testing of the model. To the extent the results in reality verify the predicted consequences, the model is a satisfactory one. To the extent that the consequences derived from and predicted by the model do not exactly fit what actually occurs, the mathematical parameters describing the physical situation must be corrected and the program iterated. If the inaccuracies are sufficiently great, in comparison with the accuracy of measurement, the model must be reformulated or different hypotheses established. Under these conditions, the experimental phase represents a reiteration of the data collection phase followed by a reformulation of the model, which then must itself be experimentally tested. This process continues until the predictions are within the accuracy of the measurements. Later, as the accuracy of measurement improves, the process must again be repeated.

Mathematical Models

In the scientific method, as we have described above, the field of mathematics occupies a unique role. It must be re-emphasized that mathematics is not a science—it is not concerned with the scientific method; it is not concerned with experimentation nor with measurement—mathematics is essentially a scholastic discipline concerned with the analysis of structure and the development of necessary consequences from hypotheses. The mathematician is essentially an analyst, not an experimentalist. Of course, it must be recognized that much of mathematics is drawn from the intuitive understanding of physical process and that most mathematical structures have resulted from the problems of modeling for a specific physical situation, but this merely represents the source of material on which the mathematician operates.

It is precisely because mathematics is concerned with the analysis of structure that it has represented the great source of models for the scientist and has been looked to for aid in the field of information systems. Mathematics provides differential equations as models of dynamic processes, probability theory as a model for statistical process, and algebra and topology as models of relationships. Each of these structures has been analyzed by mathematicians, and the resulting theory makes it easy for the scientist to determine what consequences are to be expected from particular hypotheses.

The use of a model relates to the measurement of the physical situation. It is important to understand the variety of measures available from mathematics and therefore the kind of models which can be utilized by a theory of information system design and file organization. The process of measurement has been described as the assignment of elements from some mathematical system to the set of physical objects, or events, of interest, that is, if $P = \{p_1, p_2, \ldots\}$ denotes a set of physical objects, then "measurement of P" means that a function (or rule) assigns to each element of P, such as p_i, an element b_i from some mathematical system $B = \{b_1, b_2, \ldots\}$. The nature of the set P of objects, and the process for mapping it onto the abstract space B, comprise the *operational* definition of measurement. This "explication by operation" is the point at which data gathering and the testing of predictions take place. On the other hand, the mathematical structure of the system B belongs to the formal side of measurement theory and is the domain of the mathematician. The structure of B is usually dictated by a set of rules or axioms which state the relationships among the implicitly defined elements of B.

The mathematical structures which can be utilized in this way have themselves been ranked in terms of the relative complexity of their structure, as shown by the chart in Figure 72.[4] A mathematical model is said to be "nominal" if it has essentially no structure whatsoever imposed on it. An ordinal (partial order) scale of measurement is implied if there is natural ranking of the elements in the mathematical system according to some attribute and is appropriate if the physical objects being measured can themselves be partitioned into classes in such a manner that (1) elements which belong to the same class can be considered equivalent with respect to the attributes of interest, (2) a relation can be defined between each pair of classes, such as "class x is contained in class y," and (3) there is a degree of consistency in these comparative judgments so that, if class x is contained in class y, and class y is contained in class z, then class x is contained in class z. At the far extreme in this relative scale of complexity are those models which are essentially quantified and wherein the mathematical structure consists of the real numbers.

---

[4] T. L. Saaty, *Mathematical Models of Operations Research,* New York, McGraw-Hill, 1959.

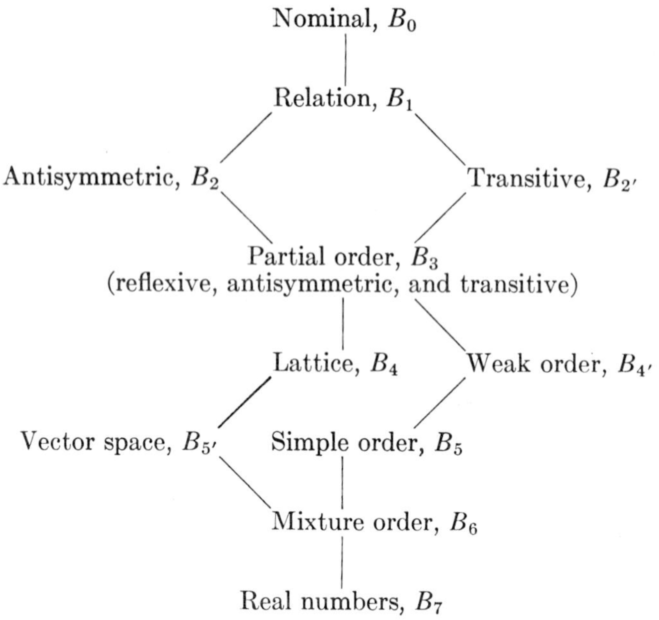

FIG. 72. Measurement scales. T. L. Saaty, *Mathematical Models of Operations Research*, New York, McGraw-Hill, 1959.

In most situations the attempt in developing a theory for a field is to increase the complexity continually, in the sense outlined above, of the mathematical structure and, in particular, to move from the purely nominal to the relational to the quantified. In this way, as the complexity of the model increases, it absorbs more and more of the complexity of the world into its own structure and correspondingly reduces the difficulties in dealing with considerations not covered by the model. In the past, the models which have appeared appropriate to information system theory have been almost solely relational. However, as we will try to show, it seems that the time is right to attempt quantification.

In the following material, we summarize the significant features of three mathematical structures—Boolean algebra, linear algebra, and probability—which have particular relevance to information retrieval theory. These summaries certainly cannot substitute for the texts in these fields, but they can serve as useful reviews and, when supported by classroom instruction, as introductions to them. For our purposes, they also serve to define the notation and approach which we will use when we apply these structures as models for information retrieval processes.

Boolean Algebra

Of the mathematical structures which have provided models for relationship, Boolean algebra—including its generalizations in the theory of sets and lattice theory—is the simplest which provides an organization of elements adequate for an information system theory, that is, it is simple in terms of requiring only the structure defined by a relationship between elements, but it is organized in the sense of exhibiting associations among elements. The foundations of Boolean algebra were developed first by the German mathematician, Leibniz, in his formulation of a system of mathematical logic.[5] Later contributions to such a systematized logic were made by Augustus de Morgan[6] and George Boole[7] around 1850. The first complete formulations were those by Russell and Whitehead in their *Principia Mathematica*[8] in about 1915 and by Hilbert and Ackermann in their classic text on the subject, *Principles of Mathematical Logic*[9] in 1928.

The concept of "classes of objects" is the cornerstone of Boolean algebra; it is impossible to conduct logical reasoning without it. As we will show, the fact that two classes of objects may have things in common describes a relationship between the classes, and the structure of this relationship is the subject matter of Boolean algebra. Similarly, the elementary logical properties of statements exhibit the same type of structure. Therefore Boolean algebra is concerned with the structure of this relationship among, for example, different sets of items or, as another example, different statements about things.[10,11]

To describe this structure we begin by defining the relations and operations of the algebra of classes. Suppose that I is a class of ob-

---

[5] *Leibnitzens Mathematische Schriften,* Gerhardt, Berlin, 1850, Abt 1, Bd2, 20–35 (espec. 21).

[6] A. de Morgan, *Formal Logic,* London 1847, reissued 1926.

[7] George Boole, *The Mathematical Analysis of Logic,* London and Cambridge, 1847.

[8] Bertrand Russell and Alfred North Whitehead, *Principia Mathematica,* 2nd Edition, Cambridge, England, University Press, 1925.

[9] David Hilbert and W. Ackermann, *Principles of Mathematical Logic,* translated from the German by Lewis M. Hammond, G. Leckie, and F. Steinhardt, edited and with notes by Robert E. Luce, New York, Chelsea Publishing Company, 1950.

[10] E. Kamke, *Theory of Sets,* New York, Dover, 1950.

[11] P. C. Rosenbloom, *The Elements of Mathematical Logic,* New York, Dover, 1950.

Logical Equation $C = f(A, B)$	Venn Diagram $C = f(A, B)$	Truth Table $C = f(A, B)$	Electronic Implemention $C = f(A, B)$
$C = A$	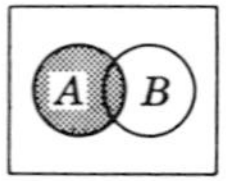	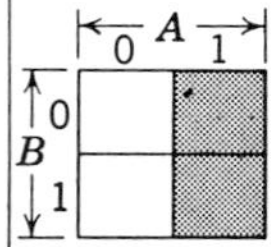	
$C = \overline{A}$	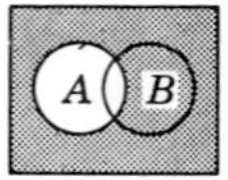		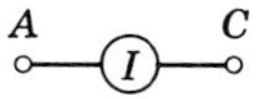 I = inverter
$C = B$	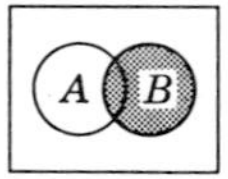	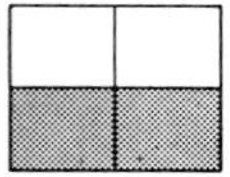	
$C = \overline{B}$	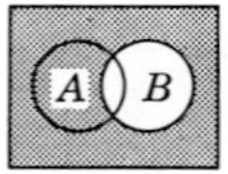	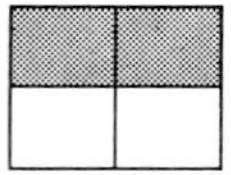	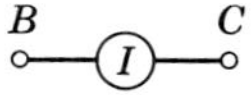

Logical Equation $C = f(A, B)$	Venn Diagram $C = f(A, B)$	Truth Table $C = f(A, B)$	Electronic Implemention $C = f(A, B)$
$C = A \cdot B$	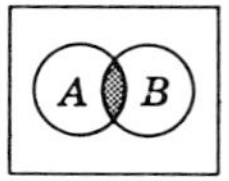	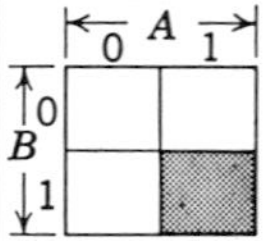	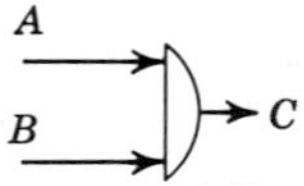 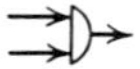 Symbol for two input AND gate
$C = A \cdot \overline{B}$	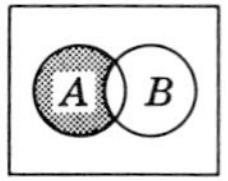	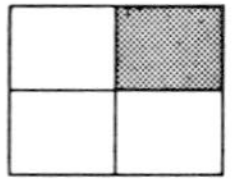	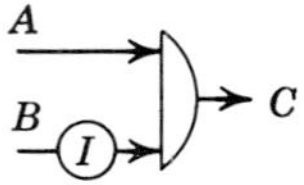
$C = A \cdot B$	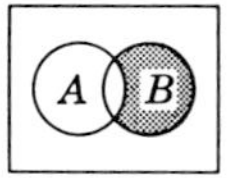	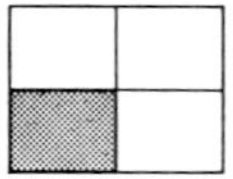	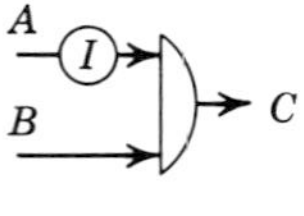
$C = \overline{A} \cdot \overline{B}$	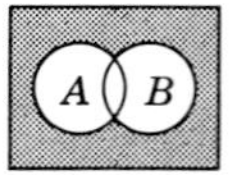	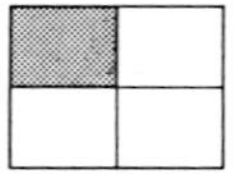	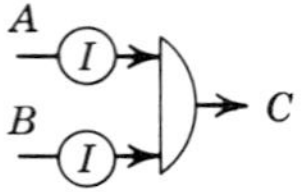

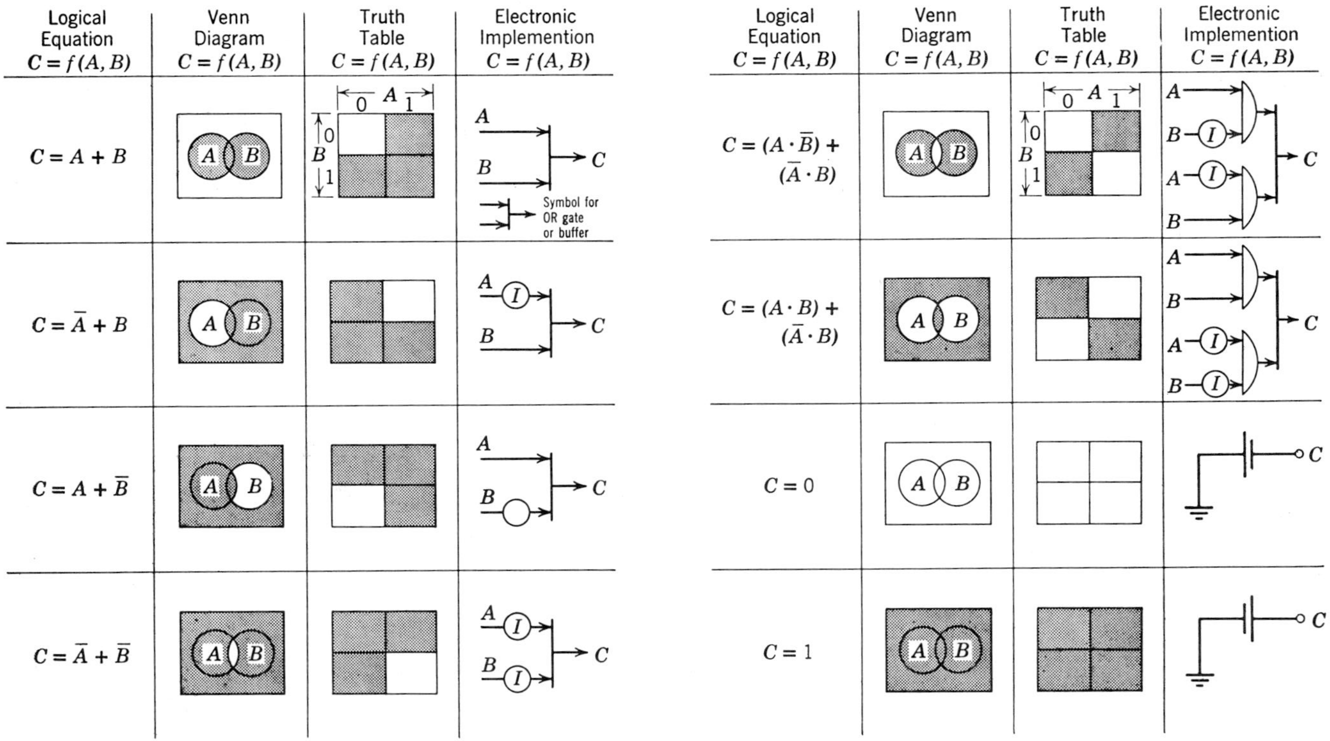

FIG. 73. Venn diagrams for all logical functions of two variables. *Symbolic Logic, Boolean Algebra, and the Design of Computing Systems,* Computer Control Co. (no date).

jects (perhaps the set of documents in a library) and that various subclasses $\{A, B, \ldots\}$ have been defined. Then, if all of the members of one subclass, A of I, are also members of another subclass B, A is said to be contained in B, and this relationship can be represented by writing $A \leq B$. Given two subclasses, A and B, other subclasses can also be defined by the application to them of the defined Boolean operations.

Conjunction: $C = A \cdot B$, the subclass of all elements which are both in A and in B.

Disjunction: $C = A + B$, the subclass of all elements which are either in A or in B.

Negation: $C = \bar{A}$, the subclass of all elements of I which are not in A.

By further combinations of these, any relation among the defined sets can be exhibited. Attempts have been made to devise a diagrammatic approach to the presentation of these relationships among classes. The first such diagrams were created by a nineteenth century mathematician, John Venn, and are called Venn diagrams. Several are illustrated in Figure 73 for the operations which have been defined above and for various combinations of them.[12]

Although we have discussed these concepts in terms of sets of things, the relationship they bear to logical statements is extremely close. For example, the logical statement "the object a of the class I is in the subclass X of I" is either true or false for each object a of I. Or, viewing this relationship between classes and statements about them in the reverse manner, the subclass of all things in I for which that statement is true defines the class X, and the subclass for which it is false defines the class $\bar{X}$. In a very real sense it is this relationship which makes Boolean algebra so applicable to information retrieval. Thus, if the class I is taken as the domain of documents of a library, then for a document to be in a subclass X might be taken as meaning that the term "X" has been applied to it. Therefore the conjunction of terms, "A"·"B," defines the conjunction of the corresponding classes of documents and thus the documents to which both "A" and "B" have been applied.

Because of this relationship between the algebra of classes and logical statements concerning the classes, the various operations which have been discussed above and represented by Venn diagrams can also be represented by what are called "truth tables." These describe whether

[12] From *Symbolic Logic, Boolean Algebra, and the Design of Computing Systems,* Computer Control Co. (no date).

or not any object in the class I belongs to a subclass, as defined by a particular relation among other subclasses, in terms of its relation to each of them. Thus, for the combinations previously described, the associated truth tables shown in the figure are applicable. In each case the relationship of an object to a subclass is defined by "1" if it is a member of that subclass and by "0" if it is not.

This means of representing membership in classes by a truth table serves to emphasize the importance which binary representation has in Boolean algebra, since membership in a class, or the truth of a statement concerning membership in a class, can be represented by 1 or 0. A very simple, but nevertheless useful, illustration of this relationship is exhibited by the situation where the class I consists of a single object. In this case two subclasses can be defined, the class I itself and the null class 0. The truth tables then simply represent operations on a single binary variable.

In the relationships among classes defined above, only operations on two classes were considered at any time. However, it is certainly possible to consider these operations as involving 3, 4, . . ., n subclasses according to the same rules of operation. This leads to the concept of a general function of n binary variables which will define a subclass as the combination, based on the three operations defined above, of n subclasses. Two of these, for $n = 3$ and $n = 4$, are shown in Figure 74. In general, these functions can be quite complicated combinations of the operations of disjunction, conjunction, and negation. One of the fundamental theorems of Boolean algebra, however, is that any binary function of n variables may be expressed as the "disjunctive combination of conjunc-

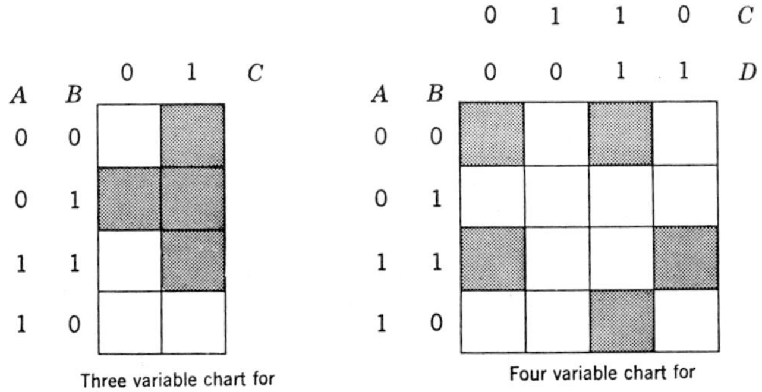

Three variable chart for $f = \bar{A} \cdot B \cdot \bar{C} \vee \bar{A} \cdot \bar{B} \cdot C \vee \bar{A} \cdot B \cdot C \vee A \cdot B \cdot C$

Four variable chart for $f = A \cdot B \cdot \bar{C} \vee \{[\bar{A} \cdot \bar{B}] \cdot [(\bar{C} \cdot \bar{D}) \vee (C \cdot D)]\} \vee A \cdot \bar{B} \cdot C \cdot D$

FIG. 74. Truth tables for more than two variables. ***Symbolic Logic, Boolean Algebra, and the Design of Computing Systems,*** **Computer Control Co. (no date).**

tions" or, conversely, as a "conjunctive combination of disjunctions." One of the critical relationships in accomplishing such a reduction is represented by a set of relations, called de Morgan's theorems, which state that for any A and B, $\overline{A \cdot B} = \bar{A} + \bar{B}$ and $\overline{A + B} = \bar{A} \cdot \bar{B}$.

The inclusion relationship and the three operations as defined above are basic to the algebra of classes. They satisfy a set of abstract properties which are, in effect, statements of the universal principles of logic involved in mathematical argument. If one were to approach this subject from the axiomatic standpoint, these principles would then be stated essentially as postulates.

1. The relation of inclusion in the algebra of sets produces a "partial order" and therefore is

Reflexive:	for all A, $A \leq A$.
Antisymmetric:	if $A \leq B$ and $B \leq A$, then A and B are the same class.
Transitive:	if $A \leq B$ and $B \leq C$, then $A \leq C$.

2. The operations of conjunction, disjunction, and negation in the algebra of sets are

Idempotent:	$A \cdot A = A$ and $A + A = A$
Commutative:	$A + B = B + A$ and $A \cdot B = B \cdot A$
Associative:	$A \cdot (B \cdot C) = (A \cdot B) \cdot C$ and $A + (B + C) = (A + B) + C$
Distributive:	$A \cdot (B + C) = (A \cdot B) + A \cdot C$ and $A + (B \cdot C) = (A + B) \cdot (A + C)$
Consistent:	the three conditions, $A \leq B$, $A \cdot B = A$, and $A + B = B$ are mutually equivalent.
Dual:	$\overline{A \cdot B} = \bar{A} + \bar{B}$ and $\overline{A + B} = \bar{A} \cdot \bar{B}$ (de Morgan's theorems).
Involute:	$\bar{\bar{A}} = A$

3. The universal set I and the null set 0 have the properties of

Universal bounds:	$0 \leq A \leq I$ for all A
Complementation:	$A \cdot \bar{A} = 0$ and $A + \bar{A} = I$
Intersection:	$0 \cdot A = 0$ and $I \cdot A = A$
Union:	$0 + A = A$ and $I + A = I$

Remarkably enough, simple though these postulates are, from them flow all the wealth of logical relations implicit in the logical design of the general purpose digital computer; in Figure 73 we have included symbolic representations of electronic circuitry for their realization. To illustrate the usage of these circuits, consider the problem of adding two sequences of binary digits representing numbers (e.g., $A = 0101$ and $B = 1011$). At each step the operation must consider the particular binary digits from each of the two sequences and the "carry" from the addition of the preceding pair. Thus addition of binary numbers (not counting the carry digit resulting) at each stage is a function of three binary variables A_i, B_i, and C_{i-1}. The successive carry digits C_i are a similar function of the same variables. The truth tables for these functions are easily generated from the rules for binary addition; they are

$f_1 = (A_i + B_i + C_{i-1})$

	C_{i-1}	
$A_i B_i$	0	1
0 0	0	1
0 1	1	0
1 0	1	0
1 1	0	1

$f_2 = C_i$

	C_{i-1}	
$A_i B_i$	0	1
0 0	0	0
0 1	0	1
1 0	0	1
1 1	1	1

$f_1 = (\bar{A} \cdot \bar{B} \cdot \bar{C}) + (A \cdot \bar{B}) \cdot \bar{C} + (\bar{A} \cdot B) \cdot \bar{C} + A \cdot B \cdot C$
$f_2 = (A + B) \cdot C + A \cdot B \cdot \bar{C}$

FIG. 75. Truth tables for add function.

Of equal importance, these simple postulates also seem sufficient to generate all the logical processes required by information retrieval. Indeed, for certain purposes, these postulates are more than sufficient, and simpler structures are adequate. One which has received a good deal of attention in this respect is the "lattice."[13] The lattice, like Boolean algebra, describes relations among sets of things or among logical statements, and indeed satisfies most of the abstract properties defined above, that is, a lattice provides an inclusion relation among its elements which defines a partial order (so that the inclusion relation is reflexive, antisymmetric, and transitive) and for any two elements, A and B, in the lattice there are elements $A \cdot B$ and $A + B$ with the prop-

[13] Garrett Birkhoff, *Lattice Theory,* American Mathematical Society, 1940.

erties, respectively, that if any element X is contained in both A and B, it is contained in $A \cdot B$, and if any element Y contains both A and B, it contains $A + B$. In lattice theory, the sets $A \cdot B$ and $A + B$ are called, respectively, the greatest lower bound and least upper bound of the two elements A and B.

Lattices can be represented graphically as structures consisting of nodes and links of the following character:

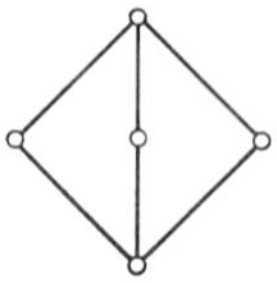

where the nodes (circles) in such a net represent the elements of the lattice and $A \leq B$ if A is below B and connected to it by a chain of links.

In summary, a lattice is a partially ordered system in which any two elements have a greatest lower bound and a least upper bound. The idempotent, commutative, associative, and consistency principles are also satisfied; however, the distributive law need not be satisfied. Lattices in which the distributive law holds are called distributive lattices. A Boolean algebra is then simply a distributive lattice in which each element A has a complement, $\bar{A}$, defined by negation, satisfying $A \cdot \bar{A} = 0$ and $A + \bar{A} = 1$.

Just as in a Boolean algebra, functions, $f(A)$, transforming elements of the lattice into other elements can be defined. If these functions preserve the order relation so that, if $A \leq B$, then $f(A) \leq f(B)$, they are said to be isotone functions. An interesting theorem is that for any isotone function there is some element in the lattice which is preserved, that is, there is some element A such that $f(A) = A$.

Given two lattices, L_1 and L_2, a combined structure called the "logical product," $L_1 \otimes L_2$, whose elements are ordered pairs (A, A') of elements from the two initial lattices can be defined. If an ordering relation for this logical product is then defined as follows: $(A, A') \leq (B, B')$ provided $A \leq B$ in lattice L_1 and $A' \leq B'$ in lattice L_2, the logical product is also a lattice. Conversely, certain classes of lattices can be decomposed into the logical product of more elementary lattices. This decomposition provides a powerful tool for the analysis of the structure of such lattices. This property of lattices provides a model of the process of "extracting" facets from a vocabulary. In this sense, facet analysis can be regarded as the decomposition of the lattice describing a given vocabulary into the logical product of the lattices describing each facet.

Even with a relational model, such as represented by a lattice, some steps toward a pseudo-quantification can be taken. Specifically, the "distance" between two points in a lattice can be defined by the smallest number of connecting links in the lattice structure required to get from one point to the other. In this way a lattice can be treated as a type of "maze," [14] and determining the distance between two points involves finding the shortest path connecting them.

Linear Algebra and Matrices

There are many possible steps which could be taken in the development of a quantified model for information system theory from, for example, the simple counting of levels in a lattice to the complete measurement by a real number scale. One particular quantified mathematical structure has been used as a model in science with particular frequency, and appears to be highly appropriate to this field of information system design. This is the structure called "linear algebra." This model has been almost universal in its application, not so much because physical processes are linear but because of the simplicity of representation when it is used. In particular, the most significant aspect of linear algebra is that the process of analysis leads to simple synthesis; that is, the effects of a combination of conditions can be determined as a simple linear combination of their individual effects.

Linear algebra is concerned with the nature of linear transformations on vector spaces,[15] that is, with the change of quantities in such a way that pre-existing linear relationships are preserved by the change. The fundamental quantitative tool of linear algebra is the matrix. Matrices are rectangular arrays of real (or possible complex) numbers, called the "elements" of the matrix, of the form

$$\begin{bmatrix} a_{11} & a_{12} & a_{13} & a_{14} \\ a_{21} & a_{22} & a_{23} & a_{24} \\ a_{31} & a_{32} & a_{33} & a_{34} \end{bmatrix}.$$

The subscript notation for the elements provides a means for defining the location of the particular elements in the array. The first subscript defines the row in which it occurs, the second defines the column.

---

[14] Gerald Estrin, Maze Structure and Information Retrieval, *Preprints of Papers for the International Conference on Scientific Information,* National Academy of Sciences—National Research Council, Washington, D.C., 1958.

[15] Paul R. Halmos, *Finite Dimensional Vector Spaces,* Princeton, Princeton University Press, 1948.

Thus the element a_{ij} falls in the ith row and jth column. The "size" of the matrix is defined as the number of rows by the number of columns: $n \times m$. When $n = m$, the matrix is said to be $n \times n$ square. For convenience, matrices are represented by shorthand, symbolic notations such as

$$A \text{ or } (a_{ij}).$$

Certain special classes of matrices are of particular interest. For example, the class of "symmetric" matrices are those square matrices which remain the same if the rows and columns are interchanged. For such matrices, $a_{ij} = a_{ji}$. A more restrictive class is the set of diagonal matrices, for which $a_{ij} = 0$ for $i \neq j$. If all the diagonal elements of a diagonal matrix are identical, it is called a scalar matrix; if they are all equal to 1, it is called the identity matrix; if they are all equal to 0, it is called the zero matrix.

Four operations are defined on square matrices: addition, product, multiplication by a scalar (real number), and transposition. These are defined as follows:

1. If $A = (a_{ij})$ and $B = (b_{ij})$ are two matrices, then $C = A + B$ is a matrix with elements

$$c_{ij} = a_{ij} + b_{ij},\ i, j = 1, 2, \ldots, n.$$

2. If $A = (a_{ij})$ and $B = (B_{ij})$ are two matrices, then $C = AB$ is a matrix with elements

$$c_{ij} = \sum_{k=1}^{n} a_{ik}b_{kj}, \qquad i, j = 1, 2, \ldots, n.$$

(Note that the sequence of elements and subscripts in this summation is critical. If they are changed in any way, totally different matrix products are involved. In general, for example

$$AB \neq BA.)$$

3. If $A = (a_{ij})$ is a matrix and c is a real number, then $B = cA$ is a matrix with elements

$$b_{ij} = ca_{ij}, \qquad i, j = 1, 2, \ldots, n.$$

4. If $A = (a_{ij})$ is a matrix, then $B = A^*$ is the transpose of A and has elements

$$b_{ij} = a_{ji}, \qquad i, j = 1, 2, \ldots, n.$$

These operations satisfy certain properties of commutivity and associativity of addition, existence of the zero and identity matrices, distributivity of addition over product, etc. Such a set of things as matrices, with these three operations satisfying such properties, is a mathematical structure called an "algebra."

The operation of matrix product can be extended to other than square matrices, provided the rows and columns appropriately match so that the summation can be defined. In particular, an $m \times n$ matrix can be multiplied onto an ordered array of n numbers. For example,

$$A\vec{x} = \vec{y} \text{ means } \begin{bmatrix} a_{11} & a_{12} & a_{13} \\ a_{21} & a_{22} & a_{23} \\ a_{31} & a_{32} & a_{33} \end{bmatrix} \begin{bmatrix} x^1 \\ x^2 \\ x^3 \end{bmatrix} = \begin{bmatrix} y^1 \\ y^2 \\ y^3 \end{bmatrix}.$$

Such matrix "equations" thus represent in compact form entire sets of simultaneous linear equations. If the ordered array $\vec{y}$ is known, solution for $\vec{x}$ requires solution of the corresponding system of linear equations. To solve these equations requires that restrictions be placed on the matrix A. In particular, A must be "nonsingular," that is, there must exist another matrix A^{-1}, called the inverse, such that

$$AA^{-1} = A^{-1}A = I.$$

A singular matrix is one that does not satisfy this condition. With a nonsingular matrix,

$$\text{if} \quad A\vec{x} = \vec{y}, \quad \text{then} \quad \vec{x} = A^{-1}(A\vec{x}) = A^{-1}\vec{y}.$$

Ordered arrays of n numbers such as $\vec{x}$ and $\vec{y}$ can be considered what are called "vectors" in a "vector space." In such vector spaces measurement of "length" and "angle" can be defined as functions of the component numbers in the vectors. In particular, the length $|\vec{x}|$ of a vector is given in terms

$$|\vec{x}|^2 = \sum_{i=1}^{n} (x^i)^2 = (\vec{x} \cdot \vec{x})$$

and the angle between two vectors $\vec{x}$ and $\vec{y}$ in terms

$$\cos(\vec{x}, \vec{y}) = \Sigma x^i y^i / |\vec{x}| \cdot |\vec{y}| = (\vec{x} \cdot \vec{y}) / |\vec{x}| \cdot |\vec{y}|.$$

The multiplication of a matrix onto such a vector then represents a transformation of the vector $\vec{x}$ into the other one $\vec{y}$. The transformation is represented symbolically by the equation $A\vec{x} = \vec{y}$, where A is the matrix, $\vec{x}$ the original vector, and $\vec{y}$ the transformed vector. Although transformations of a vector space can be quite general, one represented in this way is highly restricted and is called a linear transformation.

The problem now arises of how to measure the effect which a linear transformation has on the vector space. The most natural approach is to examine the length of the transformed vector so that if $A\vec{x} = \vec{y}$, the length of $\vec{y}$ is used as the measure of the effect of the transformation. Thus the function $f(\vec{x}) = A\vec{x} \cdot A\vec{x}$ represents this measure. This function can be equivalently represented by

$$f(\vec{x}) = \vec{x} \cdot A^*A\vec{x}$$

where A^* is the transpose of the matrix A. By its definition, $f(\vec{x})$ has the property that $f(\vec{x}) \leq 0$. Geometrically this function can be illustrated for $n = 2$ as shown in Figure 76, that is, as a bowl with its base at the origin, or zero, of the vector space and with an elliptical cross section. The height of this function at a given point $\vec{x}$, and of the bowl therefore, represents the squared length of the transform of the vector $\vec{x}$. The characteristics of this geometric picture in two dimensions can be extended to n dimensions.

Of somewhat more interest is a related measure of effect, called the Rayleigh quotient for the matrix A^*A, which normalizes the function by the square of the length of the vector $\vec{x}$ itself so that

$$g(\vec{x}) = \frac{\vec{x} \cdot A^*A\vec{x}}{\vec{x} \cdot \vec{x}} = \frac{\vec{y} \cdot \vec{y}}{\vec{x} \cdot \vec{x}}.$$

Geometrically this can be pictured in two dimensions as the intersection of the bowl defined by $f(\vec{x})$ with the cylinder defined by all vectors $\vec{x}$ of length one. As can be seen, this function achieves its maximum and minimum values for those directions lying along the principal axes of the elliptical cross section of the bowl. These directions are of par-

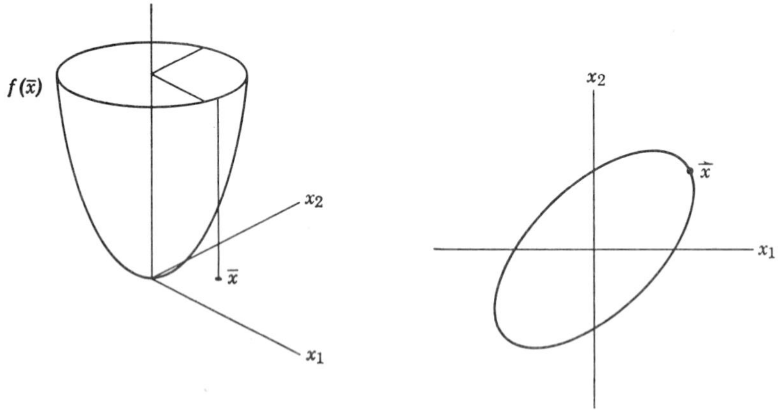

FIG. 76. Measurement of effect.

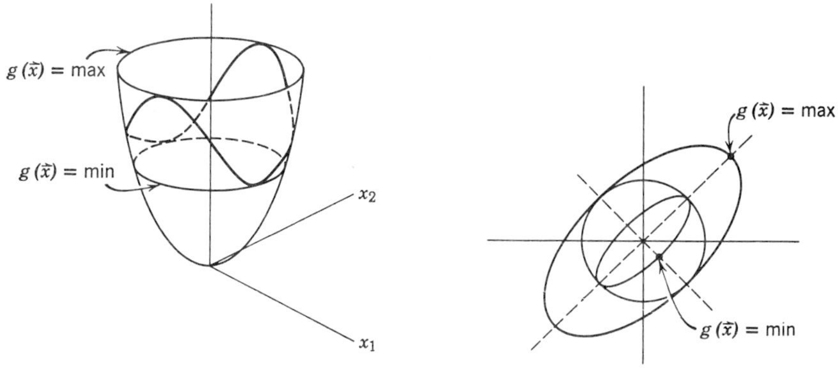

FIG. 77. Rayleigh quotient for two variables.

ticular importance. They can be determined by examining the gradient of the function $g(\vec{x})$ and setting it equal to the zero vector. This yields the equation

$$A^*A\vec{x} - g(\vec{x})\vec{x} = \vec{0}.$$

This equation is called the eigenvalue equation for the matrix A^*A. The vectors $\vec{x} \neq \vec{0}$ which satisfy this equation and the corresponding values $g(\vec{x})$ are called, respectively, the eigenvectors and eigenvalues for the matrix A^*A. The solutions to this equation thus represent those directions for which the transformed vector has maximum length, minimum length, or other critical values of length. In general, if A^*A is an $n \times n$ matrix, there are n linearly independent eigenvectors, $\vec{x}_1, \vec{x}_2, \ldots, \vec{x}_n$, and n corresponding values for $g(\vec{x})$, counting multiplicities. The eigenvectors of A^*A satisfy the desirable property that they can be made to form an orthogonal basis, so that $\vec{x}_i \cdot \vec{x}_j = 0$ for $i \neq j$, and thus they represent a coordinate system with very desirable properties.

For mathematical elegance it is sometimes desirable to use the Rayleigh quotient for the matrix A itself rather than that for the matrix A^*A. This would yield, as the measure of effect, the function

$$h(\vec{x}) = \frac{\vec{x} \cdot A\vec{x}}{\vec{x} \cdot \vec{x}}$$

and would lead to the corresponding eigenvalue equation for the matrix A, namely,

$$A\vec{x} - h(\vec{x})\vec{x} = \vec{0}.$$

Such an approach is useful when A is a matrix such that $h(\vec{x}) \geq 0$ for all $\vec{x} \neq \vec{0}$.

Probability and Stochastic Processes

Even if quantification can be introduced into information systems theory, however, significant problems arise because of the variability in the events being measured. In many cases a model cannot possibly handle the measure of an individual event because of this variability and must instead treat measurements concerned with classes of events. Probability theory is the study of the distribution of the variable measurements over these classes, and statistical techniques provide the methods for determining these distributions from the measurements made. Hence in a sense the probability distribution provides the mathematical model for variability of measurement, and statistical analysis provides the experimental tool for evaluating predictive performance.[16]

To be specific, consider the probability that a given document will, or will not, involve a class of terms, or the probability that some number k of file items must be examined to find a relevant one, or the probability that a particular type of question will be asked. In each case a probability distribution presumably can be defined describing these probabilities for each class of events (each class of terms, each number k, each class of questions). A standard example is the probability distribution for the occurrence of letters of the alphabet in English text, based on their relative frequency of usage.

Certain distributions, because of their special analytic properties and application to idealized situations, have become classic in the field. In each of these distributions, a single parameter is regarded as characterizing the entire set of probabilities. For example, one of these is the binomial distribution,

$$b(k; n, p) = \frac{n!}{k!(n-k)!} p^k (1-p)^{n-k},$$

describing the probability of the event "k successes in n occurrences" in terms of the probability p of one success in one occurrence. A second is the Poisson distribution,

$$p(k; \lambda) = \frac{1}{k!} e^{-\lambda} \lambda^k,$$

describing the probability of the event "k successes in a prescribed interval" in terms of the average density λ of successes over all intervals.

---

[16] William Feller, *An Introduction to Probability Theory and Its Applications*, New York, Wiley, 1950.

A third is the normal or Gaussian distribution,

$$\phi(x) = \frac{1}{\sqrt{2\pi}} e^{-x^2/2},$$

describing the probability of the event "x" in terms of its own magnitude alone.

In any case, except for these and a few other idealized situations, distributions are difficult to handle and even more difficult to determine in the first place. In fact, rarely is the distribution itself actually known in a given physical situation. Rather, it is the *statistics* of the distribution which are measured or calculated. Thus, given a set of actual events, or measurements, certain statistics are calculated and, from these, characteristics of the underlying probability inferred. The aim of statistical analysis is to test hypotheses concerning the probability distribution in a situation by comparing the statistics of the observed data with those of the hypothetical distribution and to establish acceptance levels of agreement between the two.

By far the most important of these "typical values" is the mean (average, or expected value), calculated in the well-known fashion (i.e., given the values $x_{i_1}, x_{i_2}, \ldots, x_{i_n}$, the average is

$$\left(\sum_{j=1}^{n} x_{i_j}\right)/n).$$

The analogy between probability and frequency leads to the definition of the expected value of a distribution $p(x_i)$ over the possible values $x_1, x_2, \ldots,$ by the equation

$$E(p) = \Sigma x_k p(x_k).$$

The calculated average is then an approximation to this expected value. For the distributions we have discussed, this expected value can be easily determined. In particular, for the binomial and Poisson distributions, $E = np = \lambda$; for the normal distribution, $E = 0$.

A second useful statistic of a distribution is the "variance." Roughly this is a measure of the "spread" in the events and is defined by

$$E[p - E(p)]^2 = \Sigma x_k{}^2 p(x_k) - [E(p)]^2 = \Sigma[x_k - E(p)]^2 p(x_k).$$

The square root of this is called the standard deviation. For the binomial distribution the variance is $np(1 - p)$; for the Poisson it is λ; for the Gaussian it is 1.

The situation gets appreciably more complicated when the successive actual events are not independent of each other. The simplest extension of this type considers events as a "simple Markov chain," wherein the outcome of any event is dependent on the immediately preceding event. This situation can be described by a "conditional probability" p_{jk} for each possible event x_k, given that x_j was the immediately preceding event. These conditional, or "transition," probabilities can be arranged in a matrix

$$P = \begin{bmatrix} p_{11} & p_{12} & p_{13} \cdots \\ p_{21} & p_{22} & \cdots \\ p_{31} & \cdots & \\ \cdots & & \end{bmatrix},$$

called a stochastic matrix, with the properties that

$$p_{ij} \geq 0 \qquad \text{and} \qquad \sum_k p_{jk} = 1.$$

An excellent example of a Markov process is again concerned with the occurrence of letters of the alphabet in English text, since it is well known that the occurrence of a particular letter (such as "q") radically affects the probability of the occurrence of any letter as the next one. It seems likely that many of the processes in information retrieval are of a similar nature. For example, if we consider a sequence of types of requests from a single requester as analogous to the sequence of letters in a word, the occurrence of one type certainly radically affects the probability distribution for the next one.

There are many types of physical situations which are most appropriately represented by a model consisting of the combination of a probability distribution with some other mathematical structure. Perhaps the best example is that of the theory of prediction, which treats the problem of extrapolating from the known past of some variable quantity to its future. The known data are in the form of a sequence of measurements taken from observations made over an interval of time in the past, and the problem is to make a reliable estimate of the future values of the variable on the basis of these data. The well-known theory of this type is that of linear prediction, developed by Weiner and Kolmogoroff,[17] wherein one compares each of the readings with a fixed linear combination of those preceding it and asks for that particular linear combination which, in some sense, minimizes the discrepancy. Having found the most consistent linear combination in this sense, the predicted value for the next reading is taken as this linear combination of the past readings. The probability distribution in this case represents the variability

---

[17] H. Furstenberg, *Stationary Processes and Prediction Theory,* Princeton, Princeton University Press, 1960.

in the observations due to "noise," including error in measurement and other behavior considered as unpredictable; the associated mathematical model is the linear algebraic approximation to sets of data and represents the predictable behavior.

This approach can be extended if one regards the concept of prediction as that of inferring information about the future on the basis of the past. This would involve predicting more than simply a "most likely value" for the future but rather an entire probability distribution. In this way the estimate for the next value may be made in a number of ways (the most natural admittedly being, perhaps, the expected value of the distribution, but other possible choices might be equally useful). The probability distribution in this case plays a role not only in representation of the past data but also in explaining the character of the future. Techniques such as these seem particularly applicable to prediction of distributions of activity of requests on a file where an "expected value" would be nearly worthless. Thus statistics of subject usage activity, in both documents and requests, should be utilized for predicting future activity distributions.

The meaning which might be attached to the concept of *information* in such a view has itself been thoroughly investigated, and the result is a mathematical model of the process involved in transmission of signals.[18] In this model the amount of information associated with the occurrence of an event x is defined to be

$$I(x) = -\log_2 \{\text{probability of } x\}.$$

The resulting unit for measuring information is the bit, which is the amount of information associated with the occurrence of an event with *a priori* probability one half. If we now consider a source of events with a probability distribution over them, the mean value of this distribution is given by

$$H = \Sigma P_i I_i = -\Sigma P_i \log_2 P_i$$

where P_i is the probability of occurrences of the ith event. This quantity H, expressed in bits per source event, has been called the "entropy" of the probability distribution.

This "theory of communication" has been utilized to determine the most appropriate coding of events under various types of probability distribution. It has also been used to measure the information capacity of a communication channel. In this case the probability dis-

---

[18] Claude E. Shannon and Warren Weaver, *The Mathematical Theory of Communication,* Urbana, University of Illinois Press, 1949.

tribution reflects the likelihood of occurrence of events; the other mathematical structure describes the costs of coding.

It should be emphasized that this measurement of information is not concerned with "semantic information" in the sense of the effects which an event may have upon the state of a receiver. For example, the occurrence of a request for a relatively unused document involves a high "information content" in the defined sense, even though the document itself may have low semantic information content. The difference is in the meaning of information in the technical sense as contrasted with the social sense. Attempts have been made to encompass both aspects into a unified theory.[19]

In certain physical situations, not only will there be variability in the measurement of the event, there will also be variability in the timing of event occurrence itself. Such considerations are significant when, although the capacity of a channel may be adequate for the "average" or expected value of this time sequence, it may not be sufficient to handle the maximum time of events. The result will be an accumulation of events in a waiting line. For example, the time sequence of requests becomes highly relevant to determining how much time can be spent on each, how many must be handled in parallel, etc. The study of such situations has been based on models combining probability distributions with other mathematical structures picturing the behavior.

Operations Research

Although we are attempting to develop quantified models for information retrieval, it can legitimately be questioned whether in fact the field of information system design has reached the stage where quantification is possible. Certainly the element of judgment is a predominant factor in this field, and judgment is, almost by definition, an ill-defined operation. Determining the relevancy of a document to a request, determining the index terms appropriate to representation of document content, determining the most appropriate position of a document in a file—each of these is highly dependent on the knowledge, experience, and intuition of competent professionals.

On the other hand, there exists, in the field of management decision making, an almost perfect example of an area wherein judgment and informed experience are fully as critical as they are in information

---

[19] Russell Ackoff, Towards a Behavioral Theory of Communication, *Management Science*, v. 4, No. 3, April 1958, pp. 218–234.

retrieval and yet one where quantitative techniques and the scientific method have been successfully applied. The development of mathematical models for the management decision process has been identified as "operations research." This work first received recognition perhaps twenty to twenty-five years ago in the attempt to quantify complex decision problems in the military field.[20] It has since found broad application throughout government and industry. Fundamentally operations research attempts to do for management decision making exactly what we are trying to do here in the area of information system design.[21]

To illustrate how mathematics has been applied to the field of management, consider the problem of deciding which of several warehouses is to distribute goods to each of several distribution points. Until operations research was developed, such a decision was made—and usually quite successfully—on the basis of experience and judgment. Operations research quantified this problem in a model called the "transportation model," which describes the problem by a matrix of values representing, for example, the cost per item for transportation from each warehouse to each distribution point

$$\text{Distribution points} \overset{\text{Warehouses}}{\begin{bmatrix} c_{11} & c_{12} & c_{13} \cdots \\ c_{21} & c_{22} & \cdots \\ c_{31} & \cdots & \\ \cdots & & \end{bmatrix}}$$

so that the element c_{ij} in this matrix represents the cost, per unit, of transportation from warehouse j to distribution point i. Based on this cost matrix, the total cost of a given distribution of shipments from the warehouses to distribution points can be calculated. The shipment problem, however, is subject to certain boundary conditions, such as limitations of warehouse capacity and the prescribed requirements at the distribution points. The problem is to find that distribution subject to these limitations which minimizes the total cost. "Linear programming" is the computational tool which is utilized to develop the solution to this problem.

This transportation problem is the classic example of the whole

---

[20] John von Neumann and Oskar Morgenstern, *Theory of Games and Economic Behavior,* Princeton, Princeton University Press, 1944.

[21] C. West Churchman, Russell L. Ackoff, and E. Leonard Arnoff, *Introduction to Operations Research,* New York, Wiley, 1957.

class of linear programming problems which are fundamental in modern operations research. The technique can be extended to any situation where the "utility" of each of a set of possible decisions can be measured. This utility is then to be optimized subject to prescribed boundary conditions of required results.

The fact that quantification has been so successfully applied in management decision making through operations research increases the confidence that it will be similarly useful in information system design.

Measurements of Value

Basic to the application of any model in the scientific method—whether to engineering, to operations research, or to information system theory—is a criterion for determining the degree to which such confidence is justified. This is done by providing as part of the model a measure of its own performance or effectiveness in predicting behavior. The aim of any mathematical model is to provide this measure of effectiveness. Most model theory follows immediately from the function chosen for measurement and the ways in which it will be maximized or minimized. Therefore any time a model is posed, the first question which should be asked is, "What is being measured, and what function is used to measure it?" And then, "How is the model maximizing or minimizing this function?"

In general, measurement produces sets of quantities, but the desire is to optimize some single objective of value. This means that the measure of effectiveness views value in terms of the established objective as a function of the set of individual measurements. Choosing the appropriate measure, and therefore the model, is not simple, particularly since there is usually a set of possible functions. Which of these possible measures of value should be used is a problem to be resolved between the physical, experimental scientist and the analytical model builder. Essentially, the model, the experimental data, and the measure relating the two cannot be divorced from one another.

Given a measure, it can be used in a number of ways. It can be used to predict, for example, that according to the measure of value, a system will perform to a certain level of effectiveness. An experiment can be used to test whether the system in fact performs to the predicted level of effectiveness. If the predictions consistently hold within the limits of accuracy of measurement, then the measure can with confidence be used as a tool for synthesis, to design a system as an optimum one according to the measure. This is, of course, a much more difficult step than the analytical creation of the model, but it is one that the scientist would like to feel can be taken.

Experimental Testing

Viewed in the light of scientific method, testing programs occupy the particularly significant role of testing the accuracy of predictions provided by the mathematical model being tested. Used in this way, the purpose of tests is to evaluate a model in the physical situation which the model is attempting to represent, that is, given a physical situation, such as a particular file structure, the mathematical model will provide the measure for the system efficiency and a testing program can then be used to test the accuracy and validity of the predictions from the model.

The other purpose for a testing program is to obtain the quantitative data concerning particular systems. Used in this way, the testing program will serve as the step of data collection to provide the raw information upon which to construct either a model for later test and verification or to provide the input to an existing model for purposes of prediction, comparison, or design.

At times, testing programs have been used by information system analysts to provide an evaluation of the relative effectiveness of two systems. However, unless this is done within the context of a proven predictive model it is fallacious to extend the results of the test to a general evaluation of the systems. Without such a model, a test merely tells which of the two systems was more effective in the particular test situation; it will not in any sense describe which of the two systems will be more effective in any other situation. In fact, all too frequently there is an inherent bias due to the very character of the test situation in favor of one or the other of the systems being evaluated. In a sense the situation is completely comparable to the description of a high IQ as merely an indication of the ability to score well on IQ tests.

Thus, whether test data can be extended to other contexts depends on the accuracy to which some model, either explicit or implicit, will predict performance in other situations. It is therefore essential, before undertaking any testing program, to state clearly the model by which evaluation and generalization are going to be made. At this stage, since no reliable model yet exists, the most desirable approach is to make the purpose of any test program to provide an evaluation of the degree to which the model does predict behavior.

Some experiments to test information systems in fact are in progress.

The ASLIB Group in Great Britain, under the direction of Cleverdon, is conducting one of these.[22] Don Swanson, at Thompson Ramo-Wooldridge Company, has also been conducting experimental tests.[23] A somewhat different approach is to examine existing information systems to determine the parameters of operation as they exist, and to verify predictions of their performance. This approach thus deals with total existing situations rather than artificially contrived ones, and has the concomitant disadvantage of including the great diversity of relationships which any real situation will exhibit. On the other hand, however, it has the advantage of dealing with systems which presumably have developed near optimum operation through the pressure of daily operation and "biological" competition and survival of the fittest.

To be specific, existing libraries and commercial data processing systems can be considered in this light. Whether these systems are actually efficient or optimum may be debatable, but if qualitative judgments of relative efficiency can be made, then the model should predict them. Unfortunately, almost traditionally, libraries have lacked a cost accounting approach. Hence, there is for example virtually no accurate data on library operations, their time and cost. If this lack can be suitably filled—and such a step appears essential if any solution is to be found to the library "problem"—then libraries can represent the most suitable of experimental testing grounds.

In most of these library systems, the human being is utilized in many roles—as a decision maker and as a user of information, but also as a "machine" and as a cog in the system. It is therefore vital, if this approach of examining existing information systems is to be successful, to develop a clear picture of the human being in each of these roles. In this respect there is a wealth of information, from psychology and elsewhere, which can be drawn on to define the quantitative characteristics of human beings as information transfer devices, viewed as a machine. It is equally important, then, to understand the psychology of the human being as it relates to the decision process or as it relates to his need for information. This view of the human being is concerned with him as a definite participant in any process in his "role as a human being."

---

[22] Cyril W. Cleverdon, Report on the Testing and Analysis of an Investigation into the Comparative Efficiency of Indexing Systems, ASLIB, Cranfield, England, September 1962, NSF Grant.

[23] D. Swanson, Searching Natural Language Text by Computer, *Science*, v. 132, 21 October 1960, pp. 1099–1104.

These data are valuable for another reason. The human being can himself be regarded as a successful information processing system, particularly in ill-defined situations requiring judgment. Any model can therefore be tested for prediction of performance for the human being in such situations. In particular, in this view, the human being is considered as an analogy—not the "machine-omorphic" analogy represented by the view of the human as a machine but the *anthropomorphic* analogy of files as similar to the brain. In this view, the human being, recognized as a successful information system, is used as a pattern for information systems. The concept is that an anthropomorphic file will also be successful on certain types of problems.

Limitations of Scientific Method

The scientific method has been perhaps the most powerful tool ever developed for increasing our knowledge. However, it has some significant limitations which must be recognized when we attempt to extend it to information system theory as it has been extended to operations research. The first concerns the availability of data and, in particular, the available accuracy of measurement. There are many situations for which the scientific method is not appropriate because the necessary data are unavailable. In other situations the scientific method is, at best, unsatisfactory because the standards of measurement would not permit adequate comparison of predicted values with observed values.

If measuring instruments cannot accurately measure the parameters involved in the model, the derived results are unsatisfactory. To raise a specific example, the mathematical structure of linear programming can be used, as we have indicated, for management decisions such as determining the optimum product mix or the optimum transportation of products from warehouses to receiving points. The accuracy of the results obtained from a linear programming problem, such as a transportation problem, are highly dependent on the accuracy of the initial data, such as the cost figures for transportation from given warehouses to given receiving plants. If these figures are inaccurate, not only are the results likely to be meaningless, they might be nonexistent. In other words, the statement from the mathematical problem might be that there is no answer to the problem whatsoever. This actually is highly likely to occur because of the size of some of these problems and the way in which error behaves in linear programming problems of high order. Therefore, in considering any application of models, and in particular to the field of information retrieval for which no accurate measurements exist, the accuracy of the data is a highly significant consideration. On the other hand, the development of models may well stimulate the development of comparably accurate measurements by providing a framework for this prescription.

A second limitation is the availability of analytical tools on which to draw for the formulation of hypotheses and models. In general, these tools are drawn from the field of mathematics; however, mathematics is itself undergoing continual growth. There are structures which can easily be defined but which present-day mathematics cannot handle because of the limitations of present-day theory. Thus, under such conditions, although the model could be defined and might be completely appropriate to the data, there would be no reasonable method of developing predictions to be tested. It appears, though, that at its present relatively unsophisticated stage, information system theory will find present mathematics completely adequate.

Even with the availability of a theory, however, the availability of tools adequate for handling the computation may represent a limitation. The computer as a tool to help in the solution of large numerical problems represented a substantial step forward and allowed the application of mathematical models in many areas where they had not been possible before. But even now certain combinatorial problems are beyond the capacity of even the largest and fastest computers, and much of information retrieval has a combinatorial character.[24]

Finally, a third limitation of the scientific method is the cost of experimental testing. There are times when it is impossible, for a number of reasons, to test the hypotheses. The cost of experimental testing is significant, particularly in the field of information retrieval. Some of the experiments which are now under way are very valuable experiments, very important experiments, very necessary experiments, but also very expensive experiments. The cost of getting literature into mechanized form for language translation, or for running experiments in information retrieval, is substantial. If any barrier really exists in the application of scientific method to this field, it is probably this one.

---

[24] John Riordan, *An Introduction to Combinatorial Analysis,* New York, Wiley, 1958.

14

Theories of file organization[1]

Many of the groups actively engaged in research in the field of information storage and retrieval have been concerned with utilizing the mathematical tools described in the previous chapter for the development of a theory for file organization. This work is described in the following pages within the framework of a general theory of file organization so that each individual contribution is shown in the context of the total problem.

The general theoretical structure within which this work will be described is based on the view that

1. Large files represent a multiple level structure whose characteristics are determined by both the physical parameters of the storage form and the logical problems in evaluating relevancy.
2. Such a structure, in order to be responsive to the usage of the file, must provide some procedure for reorganization in terms of the changing usage.

With this view, the purpose of an information system can be considered as *providing relevant responses to an environment,* that is, in a very general sense the information stored in a file, when combined with a suitable program of operations to be performed on that information, can be considered as a set of responses to the environment of activity on the file. In this sense, although the file may consist of stored information concerning inventory items, stored documents, or humanly stored patterns of response, in each case it provides a

[1] The work described in this chapter was supported in part by the National Science Foundation under Contract No. C-162.

response to some type of environment. This environment, for example, may be the set of changes, additions, deletions, interrogations, etc., involving the stored items.

The problems in designing an information system to meet this aim all revolve around the questions of *relevancy* and *economics*—first, the logical problems of determining relevancy and, second, the physical problems of providing the relevant responses at reasonable cost and time. Methods of solving these problems in the past have generally involved organizing the file in some predetermined fashion. The environment may then be examined in terms of its relationship to this predetermined organization, and logical relevancy completely determined in this way. Under these conditions, it is quite standard to "sort" the environment into the same sequence of organization as that provided for the file; in this way the successive responses for a set of environments can be provided at higher speed than a random search would provide. It is possible, on the other hand, to provide mechanisms for indexing or "random access" within the predetermined file structure and in this way solve problems where batching and sorting is precluded by the required response times.

In either event, however, economic operation is feasible only provided the predetermined pattern of the file organization corresponds to the environment. Where it is not possible to so organize the file, linear scanning of the file is a necessity and the file operation becomes hopelessly slow and uneconomic. This lack of responsiveness is the major source of difficulty in present solutions to the information storage and retrieval problem. Hence the attempt must be made *continually to fit the organization of the stored responses to that of the environment* rather than vice versa.

Attacks on this problem of file organization in response to environment have been many and varied; researchers have included librarians, documentalists, and computer specialists. For example, the librarian, with fixed classification schedules, provides, in effect, an *a priori* estimate of the environment of requests, additions, etc. However, classification schedules are quite inflexible and tend to lose contact with the changing environment. Subject catalogs have been utilized as a more flexible response mechanism and can perform reasonably well in the treatment of additions to the file, but reorganization of the *existing* file in response to changing requirements is still difficult.

The recent developments in documentation, with their newer systems for file organization, attempt to provide more flexible responsiveness of the entire file to the environment. They do this through techniques which, on the one hand, utilize more of the content of the document and, on the other, provide some degree of mechanization. Recent work in the area of "information retrieval" has therefore tended to emphasize these mechanization aspects in an attempt to increase the speed and accuracy of response through computer technology.

From this work three problem areas have become evident. The first concerns those problems involved in the recognition and representation of patterns in the environment. Thus questions relating to the selection of data to represent individual items or requests and to the recognition of interrelations among terms and items are significant pattern recognition problems. It must also be recognized that the processes of selection are required primarily for reasons of economic necessity, for the data selected must be limited, in some way, for operation to be efficient. These logical problems have been the subject of investigation by a number of research groups. Automatic abstracting, formalization of language, and so on, have all been concerned with this type of question.

The second class of problems relates to determining the relevancy to the environment of the stored patterns of response. In certain respects this also represents a logical problem of pattern recognition but of a slightly different, and probably more complex, character. Again, these problems of relevancy have also been the subject of numerous investigations. However, they have only recently gotten beyond the stage of simple Boolean logic relationships. The introduction of probabilistic techniques in the solutions of these problems has the potential of very promising results.

The third set of problems relates to the organization of the responses in such a way that physical problems of response time and accessibility can be economically solved. Attempts to attack this third class of problems when organization cannot be prespecified have led to an increasing interest in "self-organizing systems," including, for example, computer program models of the learning process, game-playing programs, theorem-proving programs, and the like. This work has been quite fruitful but has not been sufficiently extensive to represent the characteristics of mass storage problems. There has also been activity in the development of neural net models, particularly in relationship to the logical design of computers. This work has also been quite fruitful but has been almost too specific in its consideration of individual logical elements to be useful for the mass storage problem. The field of psychology has provided a whole set of models for inference, learning, and cognition in general. These models are very helpful, especially as analogies, but have the difficulty of being too dependent on the still largely unknown characteristics of the human being.

DEFINITION OF FILE ITEMS

One of the critical questions is that involved in defining what is meant by a file item and in determining how to represent quantitatively such a file item. Our approach has been based on several premises concerning the organizational character of files and the information stored in them.

The first of these premises is that the contents of a file should reflect the entire set of utilization so that file items in a library, for example, ought to consist not only of stored documents but also of some representation of requests, requesters, classes of users, indexers, words and terms, and all other things with which the library is concerned. Thus most people think of the contents of the library as a set of books or documents. We think of the contents of the library as including also the set of *requests* which have been made in the past, even the set of *requesters* represented in one way or another. It should include the words which are used in the library. Thus the subject catalog in a library contains not only representations of the documents but also representations of the words, indexes to the words, and even perhaps dissemination lists or profiles of file users.

To illustrate the significance of this premise, particularly with respect to the handling of requests, consider several factors.

1. The file must be responsive not only to requests, but also to the addition of new documents or other information, for these represent just as significant a part of the processing load.

2. The character of response to a new document can be viewed as completely analogous to that of responding to a request and it may involve an output of, say, relevant requester data from a dissemination list or profile.

3. The storage of requests is potentially as significant as the storage of documents, for it indicates the statistics of usage and aids in development of dissemination profiles and, perhaps most important, can provide past requests as responses to later requests which will be of almost as much value as formal documents.

4. The logical problems in determining the character of a request are very analogous to those in determining the content of a document,

and, in fact, one might ask a requester to state his question in the form of a small essay.

A second premise on which our definition of a file item is based is that the contents of a file should be viewed as homogeneous in its character, so that there should be no essential qualitative difference between a document, an abstract referencing that document, a request, a requester profile. The difference, if any, between items in the file in this sense should be a quantitative difference rather than a qualitative one. Furthermore, as a consequence of this premise, the response generated from a stored item may well be completely satisfied by the provision of an item from the file, such as the information from a card catalog card, which is quite removed from the information contained in the full document. Thus, with this premise, the difference between "document retrieval" and "fact retrieval" becomes a quantitative difference between various depths of acceptable response rather than a fundamental difference in the character of the file.

The third premise on which our definition of a file item is based is that a quantitative model and measure for relevancy is possible. We have therefore utilized mathematical structures based on quantified measurement. Whether this view is in fact true, particularly at this stage in the development of a theory, is highly debatable. Certainly there are not sufficient data on which to base a valid model, and therefore the picture which we present is largely an exercise in analysis. However, it is also significant that some step in this direction must be taken and that much of the most recent work in this field is consistent, as we will show, with the quantified model presented.

The fourth premise on which our view of file items is based is that there is no essential relationship between the method for representing an item and the organization of groups of items into a file. We therefore consider the two problems of item definition and file organization as essentially distinct and different problems. This we feel has been obscured in the past by the fact that the representation of items by, for example, classification numbers, seemed to predetermine automatically the organization of such items in the file. There is absolutely no reason for this to be so except to the extent that the efficiency of a file organization might be related to the choice of terms. In this way we make distinction between, on the one hand, the *logical* problems in information retrieval which are basically the problems of relevancy—the problems of item representation, the problems of matching a document and a request, the intellectual problems, if you want—and, on the other hand, the *physical* problems in information retrieval.

To illustrate this last premise, visualize some kind of mechanical or human monster which could instantaneously and absolutely accurately decide whether a given document, when looked at, was relevant to a request or not. Now ask the question would one or would one not organize the file of documents? We claim that the answer is that you *will* organize a large file, even though it is clear that we have removed all of the logical problems. The only remaining reason for organizing the file is for ease of physical access. The time to read the document, to get to the document, and so on, become the predominant considerations. The device may be able to make the decision instantaneously and absolutely accurately once it has read the document, but it still has to get the document and read it.

Basically both the logical and the physical considerations must be recognized, but, in particular, the organization of the file appears to be essentially a physical problem. The reason for pointing this out is that most of the work in this field has been concerned with the very interesting intellectual problems of how to represent the information content of the document and how to decide that it is the document wanted. But the more mundane, practical problems of how to get something out of a memory at reasonable time and cost are completely ignored.

Following from this is our fifth premise. We define organization as the grouping together of items (e.g., documents, or representations of documents) which are then handled as a unit and lose, to that extent, their individual identity. In other words, classification of a document into a classification slot, to all intents and purposes, identifies the document with that slot. Thereafter it, along with other documents in the slot, is treated as identical until they are examined individually. It would appear therefore that documents are grouped because they are in some sense related to each other, but, more basically, they are grouped because they are likely to be *wanted* together, and logical relationship is a means of measuring this likelihood. Thus the fifth basic premise is that we organize not simply for reasons of physical necessity but for the purpose of bringing items together that are likely to be wanted together. Finally, as a corollary to this premise, it seems that we organize not only on the basis of whether items are likely to be wanted together but also on the basis of whether items are likely to be wanted. Essentially this means that we make readily available those items most likely to be wanted and make relatively inaccessible those items least likely to be wanted.

Proposed Model for Item Definition

The model which we propose for definition of items is highly geometric in character, and we will therefore discuss it in such terms. Less visual approaches could also be adopted.

We interpret all items with which a file is concerned—whether stored documents, previous requests, users' profiles, words and terms—as the analog of physical bodies in a multidimensional space (not as physical documents such as a book on the shelf but as "physical documents" in an ideal sense), that is, each such thing as a document or a person, in our representation of it, is a physical body in this space in the sense that it occupies volume and has a mass distribution. We can interpret this as the volume of knowledge encompassed by the document, the mass distribution (not necessarily uniform) in some sense representing the value of the contribution made by the document to each particular point of knowledge. We further assume that there is a measure of distance and angle in this space so that, given any two points in the space, there is a determinable distance between them and an angle they subtend from any third point. There is thus, for example, the means of measuring the distance from a request, which is such a physical body, to a document, which is another physical body, as the shortest distance between these two bodies. We might call this space the space of knowledge, or the space of interest to the file system.

Such a view of file items is a highly intuitive one and certainly impossible to handle without some concrete representation. The first difficulty lies in the representation of the volume encompassed by a particular file item. The inherent problem is in representing any continuum. In general, the only way in which we can do so is by means of discrete points. However, in principle, with mass and distance as defined quantities, it is possible to determine, for example, the center of gravity and other quantities related to the moments of inertia of a mass distribution. The adequacy with which discrete points represent a volume can then be quantified in terms of the extent to which the moments of inertia of the mass distribution are matched by those of the selected points. The obvious way of attacking this problem is to choose the discrete points at appropriate centers of gravity and to represent the original mass distribution by mass concentrations at these points. In the simplest case this would mean the representation of a mass distribution by an equivalent mass at its center of gravity. More complex cases would require additional points adequate for the representation.

Thus the representation of file items can be reduced in each case to the representation of a set of points in the space of interest. Still, however, if our premise of quantifiability is valid, points in the space must be given a numeric representation. The need therefore exists to introduce a coordinate system of some kind in order to provide a basis for such quantified representation of the points. This would imply the specification of certain points in the space as coordinate points and then all other points in the space are identified in terms of them. Of course, this immediately raises the problem of the dimension of the space and the adequacy with which the points corresponding to file items can be quantitatively represented in terms of a finite number of points. In a sense this problem is related to the question of how much of the information content of a file item can be represented by a finite number of criteria. We discuss this in more detail later.

An interesting approach is to select a set of coordinate points and define the location of any other point by so-called "barycentric coordinates." In such a coordinate system, any point is represented as the center of gravity of a distribution of mass at each of the coordinate points. This allows for both the geometric location of the point and the assignment of mass at it. In particular, we can choose a set of key words in the space as our coordinate words. Each word, we recognize, is really a volume, but we will concentrate the volume as its center of gravity and choose that point as a coordinate point (realizing that, while we may choose a point as the representation of that word, the word itself is still diffuse in its meaning).

The concept of barycentric coordinates is a metric interpretation of the general concept of projective coordinate systems.[2] It is based on an ingenious mechanical idea developed by Moebius. As the coordinates for a point P in the plane, he conceived of the distribution of masses at the vertices of a triangle, chosen in such a way that the point P became the center of gravity of the distribution of masses. These masses, it can be shown, are proportional to the distances of the point P from each of the sides of the triangle as shown in Figure 78. By allowing negative masses (which we might interpret as the nega-

---

[2] W. C. Graustein, *Introduction to Higher Geometry,* MacMillan, 1946, pp. 156–173.

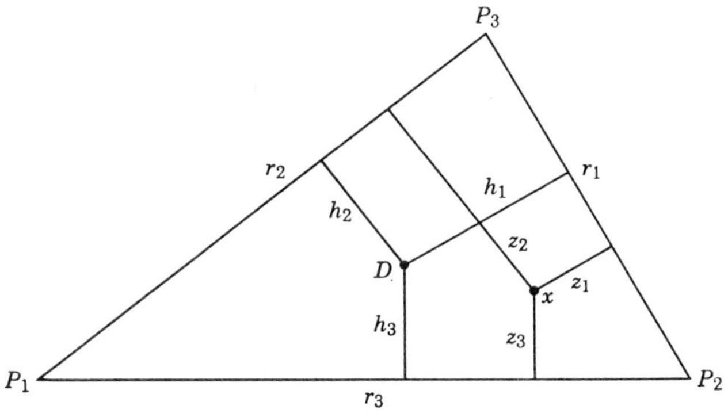

$$m_1:m_2:m_3 = \frac{z_1}{h_1}:\frac{z_2}{h_2}:\frac{z_3}{h_3}$$

FIG. 78. Barycentric coordinates.

tion of a term), points can be defined not only within the triangle but throughout the plane. Although the concept of barycentric coordinates was initially defined in terms of the plane, it can clearly be extended to n dimensional spaces.

A point of particular importance is the center of gravity of the entire mass distribution in the space because it is by choosing the center of gravity as an origin for non-projective coordinates that certain equations, particularly dynamic equations, become simplest. This point has the same character as any other point in the sense that it is a point of knowledge, but in effect, it might be considered as the center of interest of the library. Documents here may have very great value. In fact, it might be that it is the center of gravity precisely because the library has "works of . . ." located at that point and has built everything else around it.

Since barycentric coordinates describe a projective space, each point is describable by a whole set of representations (each with different masses, but the same relative proportions). It is therefore useful to embed the projective space in a Euclidean one, as described in a paper by Melvin Hausner.[3] Incidentally, it is also of some interest that a projective geometry is isomorphic to a relatively complemented modular lattice.[4] This further supports the relation between the structure of the information space and that of the vocabulary.

---

[3] M. Hausner, The Center of Mass and Affine Geometry, *Journal of the Mathematical Association of America,* October 1962, v. 69, No. 8. pp. 724–737.

[4] G. Birkhoff, *Lattice Theory,* American Mathematical Society, 1940.

Before proceeding, it is well to express this view of file items and their representation in more familiar terms. As we have indicated, the representation of a file item by a set of points is completely comparable to the representation of a document by the disjunction of a set of logical "phrases." Each such phrase attempts to represent the center of interest of some major section of the document. If the document is concerned with a fairly restricted topic, a single such phrase may be completely adequate. If the document is concerned with several unrelated topics or an extremely diffuse one, then a correspondingly greater number of phrases will be required to represent the document content adequately. Each such phrase, in a well-defined sense, corresponds to a single point in the space of knowledge which we have defined.

To represent the information content of any such point in the space, and in particular such a phrase, we have previously chosen a set of key words. Each such key word is interpreted as defining a point for assignment of mass in the space, so that the point of interest would be interpreted as the center of gravity of the mass distribution at the coordinate key word points. The degree to which a key word was itself diffuse would reflect itself in the difficulty in pinpointing its meaning to a single point in the space of knowledge. The barycentric coordinates then correspond completely to the assignments of relative importance to each key word of a phrase which is representative of the information content of some portion of a document.

The usual response to the proposal of a weighted indexing is one of shock, in the belief that indexing, classifying, and abstracting are complicated enough as it is. However, it must be recognized that even the present method of term assignment is simply a special case of weighted indexing. The assignment of one from a set of more than two weights really should not complicate judgment too much.

Several methods have been proposed for determining the weights assigned to terms. For example, Maron[5] suggested a judgmental evaluation of the probability that someone using the term wanted the document. Luhn's technique of statistical indexing,[6] since it generates a relative frequency for each term in the document, conceivably

---

[5] M. E. Maron and J. L. Kuhns, On Relevance, Probabilistic Indexing and Information Retrieval, *Journal of the Association for Computing Machinery,* July 1960, v. 7, No. 3, pp. 216–244.

[6] P. B. Baxendale, Machine-made Index for Technical Literature—An Experiment, *IBM Journal of Research and Development,* October 1958, v. 2, No. 4, pp. 354–361.

provides a mechanical process for assignment of weights. A possible generalization of this would combine the frequency values with Zipf's law [7] on probable frequency on the basis of length. Other techniques for determining the content bearing sentences, phrases, and words of a document, such as Baxendale's, Oswald's, Cambridge Language Research Unit's, can similarly be used as mechanical processes for assignment of weights. Later, we will propose a variant of the judgmental approach—not as a day-to-day operational method but as a tool for theoretical study.

With this view of document phrases as represented by assigned weights to key words, an interpretation of the role of logical conjunction and disjunction of key words is available, that is, if the possible weights are limited to "zero" or "one," the conjunction of terms is equivalent to their having the weight of "one" in the representation of a point in the document or request. The role of disjunction, that is, logical "or," in document or request representation (i.e., the document covers "A or B") can now be interpreted as implying that separate points are involved in representing the volume covered. In other words, if two points are needed in order to represent the information content of the document, the logical "or" is the tool for separation of a document into this set of points, each point being then perhaps equivalent to one phrase from the document. Thus, if a request is for

$$(A \cdot B) + (C \cdot D),$$

it is concerned with the separate concepts $(A \cdot B)$ and $(C \cdot D)$, each identified by assigning the weight "one" to its respective terms. The generalization to other ranges of possible weights doesn't change this basic interpretation of the logical operations.

Having chosen a set of key words as coordinate points, the representations of the entire set of points of interest—whether concerned with points in documents, requests, terms, requester profiles—can be compactly arranged in a matrix.

$$\begin{array}{c} \text{Key words} \\ \text{Points} \begin{bmatrix} w_{11} & w_{12} & w_{13} & \cdots \\ w_{21} & w_{22} & \cdots & \\ w_{31} & \cdots & & \\ \cdots & & & \end{bmatrix}. \end{array}$$

[7] A. F. Parker-Rhodes and R. M. Needham, *The Theory of Clumps,* CLRU Report, February 1960.

The tools of linear algebra are then available, as we will show, for manipulating this matrix and interpreting relations among the rows (i.e., among various points in the space) or among the columns.

As we have defined the quantitative representation of points in the space to date, it involves a set of weights assigned to the selected key word points. In certain cases the number of such key words may be quite large, perhaps on the order of 5000 to 10,000 words, and it would normally be expected in such a case that many of the weights would be quite small; representation in this form will therefore be extremely inefficient. Under such conditions one might establish a "cut-off" value for the weights and essentially treat all weights less than that cut-off value as 0; then the key words for which the assigned weights were greater than the cut-off value could be identified and the actually assigned weights attached to the identification. The resulting representation will be much more efficient. For example, if 5000 words are used as coordinate points and a scale of four values allowed for each weight, then the representation of any given point in the initially defined form would require at least 10,000 bits. On the other hand, using the cut-off value approach, it might be expected that, say, only 30 words would have assigned weights exceeding the cut-off value. The representation would then require $30(13 + 2) = 450$ bits, since each of the 30 words could be uniquely identified by 13 bits, and 2 bits would define the assigned weight. In summary, this approach identifies each of the significantly relevant key words together with its individual importance.

DEFINITION OF RELEVANCY

For a number of purposes—answering requests, organizing terms, classifying and grouping points—it is essential to have some measure of the degree of association, relevancy, closeness, of terms or documents. Viewed in the framework of the model for definition of file items described above, this reduces to the problem of measuring the degree of similarity between two sets of numbers, such as two rows or two columns of the point-term matrix. From the experimental standpoint, the significance which these numbers have and the extent to which the measure of their closeness coincides with the judgment of informed professionals is highly important but, from the analytical standpoint, the problem is largely independent of the interpretation which these numbers may have. Most of the work which we will describe has been of the analytical kind without serious experimental testing of the extent to which it matches informed intuition.

The approaches which have been suggested can all be viewed within the common framework of the point-term matrix which we have previously described. Usually they have limited their considerations to weights of one or zero. Considering this array of numbers, there may be reason to feel that certain pairs of the rows, or columns, appear to be similar. The effort has been to develop various measures of the degree of similarity between rows or columns.

The Cambridge Language Research Unit, in their paper on "The Theory of Clumps"[8] stated it this way: The basic step is to replace the original array by one calculated from it in which the entries are numbers measuring, in some defined sense, the "similarity," "connection," or "overlap" of pairs of columns (or rows) computed from their respective columns (or rows) in the original array. They may be set up in an obvious way in a square symmetrical array, the ijth entry being the nearness of column A_i to column A_j. The concern is with the properties of such arrays, which may properly be termed *connection* or *association matrices*.

They discussed various ways of defining the nearness function, of two columns, A_j and A_k. These included

1. $N(A_j \cdot A_k)$ = number of 1's in both columns A_j and A_k. This definition would be suitable if the number of 1's in a column was fixed or at least narrowly distributed. Otherwise it is counterintuitive, for it would, for example, make the nearness of

1110001101111 to		1110100000000 to
1111110010000	the same as that of	1111000000000

2. $N(A_j \cdot A_k) + N(\bar{A}_j \cdot \bar{A}_k)$ = number of places of agreement between 1's and between 0's, that is, the nearness in a Boolean lattice. This is simply the number of places where the two agree; it avoids the defects of definition 1 but does not resolve sufficiently unless the number of 1's and 0's are about equal, as the same weight is given to agreement in a 0 as in a 1.

3. $$\frac{N(A_j \cdot A_k)}{N(A_j + A_k)} = \frac{\text{number of 1's in both rows}}{\text{number of 1's in either row}}.$$

This attaches no weight at all to agreement in 0's and is therefore only suitable where the proportion of 1's to 0's is low. It is the most obvious definition in those cases where, at any rate in principle, the columns are indefinitely long but the number of 1's in each is fixed or (statistically) limited.

---

[8] A. F. Parker-Rhodes and R. M. Needham, *The Theory of Clumps,* CLRU Report, February 1960.

Tanimoto [9] similarly takes the document-term $n \times m$ matrix $R = (a_{ij})$. He denotes by A_j the jth column vector of R. He defines the similarity coefficient σ_{jk} of a pair of columns A_j and A_k, with respect to the given set of documents, by a form equivalent to definition 3 of CLRU:

$$\sigma_{jk} = \frac{N(A_j \cdot A_k)}{N(A_j + A_k)} = \frac{\text{number of attributes assigned to both}}{\text{number of attributes assigned to either}}.$$

In a similar way he defines the dual similarity coefficient s_{jh} of a pair of rows B_j and B_h with respect to the set of terms by

$$s_{jh} = \frac{N(B_j \cdot B_h)}{N(B_j + B_h)}.$$

The $n \times n$ matrix $S = (s_{jh})$ he calls the "matrix of the similarity coefficients" of the documents B with respect to the set of terms A. Dually, he calls $\Sigma = (\sigma_{jk})$ the $m \times m$ matrix of the similarity coefficients of the terms A with respect to the set of documents B.

Maron,[10] using the term-document matrix, suggested another of the several possible coefficients of association between columns. The particular coefficient he chose arises in the following way. Consider the columns A_j and A_k corresponding to two terms, and determine the number of elements in each of four classes, namely, documents with a one in both A_j and A_k, those with one in A_j but not A_k, those with one in A_k but not A_j, and those without a one in either. The number of elements in each class is shown most conveniently in Table 1.

TABLE 1

	A_k	$\bar{A}_k$	
A_j	$x = N(A_j \cdot A_k)$	$u = N(A_j \cdot \bar{A}_k)$	$N(A_j)$
$\bar{A}_j$	$v = N(\bar{A}_j \cdot A_k)$	$y = N(\bar{A}_j \cdot \bar{A}_k)$	$N(\bar{A}_j)$
	$N(A_k)$	$N(\bar{A}_k)$	n

Thus x corresponds exactly to the value obtained from definition 1 of CLRU, y to the corresponding value for the number of common zeros, etc. He then proposed as a measure of association

[9] T. T. Tanimoto, An Elementary Mathematical Theory of Classification and Prediction, IBM Internal Report, November 17, 1958.
[10] M. E. Maron and J. L. Kuhns, On Relevance, Probabilistic Indexing and Information Retrieval, *Journal of the Association for Computing Machinery*, July 1960, v. 7, No. 3, pp. 216–244.

$$A(A_j, A_k) = \frac{xy - uv}{(xy + uv)}.$$

Stiles [11] searched for a formula that would give a relative frequency—one that would measure the departure from the expected frequency of occurrence assuming no association. He decided on the following:

$$P(A_j \cdot A_k) = \log_{10} \frac{\left[|N(A_j \cdot A_k)n - N(A_j)N(A_k)| - \frac{n}{2} \right]^2 n}{N(A_j)N(A_k)[N - N(A_j)][(N - N(A_k)]},$$

where the expressions involved have the meanings previously defined. Stiles describes this formula as "a form of the chi-square formula using the marginal values of the 2 x 2 contingency table and the Yates' correction for small samples." If $N(A_j)N(A_k) > nN(A_j \cdot A_k)$, the association is negative. Such occurrences must be recognized during the computation process and the resultant association factors marked to indicate negative association.

Each of these cases dealt with document-term matrices whose elements are only either zero or one. It is possible to extend each possible measure, among those considered above, to the general case where the elements can take on a spectrum of values from zero to one. For example, we might take the "dot product" of the two sets of numbers, $A \cdot B = \Sigma a_i b_i$, which reduces to the CLRU first measure when values of only one or zero are allowed. This extension, incidentally, makes even more evident the counterintuitive character of this measure. Similar extensions are evident for each of the other proposed measures. To provide them, we must define a generalization of the concept of $\bar{A}$ by letting its elements be $1 - a_i$, where a_i are the elements of A.

In Maron's work this extension is implicit, for he allows a range of values to be assigned for the weight of a term with respect to a document. This weight, as we have indicated, reflects the probability of interest in documents with respect to the term.

In Osgood's book, *The Measurement of Meaning*,[12] he defines an approach of this character. He established a set of factors to which an individual is to assign weights of relevancy to various concepts. This is done by defining, for each factor, a scale of values from high negative to neutral to high positive. The value assigned by the subject can then be interpreted as a barycentric coordinate weight for the given factor with

---

[11] H. E. Stiles, The Association Factor in Information Retrieval, *Journal of the Association for Computing Machinery,* April 1961, v. 8, No. 2, pp. 271–279.

[12] C. E. Osgood, *The Measurement of Meaning,* University of Illinois Press, Urbana, Ill., 1957.

respect to each concept. These are then combined in a matrix similar to the form we have used, with a range of values possible for each element. He proposed as the measure of association the correlation between columns, computed from the sum of the products of the differences of each element from the average values for its column, that is,

$$R(A_j \cdot A_k) = \sum_i (a_{ji} - \tilde{a}_j)(a_{ki} - \tilde{a}_k).$$

This geometric type of approach has a good deal of appeal, for it introduces the possibility of a "point of view." For Osgood's measure, it was the center of interest. Thus it would seem that relevancy is not an absolute concept but is dependent on the point of view. In this way, although the concept of "relevancy" among file items is obviously highly related to the distances between points in the space, we need not interpret relevancy in such simple terms. Suppose that we consider that file items are relevant, not in any absolute sense, but to the extent that they are considered as relevant from some point of view. Thus we may measure the relevancy of two points A and B with respect to a third point P by the cosine of the angle subtended by them at that third point. This can be illustrated by the following diagram.

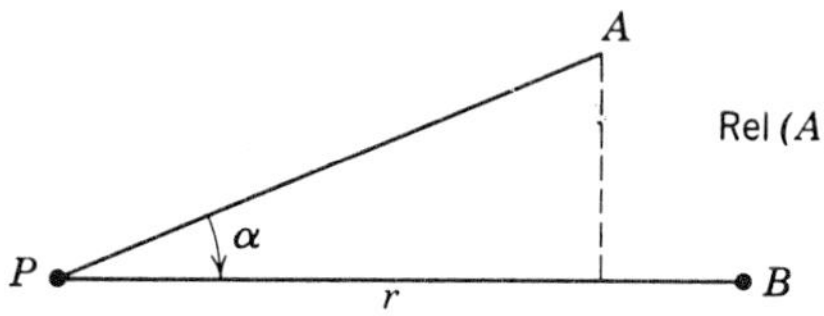

$$\text{Rel}\,(A, B; P) = \cos \alpha = r/PA$$

If properly interpreted, each of the previously described measures can be considered as a special case of this approach. For example, if the point P is chosen at the origin of coordinates, then $r = A \cdot B = N(A \cdot B)$, or the equivalent of CLRU's measure number one (extended to the dot product to accommodate a range of coordinate values).

Of more interest perhaps is interpretation in this way of the measures which were suggested by Osgood, Stiles, and Maron. To do this, define P as the center of gravity of the set of n points, so that $P = (\tilde{a}_1, \tilde{a}_2, \ldots, \tilde{a}_m)$. Then for Stiles and Maron,

$$\tilde{a}_j = \frac{N(A_j)}{n}, \qquad A_j \cdot A_k = N(A_j \cdot A_k),$$

and for Osgood,

$$\tilde{a}_j = \left(\sum_{i=1}^{n} a_{ij}\right)/n, \qquad A_j \cdot A_k = \sum_{i=1}^{n} a_{ij} a_{ik}.$$

Osgood's measure, then, provides exactly the dot product $r = (A_j - P) \cdot (A_k - P)$ necessary for calculating the angle subtended at P. It can be reduced as follows:

$$\sum_{i=1}^{n} (a_{ij} - \tilde{a}_j)(a_{ik} - \tilde{a}_k) = A_j \cdot A_k - \sum_{i=1}^{n} (\tilde{a}_j a_{ik} + \tilde{a}_k a_{ij}) + n\tilde{a}_j\tilde{a}_k$$
$$= A_j \cdot A_k - n\tilde{a}_j\tilde{a}_k.$$

Similarly, Stiles' measure can be reduced as follows:

$$\frac{(|N(A_j \cdot A_k)n - N(A_j)N(A_k)| - n/2)^2 n}{N(A_j)N(A_k)(N - N(A_j))(N - N(A_k))} = \frac{(|A_j \cdot A_k - n\tilde{a}_j\tilde{a}_k| - \frac{1}{2})^2}{\tilde{a}_j\tilde{a}_k(1 - \tilde{a}_j)(1 - \tilde{a}_k)n}.$$

To reduce Maron's measure, define $\bar{A}_j$ as we have previously discussed. If a_{ij} is the ith element of A_j, then $1 - a_{ij}$ is the ith element of $\bar{A}_j$. On this basis,

$$N(A_j \cdot A_k)N(\bar{A}_j \cdot \bar{A}_k) - N(A_j \cdot \bar{A}_k)N(\bar{A}_j \cdot A_k)$$
$$= (A_j \cdot A_k)(n - n(\tilde{a}_j + \tilde{a}_k) + A_j \cdot A_k) - (n\tilde{a}_j - A_j \cdot A_k)(n\tilde{a}_k - A_j \cdot A_k)$$
$$= nA_j \cdot A_k - n\tilde{a}_j\tilde{a}_k.$$

Thus, the three measures are closely related, differing only in the normalizations introduced by Maron and Stiles and in the minor correction for small n included by Stiles. They each relate closely to the angle subtended by two terms at the center of gravity of the points (documents) in the system.

Using this definition of relevancy, we can now define an operational procedure for determining the mass distribution required for the representation of a given point in this space. We do this in the following way. Consider a document and an indexer for that document. We ask that indexer to evaluate the importance which each of the set of specified key words has with respect to the document. We interpret the values which he assigns as his view of the relevancy of those terms to the documents and thus as the cosine of the angle subtended between each document point and the respective term points. This is illustrated by the following diagram showing two such terms, A and B, a document D, and indexer P, and the values which he would assign under this interpretation.

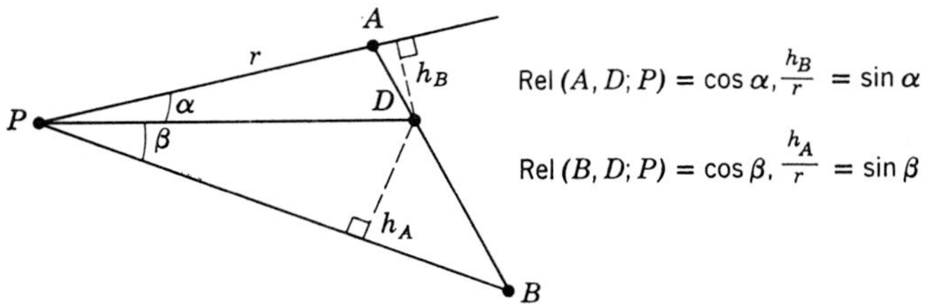

The values (h_A, h_B, 0) then are proportional to the barycentric coordinates, at the points A, B, and P, respectively, for the point D in the triangle defined by those points.

The degree to which the values, h_A and h_B, determined by the relevancy numbers assigned by the indexer, would reflect the true weights required for representing the point in the space (A-B) of interest is clearly a function of the position occupied by the indexer with respect to the space of interest and the relevancy, $\cos(\alpha + \beta)$, with which he views A and B. Thus, if his position with respect to the space of interest is relatively close to one of the key words, his evaluation will tend to be highly prejudiced. The ideal situation would be for him to be relatively equidistant from each of the points. Another observation to which this interpretation leads is the more removed—"objective"—the indexer is from the space of interest, the closer will his evaluation be to the true weights. On the other hand, it should also be observed that the more removed he is, the less able he will be to discriminate among the terms. Thus this interpretation allows for a means of measuring the degree of indexer objectivity, bias, and lack of training.

Given this operational procedure, which approximates the true weights required for representing a point by weights calculated from the relevancy values assigned by an indexer, two approaches are now available. One may ask several indexers to similarly evaluate the relevancy of key words to the same document and anticipate that an average process will eliminate the particular bias of the individual indexers. It would appear, however, that this approach would not be the most fruitful. On the other hand, one could attempt to determine the position which the indexer occupies with respect to the space of interest, by perhaps determining the importance with which he views the key terms and the mutual relevancy he assigns to pairs of them. In this way, with his position located in an absolute sense, the geometry provides a method for reducing his relevancy measures to proportional measures. Although this approach is certainly more complex than the first, it would appear to provide greater insight into the questions of relevancy. Furthermore, with this approach, the handling of requests can be similarly treated, that is, if the position of a requester could be determined in the same way (such as Luhn's profile would presumably represent), the relevancy of documents to his requests could be evaluated, not in an absolute sense but as he would view it.

LOGICAL ORGANIZATION

As we noted in our fifth premise, the purpose of organization is to bring together the items likely to be wanted together, and logical relationship is a means of measuring this. This question of establishing logical relationship can be approached in several ways, each with its own advantages in increasing the effectiveness of file organization. For example, one approach is to organize the terms on the basis of an *a priori* classification. This, of course, is the traditional approach of the various library classification schemes, such as the Dewey Decimal, Universal Decimal, or the Library of Congress classifications. It is also, moreover, the approach implicit in Ranganathan's factor analysis and Western Reserve's semantic factor analysis. In each case an intellectual examination of the field of interest to the library has resulted in an arrangement of the terms utilized to show their relationship to each other.

Although *a priori* organizations of terms have a great deal of appeal to those who believe an ideal structure to the physical world exists, they tend, as we have pointed out, to become more and more confining and to represent a strait jacket in any operational situation. Such specifications of term relationship are completely inflexible and incapable of responding to the character of changing usage. Because of this inflexibility, much of the theoretical work in the field of information retrieval has had the purpose of grouping documents or terms together on the basis of the character of usage. This work falls into two general classes, (1) those studies which consider only the relationships between terms and documents as exhibited by the document-term matrix, and (2) those studies which consider either or both of the association matrices which can be derived from the document-term matrix.

Thus the assignment of terms to documents in itself provides a means for organization of the set of documents into subclasses. In particular, one can define a cut-off value for the weight assigned to a particular term with respect to any document. Then, if the assigned weight exceeds that cut-off value, the document can be considered as a member of the subclass of documents defined by that term. In this way, if W_{ij} is the weight assigned to term A_j with respect to document D_i, and if ϵ_j is the cut-off value for term A_j, then the class S_j is the class of all documents for which $W_{ij} \geqq \epsilon_j$.

In principle, this is the approach involved in all present coordinate index schemes, recognizing that they have been based on the assignment of terms with weights of one or zero with respect to documents. It is also evident, however, in the use of a hierarchical arrangement of terms as a classification schedule for documents. In each case the method considers that a document falls within the class of documents defined by a term if the weight assigned to the term is greater than zero.

In general, the process of set definition in this way will assign a single document to many different subclasses. Therefore retrieval of documents will require specification of the particular class of interest as the logical (set theoretic) combination of the subclasses. Thus the methods of Boolean algebra or lattice theory are required for specification of the particular class of documents of interest. Robert Fairthorne has suggested that the following quotation from David Hume is appropriate in this respect, particularly as it describes the fact of language which makes necessary the use of lattice theory as opposed to Boolean algebra.[13]

> It is a universal observation which we may form upon language that where two related parts of a whole bear any proportion to each other, in numbers, rank, or consideration, there are always correlative terms invented which answer to both their parts and express their mutual relation. If they bear no proportion to each other, the term is only invented for the less, and marks its distinction from the whole. Thus "man" and "woman," "master" and "servant," . . . , are correlative terms. But the words "seaman," "carpenter," "smith," "tailor," &c. have no correspondent terms which express those who are no-seamen, no-carpenters, &c. Languages differ very much with regard to the particular words where this distinction obtains and may thence afford very strong inferences concerning the manners and customs of different nations. . . .

Powerful though the document-term relationship may be as a tool for logical organization, the relationship implied among terms or among documents by the common assignment of terms to documents seems to have deeper significance than is utilized by the Boolean algebra or lattice theory approach. Thus we may feel that two documents have very similar assignments of terms and that this is only partially revealed by their common assignment to the classes of documents defined by each of the terms. This degree of association pre-

---

[13] David Hume, Of the Populousness of Ancient Nations, Essay 11. In his *Philosophical Works,* Edinburg, 1826, v. 3, Part II, pages 421–508.

sumably would be displayed by a high value in the document association matrix, derived by one of the measures previously discussed.

The general problem is to recover information about the possible groupings of documents (or terms) from the association matrices. The typical object in doing so is to use the groups found as classes for defining a generic relationship among terms or, on the other hand, as a classification for grouping documents. CLRU phrases it in the following terms: [14] "What we want is a way of finding a partition into sub-sets with the property that there tends to be a stronger connection between two members of a group than between a member and a non-member." This would replace the rigidity of *a priori* definition of relations by the flexibility of usage determined relations.

A great variety of techniques exist for the "extraction" of significant factors from an association matrix. They include eigenvalue analysis, factor analysis, powers of the association matrix as an approximation to each, the CLRU "clump" approach, and others. Each of these produces factors, which can be interpreted as derived concepts and which are described by relative weightings of the terms or documents from the original set. Any relative weighting of the original set of points can be represented by a single point located at the center of gravity of these weights. This single point is identical in character to any other point in the space and, in particular, to any point which might have been chosen to represent a term or a file item; the only difference therefore lies in the method of derivation of it. By application of this technique, any set of points related by their degree of association can, in effect, be grouped into a box labeled with the center of gravity of the set. By a repetition of this process, groups of "abstract term" boxes can themselves be grouped and identified by a higher order abstract of the same basic character which is itself a center of gravity, etc. Therefore the technique of term or document grouping and the creation of abstract concepts provide a means for organizing the set of points in the space.

In principle, the number of new points is at least the same as in the original set, but a measure is provided of the information content loss incurred by rejecting any portion of the set of new points. Very typically, if there is any degree of association among the original set, there will be a tenfold or one-hundredfold decrease in their number with no appreciable loss of information content. Tanimoto phrased

---

[14] A. F. Parker-Rhodes and R. M. Needham, *The Theory of Clumps,* CLRU Report, February 1960.

it in the following terms.[15] Suppose that the number m of objects is fixed; what are the $k \leq m$ most important attributes of the set of objects? He answers this question by considering successive matrices in which the attributes of least significance have been eliminated. This procedure is repeated until there are exactly k attributes remaining or, alternatively, until the information loss is significant. In a similar fashion, given a fixed set of n attributes, one can find the $h \leq n$ objects which are best represented as possessing these attributes. One can also perform a reduction of both attributes and objects simultaneously if desired. In practice, one should have a sufficiently large matrix Σ so that attributes and objects may be eliminated by the above process to reduce Σ to the desired dimensions without significant loss of information content.

In particular, for example, if the eigenvalues and normalized vectors,

$$\Sigma \vec{x}_j = \lambda_j \vec{x}_j, \quad \begin{matrix} \vec{x}_1, \vec{x}_2, \ldots, \vec{x}_m \\ \lambda_1, \lambda_2, \ldots, \lambda_m \end{matrix}$$

of the term association matrix were determined and listed in decreasing order of the eigenvalue, the resulting sequence of eigenvectors would represent classes of terms extracted from the association matrix. They can be used as a basis, or coordinate system, for the space. Any point can be represented as a linear combination of them.

$$\vec{x} = a_1\vec{x}_1 + \cdots + a_m\vec{x}_m.$$

The extent to which a point could be considered as a member of the class defined by an eigenvector is measured by the magnitude of the corresponding component in its representation in such terms. In particular, the extent to which each of the original terms can be so considered is given in this way. The amount of information concerning the association between points in the space of interest which is provided by each class of eigenvector defined terms can be measured by the magnitude of the corresponding eigenvalue, that is,

$$\Sigma\vec{x} = a_1\lambda_1\vec{x}_1 + a_2\lambda_2\vec{x}_2 + \cdots + a_m\lambda_m\vec{x}_m.$$

The techniques of factor analysis, which are so commonly used in various psychological testing situations, can be regarded as generalizations of eigenvalue analysis, differing only in the character of the

[15] T. T. Tanimoto, An Elementary Mathematical Theory of Classification and Prediction, IBM Internal Report, November 17, 1958.

factors derived and the relative simplicity of the computational problem. Herbert Solomon described factor analysis in the following terms: [16]

> In the form in which factor analysis is most frequently encountered, it was motivated by the measurement of mental ability. However, factor analysis appeared in embryonic shape in connection with filing problems faced by Scotland Yard officials on the classification and identification of criminals. Galton, who was developing his ideas on correlation, became interested in the classification problem. He pointed out that the twelve Bertillon measures to be used for classification were not independent and proposed that the observed measurements be formed into a set of independent measures.

In the usual factor analysis situation, the sets of measured data (such as responses to tests of mental ability) are associated with each other and conjectures about the latent universe operating to produce the associations are mathematized. These mathematizations are the mathematical models in factor analysis. The most interesting from the standpoint of our work are the centroid method of Thurstone [17] and the principal factor method of Hotelling,[18] each for multiple common factor analysis. In each case the actual data are given the heavy burden of providing all of the information without the introduction of *a priori* hypotheses concerning relevant factors. The major difference between the two exists in the computational basis for estimation of the relationship between the original terms and the extracted factors. Details of the centroid procedure utilized by Thurstone can be found in his basic text on the subject. Fundamentally it allows the determination of an infinite number of choices for the factors, but Thurstone feels that attention should be given only to the choice for which psychologically relevant interpretation can be given. Hotelling, on the other hand, suggests that attention should be given to the factor which corresponds exactly to the eigenvectors, despite the fact that they may not have immediate psychological interpretation. Thus the eigenvalue analysis approach can be considered as a special case of factor analysis.

Harold Borko has experimentally studied the applicability of factor

---

[16] Herbert Solomon, *Mathematical Thinking in the Measurement of Behavior,* The Free Press, Glencoe, Ill., 1960.

[17] Louis L. Thurstone, *Multiple Factor Analysis,* Chicago, University of Chicago Press, 1947.

[18] Harold Hotelling, Analysis of a Complex of Statistical Variables into Principal Components, *Journal of Educational Psychology,* v. 24, 1933, pp. 417–441 and 498–520.

analysis to the generation of categories.[19] He chose as the experimental library a set of 618 psychological abstracts. Key words, from a vocabulary of 90 possible index terms, were assigned to the documents. The resulting document-term matrix was then used to produce an association matrix from the correlation between terms. Factor analysis was applied and a set of 10 factors was defined. They were shown to be compatible with terms from the classification system used by the American Psychological Association, even though they were derived empirically and without reference to that classification system.

The possibility of using powers of the association matrix is implicit in all approaches which consider second-order or higher-order effects. Thus the extent to which two terms are associated, as determined from their mutual degree of association with third terms, is described by the square of the association matrix. The behavior of high powers of the association matrix is therefore of considerable interest. This has been investigated in a number of papers,[20] one of which is by David Rosenblatt, "On the Graphs and Asymptotic Forms of Finite Boolean Relation Matrices and Stochastic Matrices." Of particular mathematical interest is the fact that powers of the association matrix provide a method for determination of its eigenvalues and thus represent an approximation to the methods of eigenvalue analysis and factor analysis.

In CLRU's theory of clumps, they propose the concept of "cohesion" across a partition of the set of terms into classes. For example, if two classes of terms, A and B, are considered, with $A_1, A_2, \ldots, A_k$ the terms in part A, and $A_{k+1}, A_{k+2}, \ldots, A_{k+h}$ the terms in part B, then the cohesion between them is given by the expression

$$\sum_{i=1}^{k} \sum_{j=k+1}^{k+h} a_{ij} \bigg/ \sqrt{\left(\sum_{i=1}^{k} \sum_{j=1}^{k} a_{ij}\right)\left(\sum_{i=k+1}^{k+h} \sum_{j=k+1}^{k+h} a_{ij}\right)}$$

where a_{ij} is the association between terms A_i and A_j. By use of this measure, the partition of the original set of terms is made in such a way as to minimize the cohesion between classes. Each class then represents a classification of the terms included within it.

The association matrices describe the similarity only between pairs

[19] Harold Borko, The Construction of an Empirically Based Mathematically Derived Classification System, System Development Corp. (Report SP-585), October 26, 1961.

[20] David Rosenblatt, On the Graphs and Asymptotic Forms of Finite Boolean Relation Matrices and Stochastic Matrices, ONR Report.

of terms or documents; similarity among groups of them must be derived by tools such as those we have described. However, similarity among groups of three, four, or more documents and terms could presumably also be defined. This would utilize more of the initial data and thus provide a firmer foundation for any process of deriving groupings of points. This approach, called "latent class analysis," has been suggested in a paper by F. B. Baker.[21]

Whichever technique may be used to generate abstract concepts from groupings of term or document points, the process of abstraction not only produces a relationship among the points but also can be utilized to reduce the complexity of representation of any given document point. Thus two separate representations of a document, one in the original form and the second in terms of the generated abstract terms, will have a qualitative difference in their character. This qualitative difference has been described by Jonker and Taube [22] in terms of their "descriptive continuum," that is, they state that the terms to be used in representing document content can be arranged in a continuum ranging from what they call "very short terms" (such as those represented by Calvin Mooers' descriptors or Taube's Uniterms) to somewhat "longer" terms (such as subject headings in a card catalog or headings produced by combinations of descriptors or Uniterms), to the "longest" type of term (this being the hierarchical classification).

The measure of "length of term" was never explicitly defined by them, but it can be interpreted as being related to the redundancy or mnemonic character of the term or the degree to which the representation of a given term shows its relationship to other terms. Specifically, "short" terms are considered as independent of each other and can be represented in binary notation by a number of bits equal to the logarithm to the base 2 of the number of terms. Combinations of terms may be represented in some compact way, such as superimposed random coding; but if their component terms are to preserve any degree of identity, representation will generally involve a larger number of bits than the actually used number of combinations would

---

[21] F. B. Baker, Information Retrieval Based on Latent Class Analysis, *Journal of the Association for Computing Machinery,* October 1962, v. 9, No. 4, pp. 512–521.

[22] Frederick Jonker, The Descriptive Continuum: A "Generalized" Theory of Indexing, *Preprints of Papers for the International Conference on Scientific Information,* National Academy of Sciences—National Research Council, Washington, D.C., 1958.

require. Similarly, description of a term defining a position in a hierarchical relationship will involve a highly redundant coding for the number of terms actually involved, particularly in comparison with the total number of terms possible in the hierarchical structure.

Jonker and Taube attempted to show that the position of a particular choice of term type in this continuum determined, to all intents and purposes, the characteristics of the information system. In particular, they felt it determined such things as the depth of indexing, the number of criteria applied to the document, and the degree to which terms could be permuted. Their results seem to be valid, particularly with respect to the number of terms applied. For example, the number of terms normally applied to a document in a library card catalog is, in practice, far fewer than the number of terms normally applied in the Uniterm system and, in fact, normally far fewer than librarians feel ought to be applied.

In any event, the problem of organizing the terms used to represent the space relates directly to the choice of coordinate system. The choice of a specific coordinate system may not turn out to be the most suitable one. Hence it may be desirable to change from one coordinate system to another, and one type of change of coordinate system is that involved in the attempt to reduce the number of coordinate points. As previously mentioned, the question exists of what the dimension of the space is and of the adequacy to which the points corresponding to file items can be quantitatively represented. Thus, how many points do we choose? How many key words are needed—10 or 10,000? Actually these questions cannot be answered, for one cannot say what the dimension of this space is; one can only say what an *adequate* set of points is for file purposes. The approach through the association matrices seems to provide a method for determining adequacy.

A final approach is to organize documents on the basis of their mutual occurrence as determined from situations of circumstance. Thus the fact that two documents have arrived at a library at effectively the same time to an extent implies a relationship between them which, in fact, is reflected by the closeness of the assigned accession numbers. Such an approach, particularly when used in conjunction with one of the others, is an extremely valuable one, although virtually unexploited, particularly where the environment has a high degree of consistency. Specifically, as new documents enter the system, a significant new parameter enters the determination of degree of document association—that of distribution of activity. This means that in some sense the organization of documents should not only reflect the degree of logical association, it should also reflect the distribution of activity. Such an approach can be made the basis of an additional, relatively unexplored, theory of file organization.

ACTIVITY ORGANIZATION

The problem in "activity organization" is to supplement the methods of logical organization by recognizing not simply the likelihood that items will be wanted together but, rather, the likelihood that items will be wanted at all. Thus it is possible, using any one of the techniques of logical organization from the previous discussion, to produce groups of related documents. In each case the question in determining how many such groups of documents should be produced, or how many documents they should contain, or how many levels of successive groupings should be produced, can only be answered in terms of the desire to maximize, or optimize, some measure of effectiveness. As a possible measure of effectiveness, the "channel rate" or information rate obtainable from the information system appears to be particularly suitable (later we will also consider a measure based on the cost per operation). Such a measure immediately makes available the great wealth of mathematical literature on information theory dealing with precisely this type of question. To utilize this mathematical structure means that very careful consideration must be given to the question of which documents, groups of documents, groups of groups, and so on, are most likely to be active. Determining this activity requires some measure of the probable distribution of activity.

To introduce the concepts of activity organization it is necessary to consider a number of "distribution functions" over the space of interest and, in particular, over the set of defined abstract patterns. The first is the universe of the space, a function $u(x)$ which is uniform over the space, and thus constant as a function over the space. The second distribution is of more interest. It is the volume $v(x)$ of items in this space; with a variable concentration of documents, $v(x)$, in effect, is a measure of the past concentration of activity. A third distribution, $w(x)$, is very similar to $v(x)$ except that it measures the worth distribution. Hence there may be a very high concentration of documents in some area, but they may be worthless, whereas a very sparse set of documents may be such that each document is of vital importance.

The *a priori* probability distribution $p(x)$, or the "probable activity," is a fourth distribution. It says that over a long period of time a large quantity of requests or documents are going to come into volumes of space where $p(x)$ is large and a relatively smaller amount where $p(x)$ is small. For example, an engineering library might get a request on "van Gogh," but most of the requests it handles are concerned with engineering topics. A related distribution, $q(x, t)$, is the conditional probable activity, given present activity at t. In other words, given the occurrence of a request in the area of knowledge t, $q(x, t)$ describes the "consistency" of the environment, since in a consistent environment the next stimulus should be fairly closely related to the immediate one.

These five functions—$u(x)$, $v(x)$, $w(x)$, $p(x)$, and $q(x, t)$—are not necessarily equivalent. On the other hand, they are very frequently used as though they were equivalent, for the more easily determined of them may be utilized as an approximation to those which are difficult to determine. In particular, the distribution $v(x)$, insofar as it represents the past frequency of activity, is very frequently used as an approximation to $p(x)$, the probability of future activity.

To illustrate the significance of these distributions, consider the space as an analog to the 26 letters of the alphabet. The information rate which we will get from the 26 letters of the alphabet, provided their usage is uniformly distributed (i.e., assuming only $u(x)$ as the distribution), is about 4.7 bits. However, it is known that usage of letters in normal English text is not uniform; $p(x)$ describes the *a priori* distribution of the letters of the alphabet: E has frequency 12%, T with frequency 10%, and so on. Finally, $q(x, t)$ describes the conditional probability that, given some letter (such as Q), another specific letter (such as U) will occur.

Utilizing the known distributions of activity has relevance throughout the entire field of information handling. Its importance in "coding" has been stressed by Fano [23] and by Wozencraft.[24] They point out the processing problem in decoding a message and the need to reduce the time for it by efficient activity organization of the relevant codes.

The aim of activity organization is to produce a hierarchical arrangement of nested "boxes," or levels of grouping, which will represent a compromise among these various distributions in such a way as to optimize the selected measure of efficiency (such as channel rate). These sets of boxes become quite analogous to the structure of a normal classification scheme, although their method of derivation is de-

---

[23] R. M. Fano, A Heuristic Discussion of Probabilistic Decoding, Preprints, *First Congress on the Information System Sciences,* November 1962.

[24] J. M. Wozencraft and B. Reiffen, *Sequential Decoding,* Wiley, 1961.

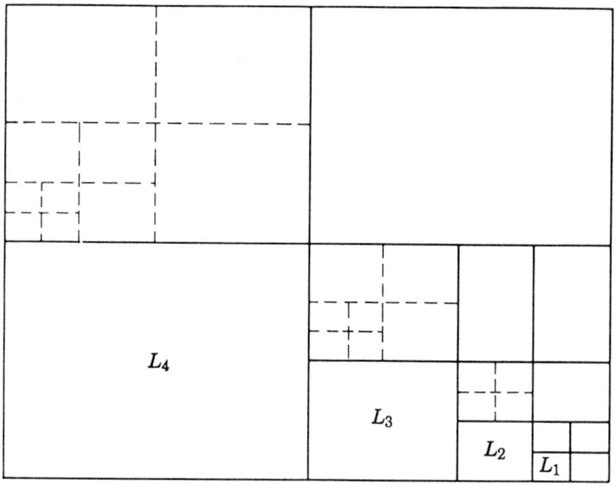

FIG. 79. Activity organized indexed file structure.

pendent on the character of usage rather than *a priori* decision. Thus they can be visualized in terms of the chart shown in Figure 79. Each box shown represents a grouping at some level of abstraction, the level being described by the relative size of the box in the diagram. Thus four levels are shown here, of which the smallest or lower level might possibly be the original documents themselves. If the cover of any box is removed, as shown in each upper left-hand corner, the interior of the box contains a nest of boxes of the same general character.

Each box is "labeled" by a pattern obtained from its contents, for example, by the point at the center of gravity of the patterns contained. In this way, what can be seen at any time is a set of patterns representing various levels of abstraction.

The actual "size" of the box at any given level is, of course, determined from the distribution of the documents themselves and the logical relationship which they bear to each other. It can be determined on the basis of any of the distribution functions, $u(x)$, $v(x)$, or $w(x)$. On the other hand, the number of levels open at any time is dependent on the distribution $p(x)$ of probable activity. The aim is to produce boxes, independent of their level of abstraction, such that the integral of the probability, $p(x)$, of each box will be equal for all boxes which can be seen at any time. In the example shown, all of the boxes which can be seen will therefore have the same probability of being utilized. This implies that the documents in the lower right-hand corner have the same probability of being requested as the entire set of documents encompassed by high level abstraction in the upper left-hand corner. If the box in the upper left-hand corner were active, then the contents would be examined and would again consist of a set of boxes of equal probable activity. This process continues until the request is answered by the pattern representing a box at some level, ultimately by a document.

Such a nested structure is characterized by two parameters:

k—the rate of growth from one level to the next (in the above example k is equal to 4)

s—the number of levels in the file (in the above example s is 4)

Based on these two parameters, the structure of the file and its activity is described by the following generating functions:

$$P(t) = p_0 + p_1t + \cdots + p_{s-1}t^{s-1}$$

$$= \frac{b_s}{b_1}\left(1 + \frac{k-1}{b_1}t\right)\left(1 + \frac{k-1}{b_2}t\right)\cdots\left(1 + \frac{k-1}{b_{s-1}}t\right)$$

where $$b_i = (k-1)i + 1, \ \& \ N = k^s.$$

Thus p_i is the probability of providing the response from the $(i + 1)^{st}$ level of the file. If we now define $m_i = (0)^ip_0 + (1)^ip_1 + 2^ip_2 + \cdots + (s-1)^ip_{s-1}$ as the *ordinary* moments of $\{p_i\}$, we can define the average search time in terms of the number of levels which must be looked at. The average time is

$$t = m_1 = p_1 + 2p_2 + \cdots + (s-1)p_{s-1}.$$

We have the following:

If $$P(t) = p_0 + p_1t + \cdots + p_{s-1}t^{s-1}$$

and $$M(t) = m_0 + m_1t + \cdots + m_jt^j + \cdots$$

then $$M(t) = P(e^t)$$

$$= \frac{b_s}{b_1}\left(1 + \frac{k-1}{b_1}e^t\right)\left(1 + \frac{k-1}{b_2}e^t\right)\cdots\left(1 + \frac{k-1}{b_{s-1}}e^t\right).$$

The determination of the actual relevancy of the given documents to an environmental situation and the selection of an adequate response involve the matching of the "request," for example, against the available box patterns and/or the location, in the space of knowledge, of the position which the request occupies. To do this involves a scanning operation in which the pattern of the request is matched against the patterns of successive boxes. The selected box is then "opened" and the contents similarly compared.

It could be considered that such an operation takes place in parallel (with all available box patterns simultaneously matched), but this would beg the question. Instead, it could be considered that the scanning operation takes place sequentially, in a preferred order. It is for this reason that organization with respect to $q(x, t)$ is imposed on the boxes, that is, the preferred sequence of scan will possibly shift with the changing center, t, of activity.

To take advantage of $q(x, t)$ we must organize the sequence of scanning of these boxes—the looking at them in their order of probable relevancy. In other words, given $q(x, t)$ as a measure of the probable activity, arrange the boxes in the order according to that measure. In this way, in scanning them, we will expect to come to the one of interest sooner than under an organization which ignores this distribution.

The set of patterns describing the boxes which can be seen at any time is equivalent to an index. The index is scanned (in the same manner) and indicates to which section of the space further attention should be paid. Access to the organization is an alternation of scanning and physical indexing repeated until access is achieved, as illustrated in Figure 80. The basis for organization by $p(x)$ is that in scanning an index at a certain level (say index_2) some of the patterns are references to groups of patterns in the next index level (index_1) and some are more basic, because of their volume of usage, and refer to patterns at a lower level (patterns_1).

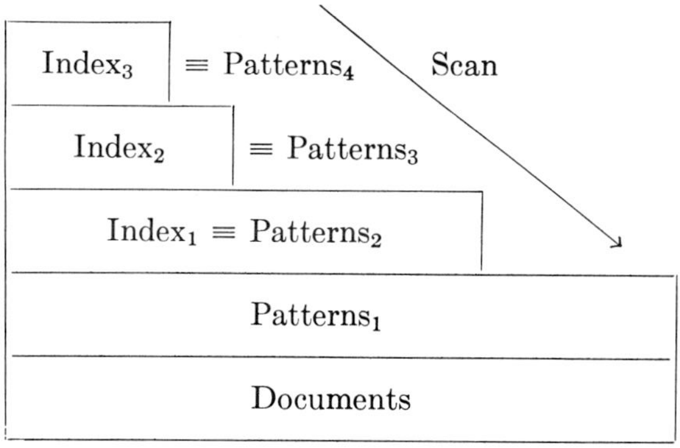

FIG. 80. Scan pattern.

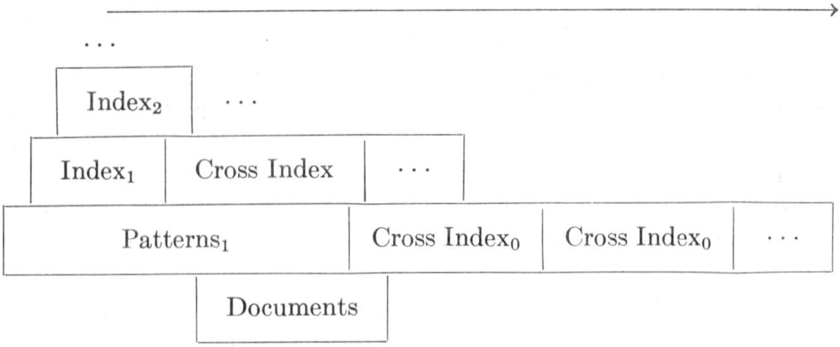

FIG. 81. Cross indexing.

As described, it has been assumed that, where multiple points were required to represent a document, multiple points are represented at the pattern level. However, it is frequently the case that this is not done (e.g., only one copy of the document is stored and that is located at the particular point defined by a classification slot). In such cases references can be stored at higher index levels in the form of cross indexes. It should be recognized that such cross indexes are basically extensions to the set of document or index pattern points. Thus the picture takes on the character shown in Figure 81.

REORGANIZATION

It is characteristic of information retrieval problems that the character of utilization is highly dynamic. Therefore, if an activity organization has been established on the basis of the distributions $p(x)$ or $q(x, t)$ at any given time, the actual distributions will themselves gradually change and the established organization will become more and more out of tune with its environment. Hence some technique would be desirable to accommodate the character of change.

Several types of change can be considered. For example, the file deals with patterns describing the information content of documents with respect to prescribed characteristics. It is to be expected that with the passage of time an improved picture of the true position and value of each document can be obtained and that this improvement should be reflected in a change in the basic pattern itself. A change of an entirely different character attempts to respond to the change in the distribution $p(x)$ of probable activity. Such a shift in probable activity should be reflected in changes in the groupings of items and their relative accessibility. Related to this is the shift in center of activity as represented by the conditional probability distribution $q(x, t)$; this should be reflected in a corresponding change in the sequence of scanning in a file search.

The need exists for a procedure which will automatically change the character, grouping, accessibility, and sequence of scan of file items. This procedure should accommodate all of these changes as a direct response to the character of the environment and, in effect, produce order as a reaction to patterns in the environment. A possible approach to such a procedure is based on the multilevel, activity-organized file structure with a set of associated logical processing. The file structure consists of a number of levels of increasing size and decreasing accessibility, as illustrated in Figure 82. On this basis, direct responses to the environment will be available only from the first level. The second level provides response to its "environment" consisting of the first level; similarly, the $K+$ 1st level provides response in terms of the Kth level. In general, it seems reasonable to assume that successive levels are of exponentially increasing size.

The information stored at any given level can be considered as patterns consisting of (1) information for selection, (2) response to be provided, and (3) index information for accessibility from one level to the next lower.

In principle, such a gross structure, suitably supported by logical processing, can provide a mechanism for economically responding to

FIG. 82. Multiple level file.

its environment. As changes occur in the environment, the position of patterns within the file structure will be correspondingly changed so that the most relevant patterns will become the most accessible. Presumably successive reorganizations of the patterns occur during some time quantum related to logical processing speed, rate of change of the environment, and so on.

There appears to be a very close relationship between the functioning of such a self-organizing large file and that of human beings. On the one hand, a file can be viewed as an analog of the mind, and, since the human being is an effective retrieval device with fantastically large capacity, any insight into the functioning of the human being would provide tools for understanding desirable structures for large files. On the other hand, the human mind can itself be considered solely as a large file mechanism and, with this view, a significantly different understanding of the heuristics of human processing is obtained.

Such a view of the human mind as a large, multiple level file is not in any sense new. In his book, *The Psychology of Invention in the Mathematical Field*,[25] Jacques Hadamard pointed out:

> The ideas that lie at any moment within my full consciousness seem to attract of their own accord the most appropriate out of a number of other ideas that are lying close at hand, but imperfectly within the range of my consciousness. There seems to be a presence-chamber in my mind where full consciousness holds court, and where two or three ideas are at the same time in audience, and an ante-chamber full of more or less allied ideas, which is situated just beyond the full ken of consciousness. Out of this ante-chamber the ideas most nearly allied to those in the presence-chamber appear to be summoned in a mechanically logical way, and to have their turn of audience.
>
> It can hardly be doubted, and we shall be able to confirm this later on, that there must even be, in the unconscious, several successive layers, the most superficial one being the one we just considered. More remote is the unconscious layer which acts in automatic writing; still more those which allow inspirations such as we reported in the preceding section. Even deeper ones will appear to us at the end of this study. There seems to be a kind of continuity between full consciousness and more and more hidden levels of the unconscious; a succession which seems to be especially well described in Taine's book *On Intelligence,* when he writes: "You may compare the mind of a man to the stage of a theatre, very narrow at the footlights but constantly broadening as it goes back. At the footlights, there is hardly room for more than one actor. . . . As one goes further and further

---

[25] New York, Dover, 1954.

away from the footlights, there are other figures less and less distinct as they are more distant from the lights. And beyond these groups, in the wings and altogether in the background, are innumerable obscure shapes that a sudden call may bring forward and even within direct range of the footlights. Undefined evolutions constantly take place throughout this seething mass of actors of all kinds, to furnish the chorus leaders who in turn, as in a magic lantern picture, pass before our eyes."

The transition of information from one level to the next, and, in particular, from the first level to the "environment," is determined on the basis of logical processes occurring, in a sense, between levels. Seven separate logical functions that must be performed can be distinguished. These can be illustrated in terms of the relationship among the environment, the first level, and the second level, as follows.

The first process is a *selection*, from the environment, of relevant data. The selected data are then used to form a new pattern to be stored in the first level. The control of the selection process, in terms of the specification of what environmental data should be considered relevant and therefore selected, may, in fact, be considered a part of the present response and thus will itself vary from time to time. The second set of logical processes involves the *matching* of the relevant data from the environment with the patterns stored at the first level. This matching may be made on the basis of complete or fragmentary agreement; it may be completely deterministic or probabilistic. Third is a *ranking* of the stored patterns in terms of their *relevance* to the environment. Fourth, as a result of the previously listed logical processes, the selected *response* (perhaps that stored as part of the most relevant pattern) is then output for control of the next processing cycle. Fifth is a process of *listing* sets of patterns, producing a new, consolidated pattern, which in some sense represents an abstraction of the original set of patterns. This is combined with the sixth logical process of *forgetting* the listed set of patterns by storing them at the next lower level (in this case the second level). In doing this an index to the location within the second level of the forgotten patterns is retained as part of the list pattern. Notice that with this mechanism, lists themselves may be included in a subsequent list and forgotten. Seventh, and finally, is a process of *remembering* wherein information is recovered from the next lower level (in this case from the second level) because of its relevancy to a new situation.

With this pattern of logical processes there seems to be a very close analogy between, for example, the process of responding to an environment and that of remembering in terms of relevancy to a new situation. It seems probable, therefore, that different sets of these seven logical processes may be analogous, if not identical, and thus each involves the processes of selection, matching, ranking, and response. The processes of listing, forgetting, and remembering at one level correspond to the analogous processes of selecting, storing, and responding one further level down.

To illustrate these fundamental considerations, the following is a well-defined process by which to organize stored patterns. At several points in this process, related to the various processes outlined, there are a variety of possible choices for detailed procedures. Any one of the procedures available at each point could be utilized without affecting the general character of the process.

The process operates on stored patterns. In order to be specific, we assume that these patterns each consist of one hundred bits. Clearly this prescribed length could be taken as any fixed value or even as a variable value. For convenience in visualization, these one hundred bits are divided into three groups called, respectively, stimulus, response, and index. In a very real sense there is no fundamental distinction among these three parts; the division is made only for descriptive purposes. Again, for the sake of being specific, we assume that the stimulus portion consists of 30 bits organized into 15 groups of 2 bits each. Each group corresponds to a single characteristic of interest; the associated two bits are used to assign a value for that characteristic with respect to a particular pattern. Similarly, the response portion of a pattern also consists of 30 bits organized into 15 groups of 2 bits each with exactly a corresponding interpretation. Thus the stimulus and response sections of the patterns together consist of 60 bits representing the value assigned to each of 30 characteristics. We make the distinction between stimulus and response only to reflect a probable difference in the degree of utilization of the two portions, that is, we call one portion the stimulus because we anticipate that these characteristics will most often be prescribed by the environment and that the response characteristics will most often be provided by the file. However, the distinction is an artificial one, and there is nothing to prevent any characteristic from being prescribed by the environment and any other characteristic from being provided by the file. The index portion of a pattern has a basically different role, and it is to be questioned whether it should, in fact, be included as part of the pattern. However, for the moment it is necessary, and its significance will be defined at a later time.

Patterns are created by a combination of the environment and file action, that is, for certain of the characteristics within a pattern, the associated value will be defined or prescribed by some mechanism external to the function of the file; the remaining portion of the pattern will be determined on the basis of file operations. As we have indicated, the distinction between stimulus and response portions of a pattern is merely a reflection of the probable source of definition for the respective characteristics. When the characteristic is not prescribed by the environment and must therefore be provided by the file operation, the lack of prescribed value is indicated by a symbol which we will interpret as "question" or "Q." Thus, in the definitive pattern as we have described it above, where the value for each characteristic is given by two bits, one of the four possible values must represent question. This, then, allows us to have three other values for any characteristic. We interpret these as high, medium, or low.

The foregoing defines the patterns (with the exception of the definition of the indexing portion of the pattern) and the environment. It is now necessary to define the operation of the file. We interpret the file as consisting of stored patterns divided into levels which, for the immediate purposes, we limit to two levels. The extension to more levels is almost self-evident. The first level is one of limited capacity, which, for the purposes of being specific, we prescribe as twenty patterns. Capacity of the second level is considered as essentially infinite. The problems of its capacity limitations and organizational processes can be treated as identical in character to those which we outline for the first level.

The operation of this two-level file involves a number of individual procedures. The first is that involved in generating a pattern from an environment and the operation of the file. As we indicated, the environment will prescribe values for certain of the characteristics, leaving questions for the remainder where the file operation must supply the values. Such a partially prescribed pattern we will call a semipattern. The environmentally prescribed semipattern is then matched according to some rule of association with the twenty patterns stored in the first level of the file. As the result of this match there is a relative ranking of these twenty patterns in their order of association, according to the defined rule, with the semipattern. If patterns are found stored in the first level and have a degree of association to the semipattern greater than some defined limit, then the values for the questioned characteristics will be provided by some relative weighting of the corresponding characteristics from the stored patterns most closely associated with the semipattern. For example, one such weighting would be to take that stored pattern most closely associated with the semipattern with a weight of one and all others with a weight of zero. Another possible weighting would be to weight each pattern by its degree of association with the semipattern. If no pattern is found stored at the first level with a degree of association to the semipattern greater than the prescribed limit, then an additional procedure called "remembering," outlined later, must be introduced.

Before describing the process of remembering, however, we must describe the process of "forgetting." The patterns, created from environmental semipatterns and file-created answers to questions, must be stored in the first level. It is clear that whatever finite limit was placed on the first level, its capacity would eventually be exceeded; therefore some process must be defined for getting rid of patterns from this first level. This is accomplished in the following way. A quantity is determined by some relative weighting of past relevancy of each pattern stored in the first level, with the immediate relevancy or association of that pattern to the environmental semipattern. For example, one such weighting would be to take the past relevancy with the value of zero and the relevancy to the immediate environment with the value of one. On the basis of this quantity, the least relevant pattern or group of patterns will be "forgotten." The process for doing so is the following. The pattern to be forgotten will be matched with the patterns stored on the first level according to the same rule of association used for determining relevancy to environment. The pattern that is found to be most relevant to the pattern that is to be forgotten will define the location in which the pattern to be forgotten will be stored. This address, or location, will be determined from the indexing portion of the relevant pattern as follows. The indexing portion will consist of three addresses—the first, a starting address; the second, the next available address; and the third, the last address assigned in the second level of memory to the relevant pattern. The pattern to be forgotten will be stored in the next available address assigned to the relevant pattern and the next available address updated.

At this point several comments should be made. The first is that, as we have pointed out, to assign an index as part of a pattern seems artificial. The desirable step would be to determine location in the second level of memory directly from the relevant pattern, not counting the index portion, that is, by some operation on the 60 bits assigned to the values associated with the characteristics. For example, by some random-number generation process on those 60 bits, an address might be generated representing the starting address for the locations assigned to that particular pattern. For the moment, however, although this represents an ideal to be aimed for, the process for achieving it is not quite clear. A second comment which might be made concerns the possible change in the relevant pattern to reflect association with it of the forgotten pattern. Thus a new pattern might be created by some relative weighting of the relevant pattern and the forgotten pattern. For the moment we do not include this, for its effects are even less clear than any of the other considerations we are attempting to handle.

To return, now, to the process of remembering: when the patterns stored at the first level do not match the environmental semipattern to the specified degree of relevancy, recourse must be had to the second level of memory by means of the indexing data stored in the most nearly relevant patterns even though they are not sufficiently relevant. Thus the index portion of the most relevant pattern at the first level provides a mechanism for obtaining information from the second level which is brought up to the first level and examined for relevancy. This process continues until either index data are no longer found or patterns are found exceeding the prescribed limit of relevancy, or until some prescribed quantum of time, such as that involved in the acceptance of a new environmental semipattern, has passed.

In the procedure as outlined above, a number of rules must be specified. The first of these relates to the determination of the degree of association between patterns or between semipatterns and patterns. A number of such rules could be defined. For example, the dot product in the vector sense in the ordered sets of numbers associated with the 30 characteristics would be one such rule. This could be generalized by providing a relative weighting of characteristics in the order of their importance. A second rule is that involved in the generation of the file-determined portions of a pattern. As we have indicated, this can be by means of some relative weighting of the stored patterns by their order of relevancy to the environmental semipattern. A third rule is the procedure for prescribing the location in the second level to which a pattern is to be forgotten.

15

Theories of system design[1]

The type of theory discussed in the previous chapter provides a structure for what is probably the basic problem in information retrieval—that of file organization. However, it fails to account for the fact that a file exists not as an isolated component but as a part of a total system of components tied together by a set of operations, that is, we might define an information (storage and retrieval) system as a collection of component subsystems which, operating together, perform a set of operations in the accomplishment of the defined purpose of the system. The aims in information system design are, therefore, to:

1. define the purpose of the system in terms so that the system can be designed to accomplish it,
2. select the component subsystems and the operations connecting them so as to carry out this purpose,
3. do this according to some criterion or measurement of "optimum."

Such system design is related to other types of system design, such as servomechanism design, but it can be distinguished from them in the following ways. The significant interrelationship among the component subsystems is the operational one rather than the physical one, so that, in an information system, the operations occupy a crucial role. Normal feedback considerations are less critical, with a relatively long-time constant compared to operating speeds. The input is generally discrete and relatively inconsistent.

---

[1] The work described in this chapter was supported in part by the United States Air Force under Contract AF 30(602)–2111.

There appear to be a number of mathematical tools applicable to information system design, and several of these have, at one time or another, been used. For example, the methods of queuing theory provide a means for designing the system in terms of the probable time sequence of events. The methods of information theory allow for the measurement of quantity of information handled. The methods of servomechanism theory allow for the evaluation of dynamic response.

However, none of these has really provided an adequate answer to the problems in information system design. In part, this has been due to the lack of an adequate criterion, or measurement of value, so basic to the design and application of any model. This criterion must provide a means of measuring value which is consistent with the accepted usage. The consequences of the measure, once it is established, cannot be ignored if the model is to be more than merely shorthand. Such a measure has been the starting point for development of the model described in this chapter.

THE MODEL

The model is based on the following set of definitions:

1. A *job,* which represents the defined purpose of the system, consists of a set of defined operations, $O_1, O_2, \ldots, O_m)$, and a volume (or traffic load) for each operation, $(v_1, v_2, \ldots, v_m)$. For the purposes of this model, the extent to which the defined set of operations actually represents the job to be performed is not evaluated, that is, once the set of operations has been defined, it, together with the associated set of volumes, is the job.

2. A *component* is a defined means of performing some parts of some of these operations. This means that its costs, operating speeds, and equipment sophistication characteristics are all well defined.

3. One can determine the *efficiency* with which a given component performs in the execution of a given operation. This efficiency is measured as a function of cost, time, and size of the operation, that is, efficiency is given by

$$a = f(C, T, N).$$

For the purposes of this model, we have chosen

$$a = \frac{CT}{N}$$

as the simplest such function. If C is in units of dollars per time, T is in time, and N is in bits, then a has units of dollars per bit—or dollars per processing unit.

4. A *total system*, consisting of a set of components, $(s_1, s_2, \ldots, s_n)$, required to perform the set of operations, is represented by a matrix of their respective efficiencies,

$$A = (a_{ij}),$$

on each of the operations. This matrix is called the "efficiency matrix" for the system. This efficiency a_{ij} is represented by the following type of formulation:

$$a_{ij} = \frac{C_{ij} \cdot T_{ij}}{N_{ij}}$$

where C_{ij} is the cost per unit time of the component when it is performing operation O_j; T_{ij} is the time during which it is required to perform on operation O_j; and N_{ij} is a measure of the size of operation O_j, generally speaking, in units of "bit."

In summary, a system is represented by a matrix of efficiency values. The rows of this matrix correspond to the individual components; the columns of the matrix correspond to the individual operations. The element a_{ij} in this matrix is then the efficiency with which the ith component performs on the jth operation.

If A is the efficiency matrix for a system and

$$\vec{v} = (v_1, v_2, \ldots, v_m)$$

is the volume vector (in processing units per unit time) for the set of operations, the equation

$$A\vec{v} = \vec{x}$$

can be defined and yields what we call the *required* cost vector (in dollars per unit time)

$$\vec{x} = (x_1, x_2, \ldots, x_n).$$

We will interpret the component x_i of this vector as the cost for component s_i required to perform the given volume of the set of operations at the defined efficiencies. In general, it will be expected that the set of *actual* costs for the components will not be given by the vector $\vec{x}$ but rather by the vector

$$\vec{c} = (c_1, c_2, \ldots, c_n), \qquad \text{where } c_i \geq x_i.$$

It should be pointed out that there is nothing really startling in this representation. It is, in fact, a very close picture of the intellectual process involved in time and cost estimation in system design.

Problems in Determining Component Efficiencies

In developing the matrix A of component efficiencies on system operations, the determination of the elements represents a significant system analysis problem. This problem has two aspects. The first relates to the problems in evaluating component performance itself. Thus, for example, the costs of a component are sometimes difficult to determine; the time a component is required to perform a given task usually involves a complete programming of the steps which the component must perform in order to accomplish the task, and no adequate measure usually exists for the operation complexity or size.

The second and more complex aspect is the evaluation of the role which the component plays in the performance of a given operation, of the degree to which the component is "tied up" during the performance of the operation, and of the relationship among components and operations. Thus we may be concerned with the question of how to handle component subsystems which are "tied up" during the performance of an operation. For example, if a magnetic tape unit cannot function independently, how should it be treated during an operation of computation?

Two separate cases can be distinguished. The first case is where some degree of independent operation is possible. A component may not be directly involved during the entire time required for performing an operation, and, in addition, there may be other tasks which the component can effectively perform during this time. In this case, the element of the efficiency matrix, for that component on that operation, will reflect only the actual time during which the component is involved. In particular, if the component is not involved on the operation at all, the element will be zero.

The second alternative would arise if, under the same conditions, there was no other operation on which the component could function even though it was free to do so. Under these conditions, the element may or may not reflect the actual time during which the component is involved in the performance of the operation, depending on the judgment of the system designer. If he wished to allow some reflection of excess capability, he might well have the element of the efficiency matrix show only the actual operating time. Then the actual costs would be greater, by that amount, than the required costs. On the other hand, if the system designer did not feel that the excess capacity should be considered, he would treat the component as though it were completely tied up during the entire time of the operation. In this case, the component is charged for the full time and the elements of the efficiency matrix reflect this fact.

To illustrate the various considerations, consider a system of components S_1, a computer, and S_2, a tape searching unit, of operations O_1 computing, O_2 searching, and O_3, a third job available to the computer in any free time. For convenience, assume $C_1 = 10$, $C_2 = 1$. As the first example, suppose that the two components are completely independent and that the tape time for searching, say T, is always greater than the computing time $T - D$ on O_1, but the computer can effectively work on operation O_3 during any free time.

$$A = \begin{bmatrix} 10(T - D) & 0 & 10D \\ 0 & T & 0 \end{bmatrix}.$$

On the other hand, if there is no alternative job O_3, the system designer has the choice between

$$A = \begin{bmatrix} 10(T - D) & 0 \\ 0 & T \end{bmatrix}$$

and

$$A = \begin{bmatrix} 10(T - D) & 10D \\ 0 & T \end{bmatrix}.$$

Thus we must distinguish between two situations. The one arises when the equipment is essentially interdependent insofar as the system is concerned, and the second occurs when the equipment is essentially independent insofar as the system is concerned, but there is a problem of time overlap because of inefficiencies in matching time loads. In the second case the basic problem is that of determining what, in fact, the required maximum time is and therefore what both the required costs and the minimum actual costs really are. This produces no problem if the time of the one unit in overlapping operation is always less than that of the other unit, as we have illustrated above. For example, see Figure 83. The problems arise when this is not so (cf. Figure 84).

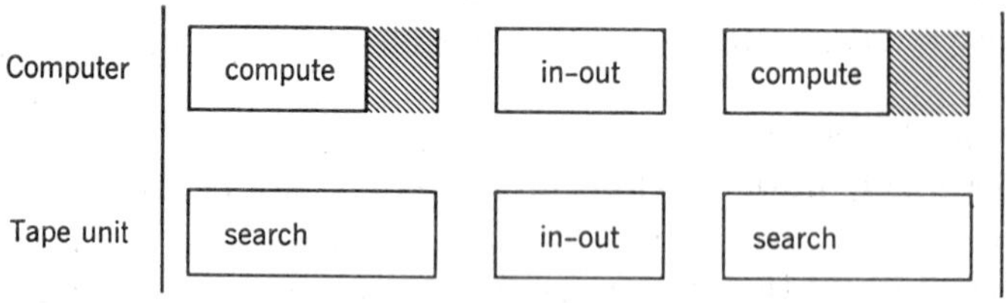

FIG. 83. Overlapping operations—one component dominant.

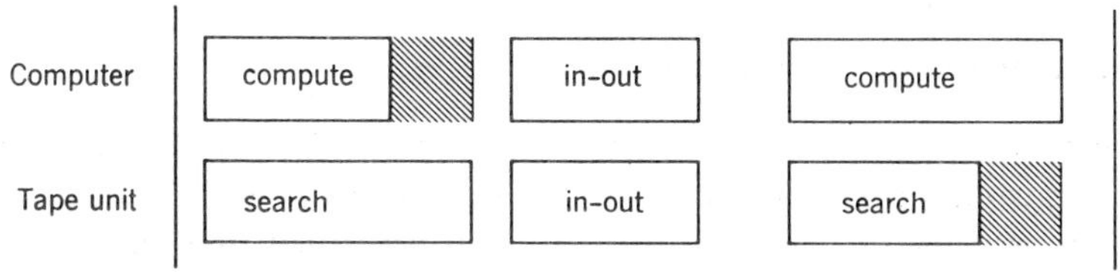

FIG. 84. Overlapping operations—neither component dominant.

To illustrate the problem, consider a set of N sorted items which are being searched for in a file containing aN items. The average searching time will then be proportional to a. However, the individual searching times will, in general, vary quite widely. The distribution of searching times is given, to a quite reasonable approximation, by the geometric distribution.

$$P(m, a) = \frac{1}{a}\left(1 - \frac{1}{a}\right)^m$$

The number of items which will require a given searching time cm, where c is some constant of proportionality, is given by $NP(m, a)$.

Now, suppose that each item also involves some fixed times—input, output, computing—and suppose we are trying to time share these operations with the searching operation. Let the fixed times total to ct. For a given item involving a searching time cm, cm might be less than, equal to, or greater than ct. In any event, the *operating* time will equal the maximum of the two.

Under such circumstances, we could choose one of the components, say the computer, as independent. Then the others, the tape in this case, would show their dependence during overlap inefficiencies but not the other way around. The required maximum time is then the maximum among the times of the other components. Another approach would handle all units as essentially functioning for the same time. Basically the decision is based on an evaluation of whether the overlap time was *potentially* usable. If it is, as may be true with the computer, then the element of the efficiency matrix will reflect the lower time and the operating efficiency will indicate the lowering in effectiveness. If the time is not potentially usable, as with a tape unit which has finished searching, then the efficiency matrix will reflect the lower time and the operating efficiency will indicate the lowering in effectiveness. If the time is not potentially usable, as with a tape unit which has finished searching, then the efficiency matrix will reflect the unavailable time by charging it to the searching operation.

Measures of Total System Efficiency

Given the matrix representation of a system, the problem now is to find a reasonable measure of "total system efficiency" in terms of the relevant parameters a_{ij}, v_j, x_i, and c_i. Several such measures can be considered, and we will review those which appear to be of greatest interest.

A natural approach is to use the normalized quadratic cost as the measure of total system efficiency. This would mean defining total system efficiency as

$$a = \frac{CT}{N} \qquad \text{where } a^2 = \frac{A\vec{v}\cdot A\vec{v}}{\vec{v}\cdot\vec{v}}.$$

This so-called "rms" measure of efficiency leads immediately, as we pointed out in Chapter 13, to consideration of the eigenvalues and vectors of matrix A^*A, since a^2 is the Rayleigh quotient for the matrix A^*A. Thus those distributions of volume, $\vec{v}$, for which $A^*A\vec{v} = a^2\vec{v}$, represent the volumes for which system efficiency will be critical, that is, maximum, minimum, or other critical values of a^2.

A more interesting variant of this, from the mathematical standpoint, is to consider the generalization of the classical eigenvalue theory to handle a non-positive-definite, nonsquare matrix A directly. It can be shown [2] that for any matrix A, there exists a unique matrix R with the property that $RR^* = AA^{-1}$ (where A^{-1} is the generalized reciprocal of the matrix A) and such that the equation $A\vec{v} = aR\vec{v}$ has for its solution positive a's and R-orthogonal eigenvectors $\vec{v}$. This yields as a measure of efficiency

$$a = \frac{R\vec{v}\cdot A\vec{v}}{\vec{v}\cdot\vec{v}}.$$

A third and fourth measure of efficiency are provided by the reciprocals of one and the other of the first two, corresponding to the reciprocal eigenvalue problems. In the first case,

$$\frac{1}{a^2} = \frac{(A^{-1}\vec{x})\cdot(A^{-1}\vec{x})}{\vec{x}\cdot\vec{x}} \qquad \text{from } (A^*A)^{-1}\vec{x} = \frac{1}{a^2}\vec{x}.$$

For the second one,

$$\frac{1}{a} = \frac{(R^*\vec{x})\cdot(A^{-1}\vec{x})}{\vec{x}\cdot\vec{x}} \qquad \text{from } A^{-1}\vec{x} = \frac{1}{a}R^*\vec{x}.$$

---

[2] Magnus R. Hestenes, Inversion of Matrices by Biorthogonalization and Related Results, *Journal of Soc. Indust. Appl. Math.*, March 1958, v. 6, No. 1.

Chebyshev-type measures can also be considered. These are generally much more difficult to handle analytically, but the tools of linear programming are available. These measures include, for example,

$$a = \frac{\Sigma |x_i|}{\Sigma |v_i|} \quad \text{and} \quad a = \frac{\max x_i}{\max v_i}.$$

None of these measures provides any consideration of the actual cost c. They might therefore be considered as theoretical efficiencies. Since an operating installation will involve actual costs greater than the required costs, we are concerned with the relationship between theoretical efficiency and operating efficiency. There are three values of interest:

$$a_1 = \frac{(A\vec{v} \cdot A\vec{v})}{(\vec{v} \cdot \vec{v})}, \quad a_2 = \frac{(\vec{c} \cdot A\vec{v})}{(\vec{v} \cdot \vec{v})}, \quad a_3 = \frac{(\vec{c} \cdot \vec{c})}{(\vec{v} \cdot \vec{v})}.$$

The first is theoretical efficiency; the second, operating efficiency; the third, rms cost per unit of rms volume. In effect, operating efficiency attempts to compromise between actual cost and theoretical cost (for the volume). Measures of operating efficiency must consider the nonhomogeneous counterparts of the eigenvalue equations. If we consider

$$b = a_2 + a_1 = \frac{(\vec{c} + A\vec{v}) \cdot (A\vec{v})}{(\vec{v} \cdot \vec{v})},$$

this leads to the equation

$$-A^*A\vec{v} + b\vec{v} = A^*\vec{c}.$$

On the other hand,

$$b = a_3 + a_2 = \frac{(\vec{c} + A\vec{v}) \cdot (\vec{c})}{(\vec{v} \cdot \vec{v})}$$

leads to the equation

$$-A\vec{v} + b\frac{(\vec{v} \cdot \vec{v})}{(\vec{v} \cdot \vec{c})}\vec{v} = \vec{c},$$

and thus is simply a different normalization of the other equation. This leads to measures of operating efficiency corresponding to the previously considered measures of theoretical efficiency.

These three classes of measure provide three separate weightings of the actual costs and the required costs. The first considers only the required cost, the second equal weighting of the two, and the third only the actual costs. Other weightings are possible, and the general form can be represented by an appropriate combination of a_1 and a_2 (or a_2 and a_3).

All of the above measures of both theoretical and operating efficiencies assume that the operations are measured in consistent units so that the normalizing value can be considered as, for example, the simple quadratic length of the volume vector. It is to be expected, however, that in practice the operations will not be defined in consistent terms but rather will have some relative weighting of importance so that we can establish a matrix B consisting of values b_{ij} reporting the relative importance of the operations O_i to O_j. The quadratic form $\vec{v} \cdot B\vec{v}$ will then provide a normalizing factor which will reflect this relative importance with which the volume vectors are to be viewed. In this way, the more important operations will receive a heavier weighting in the normalizing factor. These measures, including the different possible weightings of actual and required costs and the different possible weightings of the operations, can be summarized, for the rms case, by the measure

$$e^2 = w_1 \frac{A\vec{v} \cdot A\vec{v}}{\vec{v} \cdot B\vec{v}} + w_2 \frac{\vec{c} \cdot A\vec{v}}{\vec{v} \cdot B\vec{v}}.$$

Given a specified choice among the above available measures or others, two different systems represented respectively by efficiency matrices A_1 and A_2, volumes $\vec{v}_1$ and $\vec{v}_2$, and actual costs $\vec{c}_1$ and $\vec{c}_2$ can be compared and evaluated for their relative efficiencies. Furthermore, if in the representation of a given system certain parameters are left as variable, the specified measure of system efficiency can be maximized with respect to them.

APPLICATION TO SYSTEM EFFICIENCY

Application of the model has been made to the evaluation of the efficiency of several systems of increasing complexity. The first of these considers the single component as a part of a larger system whose characteristics, other than cost, are unspecified and thus without consideration of other system components and their characteristics. The examples within this context include core memories and drum memories.

The second set of problems is concerned with systems of several components. The first of these considers multiple level memories and provides criteria for determination of the most effective relative sizes of the levels. The second considers the organization of information contained in an indexed memory and provides criteria for determining the most suitable such organization. The third is concerned with the analysis of a particular type of file organization based on a multiple level indexing structure combined with a multiple level memory. The fourth considers this file organization in the context of other system operations and provides criteria for determining the most effective set of such operations.

The following summarizes the results of these illustrative examples. Details can be found in the referenced report.[3]

Single Component in a System

Consider the single component with respect to a single operation as part of a larger system whose characteristics, except the costs, are otherwise unspecified. It thus represents a transition stage to consideration of multiple component systems. To do this requires the use of the model to provide an evaluation of total system efficiency, for we are concerned with more than just the isolated component. The analysis showed that the factor

$$\frac{C - C_i}{C} \cdot \frac{N_i}{C_i T_i}$$

can be considered as a measure of the role which the cost distribution $\check{x}_i$ plays in the efficiency of the total system.

To illustrate this application of the model, we have examined core memories within the context of a total computing system whose characteristics, other than cost, are unspecified. The results of the analysis are shown in the form of a chart which presents a series of curves plotting the efficiency factor defined above as a function of the capacity of the core memory, with total system cost as a parameter. Each curve presents the efficiency of the core memory as a part of a system whose total system cost is a particular value of C. These curves, presented in Figure 85 are based on the following assumptions concerning the characteristics of core memories.

1. It is assumed that the cost of a core memory, as a function of its capacity, is given by the equation $C_C = 13n^{4/5}$ where n is the capacity in bits (an arbitrary approximation derived from the data presented in Chapter 12).
2. It is assumed that the access time to any bit in this memory is 15 microseconds.
3. The operation of core memory is considered solely as that of input and output, and the size of this operation is measured by the capacity, n in bits, of the core memory.

---

[3] Advanced Information Systems Company, Final Report: Mathematical Models for Information System Design and a Calculus of Operations, Air Force Contract AF 30(602)-2111, 1961.

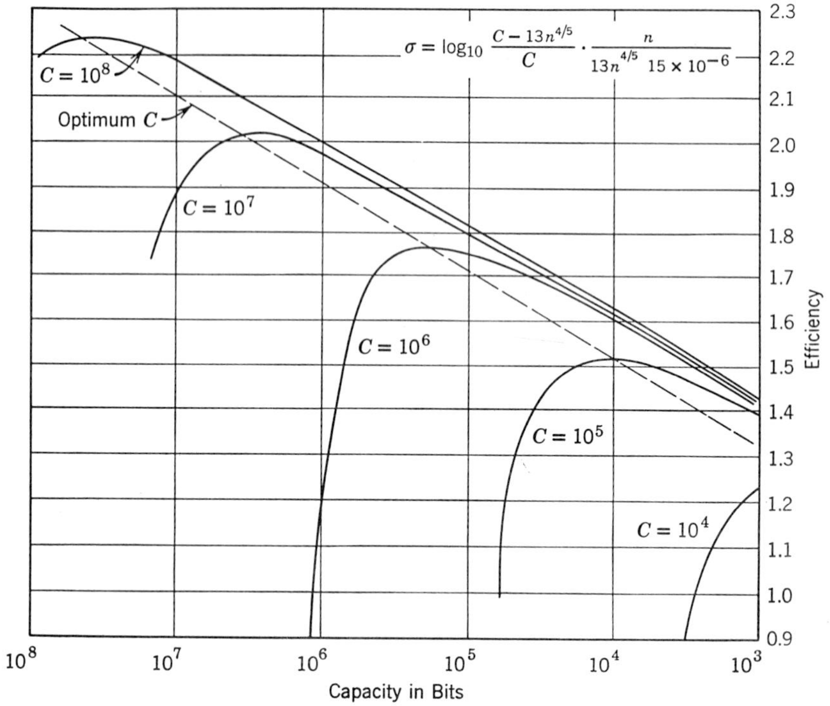

FIG. 85. Core memory efficiencies. Advanced Information Systems Company, Mathematical Models for Information Systems Design and A Calculus of Operations, Report to Rome Air Development Center, Contract AF 30(602)–2111, ASTIA Document No. AD266577, 1961.

For purposes of comparison, the same analysis has been made utilizing the same measure of efficiency and efficiency factor for viewing a drum memory within the context of a total system. The following assumptions were made concerning the characteristics of drum memories.

1. The cost of a drum memory can be expressed by the following formula: $C_D = 13n^{2/3}$ where n is the capacity of the drum memory in bits.
2. The average access time to any bit in the memory was assumed to be 15 milliseconds.
3. The operation was also only that of input and output and was measured by the capacity of the drum system.

Under these assumptions, Figure 86 presents the efficiency.

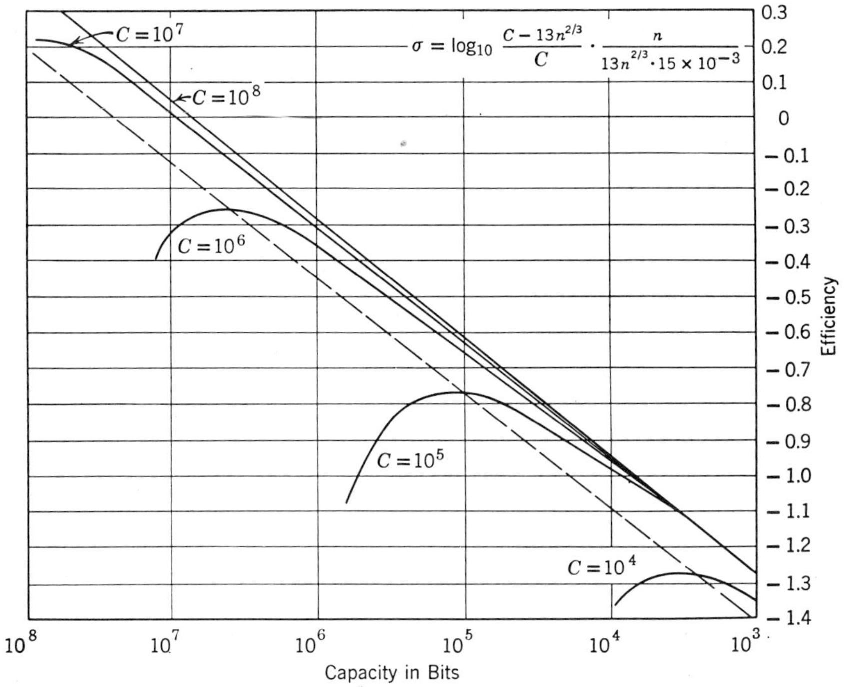

FIG. 86. Drum memory efficiencies. Advanced Information Systems Company, Mathematical Models for Information Systems Design and A Calculus of Operations, Report to Rome Air Development Center, Contract AF 30(602)–2111, ASTIA Document No. AD266577, 1961.

Memory Levels

This example considered a system with several levels of random access memory. The first and smallest level has an effective access time much less than that of the other and larger memories. In such a system, the effective random access time for the entire memory is a value intermediate to the access times of the two levels; the exact value is dependent primarily on the relative usage of the two levels. If the system includes some means for interlevel exchange of data, the effective access time becomes a function also of the number of interconnecting channels, the quantity of data transferred simultaneously, and the degree of parallel operation allowed.

Systems of this type have been discussed previously by researchers at the National Bureau of Standards Data Processing Systems Division. In a report published in September 1955,[4] R. B. Marimont of NBS investigated this type of system with the aim of determining its effective random access time. The results were as follows:

A weighting factor r is defined as the fractional usage of the slow memory; it is the number of references to the slow memory divided by the total number of references. It is a function of the sizes of the two memories and of the particular problem being computed. We have $r(x)$, the fraction of references to all cells used less frequently than x. If our fast memory includes all cells from the origin up through x, and our slow memory all those from $x + 1$ to the end, the $r(x)$ is the fraction of references made to the slow memory. If we know $r(x)$ we can predict the average operating speed of any combination of fast and slow memories, provided that all the most frequently used words are in the fast memory.

The function $r(x)$ is useful in choosing two from several memories. If we plot cost per word as the abscissa and effective access time as ordinate, any memory type is represented by a point in the plane. The effective access time of any combination of two memories is given by the $r(x)$ curve, suitably scaled so that its endpoints coincide with the two memory points in question.

The analysis utilized some of the results of these studies but extended them to include the considerations covered by the model. To be specific, the sample system analyzed consisted of a drum memory with a total capacity of words. These words are stored in some number of channels of "long lines," of specified length, and some number (to be determined) of channels of "short lines," whose length is also to be determined.

This system is called on to perform two types of operation—operation one, access to the large, slow, long lines, and operation two, access to the small, fast, short lines. The resulting efficiency matrix can then be defined.

To determine the theoretical efficiency of a given distribution of activity, we would need to examine the measure of system efficiency for that particular distribution. To illustrate this, the example chose a distribution of activity which is exponential with respect to the number of words as an approximation to the data from the NBS experiments, that is, if the words in a program are arranged in sequence from the most active to the least active, the relative utilization of the n most active words is approximated by the function

$$f = 1 - 10^{-n/g}.$$

---

[4] R. B. Marimont, Use of Small Fast and Large Slow Memories to Improve Machine Operation, National Bureau of Standards Data Processing Systems Division, Washington, D.C., September 27, 1955.

The value of the constant g provides a measure of the degree of concentration of activity; the smaller g, the more heavily concentrated is the activity in relatively few words.

The values of k and m (the number and length of short lines) could then be chosen to maximize the measure of system efficiency under this distribution of activity.

File Arrangement

In order to utilize storage devices properly, the prospective user needs to be guided by objective criteria which effectively relate the problem of indexing external file storage devices to the procedures of the user, to the characteristics of the particular application, and to the other components of the hardware system.

Moreover, not only is it important to consider indexing methods as they pertain to external storage files, but one must also consider the arrangement of the files and the processing method to be used. Thus a file may be randomly arranged or completely ordered, and processing may be random or sequential. (A randomly arranged file is one in which there is no correlation between a record's identification key and its physical location in the file. A completely ordered file is one in which every record has a key equal to or less than the following record and equal to or greater than the preceding record. Between these two endpoints of file arrangements any degree of mixture is possible.) Similarly, processing may be random, where the next record to be processed may be located anywhere in the storage file, or sequential, where all records are processed in the same sequence as they are physically located in the file. Here, too, any degree of mixture is possible and may be defined for the particular information processing job.

It is the relationships among these interdependent factors, all of which need to be considered, which are given by the tools of the model. A sequence of examples was developed to show how each of the factors in the model can be related to the others. The examples are based on hypothetical choices of equipment parameters and on specific assumptions concerning the characteristics of the application involved. They leave certain parameters of the equipment or the job as variables for which the operational system efficiency can be maximized. They all consider the problem of storing a large file in a disk-type memory.

Two types of file organization were considered for such a problem, the sequential and the random. The sequential file arrangement will involve a combination of external indexing and multiple accesses to the file in order to randomly access an item. Random access time will thus depend on the particular method of indexing chosen. On the other hand, in the randomly arranged file, address generation will be used to define the file address, and the access time will be almost solely dependent on the speeds of the disk-type memory itself.

Among the considerations on which the choice between these two methods of file arrangement would be based is the relative proportion of random activity to sequential activity, such as report preparation. The first example illustrated how criteria could be provided for making this choice objectively. It illustrated how a broad range of complexity in the size and relationship among system elements can be accommodated. The second example then illustrated how criteria can be provided for selection among various methods of indexing into a sequential file arrangement. It did this by allowing the size of an external index to the file to be a parameter and then determining the optimum size for this parameter under varying conditions. It also considered the effect of such an external index on other processing operations and, in particular, on the size of available program memory. In this way the choice of method of indexing involved not only the characteristics of the file and its activity but also the characteristics of other parts of the total processing problem. The third example then considered the relationship between file searching in a sequential file and the batching and sorting necessary to utilize it effectively.

To illustrate how the model is applied to this type of problem, we reproduce the second example—that one concerned with the size of the external index.

Several different methods of indexing, involving different sizes of external index, are to be compared. The significant factors in doing so are the cost for the external index as a function of its size, the speed of searching it, and the effective reduction in file search time as this size increases.

Consider the size of the external index as a parameter. As the size of such an index increases, the physical location of the desired item is initially approximated more closely, and the number of comparisons with file items is reduced. Thus the effect of the index is to reduce the access time by eliminating some of the more costly item accesses for comparison with file items. Using the disk-type memory as an

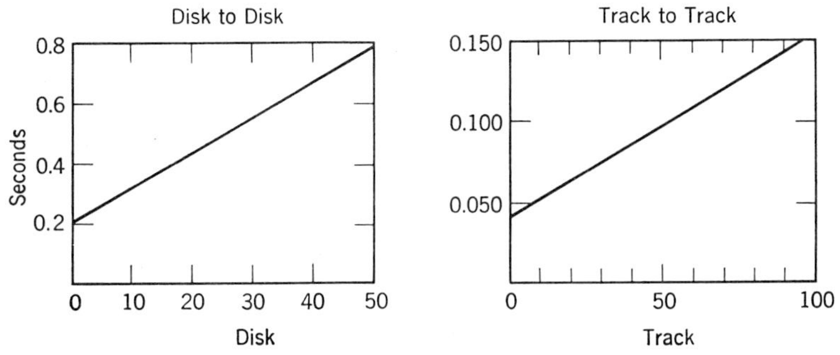

FIG. 87. Disk memory access times.

example, the access times for varying distances of search are given by the pair of charts in Figure 87. If there were no external index, a search would be required through the 50 disks, then through the 100 tracks on the disk, and then through the 10 sectors on the track. The time required for the approximately 16 accesses involved in a binary search of the file would be about 3.0 seconds, based on these charts; the first access would require 0.5 seconds; successive ones proportionally less. As the size of the external index is increased, the initial access places the accessing mechanism physically closer to the desired item so that the time for later access is reduced. The total time can be approximated by the function

$$T = 0.5 + \frac{2}{1 + \log_2 (n/32)},$$

assuming 32 bit words as suitable for comparison purposes.

If we now consider a system consisting of a disk memory and a core memory index, costs are, respectively,

$$C_1 = 5 \times 10^4, \quad C_2 = 13n^{4/5};$$

then the efficiency of the combined components will be given by

$$a = (13n^{4/5} + 5 \times 10^4)\left(0.5 + \frac{2}{1 + \log_2 (n/32)}\right).$$

Table 15 tabulates this function for various values of n.

TABLE 15

Tabulated Efficiency Values

$n/32$	n	a
0	0	12.5×10^4
30	10^3	4.5×10^4
50	1.6×10^3	4.38×10^4
60	2×10^3	4.4×10^4
70	2.24×10^3	4.44×10^4
120	4×10^3	4.5×10^4
240	8×10^3	4.8×10^4

Source: Same as for Table 10.

Optimum occurs for n about 1600 bits or 50 words. The average index time will be 0.8 second; cost of external index will be about $5000.

In doing so, the size of the external index is considered initially only in its relation to the file indexing problem and not in its effect on other operations of the total system. However, given a fixed size of memory, if some portion of it is devoted to file indexing, that portion is not available for other usage, such as program storage. Therefore the example then considers this effect by assuming that the percentage of items for which the full computational work can be performed by a memory is a function of the size of that memory. If the program memory is limited, then only a certain portion of the computational activity will be accommodated by it. To handle other percentages would then require picking up additional portions of the program (perhaps from the disk file) when they are needed.

To illustrate this, we let the size of the available program memory be a parameter and develop the matrix which represents the various components and operations. The components will be the program memory and the disk file. The operations will be, first, those transactions for which program memory space is adequate for processing and, second, those for which access to the disk memory is required. The cost per month of the program memory is assumed as given by the formula $C = 0.2n^{4/5}$ where n is in bits, a reasonably close estimate of core memory costs; that of the disk memory, as $1000 per month. The time for execution of the first class of operations will be arbitrarily assumed as 0.1 second; that for execution of the second class of operations is the same, as far as program time is concerned, but includes an additional 1.0 second for required accesses to the disk memory. The resulting matrix is given by

$$\begin{array}{l} \\ \text{Program Memory} \\ \text{Disk Memory} \end{array} \begin{array}{cc} \text{Class 1 Operations} & \text{Class 2 Operations} \\ \left[\begin{array}{c} 0.2n^{4/5} \times 0.1 \\ 0 \end{array}\right. & \left.\begin{array}{c} 0.2n^{4/5} \times 1.1 \\ 1000 \times 1.0 \end{array}\right] \end{array}$$

To determine the optimum n, the relative volumes of Class 1 and Class 2 operations must be known. We assume, as before, that there are dependent on n in the following way: $V_1 = 1 - 10^{-n/g}$, $V_2 = 10^{-n/g}$ where g is a characteristic of the type of processing activity. A typical value might be $g = 10^5$, so that 1000 words of 30 bits each would handle half the activity, and 2000 words of 30 bits each would handle three fourths of the activity, etc. Using $g = 10^5$, we obtain

$$\begin{bmatrix} 0.02n^{4/5} & 0.22n^{4/5} \\ 0 & 1000 \end{bmatrix} \begin{bmatrix} 1 - 10^{-10^{-5}n} \\ 10^{-10^{-5}n} \end{bmatrix} = \begin{bmatrix} n^{4/5} \; (0.02 + 0.2 \times 10^{-10^{-5}n}) \\ 10^{3-10^{-5}n} \end{bmatrix}$$

The value of n for which the sum of the two component costs is a minimum can be calculated as about 150,000 bits, or 5000 words of 30 bits each. Under these conditions about 2½% of the total activity will require access to the disk file. The example can be extended to other situations by varying the computing time, the relative proportions of activity, etc.

Normally, of course, we would choose the external core memory in light of the problems both of indexing the random access memory and of providing adequate space for program and data storage. With these considerations in mind, what is the effect of storing an index in the memory? Certainly, although it improves access time to the disk memory, it reduces the space available for program and data storage. To illustrate how such a situation might be analyzed, the example considers a combined system of a disk memory and a core memory with costs and so on as described previously. Normally there will be a minimal required program storage K and a remaining storage n which can be devoted to either index data, n_1, or incremental program storage, $n - n_1$. Data must be obtained from the disk memory each computational cycle, but, in addition, on some percentage of the computational cycles additional program steps must be obtained from the disk memory. There are thus three operations on which the configuration of equipment must function.

1. Computing.
2. Access to disk for additional program steps.
3. Indexing to disk for filed data.

The volume of activity for the second operation will then be a function of how large the incremental program storage is; the smaller the program storage, the more frequently additional instructions must be brought from the disk memory.

Information Retrieval

Additional examples were developed to show how the measure CT/N relates to information retrieval operations. CT/N is expressed as a function of the file organization and of the equipment and system characteristics: storage costs, processing costs, acquisition rates, processing rates, file size, search procedures, and so on. A model of information retrieval is developed and used with CT/N to provide an explicit solution for retrieval problems. One of the examples developed is presented below—the rotary card file example.

In all of the examples a retrieval file consists of a set of basic file elements R and additional elements used to refer to the R elements for search purposes. It is assumed that the individual elements in the file can be brought together in groups and referred to through their group membership. Similarly, these groups can be combined into higher order groups and again referenced by their membership. As a result, the file may be represented by a tree structure like that shown in Figure 88. The elements of R are represented by the terminal nodes and the groups by the nonterminal nodes.

Search trees have two extreme configurations. At the one extreme the tree consists of only one level containing the set R. This tree has the lowest storage requirement—that necessary to store R with no reference nodes. At the other extreme a binary tree (two nodes for each reference node) has the greatest storage requirement—space for the set R plus space for R reference nodes.

One element of R is provided in response to a search. The search steps involved are: acquire, process, and select. A search begins on the top level of the file. The nodes on this level are acquired, processed, and from them, one node is selected. The nodes on the second level referenced by the selected nodes are acquired and processed in turn. The selected node determines the nodes to be examined on the

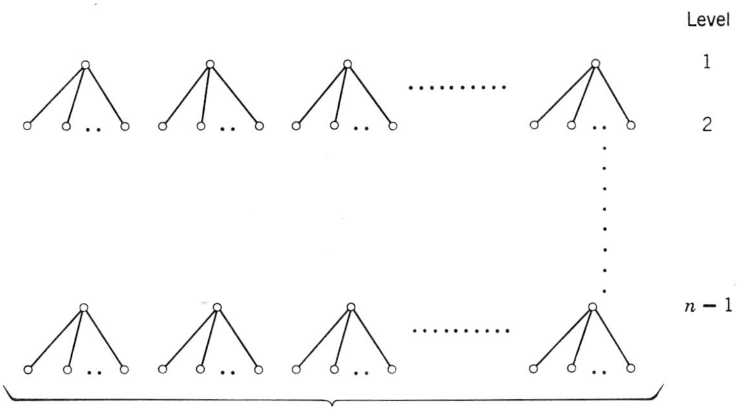

FIG. 88. Tree structure of a file.

third level, and so forth, through the file levels. When a terminal node is selected, the search terminates with this R element as the search result.

As a search progresses through the levels of the file, the selection control need not be the same. For example, it could be determined by the results of the search on the previous level. The file model requires only that there be available some method of search and some scheme of connection between a group and its members. The present concern is the implication of such connection for the total system organization and efficiency. As such, the relations that are obtained are compatible both with present techniques (library classification systems) and with more recent developments, for example, probabilistic indexing.

The average time required for a search is

$$\frac{T}{N} = \sum_{i=1}^{L} \left(\sum_{k=1}^{g_i} Pr_{i,k}(t_{ak} + t_{rk}) \right)$$

where Pr_{i_k} = probability of selecting kth group level i.
t_{a_k} = time to access kth group.
t_{r_k} = time for selection process kth group.
g_i = number of groups on level i.
L = number of file levels.

Given an estimate of the file activity, the tree structure may be modified to reduce the average time required for a search. There are two methods by which such a reduction can be accomplished. The order in which the nodes in a group are processed may be revised, thereby allowing a reduction in either or both of the access and process times. A reduction in the process time will then be accomplished if not all nodes of a group are processed for a selection. Even where all nodes are processed, the numbers of the most likely node may be positioned most accessibly. The second method of reducing the expected time is to move terminal nodes higher in the search tree. This allows the possibility of terminating search without processing all the levels of the file.

The above described analysis can be illustrated with a rotary card file system. The components and costs of the rotary card file system are represented in Table 16. Each of the basic file elements is written

TABLE 16

Rotary Card File System

Component and Associated Costs

		Dollars per Month
Raw cards	R	$\$4.10^{-5}R$
Guides	G	$2.10^{-3}G$
Trays	T	$0.2T$
Cradles	D	$0.4D + 0.8\,\frac{T}{D}$
File unit	U	40
Operator	O	400

$$C = 400 + 40 + 0.2T + 0.8\,\frac{T}{D} + 0.4D + 2.10^{-3}G + 4.10^{-5}R$$

Constraints

a. $D \leq 20$

b. $4 \leq \frac{T}{D} \leq 20$

c. $\frac{R + 5G}{T} \leq 100$

(all values are integer)

Source: same as for Table 10.

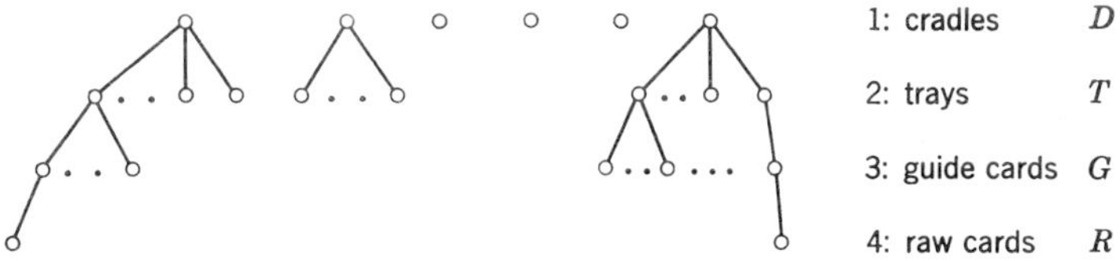

FIG. 89. Tree structure of rotary card file.

on a card. The cards are placed in trays with the guide cards interspersed. The guide cards are used to identify the groups. They are higher than the other cards and are searched before the individual cards. The trays are placed side by side on a cradle, and the cradles are mounted in a continuous loop within the file unit. The appropriate cradle is obtained by revolving the file until the cradle is in front of the operator. Figure 89 is an illustration of the tree representing this file. Table 17 lists the search procedure and the associated times. These times are average values. The efficient system

TABLE 17

Rotary Card File

Time and Procedure

	Time (seconds)
0. The operator starts a search.	
1. Scans the index to determine the proper cradle.	$0.1D$
2. Activates the file to position the proper cradle.	$0.5 \dfrac{4D}{30}$
3. Scans the trays on the cradle.	$0.05T$
4. Determines the proper tray and looks into it.	0
5. Scans the guides in the tray.	$0.05 \dfrac{G}{T}$
6. Grasps and withdraws a set of cards.	0.5
7. Searches the raw cards for the appropriate card. End.	$0.1 \dfrac{R}{G}$

$$\frac{T}{N} = 0.1D + 0.5 + \frac{4D}{30} + 0.05\frac{T}{D} + 0.05\frac{G}{T} + 0.5 + 0.1\frac{R}{G}$$

Source: same as for Table 10.

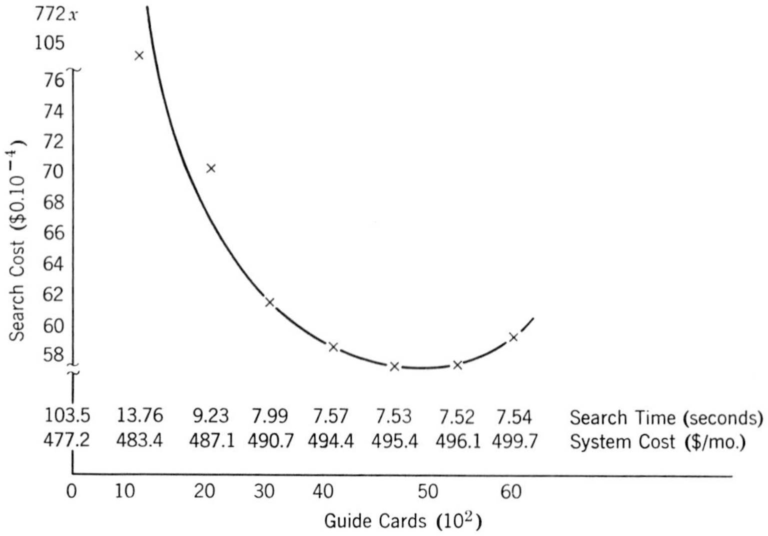

FIG. 90. Rotary card file efficiencies.

is obtained by determining the values of the system variables, D, T, G, and so on, which minimize CT/N. Inspection of the functions indicates that as a variable is changed, a trade off occurs between cost and time. For example, as the number of trays per cradle, T/D, is increased, the cost of the system is increased. On the other hand, reducing the number of cradles, for a fixed number of trays, allows a reduction in the amount of time required for a search. In general, it will be true that faster search will require a higher cost system. The object is to find that set of values which minimizes the product of cost and time. Figure 90 is a plot of the minimum obtainable cost of a search as a function of the number of guide cards G in the file. The two rows below the plot indicate the average time required for a search and the monthly system cost associated with each of the plotted points. In these calculations the trays were assumed to be completely filled with cards, that is, $T = R + 5G/1000$ was held as a strict equality. Thus the two free variables in the system were the number of guides G and the number of cradles D. Having obtained a minimum of CT/N on this basis, there are two adjustments yet to be made; all values must be integer, and the inequality relation on T must be reintroduced.

The system values for a minimum cost organization are $G = 4800$, $T = 140$, $D = 7$, $T/D = 20$, and the results are $C = \$500.4$ per month and $T/N = 7.42$ seconds per search. This result contains numerous implications. A minimum monthly cost system costs $475 per month, but the associated search time is 103 seconds. By properly balancing the system the time can be reduced to 7.42 seconds with a total system cost of $500.4 per month. The new time is 7% of the old and the monthly cost 105%. The efficient system yields a cost per search of $0.0059 as opposed to $0.0772 with the minimum monthly cost system. When about 5000 guides have been added to the file, the time saved through the reduction in number of raw cards searched is offset by the increased time in searching the guide cards. Thus no further time will be saved by adding guide cards. The longer the cradles, the more expensive they are but the shorter the search time because of faster access to the trays. Examination of the functions indicates that the maximum width (20 trays per cradle) cradles are most efficient. Even where this width is not required to hold the basic number of trays (e.g., where $T = 125$, $D = 7$, there need only be room for 18 trays per cradle), it is more desirable to carry 20 trays on each cradle and reduce the number of cards in each tray, thus reducing search time on the tray. However, it is not desirable to have more cradles than necessary, so there will be an attempt to avoid spilling over into another cradle by having a slight excess of cards.

In this particular system the costs are extremely responsive to the times. There is no reason why this should be the usual case. The reason it holds here is that a very considerable portion of the system costs are fixed; the operator salary alone is $400 per month. In addition, the guide cards are relatively inexpensive and minimize the time before much cost has been added. Finally, the trays are limited in the maximum number that can be added without adding a cradle, and a cradle addition increases the search time. As a result, increasing the system in this manner increases both cost and time.

The system that has been developed takes no advantage of the special usage characteristics that may exist. The search times were developed on the assumption that all the file would have about the same use; thus search time was assumed to be the sum of one-half the maximum cradle index time, one-half the maximum cradle access time, one-half the tray scan time, and so forth.

Where the usage on the raw items of the file is not about the same, one would wish to obtain the highly used items with less effort than the others. There are numerous ways one might accomplish this. One may move the highly used cards in front of the others; one may move a highly used group and its guide card up in the tray; one may position the highly used tray to be scanned first; and one would wish the cradles to be most accessible which are used most.

It is clear from these statements that, in order to accomplish an efficient organization along these lines, an estimate of the usage, for example, a probability distribution, must be available to the designer. It will be assumed that such knowledge is on hand. With this knowledge, each of the above changes could be made and the associated time function could be modified accordingly by changing the average times for each of the operations. Depending on the particular criterion of organization that is used in the file, it may be possible to actually change the organization of the file in order to bring the highly used items together to be searched first. In the problem at hand, however, this would not be too helpful because one of the time-consuming tasks is that of grasping a group of raw cards and searching through them one at a time.

All the techniques mentioned so far are examples of one type of activity organization. The lower cost for a search is obtained by changing the order in which the nodes on a level are arranged and processed. The guide cards stand above the others and are scanned first. The information normally on a raw card could be transcribed on a guide card. It would then be read during the guide scan. If the card were the one desired, search would terminate without performance of the grasp and search steps (numbers 5 and 6 of Table 3). Since knowledge of usage is required by both methods, both may be instituted in the same file. In organizing a particular file, type one organization is developed first. This organization is then modified by moving terminal nodes up in the tree. The first organization is dependent on the average usage of a group of nodes, whereas the second type depends on usage of single nodes. As a result, the first organization is likely to be more stable than the second when the usage estimates are subject to error.

PROGRESS TOWARD A CALCULUS OF OPERATIONS

In the model whose application has been illustrated, it has been assumed that the choice of operations and the assignment of performance of them to the component subsystems have been completely prespecified. This essentially begs the question of (1) what the choice of operations should be for the performance of some desired task, (2) what the component subsystems should be, and (3) what the assignment of tasks to components should be. The purpose of a calculus of operations is to provide a tool for answering these three questions.

The methodology presented in this section represents a preliminary step toward the development of such a calculus of operations. It is based on a picture of information systems involving highly structured relationship among the component subsystems. Specifically it considers the equipment configuration in a system as consisting of a set of points arranged in a hierarchy of echelons to each point of which operations of the system may be assigned. The procedure presented in this section provides a mechanism by which the potential assignment of pieces of equipment to points can be evaluated for their effectiveness in performing combinations of operations assigned to those points. In this way it results in a ranking in order of effectiveness of operation assignment and equipment facility selection. The fact that the approach is essentially combinatorial in nature represents a substantially different technique for optimization from the more analytic, functional approach described in the previous sections.

This view of a system as a network of points to which tasks can be assigned is particularly applicable to a broad class of large-scale problems. One of these is the typical management center, depot warehouse, base level distributing point class of problems. However, the technique is also of importance at a more detailed level of system design, such as is involved in the master-satellite computer configuration, and at even more finely detailed levels of analysis.

In fact, this hierarchical picture of system structure and operation assignment can be utilized in a nested iterative procedure illustrated in Figure 91. As shown, the procedure for operation assignment and the model for system evaluation interact with each other at each of several multiple levels.

1. Define points and requirements for each.
2. Determine those operations involved in meeting requirements.
3. Determine efficiency of selected facilities on each operation.
   a. Define points (within facility) and operations and requirements for each.
   b. Determine suboperations involved in performing operations.
   c. Determine efficiency of selected equipment in performing suboperations, etc.
   → *d*. Assign operations to points at which pieces of equipment are located.
   e. Select optimum set of equipment for this assignment.
   f. Evaluate its efficiency.
   g. Repeat until optimum assignment of operations is made.
4. → Assign operations to points.
5. Select optimum set of facilities for this assignment.
6. Evaluate its efficiency.
7. Repeat until optimum.

FIG. 91. Assignment and evaluation procedure.

The type of combinatorial assignment presented in this sequence of procedures represents a problem of potentially enormous magnitude. It is therefore essential that some restriction be placed on the assignment of operations and facilities to points in the system structure. The operations may be tied together in a network of assignment so that if one operation is assigned to a given point, others must be similarly assigned. Furthermore, the assignment may be further restricted by arbitrarily limiting the points to which certain operation assignments can be made. Similarly, restrictions could be placed on the assignment of potential equipment facilities to points.

In the study to date, the steps taken toward the development of a calculus of operations have therefore included the following:

1. A model for measurement of system efficiency.
2. A hierarchical picture of system structure.
3. A procedure for operation definition and assignment.

Even with the capability represented by this technique for operation assignment and facility selection, the problem remains of determining the operations involved in meeting requirements and, of even more significance, the most suitable selection of equivalent sets of operations in terms of the facility under consideration. In the work described in this chapter, the operations have been completely prespecified. This could be extended to allow consideration of the assignment of alternative but equivalent operations, controlled by the rules for assignment as discussed above, for the most effective matching of operations and equipment. In this way a further step would be taken in the development of a true calculus of operations. On the basis of this approach it seems that the definition of "equivalent class of operation" is required to allow the further development of the calculus for assignment of sets of operations appropriate for assigned facilities.

In detail, the approach involves the definition, in terms similar to those used in this chapter, of the concept of a task T. Fundamentally this definition will reduce to that of "a required output from a prescribed input." Given any task defined in this way, a set of operations $\{O_1{}^T, O_2{}^T, \ldots, O_n{}^T\}$ which will essentially perform the defined task is called a "feasible" set. However, in general, a given set of operations, although it will perform the task, will be completely unsuitable because of inefficiency. Therefore the next step is the determination of that particular set of operation, $O^{TF} = \{O_1^{TF}, \ldots, O_{nF}^{TF}\}$, which is maximally efficient for a given specified facility F. If the facility is changed, then very probably the associated set of operations will be correspondingly changed. However, the class $\{O^{TF_1}, O^{TF_2}, \ldots\}$ of all such sets of operations for all possible choices of facility $\{F_1, F_2, \ldots\}$ is a class of *equivalent sets of operations* in terms of maximal effectiveness for the associated facilities. In a sense this class of equivalent sets of operations can be considered as identical, from an operational standpoint, to the originally defined task.

In order for such a definition of equivalence to be useful, a procedure must be provided by which to translate from one set of operations defined in terms of one facility to any other equivalent set of operations for any other facility. The procedure outlined in this section, at least in a preliminary fashion, provides this capability. Each such class of equivalent sets of operations can be defined and, if the procedure in this section is suitable for translation from sets of operations to equivalent sets of operations, the capability exists for problem statement in a form essentially independent of the choice of equipment. The next step would be the manipulation of the tasks in such a problem-oriented language so as to be able to change from one problem to another without the necessity of considering details of implementation.

Periodicals and journals relating to information storage and retrieval

ASLIB Proceedings, incorporating ASLIB information. ASLIB, 3 Belgrave Square, London S.W. 1. Monthly.

Administrative Management, 212 Fifth Ave., New York 10, N.Y. Monthly.

Advanced Management—Office Executive, 1927 Old York Rd., Willow Grove, Pennsylvania. Monthly.

American Documentation, a review of ideas, techniques, problems and achievements in documentation. American Documentation Institute. 1728 N St., N.W., Washington 6, D.C.

American Institute of Electrical Engineers, *Joint Computer Conference Proceedings.* 29 West 29th Street, New York 18, N.Y.

Association for computing machinery. Communications. 14 E. 69th St., New York 21, N.Y. Monthly.

Association for Computing Machinery. Journal. 2 East 63rd Street, New York 21, N.Y. Quarterly.

Association for Computing Machinery. Computing Reviews, 14 E. 69th St., New York 21, N.Y. Bimonthly.

Automatic Control, the applications magazine of systems engineering. Reinhold Publishing Corp. 430 Park Avenue, New York 22, N.Y. Monthly. Free to engineers and technical organizations; others, $10.00.

Automatic Data Processing. 109–119 Waterloo Road, Mercury House, London S.E. 1. Monthly.

Automation, the magazine of automatic operations. Penton Publishing Company, Penton Building, Cleveland 13, Ohio. Monthly.

Automation Express, new comprehensive digest of current Russian literature dealing with automation topics. International Physical Index, 1909 Park Avenue, New York 35, N.Y. 10 times a year.

Automation Progress. Morely House, Holborn Viaduct, London, E.C. 1, N.W. 1. Monthly. 60s.

Babel, international journal of translation. International Federation of Translators, Hausdorffstr. 23, Bonn, Germany. Quarterly.

British Communications and Electronics. Heywood & Co., Ltd., Drury House, Russell Street, London W.C. 2. Monthly.

British Institution of Radio Engineers. Journal. 9 Bedford Square, London W.C. 1. Monthly.

Business Automation, 288 Park Ave., West, Elmhurst, Illinois. Monthly.

Chemical and Engineering News. American Chemical Society, 1155 Sixteenth Street N.W., Washington 6, D.C. Weekly.

College and Research Libraries. ALA, 50 East Huron Street, Chicago. Bimonthly.

Communication and Electronics. American Institute of Electrical Engineers, 33 West 39th Street, New York 18, N.Y. Bimonthly.

Computer Abstracts (includes *Computer News*). Technical Information Company, Ltd., Chancery House, Chancery Lane, London W.C. 2. Monthly.

Computer Bulletin. The British Computer Society, Ltd., Finsbury Court, Finsbury Pavement, London E.C. 2.

Computer Journal. The British Computer Society, Ltd., Finsbury Court, Finsbury Pavement, London E.C. 2. Quarterly.

Computer News. Technical Information Company, Ltd., Chancery House, Chancery Lane, London W.C. Monthly. Included as a 4-page insert with issues of *Computer Abstracts.*

Computers and Automation, data processing, cybernetics, robots. Berkeley Enterprises, 815 Washington Street, Newtonville 60, Mass. Monthly.

Computing News. Box 261, Thousand Oaks, Calif. Semimonthly.

Current Research and Development in Scientific Documentation. U.S. National Science Foundation, Washington 25, D.C. Semiannually, May and November.

Data Processing Digest. Canning, Sisson and Associates, 1140 South Robertson Boulevard, Los Angeles 25. Monthly.

Data Processing. Iliffe & Sons, Dorset House, Stamford Street, London S.E. 1. Quarterly.

Data Processing, Gille Associates, 22nd Floor, Book Tower, Detroit 26, Michigan. Monthly.

Data Processor. International Business Machines Corp., 590 Madison Avenue, New York 22, N.Y.

Datamation. 10373 West Pico Boulevard, Los Angeles 64. Bimonthly.

Digital Computer Newsletter. Office of Naval Research, Code 437, Washington 25, D.C. Quarterly.

Electronic News. 7 East 12 Street, New York 3, N.Y. Weekly.

Feedback, abstracting journal of computers and automation. 5419 North Kenmore Street, Chicago 40, Illinois. Monthly.

Filmsort Facts. Minnesota Mining and Manufacturing Company, St. Paul. Monthly.

IBM *Journal of Research and Development.* International Business Machines Corp., 590 Madison Avenue, New York 22, N.Y. Quarterly.

IBM *Technical Disclosures Bulletin.* International Business Machines Corp., 590 Madison Avenue, New York 22, N.Y. Irregular.

Information and Control. Academic Press, 111 Fifth Avenue, New York 3, N.Y. Quarterly.

Institut Tochnoy Mekhaniki i Vychislitel'noy Tekhniki Akademii Nauk SSSR. Trudy. (Transactions of the Institute of Precision Mechanics & Computer Engineering of the Academy of Sciences, USSR.) Akademeya Nauk SSSR. Institut Tochnoy Mekhanika i Vychislitel'noy Tekhniki. Moscow. Irregular.

Institute of Electrical Communication Engineers of Japan. Journal. (Denki tsushin gakkai zasshi.) Charles E. Tuttle Company, Tokyo. Monthly.

Institute of radio engineers. *Transactions.* (In 22 parts. Particularly relevant are: Information theory, Quarterly; Electronic Computers, Quarterly; IRE convention record, Annual.) 1 East 79th Street, New York 21, N.Y.

Journal of Cataloging and Classification. ALA. 1407 Sherwood Avenue, Richmond 5, Virginia. Quarterly. (Ceased publication.)

Journal of Chemical Documentation. American Chemical Society, 1155–Sixteenth Street N.W., Washington 6, D.C. Quarterly.

Journal of Documentation. ASLIB, 3 Belgrave Square, London S.W. 1. Quarterly.

Journal of Electronics and Control. Taylor and Francis, Ltd., Red Lion Court, Fleet Street, London E.C. 4. Monthly.

Journal of Machine Accounting, systems and management. 1750 W. Central Ave., Mt. Prospect, Ill. Monthly.

MT. *Mechanical Translation,* devoted to the translation of languages with the aid of machines. Massachusetts Institute of Technology, Cambridge 39, Mass. Irregular.

MULL (Modern use of logic in law) Mull, Yale Law School, New Haven, Conn. Quarterly newsletter of the Electronic Data Retrieval Committee of the American Bar Association.

Management Science. Institute of Management Sciences, P. O. Box 273, Pleasantville, New York. Quarterly.

Management Technology. Institute of Management Sciences, P.O. Box 273, Pleasantville, New York. Quarterly.

O and M Bulletin. Treasury Chambers, Great George Street, London S.W. 1.

Office, magazine of management, equipment, methods. Office Publications Company, 232 Madison Avenue, New York 16, N.Y. Monthly.

Office Administration. 146 Bates Road, Montreal 8, Canada. Monthly.

Office Executive. National Office Management Association. Willow Grove, Pennsylvania.

Operations Research. Operations Research Society of America. Mt. Royal & Guilford Avenues, Baltimore 2. Bimonthly.

Patent Office Society. Journal. 104 Academy Avenue, Federalsburg, Maryland. Monthly.

Provisional International Computation Centre. Bulletin. 1958. Istituto Nazionale de Alta Matematica, Palazzo degli Uffici, Rome. Established by contract between UNESCO and the Istituto. Quarterly schedule (issues frequently combined).

Research for Industry. Stanford Research Institute, Menlo Park, Calif. Bimonthly.

SRI Journal. Stanford Research Institute, Menlo Park, Calif. Quarterly.

Science. American Association for the Advancement of Science. 1515 Massachusetts Avenue N.W., Washington 5, D.C. Weekly.

Science Information Notes, National Science Foundation, Superintendent of Documents, Government Printing Office, Washington 25, D.C.

Scientific Information Activities of Federal Agencies. National Science Foundation, Washington 25, D.C. Reports in this series available for purchase from the Superintendent of Documents, Government Printing Office, Washington 25, D.C.

Special Libraries. Special Libraries Association. 31 E. 10th Street, New York 3, N.Y. Bimonthly (May–August).

Systems and Procedures Quarterly. Systems and Procedures Association of America, 4463 Penobscot Building, Detroit 26.

Systems. Remington Rand, 315 Fourth Avenue, New York 10, N.Y. Bimonthly.

Systems Management, 10 E. 40th St., New York 16, N.Y. Bimonthly.

U.S. National Bureau of Standards. *Technical News Bulletin.* U.S. Superintendent of Documents, Government Printing Office, Washington 25, D.C.

Vestnik svyazi, proizvodstvenno-tekhnicheskiy zhurnal. (Journal of communications.) Ministerstvo Svyazi SSSR. Svyaz'izdat, Chistoprudnyy Bul'var 2, Moscow. Monthly.

Vychislitel'naya matematika i vychisilet'naya tekhnika. (Computer mathematics and computer techniques) Published by Akademiya Nauk SSSR. Institut Tochnoy Mekhanika i Vychislitel'noy Tekhniki, Moscow.

Zator Tech. Bulletin. Zator Company, Boston.

Index

As we prepared the index for this book, it became evident that certain words and concepts appeared with particularly high frequency and in a variety of different contexts. For each of these words—which evidently represent the vocabulary we have tended to use—we have provided in the index an indication of each context within which it was used. In addition, however, it has seemed to be of value to bring these terms together and to group them in major categories to provide a rudimentary sort of word association list. The user of the index may well find this of value in presenting alternative words and concepts whose association is too tenuous to warrant a "see also" reference.

The first four groupings appear to be related to the orientation of the book to the explication of the interdisciplinary character of the information retrieval problem. They therefore relate to the areas of usage, operation, organization, and equipment as follows:

The first grouping of terms seems to be generally concerned with *communication as a human process:* communication, concepts, human, information, language, language translation, meaning, semantic, subject, usage, user, word.

The second major grouping seems to be concerned with *communication as a library process:* abstracts, alphabet, bibliography, code, data, descriptive, dissemination, document, input, publication.

The third major grouping seems to be concerned with *organization:* address, classification, file, format, grouping, index, library, operation, organization, pattern, procedures, processes, program, sequence, sorting, standardization, systems, uniterm.

The fourth major grouping is quite evidently concerned with *equipment:* computer, electronic, equipment, IBM, machine, magnetic, manual, mechanization, minicard, photo, physical, punched, technical.

The remaining four groupings appear to be concerned with some of the detailed technical problems in the research and experimentation in this field:

Thus the fifth grouping appears to be generally concerned with the *intellectual* character of information retrieval: ambiguity, analysis, combination, comparison, criteria, decision, intellectual, judgment, logical, matching, relevancy, scanning, searching.

The sixth grouping appears to be generally concerned with the *numerical* measurement problem: accuracy, costs, digital, efficiency, errors, linear, measurement, numerical, parameter, probability, statistics, time.

The seventh grouping relates to the need for *research:* difficulties, experiment, mathematics, research, spectrum, theory.

Finally, the eighth grouping describes the conflicting character of information retrieval in serving both specialized needs and multiple purposes: *a priori,* change, flexibility, multiple, special, specialization, general.